The
Emergence of Folklore in Everyday Life

The Emergence of Folklore in Everyday Life

A Fieldguide and Sourcebook

edited by
George H. Schoemaker

TRICKSTER PRESS
Bloomington, Indiana

Cover design by CompuType, Bloomington, Indiana 47401.

Cover Photo: Nashville House Country Store, Nashville, Indiana. Hohenberger Collection. Courtesy of the Indiana University Foundation and the Lilly Manuscript Library.

This book is dedicated to all frustrated folklore students

. . . past, present, and future.

Library of Congress Cataloging-in-Publication Data

The Emergence of folklore in everyday life: A fieldguide
        and sourcebook / edited by George H. Schoemaker.
                p.   cm.
        Includes bibliographical references.
        Includes index.
        ISBN 0-915305-03-8
        1. Folklore—Fieldwork. 2. Folklore—United States.
        I. Schoemaker, George H.
        GR45.5.E48 1989
        398'.0973—dc20   89-50953
                                                              CIP

TRICKSTER PRESS
Indiana University
504 North Fess
Bloomington, IN 47405

TABLE OF CONTENTS

Preface

The conceptualization of this book was the result of several informal discussions with several graduate students at the Indiana University Folklore Institute. The impetus for such discussions originated from the frustration that we had encountered as Associate Instructors of Introduction to Folklore, American Folklore, or Introduction to World Folk Music courses. Each semester students were required to obtain data, document, analyze, interpret, and present the fruits of their fieldwork in some coherent, and informed manner. The resources available to teachers of undergraduate courses in Folklore were either too general, too pedantic, or too dated, hence the production of this volume.

The book that I envisioned was one that would not only serve as a fieldguide, but would also stand alone as a resource guide to complement the other basic textbooks which are currently available for use in undergraduate courses. There are basically two approaches which have been employed in these folklore textbooks. The first is a *generic approach*, that is, to teach folklore in terms of the stuff, the material, the expressive forms. The second is to teach folklore in terms of the *social processes* of human beings, the expressive forms which emerge from social interactions.

Jan Brunvand's *The Study of American Folklore: An Introduction*, (1986) is probably the most widely used introductory Folklore textbook. The printing of its third edition attests to this fact. Brunvand defines folklore as "those materials in culture that circulate traditionally among members of any group in different versions, whether in oral form or by means of customary example; as well as the processes of traditional performance and communication" (7). As such, Brunvand divides his book into three large categories, namely, oral lore, customary lore, and material folk traditions, within which are the numerous genres of folklore. The generic approach to teaching folklore or any other discipline for that matter is probably one of the most useful in colleges and universities today. It allows students to learn the language and also to come to terms with the materials—the stuff of the new discipline. A valuable aspect of Brunvand's book is the Bibliographic Notes at the end of each chapter. Conspicuously absent from Brunvand's textbook, however, is any discussion of the social processes which play a part in the performance and communication of folklore, as well as any suggestions of how to engage in fieldwork so that such processes might be observed and documented.

Richard M. Dorson's *Folklore and Folklife: An Introduction* (1972), also takes a generic approach to folklore material. The Introduction to this book provides an excellent historical framework for folklore scholarship and an introduction to most of the major schools of thought in folkloristics. Most underclassmen, however, find this book extremely pedantic and complex. There are three fairly good chapters on how to do fieldwork within three large categories: oral literature, material culture, and traditional music. There are many good, albeit very general, suggestions in these chapters and the bibliographies also provide good sources for further investigation of fieldwork techniques.

Folk Groups and Folklore Genres: An Introduction (1986) and *Folk Groups and Folklore Genres: A Reader* (1989), Elliott Oring ed., are both instructive books for introductory folklore courses. While there are no specific chapters on fieldwork techniques per se, each book has essays based on fieldwork and provides good examples of how to document and annotate fieldwork data. However, as Oring has pointed out in the most recent text, "As folklore projects are generated by students working within constraints imposed by an academic quarter or semester, they tend to be carried out within groups or environments that are a part of everyday student experience: student residence units, special interest clubs, student arts and political organizations, or student occupational settings" (1989:339).

This fieldguide concerns itself with everyday student life and the possible topics which can be selected in close proximity to a university campus. The contributors have tried to use examples of fieldwork from several different regions of the country and include not only rural but urban centers. This fieldguide will complement any of the above texts because in part it takes a generic approach. While it is not intended to be comprehensive in its treatment of genres, it uses genre and social base as a framework for talking about fieldwork and the social processes of folklore.

As an underclassman one learns the language, categories, classifications, and a feel for the material of a discipline. Pedagogically, it is a way of trying to bridge the gap between confusion and understanding. These bridges are built as underclassmen so that they might be destroyed and rebuilt again as upperclassmen. That is, one learns that the structures built in classrooms rarely conform to the stuff of everyday life. The lesson: underclassmen need some way of recognizing, relating to, and eventually as upperclassmen understanding the processes by which human beings construct meaning in their lives.

It is this latter concern that is addressed by Barre Toelken in his book *The Dynamics of Folklore*, (1979). Toelken's concern is not the generic categories that folklore may fit into, although, he is quick to point out that he is not trying to dismiss the concept of genre completely. Rather, his concern is with the dynamic processes by which the social lives of human beings are shaped. Toelken's book is an excellent text for upper division folklore courses mainly because he presupposes the student will have some kind of prior knowledge of the language, categories, classifications, and the genres of folklore. Toelken devotes a small section of his book to fieldwork, and while extremely useful, it is for the most part, very general.

This fieldguide will complement Toelken's book because it deals with specific generic categories or folk groups while still emphasizing the social processes which determine the emergence of folklore in our everyday life.

Many fieldguides have been written for the novice to the seasoned professional fieldworker. Kenneth Goldstein's *A Guide for Field Workers in Folklore* (1964) has useful chapters on the processes leading up to the interviewing of informants including pre-field preparations, rapport establishment, and observation methods. The section of his book entitled "The Induced Natural Context" describes how a collector can induce or create a *natural context* by employing a three-step method including: 1) determine what the natural context(s) are for the performance of any genre of folklore, 2) find an accomplice from the group, preferably a performer of folklore, and 3) have the accomplice introduce the fieldworker to the members of the group, and then the fieldworker can either observe from a distance or participate in the performance (87-90). While the sections on technical aspects are extremely dated, the book is still a good source for general information.

Folklife and Fieldwork: A Layman's Introduction to Field Techniques published by the American Folklife Center in Washington is, as the title suggests, a simple and unsophisticated fieldguide for laymen. The major sections of the book include some useful suggestions on how to choose informants, what to collect, how to interview, and what to do with results.

Interviewing informants for the purpose of doing oral histories or folklore fieldwork is the purpose of Edward D. Ives' book *The Tape-Recorded Interview* (1974). This book has useful, practical information on the complexities of tape recorder technology, the choosing and interviewing of informants, and the processing and transcribing of data. Bruce Jackson's *Fieldwork* (1987) is a practical book that looks at the mechanical, ethical, and human components of doing fieldwork, and in particular the ethnographic interview. Jackson's book is divided into four major sections dealing with various aspects of fieldwork. Within these sections are included various aspects of doing fieldwork, for example: collecting, planning, finding informants, points of view, the actual interview process, developing rapport, controlling the interview situation, mechanical considerations, and certain ethical issues.

Centered upon the interview are two works, by James Spradley (1979) and Charles Briggs (1986). Spradley's *The Ethnographic Interview*, is an approach to the ethnographic (describing culture) interview based on language models. For the ethnographer, it is necessary to learn emic or native categories and taxonomies. Spradley recognizes the problems in doing this in a foreign language. Similar problems are well documented in Américo Paredes' article in *New Scholar*, called "On Ethnographic Work Among Minority Groups: A Folklorist's Perspective" (1977). For Spradley, problems in semantics, mind set, and translation competence offer many challenges for the ethnographer.

Charles Briggs' book *Learning How to Ask: A Sociolinguistic Appraisal of the Role of the Interview in Social Science Research* (1986) is a rich and useful book. The focus of his book are the faulty assumptions upon which fieldworkers perform interviews. The assumptions deal with the perceived structure of the interview and not a realization that there are a number of dynamic relations at work simultaneously. For example, there are shifting roles, shifting contexts, shifting and emerging genres, shifts in relations of power and dominance, shifts in time and space. The discourse lacks formal structure because of these constant shifts. What is said is seen as a reflection of what is out there, rather than an interpretation which is jointly produced. Briggs also challenges earlier

The Emergence of Folklore in Everyday Life

methods of doing fieldwork, in particular Goldstein's notion of *induced natural context* which gained popularity during the 60s and 70s (see 1964:87-90). The problems he sees with this notion are two-fold. First, the nature of ethnography is misconstrued, that is, the fact that the ethnographer or fieldworker is interacting, even unobtrusively, is overlooked as somehow creating a natural context for the performance of expressive forms of folklore. Second, the notion of *context* is one which is said to be given and not constructed, that is, the assumption of the *induced natural context* is that by providing the elements for a performance made from a list of ideal or composite contexts, that one might be able to approximate the *actual* context of a certain expressive form. To Briggs and other sociolinguists, contexts are interpretive frames that are constructed and negotiated by participants including the fieldworker, not given through a checklist of elements in the social and physical setting (1986:12). The result is to create a "dangerous chasm between text and context" (13). Briggs book should be consulted by students and instructors before engaging in fieldwork of any kind.

There are two regional fieldguides, one for Pennsylvania and the other for Utah. *A Guide for Collectors of Oral Traditions and Folk Cultural Material in Pennsylvania* (1968), by MacEdward Leach and Henry Glassie, was written to help those who were interested in working on Pennsylvania Historical and Museum Commission's Ethnic Culture Survey Collections project. It offers suggestions on how to collect tales, songs, games, riddles, customs and beliefs, and material culture. The other regional guide is Jan Brunvand's *A Guide for Collectors of Folklore in Utah* (1971). It too was commissioned by state organization, the Committee on Folk Culture of the Utah Heritage Foundation. It has a good introduction to folklore and the study of folklore materials. It then suggests the range of folk groups found in Utah, the kinds of materials that can be collected in Utah, and how to document the material for an archive.

The predecessor of the present fieldguide is Lindahl, Rikoon, and Lawless' *A Basic Guide to Fieldwork for Beginning Folklore Students*, (1979). The production of this new fieldguide is, in part, due to the popularity of *A Basic Guide*. As stated by the authors, its goals were to "familiarize beginning folklore students with contemporary American Folklore genres, to outline collection techniques and fieldwork methods, and to suggest means for the presentation and analysis of a finished field collection" (iii). While this fieldguide follows similar goals as its predecessor, it has been updated and improved in a number of ways.

HOW THE BOOK IS SET UP

In addition to covering the kinds of projects that can be done in any given category, it provides students with other resources for their particular course. Most chapters include:

1) Brief working definitions of key terms in **bold italics** which are in turn found in the Glossary.
2) A Selected Annotated Bibliography at the end of each chapter with other relevant sources to allow students to research their topic.
3) Suggestions for documenting and organizing data.
4) Topic headings in BOLD SMALL CAPS and subheadings in **bold upper/lower** so that students can focus quickly on a particular section without having to re-read through the introductory material.
5) Photographs of fieldwork done in various regions of the country.
6) An integrative index.
7) An appendix with examples of some good student papers.

G.H.S.

Acknowledgements

This book was the culmination of ideas and efforts on the part of many people. First, for his encouragement, confidence, and friendship, and the numerous discussions of this and many other related projects I would like to thank Bob Walls. Second, I'd like to thank the contributors for their cooperation and enthusiasm during the past year.

For advice and suggestions during the conceptualization of this book, I thank Richard Bauman and Sandra Dolby-Stahl.

Finally, thanks to Jennifer Livesay for proofing and helping with the index; Guntis Šmidchens, Bob Walls and Katherine Borland for proofing, encouragement, and suggestions; Linda Kinsey Adams for help with formatting of the photographs; Patricia Sawin and Ken Pimple for suggestions on the glossary; and Laraine Wilkins Schoemaker for her willingness to type those chapters which were supplied without floppy disks.

References Cited

Bartis, Peter. 1979. *Folklife and Fieldwork: A Layman's Introduction to Field Techniques.* Washington, D.C.: American Folklife Center.

Briggs, Charles L. 1986. *Learning How to Ask: A Sociolinguistic Appraisal of the Role of the Interview in Social Science Research.* Cambridge, MA: Cambridge University Press.

Brunvand, Jan Harold. 1971. *A Guide for Collectors of Folklore in Utah.* Salt Lake City, UT: University of Utah.

_____. 1986. *The Study of American Folklore: An Introduction.* Third edition. New York: W.W. Norton and Company Inc.

Dorson, Richard M., ed. 1972. *Folklore and Folklife: An Introduction.* Chicago: University of Chicago Press.

Goldstein, Kenneth S. 1964. *A Guide for Field Workers in Folklore.* Hatboro, PA: Folklore Associates, Inc.

Ives, Edward D. 1974. *The Tape-Recorded Interview.* Knoxville: University of Tennessee Press.

Jackson, Bruce. 1987. *Fieldwork.* Urbana: University of Illinois Press.

Leach, MacEdward and Henry Glassie. 1968. *A Guide for Collectors of Oral Traditions and Folk Cultural Material in Pennsylvania.* Harrisburg, PA: Commonwealth of Pennsylvania Historical and Museum Commission.

Lindahl, Carl, J. Sanford Rikoon, and Elaine J. Lawless. 1979. *A Basic Guide to Fieldwork for Beginning Folklore Students.* Bloomington, IN: Trickster Press.

Oring, Elliott., ed. 1986. *Folk Groups and Folklore Genres: An Introduction.* Logan, UT: Utah State University Press.

_____., ed. 1989. *Folk Groups and Folklore Genres: A Reader.* Logan, UT: Utah State University Press.

Paredes, Américo. 1977. On Ethnographic Work Among Minority Groups: A Folklorist's Perspective. *New Scholar* 6:1-32.

Spradley, James P. 1979. *The Ethnographic Interview.* New York: Holt, Rinehart, and Winston.

Toelken, Barre. 1979. *The Dynamics of Folklore.* Boston: Houghton Mifflin Company.

CHAPTER 1
Introduction: Basic Concepts of Folkloristics

George H. Schoemaker

When you first hear the word *folklore* it immediately conjures up images similar to those depicted in the photograph on the front cover of this book. Adjectives used to describe this photograph might include quaint, old-fashioned, rustic, rural, grass-roots, common, and backward. Or you may have heard the word *folklore* when it was incorrectly used to denote something as being *nonsense* or a *falsehood* as in a phrase like, "Oh, that's just *folklore!*" You probably have some kind of preconception of what folklore is, and it might be correct——but then again, it might not.

This book has two basic goals. The first and most important is to show how folklore is part of the experiences and practice of our everyday life, that we are all involved in the processes of performing folklore even though we may not always be aware of it. The other goal of this book is to provide you with the information you need to design, carry out and interpret a fieldwork project in a manner which is both effective and meaningful for you.

In this chapter, I want to introduce you to some of the basic, but important, concepts of the study of folklore or *folkloristics*. Before I do this however, I think it will be useful to put folklore within a larger context, that of culture.

THE CONCEPT OF CULTURE AS PROCESS

The term *culture* is problematic, because as with many other abstract terms, *culture* has many different meanings depending on the particular disciplinary perspective one takes. For example, in the sciences *culture* denotes growth or cultivation as with "a culture of bacteria." In fact, the ancient roots of *culture* (cultivation) are tied closely to the agrarian world, the world of farming and plant husbandry.

In the arts and humanities, *culture* still retains the influence of the late nineteenth-century Victorian poet

and philosopher, Matthew Arnold, who wrote that culture was "the study of perfection . . . to conceive of true human perfection as a harmonious perfection, developing all sides of our humanity; . . . developing all parts of our society" (1988[1869]:11). To Arnold, culture was a process defined in terms of the development of the total human being. Implicit in this definition is a conscious pursuit of knowledge for the purpose of "becoming something rather than in having something, in an inward condition of the mind and spirit, not in an outward set of circumstances. . ." (48). Culture, then, becomes the process of cultivating the mind and spirit, a process of *refinement*.

In the social sciences, culture is seen in terms of the totality of human expressions in a particular society. Human expressions take many forms, from behavior such as habits, fears, attitudes, or customs, to conscious constructions like art, music, literature, architecture, thought, language, and symbols. The eminent nineteenth-century British anthropologist, Edward B. Tylor, took this idea further. Tylor wrote that *culture* is a whole way of life, those aspects of society that are learned and acquired by its members. *Culture* has also been used to mean a particular civilization or group who share certain traits which are distinct from other groups. We will use a working definition of culture combined from anthropology and the social sciences, but be conscious of the fact that the word has many meanings. In this book, *culture* is defined as a whole way of life and the human expressions of individuals in a particular society. For example, when I say African American culture, I mean everything that makes up the African American way of life, the way African Americans think, the way they express those thoughts through things they say, things they do, and things they make.

Culture is learned through familial, religious, political, educational, and even economic conventions, as well as through the informal daily interactions we have in face-to-face communication. The process of learning and acquiring culture is called *enculturation*. Everything that you can characterize as being American, Canadian, or Chinese (for example) can be termed American, Canadian, or Chinese culture. But as you already know, American culture is made up of many different ethnic groups each of which have their own culture. In this book you will read chapters on the folklore of African-American, ethnic and immigrant, and Latino cultures. These are called *subcultures*, that is, cultures within a larger culture that are not confined to any specific locale. For example, you are probably aware of Chinese-American cultures in large cities like New York, Chicago, San Francisco or Los Angeles. While members of this culture group are American citizens, and share many of the same culture traits as you and I, nevertheless, they also retain a sense of their own cultural identity.

Since culture is a process, one of its characteristics is that it rarely remains the same. It is dynamic and constantly changing due to many different factors, including conflict, contact with other cultures, advances in technology, or war—just to name a few. For example, some of you may have heard your parents talk about the *counter-culture* of the sixties, the flower-power generation with its anti-war protest marches, bohemian lifestyles, protests on college campuses, free love and experimentation with drugs of all kinds. After the flower children became adults, some of them abandoned the culture traits and practices they earlier upheld and became part of the very establishment that they were initially fighting and protesting against. The long-haired, jean and T-shirt clad hippies of Haight Ashbury in San Francisco became short-haired, three-piece suited, property owners and real estate investors of the eighties. Others directed their energies into other kinds of projects. Attitudes change, and when this happens, you can expect a shift in culture.

Sometimes when two different cultures come into contact and live in the same proximity, a process will occur called *acculturation*. *Acculturation* refers to the massive borrowing of cultural components by one group from another group with which it has had prolonged contact. In effect, the smaller or less powerful group adapts to the ways of the dominant society. I am sure that if you were to do a *diachronic* study of Chinese-Americans—that is, a long-term study of how a culture develops and changes over time—you would probably find that many American culture traits and practices would be found within the Chinese-American culture.

As you have seen in the above example, another characteristic of culture is that it has continuity over *time and space*—that is, it has temporal continuity (time), and can be studied over a certain period or at one particular moment (*synchronic*). Culture also shows continuity in *space* (location, geographic space) because expressions of culture which are the same or similar can be found in several different locales. For example, something as fundamental as a family dwelling can be found in most societies in one form or another. Cultural aspects of these dwellings would include style, materials used for construction, size, and features, to name a few. These cultural aspects *vary* from one society to the next, thereby exhibiting continuity over *space*.

ON CLASSIFICATION, CATEGORY, AND GENRE

Classifications are used to try and make sense of the world. In our everyday activities, we are involved in classification; from arranging our Compact Disc collection alphabetically according to performer (Beethoven, Bob Dylan, Genesis, Led Zeppelin, Mozart, Neil Young, The Sugarcubes, Tears for Fears) or type of music (classical, folk, heavy metal, alternative), to classifying the kinds of food we eat (fruits, vegetables, grains, dairy products), the places that we perform certain activities in the home (kitchen, dining room, bedroom, recreation room), and so forth. We may classify the world according to the *kinds* of expressive materials, the *method* by which materials are expressed, or the socio-cultural *group* to which the expressions of culture belong. These are ways by which culture may be classified, and because of these classifications, culture may be called high or elite, popular, mass, folk, or peasant, just to name a few. But what these classifications mean is always open to debate, for where are the boundaries between high and folk culture, for example? Classifications are only tools for the purpose of comparison and analysis. Classifications and categorizations are ways to organize the *stuff*, the *expressive materials* of a new field of study.

As such, you will need to learn how folklore is organized so that you can make sense of the different kinds of materials that are transmitted and performed on a daily basis.

There are two systems of classification that a person can use. One system is based upon *etic* categories. *Etic* categories developed by scientists studying culture, describe that culture interms relevant to traditional Western scientific thought, but possibly not in ways that make sense to members of the society in question. In contrast, *emic* categories are native or indigenous to a specific culture group. They are derived by members of a particular group and are not usually found outside of that particular culture group.

Etic cultural categories such as elite, popular, mass, and folk culture include many expressive forms. An expressive form of culture is called a *genre*. In folkloristics, *genres* are categories of culture which can be distinguished from each other by standards of form, content, style, and function. Fairy tales, jokes, ballads, festivals, folk art, and so forth, are different genres of folklore. Each of the subsequent chapters deals with certain genres which may be found in your fieldwork situation.

THE CONCEPT OF FOLKLORE

The term *folklore* was coined by William John Thoms in 1846. *Folklore* referred to both the *materials* and the disciplinary *study*, but currently the term *folkloristics* is used to denote the study of folklore. *Folklore* is a synthesis of two conceptual terms, *folk* and *lore*. *Folk* is a sociological entity, as with a group of people, while *lore* pertains to a category of culture. Any definition of *folklore* would have to deal with both the sociological and cultural aspects of the term. This book will operate with a definition which was formulated by the folklorist, Dan Ben-Amos, "*folklore is artistic communication in small groups*" (1971:13). This very short and concise definition is packed with meaning.

Artistic Communication

As human beings, we are all involved in the process of *socialization*——that is, the process by which human beings become social beings, capable of interacting one with another, and capable of interacting within a particular society. We are involved in communication on an ongoing basis in our everyday life. This may be as simple as telling somebody your name, address, and Social Security Number, or as complex as explaining how a law of physics works. We use different modes of communication depending on the situation and the person with whom we are talking. For example, you may communicate to your mother in one mode, but you may not communicate in the same mode with your employer.

A mode of communication which is specially marked and calls attention to itself is called *artistic communication*. *Artistic communication* is specially marked because it informs the person(s) receiving the communication that there is something out of the ordinary transpiring and that one should take notice. Artistic communication can be classified into three major categories: things people say, things people do, and things people make. Festivals, theatrical events, musical performances, parades, and art exhibits are examples of things people do. They are expressive forms of culture that are specially marked, distinct, and fairly obvious.

Other forms of artistic communication are less distinct and less obvious. You are less likely to be able to recognize artistic communication in things people say because you have never stopped to think about how people talk unless they are blatantly calling attention to their own speech. For example, suppose you have been consoling a friend about a poor grade he or she received on a college biology exam. At a certain point during the conversation you say "*well, there is no use in crying over spilled milk, so just forget about it and study harder for the next one.*" While what you said is important, it is *how* you said it that is of most interest to folklorists. You have artistically marked your discourse with a proverbial expression instead of expressing your thoughts in any number of different ordinary ways. A proverbial expression could have been substituted with a fairy tale, "well your experience reminds me of a story that goes something like this, *Once upon a time . . .*" or a joke, or a legend, or a personal experience narrative, or a metaphor, or any number of figures of speech. The point is this: we all have moments during the course of communicating with another person or a group of people, when we break through into a performance of some kind——a performance that demonstrates a certain degree of artistic competence, is specially marked, and invites another person(s) to take notice.

Artistic communication is not exclusively the doing or saying of things. It can also be expressed as things people make or what is called material culture. Things that are human-made communicate something about that human being to another. A hand-made ceramic pot has a function——to carry or hold something——and a certain degree of artistry. But, once a person paints some kind of design on the pot, it has more than just a utilitarian function. The degree of artistry has been raised to a level where it becomes the dominant point of attraction, it calls attention to itself, first to take notice of the design , second to take notice of the pot. It now communicates something about the individual——about his/her identity, his/her beliefs, his/her attitudes, and his/her culture. (See Chapter 12 **Folklife and Material Culture**)

Who Are the Folk?

The second part of the definition of *folklore*, "artistic communication *in small groups*," focuses on a social base. The term *folk* has had many meanings. It can denote:

1) *A nation*, as in the German *das Volk*, and *Volkskunde* (folk knowledge) characteristic of the German Romantic-Nationalism of Johann Gottfried von Herder, and Jacob and Wilhelm Grimm.

2) *A social group* connected by a common tradition and a unique sense of communion, characteristic of the work of Ferdinand Tönnies, and Émile Durkheim.

3) That portion of society that has not evolved to the point of being *civilized*, as characterized by the writings of *cultural evolutionists* like Edward B. Tylor. Tylor's idea was that culture evolved through three stages of social development:

savagery——> *barbarism*——> *civilization*

Folklore in these terms is the remnants or survivals of an earlier stage of social development.

4) A group that is "*small, isolated, nonliterate, and homogeneous, with a strong sense of group solidarity. . . .*" writes Robert Redfield about the folk. This notion contrasts the folk with modern, and urban populations.

5) *The lower stratum*, the old-fashioned, rustic, rural segment of society.

6) *Anyone*. As formulated by Alan Dundes, "The term *folk* can refer to any group of people whatsoever who share at least one common factor" (1980:6).

For our purposes we will use and expand upon the definition proposed by Alan Dundes: "The term *folk* can refer to any group of people whatsoever who share at least one common factor." If we think about Dundes' definition, we come to the realization that we all interact and communicate with members of several different folk groups, and that we are ourselves members of several different folk groups—a family, an occupation, a religion, an age set, and so on. There are probably any number of different ways to categorize folk groups. Here are eight ways that may be useful (Stahl 1989:35):

1) Sex (Gender)
2) Family
3) Occupation
4) Social Network (Class affiliation)
5) Age Set
6) Religion
7) Place (region)
8) Ethnicity

Shared social identity is only one factor contributing to the proliferation of artistic communication in situations of social interaction. Differential identity is another way (Bauman 1971). Social interactions among people with differing (and occasionally opposing) social identities and role relationships can actually provide situations where folklore is produced and disseminated. For example, race conflicts, border disputes, gender differences, religious conflicts, or socio-economic differences can provide the spark for the creation and performance of artistic communication. In the above cases, folklore may be the only reason that people interact with each other.

High and Low Context Groups

Some groups you may be aware of have a strong sense of social identity and social solidarity (are closely knit), are highly organized, and have a strong code of conduct (rules of behavior and means to enforce desirable behavior). These groups may share a high degree of cultural context, cultural practices, and culture-specific information. Groups exhibiting these characteristics are called *high-context* groups. Groups with fewer of these characteristics are called *low-context* groups. Examples of *high-context* groups might include: the military; certain occupations with a high degree of risk and danger associated with them such as loggers, miners, and steelworkers; religions whose teachings and beliefs pervade the whole way of life of their adherents, are highly regimented, with a high degree of organization and emphasis on hierarchy such as Catholics, Mormons, Jews, or Pentecostal; and certain ethnic or immigrant groups who have a strong sense of social identity and social solidarity, such as eastern Europeans, Latinos, African Americans, or Asian Americans. High-context groups like these have a strong sense of *groupness* and as a result are more inclined to express this sense of *groupness* in ways that are highly marked—through artistic communication—through folklore.

On the Esoteric/Exoteric Factor

Groups that are closely-knit and have a strong sense of social identity and social solidarity express attitudes, beliefs, and concerns about themselves and others (Jansen 1959). Attitudes, beliefs, and concerns a group has about *itself*, and those the group supposes *others* to have about itself constitute what is called the ***esoteric factor***. For example, a religious group may hold to the attitude that only they are the *chosen people* of God. The attitude this religious group has about itself is the esoteric factor. Attitudes, beliefs, and concerns that a group has about another group, and those it supposes the other group to have about itself make up the ***exoteric factor***. If the religious group mentioned above holds the attitude that all other religious groups are somehow in error, this would be an example of the exoteric factor. The exoteric factor can also be exemplified by the attitudes and beliefs held by *whitemen* about Native Americans (Indians), while the esoteric factor is illustrated by those attitudes that *whitemen* suppose Native Americans have about *whitemen*. In either case, the attitudes that are expressed about each *other* will be stereotypical, and most likely, will be an inaccurate portrait of either group. But beyond the accuracy of the portrait, the attitudes a group has about the *other* may actually reveal ***ethnocentric*** attitudes about the group. The condition where a culture group believes that it is superior and that other groups are inferior is called ***ethnocentrism***.

Summary

Accordingly, the term *folklore* is one that is pregnant with meaning. It has a cultural and a sociological dimension. The cultural dimensions deal with a type of expressive culture and the sociological dimension deals with the concept of the folk group, and who constitutes the folk. As a consequence of these dimensions, folkloristics brings together and is influenced by several disciplines including: literature, literary criticism, sociology, psychology, symbolic and cultural anthropology, semiotics, history, and sociolinguistics just to name a few. Folklore also exhibits several characteristics which will be explained below.

CHARACTERISTICS OF FOLKLORE
Traditionality

One characteristic of folklore is its ***traditionality***. Like culture this term has many meanings and applications to folklore. Tradition has been used synonymously with culture, as when one speaks of a particular cultural tradition—the African-American tradition—for example. However, the predominant uses of the term tradition have been in a dual sense: tradition as the lore or materials of a culture, and tradition as a process of dissemination and transmission. In the latter case culture exhibiting the

characteristic of continuity over *time* (generation to generation) and *space* (place to place) is said to be ***traditional***. For example, the practice of using miniature toy sleighs instead of the usual Christmas stockings (as explained in Chapter 18 **Family Folklore**) can be seen as both a tradition in terms of the material (the sleigh is a Christmas tradition), and a tradition in terms of the process of transmission—the way the practice was passed on from parent to child through informal means of imitation and repetition.

Tradition as a process—the transmission of an item of folklore through time and space—has been a standard by which culture and even folklore are defined. Cultural practices and traits which have continuity over time and space are considered ***traditional culture***, and hence, folklore. Cultural practices and traits which only have continuity over space are considered ***fads*** and make up ***popular culture***. For example, the hoola-hoop, clothing styles, disco music, mood rings, the practice of using tanning salons and other items and practices seem to spread like wildfire all over the country (continuity over space), but are very short-lived and die out quickly (lack of continuity over time).

Recently, there has been another way of regarding tradition that de-emphasizes the idea of continuity over time and space, and emphasizes instead the interpretation of practices of the present in terms of its connection (sometimes real, sometimes symbolic) with the past. In other words, some practices are invented traditions—made to have a link with the past in order to validate and legitimate them in the present.

Regardless of how you view tradition, it is a central concern for folklorists because it raises questions about the preservation and innovation, repetition and variation, and conservatism and dynamism of artistic communication.

The Concept of Variation

I mentioned earlier that culture is a dynamic process—one that is constantly changing. As a result, expressions of culture change, folklore changes. I also mentioned that informal transmission of artistic communication is considered traditional if the artistic communication has continuity over time and space, that it is resistant to change and will retain more or less its content and form. These seemingly paradoxical characteristics of folklore—one dynamic, the other conservative—are what folklorist Barre Toelken calls the ***twin laws of folklore process***. Says Toelken, "Conservatism refers to all those processes and forces that result in the retaining of certain information. . . and the attempted passing of those materials, intact, through time and space in all the channels of traditional expression" (1979:35). On the other hand, "Dynamism comprises all those elements that function to change features, contents, meanings, styles, performance, and usage as a particular traditional event takes place repeatedly through space and time" (1979:35). In any kind of artistic communication, there will be a constant interplay between conservatism and dynamism, between tradition and innovation. As a result of the twin laws of folklore process, items of folklore exist in numerous versions and variants as they are performed in different situations, at different times. A *version* is created when an item of folklore is performed in a certain way so that certain *motifs* (the smallest identifiable unit of an item of folklore), stylistic devices, and structural features differ from other renditions. A *variant* is a radical deviation from the standard text of a folklore item. A person may have a certain *repertoire* of folklore that he or she can perform in any given situation, but that person will never perform the item in exactly the same way twice because the interplay between tradition and innovation, between conservatism and dynamism, between continuities and discontinuities always affects the performance. What becomes interesting for folklore fieldworkers are the reasons for the discontinuities of a folklore performance. Why does the performer vary his or her performance? What conditions have changed from one performance to the next? What changes or discontinuities exist between performances of the same material by different performers? What do these changes reveal about the performer(s), about the situation(s), about the folk group to which the performer(s) belongs, or about the audience(s)? In every item of folklore there will be both aspects of tradition and aspects of innovation. Learning to recognize both aspects will require some practice and a little time, but you will soon understand how these forces work in folklore performances.

ON DOING FOLKLORE FIELDWORK
Methods of Ethnographic Inquiry

Ethnography is the act of describing culture. When you embark on your fieldwork assignment, you will be performing ethnography and will need to be attentive to every interaction, every gesture, every word uttered by your informants, and every little detail of the physical surroundings. Sound impossible? Don't worry, it is, and even the best ethnographer will miss large amounts of data! The reason for this is that when you step into your field site, unless you know exactly what you want to do, you will be confronted with chaos. There will be so much going on that you will likely miss everything. This is why good planning and preparation are essential to combat confusion. It won't guarantee success, but it will lessen the anxiety you will feel and will ensure a well-executed field project.

I want to suggest some very basic methods of ethnographic inquiry so that you can make the essential preparations and be able to compile some good, quality data.

Questionnaires. Questionnaires have limited use in ethnographic fieldwork, but as a way to obtain a sampling of attitudes and demographic information, they are useful. One of the problems with questionnaires is that they do not allow you to interact with people. In some culture groups, questionnaires may not be a recognized means of obtaining information. Sometimes people will answer the questionnaire in a way that they think the fieldworker would like. This is also the case, sometimes, with the interview.

Interviews. Interviews can actually be a very good way of obtaining data, and for the most part, you as a student of Folklore will employ this method since it is easily accessible to you. In doing interviews, you need to determine just what it is you are trying to accomplish, what your goal is. Most likely you will already know the person(s) you have chosen to interview, but even if you do, you will need to establish some kind of rapport with them—to break the ice. Let's face it, how comfortable would you be knowing that every word you say was being recorded for all time? I think that we would all be a little self-conscious. Keep this in mind as you approach the situation. What I have done in the past is to meet with my informants or collaborators a few days before the interview and just run through, in a general way, the interview scenario. This way the informants know exactly what will transpire and can put themselves at ease. Before going to the interview, make a skeleton list of questions that you may ask. This is good practice because if you have an informant who is unresponsive, you can fall back on your list of questions. Most likely what will happen is that after the first question, your informant will talk and talk and you will find yourself unable or unwilling to guide the direction of the interview. Remember that the interview format itself is unintentionally designed to put someone in a superior and dominant position. On the one hand, the person asking questions is in a dominant and superior position, but on the other the informant is dominant because he/she possesses the

The Emergence of Folklore in Everyday Life

desired information. This relationship is constantly being renegotiated every time there is a change in turn-taking. Being able to navigate the interview in a particular direction requires skill and sensitivity. If your informant is totally off the subject, but is divulging some information that reveals a different side of his or her personality, then why not let the informant continue and finish the thought. Believe it or not, everything that your informant says and does will be able to tell you something.

After you have done an interview, you may want to listen to the results and take notes on the kinds of things that were talked about. Often there will be things that you may not have understood completely or things you'd like to know more about. Write these down and ask your informant for a follow up interview. This will be a valuable practice and will help clarify any confusing or inconsistent information.

Observation. Combined with interviewing, you will be using observation skills. The problem with observation is that most times, you are not in a position to record or write down your observations until much later. When I walk into an interview situation, I usually like to observe things like the type of reading material on the bookshelves, magazines on the coffee tables, what kind of things are on the wall (photographs, paintings, degrees, etc.), the arrangement of the furniture or whatever physical objects may be present, the presence or absence of plants, the intensity of light, and so forth. Of course, this kind of information will differ depending on the location of the interview. Sometimes the information you receive from your observations can either break the ice or provide you with a springboard into the interview itself.

In addition to the physical surroundings, you need to observe what your informant is doing. Things like gestures, voice quality, whether the person maintains eye contact or not, and so forth, all tell you something about the person. Observations will give you another kind of data that will supplement your interview and permit you to paint a more complete picture of your informant.

Participant/Observation. On occasion you may have the opportunity to participate in some kind of cultural expression; a festival, a musical performance, a storytelling session, a barn-raising, etc. If this happens, you will become a participant observer, that is, you will be participating in the event while at the same time making observations that you will record or write down at a later time. Being a participant observer requires striking a fine balance between being the active participant and the passive observer; however, the experience will give you a completely different insight into the culture group you are studying than if you simply observe other people performing. Often, your entry into a situation like this can be facilitated by already knowing someone from the group. With your friend as a mediator, you can interact with other people from the group with less self-consciousness. Your friend can also alert you to practices and taboos that the culture group may have, saving you embarrassment and helping you avoid jeopardizing your fieldwork experience.

Texture, Text, and Context

Once you understand the methods of fieldwork, you need to know the kind of data to look for. The three basic elements of an item of folklore that you'll need to take account of are *texture, text* and *context* (Dundes 1980).

Texture. By this, we mean how any item of folklore is presented. It is based heavily on the study of language and takes into account many formal features, how the item is structured and how it is presented. It is that part of folklore that is untranslatable.

In verbal or aural forms (narrative forms, music, folk speech) this would include:

1) Tempo of speech (how fast or slow)
2) Dynamics (loud or soft)
3) Pitch (high or low)
4) Repetition of sounds (alliteration, rhyme, assonance, consonance, repetition of words and phrases)
5) Types of comparisons (simile and metaphor)
6) Figures of speech

In visual, performance, or mixed-media forms (dance, festival, material culture, etc.) texture would also include:

1) Tempo
2) Color
   a) intensity
   b) value
   c) hue
3) Repetition of motifs and patterns (the interplay between repetition and innovation)
4) Use of textures in material objects
5) Use of space and line
6) Movement

The texture of an item will often be the most difficult information to describe, but it can tell you much about the performer, the group, and the item itself.

Text. Is the actual item itself (a joke, a proverb, a

legend, a one and a half-story I-house, a carpet) or as Dundes writes, a version or telling. A folklore text contains the content of the folklore item (on how to transcribe a text, see Chapter 20 **Documenting the Fieldwork Project**).

Context. Context has many dimensions. In a general sense it has to do with the situation in which an item of folklore is performed or everything that is going on at the time an item of folklore is presented. But this definition is misleading because a performance of folklore is embedded in many different levels of context, stretching from the most immediate social/physical surroundings to the over-arching context of the entire culture. In an informative essay called "The Field Study of Folklore in Context," Richard Bauman identifies two different categories of context: *cultural context*, "having to do with systems of meaning and symbolic interrelationships, and *social context* having to do with matters of social structure and social interactions" (1983:363). Within the *cultural context*, Bauman writes about *context of meaning, institutional context*, and *context of communicative system*. By *context of meaning*, Bauman means the information and knowledge necessary to "understand the content, meaning, the 'point' of an item of folklore, as the people themselves understand it" (363). *Institutional context* deals with how cultural institutions (familial, economic, religious, educative, and political) influence or inform behavior, ideology, worldview, belief systems, expressions of culture, etc. Finally, the *context of communicative system* has to do with *emic* categories (native categories, categories from the point of view of the folk) of genres, and ways of organizing the world. The question to ask within this context is "how a particular form of folklore relates to other forms of folklore within the culture" (364).

The *social context* is divided into three subcategories *social base, individual context*, and *situational context*. By *social base*, Bauman means the group or the kind of people who use the folklore. How does the performance fit into the social network? The *individual context* has to do with how an item of folklore relates to an individual. It may be an item that is well-known among members of a collective group, but the item and its performance also have meaning for the individual, and, on occasion, this may be different or in opposition to the collective meaning of the item. The *situational context* is understood to be how the item of folklore operates in actual situations of everyday interaction. How does it work in a particular situation or event? What social work does it accomplish.

In sum, the cultural and social contexts deal with six broad categories: "a)*context of meaning* (what does it mean?); b)*institutional context* (where does it fit within the culture?); c)*context of communicative system* (how does it relate to other kinds of folklore?); d)*social base* (what kind of people does it belong to?); e)*individual context* (how does it fit into a person's life?); f)*context of situation* (how is it useful in social situations?)" (367).

With this in mind you may want to formulate questions about the different kinds of contexts that you can ask your informants, the audience, cultural specialists, and so forth. By doing this, you will be able to paint a more complete picture of your informants, their folklore and what it means in their lives, in the context of the culture group, and so on. As you can see, ethnography is quite involved and requires much preparation. Once you have made the necessary preparations, and completed your fieldwork, you will be ready to write up your data. (See Chapter 20 **Documenting the Fieldwork Project**)

Thin and Thick Description

Traditionally, ethnography was establishing rapport, selecting informants, collecting and transcribing texts, and writing about culture. To Clifford Geertz, ethnography is all this and much more. Geertz distinguishes between two types of description which you should keep in mind while you do fieldwork.

Thin description would be describing culture on a very surface, descriptive level, as one saw it exactly. *Thick description* would engage in a more detailed *analysis of culture* and attempt to interpret data in some meaningful way. Geertz provides an example: *three boys in a room contracting their eyelids* would constitute an example of thin description, a description of what is going on. Thick description would attempt to distinguish, analyze, and interpret the contractions *as a blink, a wink*, or *a parody* of a wink (an attempt to deceive one of the other boys), and attempt to answer why? what does this mean? what is really going on here beyond the descriptive facade?

The object of ethnography, then, is the development of observational, analytical, and interpretive skills. It is to develop a hierarchy of meaningful patterns from culture. It is a mistake, however, to think that analysis is a reflection of what others really think. Remember that you—the fieldworker, the ethnographer—are creating culture with yourself interacting with your informants. With this in mind, hopefully you will be able to approach folklore fieldwork and ethnography with a certain degree of preparation, sensitivity, and a sense of what it is you are trying to do. Each of the following chapters in this fieldguide will help you in this way.

Acknowledgement

This chapter was influenced, in one way or another, by many people including Hasan El-Shami, Sandra Dolby Stahl, Richard Bauman, William A. Wilson and Richard C. Poulsen. I would also like to thank Laraine Wilkins Schoemaker, Phillip McArthur, Bob Walls, and Katie Borland for reading and commenting on earlier versions of this chapter.

References Cited

Arnold, Matthew. 1988[1869]. *Culture and Anarchy*. Ed. J. Dover Wilson. Cambridge: Cambridge University Press.

Bauman, Richard. 1971. Differential Identity and the Social Base of Folklore. *Journal of American Folklore* 84:31-43.

_____. 1977. *Verbal Art as Performance*. Prospect Heights, IL: Waveland Press.

_____. 1983. The Field Study of Folklore in Context. IN *The Handbook of American Folklore*, ed. Richard M. Dorson, pp. 362-368. Bloomington, IN: Indiana University Press.

Ben-Amos, Dan. 1971. Toward a Definition of Folklore in Context. *Journal of American Folklore* 84.3-15.

Dundes, Alan. 1980. Texture, Text, and Context. IN *Interpreting Folklore*, pp. 20-32. Bloomington, IN: Indiana University Press.

_____. 1980. Who Are the Folk? IN *Interpreting Folklore*, pp. 1-19. Bloomington, IN: Indiana University Press.

Geertz, Clifford. 1973. Thick Description: Toward an Interpretive Theory of Culture. IN *The Interpretation of Cultures*, pp. 3-30. New York: Basic Books.

Jansen, William Hugh. 1959. The Esoteric-Exoteric Factor in Folklore. *Fabula: Journal of Folktale Studies* 2:205-211.

Redfield, Robert. 1947. The Folk Society. *The American Journal of Sociology* 52:293-308.

Stahl, Sandra Dolby. 1989. *Literary Folkloristics and the Personal Narrative*. Bloomington, IN: Indiana University Press.

Toelken, Barre. 1979. *Dynamics of Folklore*. Boston, MA: Houghton Mifflin Company.

Tylor, Edward B. 1958[1871]. *The Origins of Culture*. New York: Harper and Brothers Publishers.

Selected Annotated Bibliography

Bauman, Richard. 1971. Differential Identity and the Social Base of Folklore. *Journal of American Folklore* 84:31-43.
Influential essay bringing the social base of folklore under scrutiny. Current theories point to common and shared features as determinants for the formation of social groups and ultimately the performance of folklore. Bauman points out that difference can sometimes be the only reason for the performance of folklore.

_____. 1983. The Field Study of Folklore in Context. IN *The Handbook of American Folklore*, ed. Richard M. Dorson, pp. 362-368. Bloomington, IN: Indiana University Press.
This essay examines *context* in terms of social and cultural frameworks. Within these frameworks are six types of context that fieldworkers should be aware of in order to interpret the social and symbolic significance of cultural forms of expression.

_____. 1989. Folklore. IN *International Encyclopedia of Communications*, ed. Erik Barnouw, pp. 177-181. London, England: Oxford University Press.

Ben-Amos, Dan. 1971. Toward a Definition of Folklore in Context. *Journal of American Folklore* 84:3-15.
Seminal essay which looks at history of folklore definitions and proposes yet another, one based on context and emphasizing the doing of social life, folklore as everyday practice, as artistic communication in small groups.

_____, ed. 1976. *Folklore Genres*. Austin: University of Texas Press
Excellent book investigating the concept of genre and focusing attention of the major genres of verbal folklore.

_____. 1984. The Seven Strands of Tradition: Varieties in Its Meaning in American Folklore Studies. *Journal of Folklore Research* 21:97-131.
The author critically examines the numerous uses of the concept of tradition in American folkloristics.

Briggs, Asa. 1989. Culture. IN *International Encyclopedia of Communications*, ed. Erik Barnouw, pp. 435-438. London, England: Oxford University Press.
The author provides a good introduction to the concept of culture is a communicative process.

Brunvand, Jan Harold. 1986. *The Study of American Folklore*. Third edition. New York: W.W. Norton and Company Inc.
A good introductory textbook covering basic concepts of folklore, folk groups, and an introduction to different genres of folklore.

Burke, Peter. 1981. The Discovery of Popular Culture. *People's History and Socialist Theory*, ed. R. Samuel, pp. 216-221. London: Routledge and Kegan Paul.

_____. 1984. Popular Culture Between History and Ethnography. *Ethnographia Europaea* 14:4-13.

Burns, Thomas A. 1989[1977]. Folkloristics: A Conception of Theory. IN *Folk Groups and Folklore Genres: A Reader*, ed. Elliott Oring, pp. 1-20. Logan, UT: Utah State University Press. Also in *Western Folklore* 36:109-134.
This essay develops the main lines of diachronic and synchronic thought which have gone into folklore studies. Essential reading to contextualize the discipline in nineteenth and twentieth century cultural thought.

Dorson, Richard M. 1972. Concepts of Folklore and Folklife Studies. IN *Folklore and Folklife: An Introduction*, ed. Richard M. Dorson, pp. 1-50. Chicago: University of Chicago Press.
An introduction to folklore concepts and a history of the discipline, including the important schools of thought and figures who have helped to shape the discipline. The rest of the book takes a generic approach to folklore.

Dundes, Alan. 1965. *The Study of Folklore*. Englewood Cliffs, N.J.: Prentice-Hall Inc.
This book contains many influential previously published articles dealing with the history of folkloristics, theoretical issues, forms of folklore, and functional aspects of folklore.

_____. 1975. *Analytic Essays in Folklore*. The Hague: Mouton.
Emphasizes folklore analysis based on structural and psychoanalytic approaches.

_____. 1980[1964]. Texture, Text, and Context. IN *Interpreting Folklore*, pp. 20-32. Bloomington, IN: Indiana University Press.

_____. 1980a[1977]. Who Are the Folk? IN *Interpreting Folklore*, pp. 1-19. Bloomington, IN: Indiana University Press.

Foster, George. 1953. What is Folk Culture? *American Anthropologist* 55:159-173.

Geertz, Clifford. 1973. Thick Description: Toward an Interpretive Theory of Culture. IN *The Interpretation of Cultures*, pp. 3-30. New York: Basic Books.
Traditionally, ethnography was establishing rapport, selecting informants, collecting and transcribing texts, and writing about culture. To Geertz, ethnography is all this and much more. To illustrate his point he distinguishes between thin and thick description.

Georges, Robert A. 1969. Toward an Understanding of Storytelling Events. *Journal of American Folklore* 82:313-328.

Handler, Richard and Jocelyn Linnekin. 1984. Tradition, Genuine or Spurious. *Journal of American Folklore* 97:273-290. A condensed version of this article also appears IN 1989 *Folk Groups and Folklore Genres: A Reader*, ed. Elliott Oring, pp. 38-42. Logan, UT: Utah State University.
This essay looks at tradition as not having boundedness, but as being a process of symbolic interpretation in order to link the present with the past.

Hobsbawm, Richard and Terrence Ranger, eds. 1983. *The Invention of Tradition*, pp. 1-14. Cambridge: Cambridge University Press.

Hymes, Dell. 1981. Breakthrough into Performance. IN *"In vain I tried to tell you: Essays in Native American Ethnopoetics*, pp. 79-141. Philadelphia, PA: University of Pennsylvania Press.

Jansen, William Hugh. 1959. The Esoteric-Exoteric Factor in Folklore. *Fabula: Journal of Folktale Studies* 2:205-211. Also in *The Study of Folklore*, ed. Alan Dundes, pp. 43-51. Englewood Cliffs, NJ: Prentice-Hall, Inc.
This essay addresses perceptions groups have about themselves and others, and the implications these perceptions have on other aspects of culture, including folklore.

Redfield, Robert. 1947. The Folk Society. *The American Journal of Sociology* 52:293-308.
Early article which conceptualized folk culture in terms of size, literacy, homogeneity, social solidarity, and isolation. This conception contributed to his formulation of the folk—urban continuum.

Spradley, James P. 1980. *Participant Observation*. New York: Holt, Rinehart and Winston.

Toelken, Barre. 1979. *The Dynamics of Folklore*. Boston, MA: Houghton Mifflin & Company.
Excellent textbook approaching folklore as a dynamic cultural process rather than as static, text-oriented collections.

Wilson, William A. 1989[1973]. Herder, Folklore and Romantic Nationalism. *Journal of Popular Culture* 6:818-835. Also in *Folk Groups and Folklore Genres: A Reader*, ed. Elliott Oring, pp. 21-37. Logan, UT: Utah State University.
Good essay to contextualize the emergence of folklore during late eighteenth-century German and Finnish nationalist movements.

CHAPTER 2
Ethics and the Student Fieldworker

Guntis Šmidchens and Robert E. Walls

In December 1930, Franz Boas watched a potlatch feast at Fort Rupert, British Columbia. He had seen his first Northwest Coast feast forty-five years earlier and he now noted some of the changes that had occurred. The host chief, Boas wrote, made a speech while the meat was distributed, saying "'This bowl in the shape of a bear is for you,' and you, and so on; for each group a bowl." The speech was the same one that he had heard often before, "But the bowls are no longer there. They are in the museums in New York and Berlin!"[1]

Fieldwork is something of a *rite of passage* for most folklorists, an experience in which they must endure, learn and, they hope, succeed. It is a craft at which they, as professionals, are expected to become highly proficient. All too often though, the consequences—positive or negative—of their actions in the course of field research are buried beneath the final results, on which, ultimately, their work as scholars will be judged. Unfortunately, erudition on the campus does not necessarily beget a strict adherence to local proprieties in the field, and under the pressure to succeed in fieldwork, decisions can be made which benefit the scholar but not the individuals being studied. The consequences may be seen immediately, but just as likely will be seen much later on, perhaps years later, as in the case of Boas.

The question of ethics and the moral implications of research during and after *the field* has engendered considerable discussion in the social sciences and humanities recently, fueled, in part, by ethical concerns in wider American society. The American Folklore Society, to which most professional folklorists belong, is one of the many professional societies which has addressed the issue of the fieldworker's responsibilities toward those people being studied, the public, the discipline, students, sponsors, and governmental agencies.

Yet such ethical concerns are not limited to only professional folklorists: you, as a *student* of folklore who is endeavoring to study the traditions of a specific group of people, should also be aware of the potential consequences of your actions. While you may lack professional status and are doing the project only because it is a class requirement, your interaction with people can nonetheless still influence their lives in a way they find undesirable. Therefore, it would be wise to carefully consider some of the following questions in advance of your fieldwork project in order to anticipate or recognize ethical problems as they emerge in the process of fieldwork. Such preparation will help you to avoid embarrassing or distasteful situations, and to treat the people you are studying in a manner that is fair and just.

HONESTY AND FAIRNESS

The folklorist should accurately portray the lives of real people. How much time must be spent on fieldwork if it is to be *fair* to the group concerned? Can transient collecting or any form of short-term field survey fairly represent a group's traditions? How is long-term fieldwork any different? At what point should fieldworkers emerge from the shadows of anonymous observation and announce their presence to a person or group, possibly hindering the observance of a folkloric event in its *natural context*? Is a folklorist *always* on the job? How honest or dishonest is a certain amount of role-playing in order to gain information? How should you introduce yourself to an individual or group who may not fully understand what a folklorist does: as a *folklorist, student, anthropologist, historian, interested person*? What do you tell people about your work when asked? How do you know if subjects fully understand the aims of the investigation and its possible conse-

Scenario 1:

Your extended family (aunts, uncles, cousins, grandparents) gather annually for a special family Christmas or Hanukkah celebration. Your family celebration involves certain secular and religious traditions which seem quite different from those traditions of other family celebrations. You want to document your family's traditions for your project. Do you tell your family members in advance what you plan to do and why? What if some members object? How do you reassure them, or do you?

quences? Should you send the people you study copies of the work resulting from your fieldwork?

RIGHTS AND RESPONSIBILITIES

Folklorists must respect the integrity of the people they study. Should people interviewed be called *informants, assistants, associates, consultants, interviewees,* or *participants*? What are the limits of sole-authorship, and when should members of the folk group be listed as co-authors? Is it fair not to reveal your true feelings on a controversial subject only to satisfy informants' wishes and avoid a confrontation? Who *owns* the information or performance which a folklorist has recorded? What are the rights of the individuals who create or perform products or activities which are based on tradition? Who has control over what is filmed or photographed? Should you be responsible for the protection, privacy, or consent of individuals who are filmed or photographed, especially at a public event?

Reciprocity is about as universal to social behavior as one can get, so it should be natural to the human interaction involved in fieldwork. But what is the nature of reciprocity between fieldworker and folk, and what forms should it take (e.g., money, gifts, prestige, psychological gratification)? Even where monetary gain is not involved—for either the field-

Scenario 2:

Some folk musicians have given you permission to video-tape their highly original music being performed at a small community festival. Later, someone offers to incorporate a portion of your video into a documentary, for which you will receive money or recognition. The documentary becomes very popular and is sold on videotape. Do the musicians deserve compensation for their part in this documentary, and if so do you give it to them? Did they know precisely what you were going to do with this video? Are the rights to their original music protected?

worker or the folk—what is *fair return* when the fieldworker's success brings good grades and academic recognition?

THE FIELDWORK SITUATION

Folklorists strive to describe tradition in the real world—accurately and fairly. Is the tape-recording and photographing of an individual or group without their knowledge permissible? What is the difference between secretly taping someone and writing down their words in a fieldbook shortly afterwards without their knowledge? At what point does gentle prodding or requests (to achieve an induced natural context) leave the realm of encouragement and become a subtle form of coercion? While folklore studies demand precision and accuracy of contextual details, is it right to record and then write about a story which may be a narrator's account of the most personal and emotional experience of their life (e.g., a supernatural encounter; the death of a loved one) even if the narrator, at the time, had given per-

Scenario 3:

During the course of an interview you are tape recording, the narrator tells some traditional stories of a bawdy nature, using some obscene language. This is exactly what you need for your project; however, at the end of the interview the narrator says, "I hope you didn't record those (bawdy) stories." What do you do?

mission to do so? Should you approach controversial topics (ethnographic dynamite such as sex, criminal acts, etc.) even if you know an individual or group will be offended or object? What if the information they reveal could harm them in some way?

THE POLITICS OF FIELDWORK

Folklorists must always be aware of the potential consequences of their work in the wider sphere of social relationships—within a community, a region, and beyond.

To what extent should gossip (or what one thinks may be gossip) be recorded in your field records? Do you record in your fieldbook *everything* that is observed? Should a written record be kept of those things which a group prefers not to be recorded, even if it's done in an anonymous, disguised fashion? How do you deal with political or social factions? At what point is suppressing the writing down of certain information, sensitive or not, censorship or accommodation for the protection of privacy? Something in

---

Scenario 4:

You are documenting a Finnish-American farmstead. One building on the farm is an old milkhouse converted into a sauna. The owners tell you how much this sauna means to them, but they also tell you that few people know about this because if the local government found out the owner's property taxes and insurance rates would increase. This kind of information, however, would be a crucial detail to include in your paper because saunas are so much an important part of Finnish-American identity. What do you do?

Scenario 5:

In the course of a taped interview, someone describes local criminal activities (e.g. moonshining, drug-related activities, graffiti writing on public property) and actually names people involved. This is very revealing information and certainly enhances the value and color of your paper. Do you erase this information from the tape, or try to disguise the identities of the people or local community involved? What if the information is not criminal but only potentially embarrassing to the people or community involved?

---

every report is bound to be disapproved of by somebody in the group studied. How do you gauge what is truly "sensitive" information? Is it really possible to foresee potential misuse of field-collected data, and should you be held accountable if it is misused?

Individual traditions may change drastically if hordes of folklorists repeatedly descend upon an area to collect, question, and otherwise intervene in the everyday lives of folk groups and performers. To whom do the "folk" belong? Can they be "kept" from other fieldworkers or others interested in their knowledge or abilities? To what extent can the descriptions of people and places be modified to protect confidentiality or privacy and yet still present a responsible and informative piece of scholarship that can be read confidently by your teacher and possibly others? Should you become involved in public controversies in any way? What if your view was based on sound scholarship, but was potentially contrary to the welfare of the group or some of its members?

Questions regarding the politics of fieldwork are of particular importance if your project will be seen by individuals other than yourself and your instructor, and especially if your paper will be deposited in a public folklore archive.

CONCLUSION

Wrestling with at least some of these questions is nothing new for experienced fieldworkers. Many have probably come up with their own personal answers, or have relied on the advice of co-workers. Still others may see the issues as unresolvable.

However, as students, these issues may be new to you, and therefore we urge you to take time and seriously consider and reconsider these ethical concerns before, during, and after your fieldwork experience. Should a problem emerge that seems particularly difficult, consider discussing it with your friends and especially your instructor. Such dis-

cussion will no doubt provide valuable feedback.

Obviously the exigencies of many fieldwork situations don't permit sufficient time to consider the possible consequences of decisions which you might have to make. However, some advance consideration of the ethical choices and ethical imperatives involved in the issues of deception, privacy, consent, and reciprocity cannot help but make you a better and more conscientious fieldworker in the long run as you, like Franz Boas, attempt to "capture" the traditional heritage of people and observe the consequences of your actions.[2]

Notes

[1] From a letter Boas wrote to his children, December 14, 1930, in the Boas Family Papers, American Philosophical Society. Quoted in *Captured Heritage: The Scramble for Northwest Coast Artifacts.* By Douglas Cole (Seattle: University of Washington Press, 1985), p. xiii.

[2] An earlier version of this essay—directed towards professional folklorists—appeared in *Folklore Forum* 19(1986):117-24.

Selected Bibliography

Adler, Patricia A., Peter Adler, and E. Burke Rochford, Jr. eds. 1986. The Politics of Participation in Field Research. *Urban Life* (Special Issue) 14(4).

Appell, G.N. 1978. *Ethical Dilemmas in Anthropological Inquiry: A Case Book.* Waltham, MA: Crossroads Press.

Beauchamp, T.L., R.R. Faden, R.J. Wallace, and L. Walters, eds. 1982. *Ethical Issues in Social Science Research.* Baltimore: Johns Hopkins University Press.

Buckley, Thomas. 1987. Dialogue and Shared Authority: Informants as Critics. *Central Issues in Anthropology* 7(1):13-23.

Bunch, John B. 1973. The Legal Consideration of Privacy, Property, Copyright, and Unfair Practices, in the Publication of Folklore Material. *Folklore Forum* 6(4):211-216.

Carpenter, Inta Gale, ed. 1978. Folklorists in the City: The Urban Field Experience. *Folklore Forum* (Special Issue) 11(3).

Cassell, Joan and Sue-Ellen Jacobs, eds. 1987. *Handbook on Ethical Issues in Anthropology.* (Special Publication No. 23) Washington, D.C.: American Anthropological Association.

Cassell, Joan and Murray L. Wax, eds. 1980. Ethical Problems of Fieldwork. *Social Problems* (Special Issue) 27(3).

Chesley, Cataline. 1988. An Anthropologist Trying to be Ethical and Still Getting the Job Done: Ethics and the Human Dimension in Fieldwork. *The Turkish Studies Association Bulletin* 12(2):79-90.

Dufresne, Colette, et al. 1980. Vers une déontologie du folkloriste. (Toward a professional code of ethics for folklorists) *Bulletin of the Folklore Studies Association of Canada* 4(3/4):22-36. (With English summary.)

Farrer, Claire. 1977. Fieldwork Ethics. IN *Trends and New Vistas in Contemporary Native American Folklore Study.* Ed. by Stephen Mannenbach, pp. 59-63. Folklore Forum Bibliographic and Special Series No. 15.

Fry, Amelia. 1984. Reflections on Ethics. IN *Oral History: An Interdisciplinary Anthology*, ed. by David K. Dunaway and Willa K. Baum, pp. 150-161. Nashville: American Association for State and Local History.

Georges, Robert A. and Michael Owen Jones. 1980. *People Studying People: The Human Element in Fieldwork.* Berkeley: University of California Press.

Goldstein, Kenneth S. 1964. *A Guide for Fieldworkers in Folklore.* Hatboro, PA: Folklore Associates.

Howell, Nancy. 1986. Occupational Health and Safety: An Issue in the Culture of Anthropology. (Letter to the Editor) *Anthropology Newsletter* 27(5): 2,10.

Ireland, Tom. 1974. Ethical Problems in Folklore. IN *Conceptual Problems in Contemporary Folklore Study*, ed. Gerald Cashion, pp. 69-74. Folklore Forum Bibliographic and Special Series No. 12.

Ives, Edward D. 1980. *The Tape-Recorded Interview: A Manual for Fieldworkers in Folklore and Oral History.* Knoxville: University of Tennessee Press.

Jackson, Bruce. 1987. *Fieldwork.* Urbana: University of Illinois Press.

Jansen, Wm. Hugh. 1983. Ethics and the Folklorist. IN *Handbook of American Folklore*, ed. by Richard M. Dorson, pp. 533-539. Bloomington: Indiana University Press.

Jones, Michael Owen. 1977. In Progress: Fieldwork—Theory and Self. *Folklore and Mythology Studies* 1(Spring):1-22.

King, Thomas F. 1983. Professional Responsibility in Public Archaeology. *Annual Reviews in Anthropology* 12:142-164.

Long, Gary L. 1982. An Assessment of the ASA Code of Ethics and Committee on Ethics. *American Sociologist* 17:80-86.

Myers, James E. 1969. Unleashing the Untrained: Some Observations on Student Ethnographies. *Human Organization* 28(2):1-55-159.

Oring, Elliott. 1987. Letter to the Editor. The American Folklore Society *Newsletter* 16(2):3-4.

Paine, Robert, ed. 1985. *Advocacy and Anthropology, First Encounters.* St. Johns, Nfld: Memorial University of Newfoundland.

Punch, Maurice. 1986. *The Politics and Ethics of Fieldwork.* Beverly Hills: Sage Publications.

Reece, Robert E. and Harvey A. Siegal. 1986. *Studying People: A Primer in the Ethics of Social Research.* Macon, GA: Mercer.

Reynolds, Paul Davidson. 1982. *Ethics and Social Science Research.* Englewood Cliffs, NJ: Prentice-Hall.

Rynkiewich, Michael A. and James P. Spradley, eds. 1976. *Ethics and Anthropology: Dilemmas in Fieldwork.* New York: John Wiley and Sons.

Santino, Jack. 1986. Statement on Ethics: Principles of Professional Responsibility. The American Folklore Society *Newsletter* 15(5):8,4-5.

Seiler, Lauren H. James M. Murtha. 1980. Federal Regulation of Social Research Using "Human Subjects:" A Critical Assessment. *American Sociologist* 15:146-157.

Sherman, Sharon R. 1986. "That's How the Seder Looks": A Fieldwork Account of Videotaping Family Folklore. *Journal of Folklore Research* 23(1):53-70.

Stahl, Sandra K., ed. 1973. Folklore Archives: Ethics and the Law. *Folklore Forum* 6(4):197-210.

Titon, Jeff Todd. 1985. Stance, Role, and Identity in Fieldwork Among Folk Baptists and Pentecostals. *American Music* 3(1):16-24.

du Toit, Brian. 1980. Ethics, Informed Consent, and Fieldwork. *Journal of Anthropological Research* 36(3):274-286.

Toelken, Barre. 1979. *The Dynamics of Folklore.* Boston: Houghton Mifflin Co.

Washburn, Wilcomb. 1985. Ethical Perspectives in North American Ethnology. IN *Social Contexts of American Ethnology, 1840-1984*, ed. by June Helm, pp. 50-64. (Proceedings of the American Ethnological Society 1984) Washington, D.C.: American Ethnological Society.

Wax, Murray. 1986. Reflections on Fieldwork Reciprocity and Ethical Theories. *Anthropology and Humanism Quarterly* 11(1):2-7.

Wax, Rosalie, H. 1971. *Doing Fieldwork: Warnings and Advice.* Chicago: University of Chicago Press.

Yocom, Margaret. 1982. Family Folklore and Oral History Interviews: Strategies for Introducing a Project to One's Own Relatives. *Western Folklore* 41:251-274.

CHAPTER 3
Gender Issues in Folklore Fieldwork

Jennifer Livesay

In this chapter I will be discussing the importance of gender issues in folklore, both in the material itself and in the approaches that people have taken to it. Since much of the history of folklore studies has arguably been about *men's folklore*, I will be talking mostly about women and folklore. I will not give specific examples of fieldwork projects in women's folklore or folklore and gender. Instead, I will try to provide an overview of general things to keep in mind while designing and carrying out such a study.

GENDER VS. SEX

First we need to define what is meant by gender and how this concept differs from that of sex. Put most simply, gender is cultural and sex is biological. *Sex* refers to a biological classification as male or female, based largely on chromosomal differences. *Gender* refers to the totality of cultural attitudes and definitions of maleness and femaleness, the ways that the members of a culture understand what it is to be a woman or a man and what the rules of interaction between the two are. The distinction is not really this simple: in the first place, biology and culture influence each other profoundly; in the second, the extent of biological differences between the sexes is still a hotly contested issue; and in the third, biology as a science represents a particular cultural way of thinking about the world, which has been influenced by the gender understandings of its *founding fathers*. The important point is that gender is a system of beliefs about the capacities and limitations of women and men, and a body of knowledge about how to act appropriately as a woman or a man. These beliefs seem to be based on nature, on physical differences between men and women, but in fact there is a great deal of variation from one culture to another in the ways that men and women are expected to behave and in what they are considered capable of doing, by virtue of their sex. In

some societies most of the heavy physical labor is deemed *women's work*, while in others women are not considered capable of such labor. In some societies, women are considered to make good doctors and bad poets, while in others quite the opposite is true. Some societies consider men more emotional, or more spiritual, than women; others make the opposite assessment. If concepts of men's and women's roles were indeed based simply on nature, we would not see this cross-cultural variation in roles.

FOLKLORE AND GENDER

If gender is an aspect of culture, rather than a biological fact, we can begin to see that folklore might play important roles in its expression and reinforcement. In this guide we are drawing on one of the major definitions of folklore, as *artistic communication in small groups*. It is important to realize that much of our sense of identity, sexual and otherwise, is developed and expressed through just this form of communication. A second definition of folklore that is often used has to do with the way that it combines traditional knowledge with personal innovation. For example, you might retell a joke you heard, but change it a bit to fit the circumstances or because you don't remember it exactly as told. This combination of tradition and innovation means folklore can be a place where we check our own experiences against cultural expectations.

Folklore to Reinforce Gender Stereotypes

Folklore, then, can be an important way of learning and expressing cultural values and beliefs. Many forms of children's folklore, from jump-rope rhymes, to jokes and riddles, to playing house, can send messages about what boys and girls and men and women are, and what they can do. Another important place where gender identity is often learned and expressed is in family folklore, where family stories and rituals may convey unspoken attitudes about gender. Both family folklore and children's folklore are discussed in separate chapters in this guide. A collection project in either of these areas can and should include questions like the following: are gender beliefs being expressed, either implicitly or explicitly, in this folklore? is this form of folklore usually or always performed by one sex or the other? to the same or the opposite sex? You might look at your own family's rituals, and ask, for instance, whether your mother or father usually cooks or carves the Thanksgiving turkey, or tells the stories about how they met, and so on. You might listen to small children playing house for what they have to say about what *Mommy* and *Daddy* are supposed to do. Of course this in itself is not a collection project, only the first step. I'll talk more about this later.

Folklore to Challenge Gender Stereotypes

Folklore can serve to teach and express the dominant cultural expectations about gender roles, but it can also serve to question them or to protest against them, and to express alternate beliefs. Many folklorists suggest that folklore allows us to express ideas that cannot be expressed directly, because they don't match with official cultural messages, or because we aren't consciously aware of these ideas. Studying folklore may help us to understand what people believe but are politically unable to say or psychologically unwilling to admit. Consider that although there are many different ways of seeing the world, only a limited number of these ways are actually encouraged by our schools, television, and authority figures. The other ways of seeing the world exist in informal channels, such as in *artistic communication in small groups*, which is to say, folklore. One example of this from children's folklore which most people will be familiar with is the song, sung to the tune of *The Battle Hymn of the Republic*, which begins "Mine eyes have seen the glory of the burning of the school." Here is a joke that works by upsetting one of our conventional assumptions about gender:

> A man dies and goes to purgatory, and sees an old friend of his walking around with a beautiful woman on his arm, so he asks his friend, "What did you do in life that was so good that you should be rewarded this way?"
>
> "Nothing," his friend answers. "I'm her punishment."

This joke, which could be told by either a man or woman, works because it plays with our tendency to see the man in a couple as the active subject, and the woman as the passive object; the joke offers an alternative reality.

WOMEN AND FOLKLORE

As I mentioned above, *gender issues in folklore* apply to studies of both male and female genders. For instance, studies on the folklore of masculinity, and the ways in which men's experiences may differ from the cultural norm, are important and worthwhile. However, many people argue that folklorists have tended to look primarily at folklore performed or valued by men, and at women's folklore only when it is performed in front of men or otherwise matches male assumptions about appropriate female behavior. To redress this situation, studies of gender issues often focus on women's expressions, as I will do in this chapter. At first glance, it might seem strange to assert that folklore has traditionally meant men's folklore, or that women have been underrepresented in folklore studies. For most of the history of folklore as a discipline, many of its most talented researchers have been women. Women, and women's folklore, have also been present in the pages of the books folklorists have written. The problem, then, is not simply a lack of women in the field or in the literature. Rather, it is a question of what about women's lives and expressions is deemed worthy of study, and what our discipline has been unable to see and hear about these lives and expressions. A number of writers have suggested that women's folklore is not noticed or valued unless it corresponds to society's concepts of what women are about. Below I will give some examples of what these writers mean.

Many recent researchers have suggested that our culture's dominant ways of viewing the world represent a male perspective, or rather the perspective of men of a particular age, class and ethnicity (these researchers refer to this as a *male-centered ideology* or a *patriarchy*). These ways of viewing the world are largely accepted and internalized by most people, whether or not they are members of this class and gender. However, there are times when these views on the world do not match up with the experiences of many women (or of men who don't belong to the dominant class and ethnic group). Women's folklore may express those experiences that don't fit in our dominant cultural ideas of what life is about. Some of the folklore performed by women, then, will be different both from folklore performed by men, and from other forms of artistic communication found in popular culture, high art, and literature.

Not just the *stuff* of women's folklore, but the very way in which women communicate this folklore may differ from the standard, as well. In one influential study of woman's verbal folklore, Susan Kalcik (1986) suggested that women are more likely than men to build a folkloric performance together, by contributing elements based around a central idea she terms a *kernel*. In this style of performance there is no clear distinction between audience and performer, as all the people in the room may contribute pieces to the story being created. This type of folklore-telling session differs from the more classical notion of a story-teller performing traditional stories to an attentive audience. It is the latter which is the sort of folklore that has been most sought after and emphasized by folklorists, and which may in fact be more of a *male* style of folklore performance. This has important implications for the student who is going out to collect folklore. How do you know when you've found it? Starting out with strong preconceptions about what a folklore performance *looks like* may cause you to overlook instances of folklore that don't fit this model.

Two Studies of Women's Folklore

A related problem is overlooking folklore that you don't expect people of one or the other gender to be performing. Be aware that the use of folklore to reinforce gender distinctions also includes ideas about which sex characteristically performs certain kinds of folklore, and the different values we ascribe to each of those kinds. What do we mean when we call something "just an old wives' tale"? Why is gossip considered to be a *female* activity in our society, thus making it necessary for people to claim that *men gossip, too*? To help explain what I'm saying here, I will discuss two chapters written on women's performances of folklore; the first is an article written by Richard Dorson in the *Handbook of American Folklore* (1983), the second is an article by Rayna Green (1977).

In "Folktale Performers," Dorson compares two female performers, whom he characterizes as "Mountain Woman" and "Faculty Wife," respectively. For the "mountain woman" he uses the work of a folklorist named Willard B. Moore who, along with his wife and children, spent a week at the home of a storyteller named Sara Cowan in an Appalachian town in Kentucky in 1977. Out of this week of study, Dorson tells us, came "the fullest statement yet of an American female storyteller" (1983:295). Immediately following his discussion of Sara Cowan, Dorson tells us about a woman he calls Jennie Clifton (a pseudonym). Jennie Clifton was the wife of a colleague of

Dorson's and a member of his circle of friends and acquaintances. Dorson discusses a number of off-color jokes which Clifton was in the habit of telling at cocktail parties and dinners. Then he compares Jennie Clifton's repertoire to Sara Cowan's and notes that they are "as far apart as the poles." Sara Cowan, he claims, stayed away from off-color jokes, preferring the "serious and didactic." She most often told true stories about local occurrences, and she usually used them to prove a point or teach a lesson. Dorson notes that she did, according to Moore, once share an off-color joke with Moore's wife. However, Dorson considers this an exception which is not worth pursuing. Jennie Clifton, on the other hand, tells mostly vulgar jokes with sexual and racial themes which are meant to amuse and shock her audience, relying in part on what Dorson describes as the contrast between her "ladylike appearance" and the crudeness of the jokes.

What are the differences between these two women and the situations in which their stories and jokes are collected? Sara Cowan is 75 years old, from a rural, conservative, religious background. Jennie Clifton is in her late thirties and a member of upper-middle class, mainstream American society. Certainly they are very different women in a number of ways. But in characterizing their story-telling preferences as he did, Dorson overlooked crucial differences in the situations in which each woman's stories were collected. The fact that such an experienced folklorist as Richard Dorson was able to overlook these important factors suggests that he was allowing himself to be influenced by cultural attitudes of what certain women are supposed to act like, to the detriment of his scholarship.

One important distinction Dorson failed to take into account is the difference between public and private. Sara Cowan was performing her stories for a fieldworker who was an outsider in her community and her house. Jennie Clifton, on the other hand, was within her circle of friends when she told her jokes. Although this did not necessarily influence these particular women's choices of stories and jokes, it is an important point to keep in mind as you do your fieldwork. The people you choose to work with may not feel comfortable sharing parts of their joke or story-telling repertoire with you. This is particularly true in instances where the fieldworker is male and the informant female, or vice versa. In other words, be aware that your presence may influence the performer in ways you may not have anticipated.

Mixed company can be considered an obstacle to folkloric performance in some parts of our society, but not in others. The issue of gender should be seen as working together with other issues such as age, ethnicity, and class. You've probably noticed that what is considered proper behavior for men and women, and what is okay for mixed company, is not always the same for old people and young people, for people of different ethnic backgrounds, and in different regions of the United States. For Jennie Clifton, performance of off-color folklore in mixed company was amusingly scandalous, not outrageously inappropriate. Remember that Sara Cowan shared such a joke with the fieldworker's wife, but not with the fieldworker himself. Her reluctance to do so might have come from a different concept of appropriate mixed-company behavior as much as from the fact that the fieldworker was a relative stranger. Did she commonly share such jokes with her female friends? Of course, we can't say. Dorson assumes she did not, and would probably have been surprised had such a "nice old lady" been telling off-color jokes. You may be able to recall a time when you were surprised to hear your grandmother, or someone else, tell a joke that seemed shocking coming from a "nice old lady." However, Rayna Green has collected what she calls "bawdy lore" from the nice old (and not-so-old) Southern ladies of her family in East Texas, and she suggests that for many women of all ages "racy" folk wisdom and humor is far from unusual. The folklore Green collected, jokes and stories pertaining to sex and scatology (i.e. bathroom humor), is performed out of the hearing of the men and represents an unofficial response to the official code of behavior for Southern ladies.

In her article, Green presents examples of the humor of Southern women as well as telling us something about the culture to which they are reacting. For instance, pointing out that the Southern church exerts powerful control over women's lives, she notes that much of Southern women's bawdy lore pertains to preachers (1977:31). Other examples ridicule male egos, the institution of marriage, and sexual miscues (particularly on the part of newlyweds and old or drunk men who are unable to perform). Through the channel of folk humor, women are able to express a reality very different from the official version of reality, and to pass their version on to their daughters.

In presenting these examples, I do not mean to suggest that all of the folklore specific to women deals in sexual humor, or that all women have their secret store of bawdy folklore to be brought out in get-togethers such as Green describes. Instead, I want to stress the point that many of the prevailing images of women and women's folklore are based on male perceptions of women. Many people (men and women) accept the idea that women do not tell jokes as well as men. Based on the evidence presented, perhaps we can replace this notion with the idea that women are often reluctant to perform their jokes in front of men, and that many women perform their jokes in a different style than what might be considered standard for male joke-telling. Green notes that in her experience women's dirty jokes differ from men's: the jokes she hears from women are seldom "deeply derogatory to women or men"; rarely do they make use of racist themes; they emphasize different aspects of situations and draw different conclusions (1977:32).

IDENTITY AND FIELDWORK INTERACTIONS

Rayna Green is able to collect such folklore because, in the first place, she is female, and in the second place, she is related to the women she studied for this article. (This fact doesn't necessarily make one privy to all of a person's intimate secrets—we've all had the experience of telling a cab driver or other stranger something we wouldn't tell our close kin. Nonetheless, for many types of folklore, studying people close to you can be a definite advantage.) The sort of folklore Green is studying is performed in situations where female friends and relatives get together after dinner or at other times when the men are gathered elsewhere. That is to say, its *natural context* is in all-female, extended family get-togethers. Green is able to study this "bawdy lore" in its natural context because she is a member of this folk group. Dorson was able to collect jokes from Jennie Clifton, the "faculty wife," in their natural context because she was comfortable performing her jokes for female *and* male friends, and thus he was a part of the folk group in which she performed.

It is important to keep in mind that gender identity neither automatically qualifies or disqualifies you from most types of folklore study. Women should not assume that women's folklore will be automatically accessible to them any more than men should. In the first place women may be outsiders among other women for various reasons, such as age, class, ethnicity, or simply being strangers. In the second place, most women basically accept official cultural ideas about what kinds of expression are valuable and important, and thus may have a hard time seeing and appreciating women's folklore when it differs from the official version. This is not meant to discourage you, but to urge you to consider your relationship to the person or people whose folklore you wish to collect.

In what ways might your identity influence the type of folklore they feel comfortable performing, or you feel comfortable collecting? Are you a part of their usual folk group for this sort of performance or not? You should take these questions into account at the time you collect the folklore and also at the time you write about it.

CONTEXT AND MEANING

Regardless of whether you are fortunate enough to collect the folklore item in its natural context, it is important to include as much information about context as you can. Having the contextual information about an item of folklore helps in trying to understand what this folklore means to the person who performed it, how it fits in with major issues in her or his life, why she or he might have performed it at this time. You've probably had the experience of having a joke take on new meanings when told by a woman instead of a man, or when the context is changed in some other way. In a project that deals with gender issues in folklore, you will need to explore how and why this change in meaning takes place. To do this you should take down as much information about the context as you can: the age, sex, and other background information on the performer; the audience he or she was performing to; what came immediately before and after this item; the time of day, time of year, location, and so on. You will also need to find out from the performer what this item means to her or him, and why she or he chose to perform it at that time. You might be surprised by what you come to understand about that person or that item of folklore.

Rachelle Saltzman has written an article in which she makes clear the importance of filling in this contextual information (1986). I will quote one of her examples at length because it will help to explain this process. She was talking with an elderly Scottish woman, Rose Kerrigan, who had considered herself a staunch feminist for most of her life. During the course of conversation, Rose related the following joke:

> This girl told me this. She worked in the factory. She said, this man met his friend and as he was getting on a bit his friend said to him,
> "Why don't you get married?" he said.
> "Oh well, I'm waiting for my ideal wife."
> And he said, "Well, what is your ideal wife?"
> He says, "Well, my idea of a good wife would be one when she walked down the street she would look like a lady, in bed she would act like a prostitute, and in the kitchen, she'd be economical."

> A few years later he met his friend again and he said, "Did you get your ideal wife?"
> "Ah, no, not exactly," he says. "My wife, when she walks down the street, she looks like a prostitute. In the kitchen, she acts like a lady. And in bed she's economical."

Saltzman tells us that she was surprised to hear this joke coming from Rose, because it seems to reflect a very unfeminist way of thinking about women, as objects. But when Rose explains the joke, it becomes clear that the joke as the women shared it at work had a very different meaning. For Rose, it was a joke on chauvinistic men, on a man who gets his comeuppance because "he wants perfection, but he's not always prepared to give perfection! . . . You see they're always looking for perfection in the female" (552). Think about the different things this joke could mean if it were told by a man in a group of all men, or by a man to women, and you can understand how important it is to get the context of a performance of folklore. In any sort of folklore collection you embark on, this is an important part of the job. For a collection dealing with gender issues it is crucial. It is not enough to simply collect folklore from women and call it *women's folklore* or from men and call it *men's folklore*. You should be asking how it fits in with questions of gender identity and relationships with the opposite sex, either in reinforcing or challenging the dominant cultural ideas.

CONCLUSION

By way of example, in this chapter I have concentrated on the ways gender may be involved in folk narrative and folk humor, and I have alluded to the importance of gender in family folklore and children's folklore. However, I do not mean to suggest that gender issues are involved only in these genres and contexts. Later chapters in this book discuss other genres of folklore such as material culture, dance, narrative, and festival; and other kinds of diversity such as age and ethnicity. All of these are areas in which gender issues may play important, but not necessarily obvious roles. You should turn to these chapters for information on the specific form of folklore you plan to collect. Keep this chapter in mind as you consider the ways in which gender identity may be involved in the form and use of an item, as well as your own reaction to it.

Acknowledgements

I am grateful to Katherine Borland and Jan Tarlin for critical readings of previous drafts. The research and writing of this chapter were supported in part by a Jacob Javits Fellowship from the U.S. Department of Education.

References Cited

Dorson, Richard M. 1983. Folktale Performers. IN *Handbook of American Folklore*, ed. Richard M. Dorson, pp. 287-300. Bloomington: Indiana University Press.

Green, Rayna. 1977. Magnolias Grow in Dirt: The Bawdy Lore of Southern Women. *Southern Exposure* 4(4):29-33.

Kalcik, Susan. 1986 [1975]. '. . .like Ann's gynecologist or the time I was almost raped':Personal Narratives in Women's Rap Groups. IN *Women and Folklore: Images and Genres*, Claire Farrer, ed. pp. 3-11. Prospect Heights, IL: Waveland Press.

Saltzman, Rachelle H. 1987. Folklore, Feminism, and the Folk: Whose Lore Is It? *Journal of American Folklore* 100:548-562.

Selected Annotated Bibliography

This bibliography is intended to provide sources in four distinct but overlapping areas. Since many of the sources included cover more than one of these areas, it will be useful to look in each section.

1) Gender Issues in Fieldwork

Folklore Fieldwork: Sex, Sexuality, and Gender. 1990. Special Issue, *Southern Folklore* 47:1, Camilla Collins, ed.
With articles covering a range of topics relating to sexuality and gender in fieldwork, this collection promises to be a valuable source. Articles cover a variety of genres of folklore from narrative to folk architecture.

Golde, Peggy, ed. 1986. *Women in the Field: Anthropological Experiences*, 2nd ed. Berkeley and Los Angeles: University of California Press.
A collection of articles by women anthropologists on their fieldwork experiences in a large number of cultures around the world. This would be a useful book for anyone planning an extended fieldwork project, or just wanting to know more about the process; and its usefulness should not be limited to female students.

Kodish, Debora. 1987. Absent Gender, Silent Encounter. *Journal of American Folklore* 100:573-578.
An excellent chapter about how implicit assumptions regarding gender influence a fieldworker's first encounter with "the folk."

Saltzman, Rachelle H. 1987. Folklore, Feminism, and the Folk: Whose Lore Is It? *Journal of American Folklore* 100:548-562.
An excellent chapter which discusses the importance of listening to the informant's own interpretation of her folklore, as well as paying heed to the context in which it is performed.

Whitehead, Tony Larry and Mary Ellen Conaway, eds. 1986. *Self, Sex and Gender in Cross-Cultural Fieldwork*. Urbana and Chicago: University of Illinois Press.
A collection of articles dealing with gender issues involved in working with foreign cultures.

Yocom, Margaret R. 1985. Woman to Woman: Fieldwork and the Private Sphere. IN *Women's Folklore, Women's Culture*, eds. Jordan and Kalcik, pp. 45-59. Philadelphia: University of Pennsylvania Press.
Yocom discusses folklore which is performed in the private sphere, and necessity for the fieldworker to be accepted into that private circle before beginning to study these folkloric performances. A useful article for anyone planning to study women's folklore; also relevant for a project in family folklore.

2) Gender in Culture and Society

Baker, Russell. 1982. *Growing Up*. New York: Congdon & Weed, Inc.
Although this is not a book about folklore, fieldwork, or gender, I highly recommend it because Baker, in telling his life story, shows how his role as a male was constructed through proverbs, stories, and other forms of conventional expression used by his mother and other adults in his life. A fascinating look at how folklore shapes gender.

Goffman, Erving. 1979. *Gender Advertisements*. Cambridge, MA: Harvard University Press.
By examining magazine and television ads and publicity photos, Goffman has provided us with a fascinating look at the ways in which gender is socially constructed. The brief essays at the beginning of the book are written for a general audience, and although the photos are somewhat dated, the observations are still powerful.

Ortner, Sherry B. and Harriet Whitehead, eds. 1981. *Sexual Meanings: The Cultural Construction of Gender and Sexuality*. Cambridge and London: Cambridge University Press.
A collection of chapters on issues of gender and sexuality in various cultures, looking at gender as a set of cultural symbols. Good collection of chapters to show some of the range of ways different cultures conceptualize gender.

Brandes, Stanley. 1980. *Metaphors of Masculinity: Sex and Status in Andalusian Folklore*. University of Pennsylvania Press: American Folklore Society.
Brandes examines a variety of genres of folklore among Andulasian men, exploring ways in which masculine identity is created and expressed.

Weigle, Marta. 1982. *Spiders and Spinsters: Women and Mythology*. Albuquerque: University of New Mexico Press.
This very readable book looks primarily at how women are depicted in (mostly male) mythologies from around the world. It also suggests ways of studying women's mythologies, of which less is known. Contains many examples and illustrations, and a large bibliography.

3) Women and Folklore

De Caro, Francis A. 1983. *Women and Folklore: A Bibliographic Survey*. Westport, CT: Greenwood Press.
This bibliographic guide contains over 1600 references in all areas of folklore pertaining to women, female folklorists, etc. There is also a brief but helpful introduction, and a forty-five page bibliographic essay.

DeCaro, Rosan Jordan. 1973. A Note on Sexocentrism in Folklore Studies. *Folklore Feminists Communication* 1:5-6.
A brief note cautioning folklore researchers to be aware of their own biases and preconceived notions when analyzing materials.

Farrer, Claire R. 1986 [1975]. *Women and Folklore: Images and Genres*. Prospect Heights, IL: Waveland Press.
An important early collection of articles discussing women's folklore and women in folklore, covering a broad range of topics.

Feminist Revisions. 1988. Special Issue, *Journal of Folklore Research* 25:3. Beverly Stoeltje, guest editor.

Folklore and Feminism. 1987. Special Issue, *Journal of American Folklore* 100:398.
These two special issues both came out of a "Folklore and Feminism Symposium" at the 1986 meetings of the American Folklore Society. Both contain papers addressing a wide variety of concerns and will give a good idea of current scholarship on women and folklore.

Folklore Women's Communication. (formerly *Folklore Feminist Communication*). 1973-.
The newsletter of the Women's Section of the American Folklore Society; often contains useful notes and brief articles on gender issues in folklore research.

Green, Rayna. 1977. Magnolias Grow in Dirt: The Bawdy Lore of Southern Women. *Southern Exposure* 4(4):29-33.
A brief, extremely readable article on an example of women's folklore which, in part because it is not performed in front of men, has not been recognized or studied by folklorists before.

Jordan, Rosan A. and Susan Kalcik. 1985. *Women's Folklore, Women's Culture*, Publications of the American Folklore Society, New Series, vol. 8. Philadelphia: University of Pennsylvania Press.
A collection of chapters on women's folklore in the public and private spheres, with a final section comparing men's and women's forms. Also has a very helpful introduction.

Kalcik, Susan. 1986 [1975]. '. . .like Ann's gynecologist or the time I was almost raped':Personal Narratives in Women's Rap Groups. IN *Women and Folklore: Images and Genres*, Claire Farrer, ed. pp. 3-11. Prospect Heights, IL: Waveland Press.
In this chapter, Kalcik discusses the collaborative nature of some women's personal narratives and suggests this may be a women's style of narrative.

Sawin, Patricia. 1988. Women's Identity and Ethnic Identity: An Exploratory Bibliography. *Folklore Forum* 21(2) (In Press).

Weigle, Marta. 1978. Women as Verbal Artists: Reclaiming the Daughters of Enheduanna. *Frontiers* 3:1-9.
An excellent discussion of the study of women's verbal art, why it has been neglected until recently, and general suggestions which should be helpful in designing a project.

Women as Verbal Artists. 1978. Special Issue, *Frontiers* 3:3. Marta Weigle, Special Editor.
Contains short articles on women's verbal art in several cultures.

4) Women's Studies and Feminist Scholarship

The following women's studies and feminist journals are a good source of articles on gender: *Differences: A Journal of Feminist*

Cultural Studies, 1988- ; *Frontiers: A Journal of Women Studies*, 1975- ; *Signs: A Journal of Women in Culture and Society*, 1975- ; *Womens Studies: An Interdisciplinary Journal*, 1972- .

Du Bois, Ellen Carol, Gail Paradise Kelly, et al. 1985. *Feminist Scholarship: Kindling in the Groves of Academe*. Urbana: University of Illinois Press.
This book looks at feminist scholarship and how it has influenced, and been influenced by, the academic disciplines in which it is practiced. Good reading for students interested in feminism or women's studies.

Jaggar, Alison M. and Paula Rothenberg Struhl. 1978. *Feminist Frameworks: Alternative Theoretical Accounts of the Relations Between Women and Men*.
A collection of articles meant to show the variety of approaches that have been taken to studying the situation of women in society. Shows the range of feminist approaches as well as more conservative approaches. A fairly "heavy" collection, but useful for anyone trying to understand the range of ways of thinking which are included within *feminism*.

Reiter, Rayna R. 1975. *Toward an Anthropology of Women*. New York: Monthly Review Press.
This is an early work on the anthropological study of women which will provide a very readable introduction for anyone beginning to think about a project involving either women's folklore or gender issues.

CHAPTER 4
Folk Narrative

Linda Kinsey Adams

A *narrative* is a story. Narratives can be told, written, sung, acted out, danced, or performed in many other ways. You can find narratives in conversations, in speeches, in songs, in books, in magazines, in films, on television shows, on the radio, and in other media. Some narratives are widely known all over the world, while other narratives are highly personal or limited to a particular community. In this chapter I will discuss several kinds of *oral prose narratives*, the stories that people tell each other in face-to-face interaction.

Like a story you read in a book, an oral prose narrative contains a plot; that is, it contains a series of events that unfold in a definite sequence over time. It has a beginning, a middle, and an end. Sometimes these narrative elements are strongly marked. For example, if someone says "Once upon a time," you immediately know that you are about to hear a story, a particular kind of story that folklorists call a *Märchen*. Sometimes a story is less obviously marked, emerging almost imperceptibly in the course of a conversation. In this case, you will have to listen carefully to discover how the story is framed or set off from the surrounding flow of talk.

Oral prose narratives, however, differ from written texts in fundamental and important ways. First, their overall form and content are not fixed. In other words, an oral narrative exists in as many *versions* as there are tellers or tellings, and no two versions will be exactly alike. Second, their *style* differs from that of a written text, because the *medium of expression* is different. Since the spoken word is fleeting, storytellers tend to use repetition and other techniques to emphasize key elements and keep the story thread present in the minds of their listeners. Moreover, *paralinguistic* features or what Alan Dundes calls *texture*, such as loudness, tone, gesture, speed of delivery and facial expression, allow storytellers to convey with a few words ideas that an author, working with the printed page, must use many more words to say.

Finally, a storyteller must always take into account the *context* in which she or he is performing a narrative. Storytellers may shorten or fill out their narratives to fit the needs and expectations of their audience. For example, a man who delights in recounting a particular hunting adventure to his circle of friends may produce a much more elaborated version of the same story to a group of interested outsiders. This new audience cannot be counted on to understand the allusions to local terrain, personalities, and hunting practices that would be common knowledge among the teller's friends. These new listeners must be "filled in" about important background information if the story is to be effective.

Like folklore in general, folk narratives are traditional; that is, they have been performed over time and through space. Some folk narratives are very old and have been disseminated over a wide geographic area. Others have a more limited temporal/geographic distribution. For our purposes, a *folk narrative* can be any oral prose narrative that has been repeated at least twice and therefore exists in at least two versions. "But," you may ask, "if I record a story, how do I know whether it is unique to the teller or whether it is just one version of a traditional folk narrative?" The answer is that folklorists, over the last hundred and fifty years, have built up great collections of traditional narratives of all kinds. By checking the indexes to these collections for analogues to your story, you can determine to what degree it is traditional.

Let's take an example of a *tall tale* I collected during a call-in radio program in West Texas a few years ago. A caller told the story like this:

23

Listen, I've got a tale that my grandfather used to tell me. He was from out in Tom Green County, and telling about back when he was a boy, they used to take their wagon into town, you know, when they got the chance to go in. And he said they had gone into town one weekend and come back and they were getting pretty close to the house, and said that the horses jumped all of a sudden, and said this humongous rattlesnake came out of the bushes from the side of the road and struck at the horses. And said that he missed the horses but he hit the tongue of the wagon. And they didn't think much about it and went on back down to the house, and by the time they got there, that wagon tongue had started swelling up so big that they were plumb afraid of it, that it had swole up so big that they cut it up and built a four-room house with it. [Laughter.] It was amazing. He said that about two weeks later, too, said there come a big ole rainstorm, and said luckily they was out of the house 'cause it drained all that venom out of there and that thing just shrunk up about the size of a matchbox.

Reviewing this story, I might have assumed that it was unique to my storyteller, since, as he tells it, the events actually happened to his grandfather. On the other hand, these events are rather implausible, and I would be very gullible to accept the story as a faithful recounting of a true experience. In fact, the exaggeration in the tale tells me that I am probably hearing a *tall tale* or *windy*. Therefore, I consult the folk narrative indexes to see whether other versions of the same tale have been collected.

What do I look under? Well, the tale has several striking elements or *motifs*. It recounts the effect of *snakebite* on a *wagon tongue* which produces *swelling*; the construction of a *house* from the swollen *wood*; and its subsequent *shrinking* to the size of a *matchbox* after a heavy *rain*. Now we need to consult the folk narrative indexes for stories with similar motifs. We start by checking the back of the Aarne-Thompson tale type index, *The Types of the Folktale*. By looking under *Snake* we find: *bites objects (they swell)*, 1889M. We now know that this motif has been numbered. We also could have looked under the word *swelling* and found *Swelling objects (snake bite, bee sting)*, 1889M. By turning to 1889M in the actual index, we find that this story can be found in the tall tales of Baron Munchausen, which means the tale type is at least 200 years old, as Munchausen's tales first appeared in print in 1785. We also learn that the type is related to motif X1205 which is indexed in Ernest Baughman's *Type and Motif Index of the Folktales of England and North America*. By turning to this index, we will find dozens of related motifs. For example, one of the variations listed by Baughman in his index is X1205.1(c)——*Snake strikes man's wooden leg*. Mody Boatright's work, *Tall Tales of Texas Cow Camps* (1946), is listed as one of the places where this motif is discussed.

In Mody Boatright's version, the effects of the snake venom causes the man's leg to swell; it swells so much that three men have to chop on it for three days. The victim finally dies from suffocation, but his leg has produced enough kindling wood to last all winter (6-9). In other versions, a man decides not to commit suicide after his hoe swells and provides enough wood to put new shingles on all his buildings (Pennsylvania). An old mattress "was so plum swole up that I used it for a feather bed for two weeks," said another teller. In a California version of the tale, a man is losing a car race because a cactus has punctured his tires. However, the day is saved when he runs over a rattlesnake nest. The venom from the snakes causes the tires to swell back to their normal size.

In Baughman's index you would also find other shrinking examples: A sapling which was used as a tent post swells into a log big enough to be sawed into "several hundred thousand feet of lumber." However, after the venom wore off, "the dang stuff shrank up" to the size of toothpicks, and the boss was really upset at the men. A cypress club swelled, providing enough wood for almost a mile of railroad track; but rain caused the railroad ties to shrink to the size of toothpicks. Note that these versions correspond with our West Texan version in which the house shrinks to the size of a matchbox.

You could also find other versions by checking archives, such as that at Indiana University. In a version collected at IU in the 1940s, a snake-bitten fork handle swells so much that enough wood for twenty five-room houses is provided. In another Indiana version, we learn that what swells must *unswell*, as when a rattlesnake bites at a toothpick hanging from a man's mouth. The toothpick swells to such an extent that enough wood for a 12-room house was provided; however, when paint is applied, the house shrinks back to the original toothpick.

Finding other examples that correspond with your data can give you valuable background, but such a task is not your primary mission. Our hunt through the indexes was merely to determine if the motif is well established as a tradition. However, our primary goal in analyzing the data is to find out what the data means *now* to the people who perform it. This information cannot be gleaned from a book. Understanding the context of the situation as the folklore is currently performed is the most important key to understanding the current meaning of the lore.

Before we can discuss meaning, however, we need to understand the forms of oral prose narratives. Folklorists have identified four major genres of folk narrative that are told in different contexts and convey different kinds of messages. Each of these genres is divided into smaller subgenres of narratives that have their own particular characteristics. Once you know the general features of these genres, you will become attuned to the abundance of oral prose narratives in everyday life. Many students are surprised to discover how commonly oral prose narratives are performed. But if you think of it, this is really not very surprising at all. As social beings, we communicate constantly in stories to amuse, entertain, warn, preach, question, console, project our point of view, or preserve aspects of our experience. Yet storytelling is so natural, so much a part of the way we relate to one another, that it often goes unnoticed. After reviewing the definitions for the four major genres of oral prose narrative below, you may want to test this assertion by informally taking note of all the narratives you hear in the course of a week. See how many narrative genres you can identify during your everyday interactions with friends, family, and coworkers.

Genres of Oral Narrative
Myth

A myth is a sacred narrative set in the primordial past. The word *myth* is sometimes used by nonfolklorists to mean something that is fallacious or silly, but folklorists do not use the word in this sense. *Myths* are the tales people tell about the beginnings of things. They are powerful social forces, often connected with a person's religion, and as such, are associated with ritual and ceremony. The characters in myths are believed to be real, even though they may exist in a time and space remote from ordinary life. Myths explain the creation of the earth and all things in it; they explain why things are the way they are. For instance, the story of the Tower of Babel attempts to explain why there are different races in the world. The story of Adam's rib attempts to justify the domination of males over females. Myths govern the way people live, but they are not often articulated in everyday life. One place you may hear myths performed orally, however, is at a religious service. (See Chapter 7 **Folklore and Religion**. See also *aetiological legends* in the glossary of terms.)

Folktales

Folktales are stories that are completely fictional. The characters are not believed to be real people, and the purpose of folktales is usually to entertain, although they may also be instructive. *Complex* tales are those which have more than one episode: these

include *Märchen, religious tales*, and *novella*. *Simple* tales have only one episode or a simple formula: these include *animal tales, fables, exempla, jokes, humorous anecdotes, Numskull tales, schwank, tall tales, shaggy dog stories*, and *formula tales*. (See glossary for definitions.)

Märchen. This is probably the most familiar complex genre of folktales. Folklorists often use this term instead of *fairy tale*, while the term *fairy tale* is more and more being used to refer to a Märchen that has been printed in a book. Märchen means *little short story* in German, and the German term is used because the first great collection of this type was made in Germany by the Grimm brothers in 1812. Other terms that have been used in the past for this type of tale include *magic tale, ordinary tale, hero tale*, and *conte fabulaire*. A märchen has a distinctly recognizable beginning, such as "Once upon a time, . . ." as well as a standard ending, such as ". . . And they all lived happily ever after," or "A rat went in a hole, and now my story's whole." Set in a world of fantasy, the stories are highly complex, with multiple episodes, high adventure, and magical acts. People willingly suspend disbelief when listening to these stories. Other stylistic characteristics of the folktale have been well described by Max Lüthi (see bibliography).

Before radio and television, Märchen used to be performed for both adults and children in evening gatherings after the day's work had been done, and they still are in some countries. In modern America, however, you are not likely to come across many Märchen performers. In American society, you most likely will find Märchen told to children at bedtime. Examples of Märchen include Little Red Riding Hood, Snow White and the Seven Dwarves, and Cinderella. You will also find thousands of allusions to Märchen in the mass media, in advertisements, television sketches, cartoons, and movies.

Legends

Legends are stories people tell about events that purportedly really happened. However, one of the identifying marks of a legend is that, in the telling, people bring up the issue of whether or not the story is true. Some people will swear that the story is true; others are just as sure that it is a "bunch of baloney," while other people's reactions fall somewhere in between: "I don't know whether this story is true or not, but I've always heard that . . . ." Legends can be transmitted regardless of the belief factor; i.e., a believer can pass the story on to a skeptic who can then pass the story on to another believer (Dégh and Vazsonyi 1971).

The legend is also a conversational genre. In fact, several people may contribute parts of the story in any particular telling. It has no stylized opening formula, although, as mentioned, there is usually reference to the truth element of the story. Evidence, such as witnesses, buildings, or natural sites may be cited. Pseudoevidence may also be cited: "And I can prove it happened because the bruise is right here on my arm."

Legends are not as stylized as folktales, and they are so numerous, constantly being born, that a successful system for indexing them has not been developed. However, some common types of legends that you may run across are supernatural legends, memorates, urban legends, and local legends. (For *historical, place-name,* and *religious legends,* see glossary.)

Supernatural legends (also known as *belief legends* or *belief tales*) include stories of ghosts, spirits, witches, the dead, haunted places, voodoo, and other supernatural creatures and events. Supernatural legends flourish at night, in the shadows, when people are most susceptible to their fears, and when they are mentally prepared to be scared. Gloomy weather, old abandoned houses, caves, ditches, tunnels, bridges, cemeteries, scenes of fatal accidents, Halloween parties, or the darkness around a campfire are perfect settings for supernatural legend-telling. Legends also flourish at slumber parties.

A *memorate* is a narrative told in first person that usually expresses a personal encounter with the supernatural. These stories may involve an individual's encounter with a dead relative or friend (a *revenant*) or may contain more traditional supernatural characters. A person who tells about the time that a witch invaded his bedroom, sat on his chest and paralyzed him so that he was unable to cry out, is telling a memorate. Dozens of versions of this legend exist cross-culturally; the individual first-person version is a memorate. A memorate is sometimes thought of as a *pre-legend,* the stuff from which legends are made.

Urban legends are also stories of horror or eeriness that involve weird happenings, close calls, horrible deaths, and other real-world phenomena. These stories have developed out of the contemporary urban and industrial setting and may center on people's fears about technology. Stories about microwaved cats and babies cooked in the oven are examples of urban legends. A recent urban legend involves tanning parlors. A woman who wanted a "quick tan"

decided to visit three tanning parlors on the same day. Later that evening, people around her noticed a peculiar smell; it turned out that the woman had "cooked" her insides and was doomed to die.

Many urban legends involve automobiles. The economical carburetor, which causes a car to get 100 miles to the gallon, but which the gas companies are allegedly withholding with huge bribes in order to maintain profits from gasoline sales, is an urban legend that has gotten a lot of mileage. People who tell such stories often back up their claims with *pseudowitnesses,* such as "my girlfriend's dentist's wife." If you try to track down these witnesses, you will find you can never get back to the original source. One of the most famous urban legends is known as "The Vanishing Hitchhiker." In one version of this story, a motorist picks up a hitchhiker who later mysteriously vanishes from the car seat. Upon arriving at the hitchhiker's destination, the motorist learns that the hitchhiker had died years previously (Brunvand 1981, 1984, 1986).

Local legends are connected with a particular locality. For example, in Eastland, Texas, a live horned toad was sealed in the cornerstone of the courthouse in 1897. In 1928, when the courthouse was being razed to make way for a new one, 1,500 people gathered to see if the horned toad had survived. A man removed the toad from its metal container, handed it to the county judge, who held it up for the crowd to see. According to various accounts, as the toad began to breathe, the crowd pressed in, and a law officer grabbed the animal, mounted his motorcycle, and raced to the edge of town lest the horned toad be crushed by the mob. The toad was known as Old Rip because he outslept Rip Van Winkle. The story was picked up by news wires all over the country. The toad was shown at conventions from Dallas to New York, and was even shown to President Calvin Coolidge. When Old Rip died in 1929, his body was embalmed, placed in a red velvet casket and enclosed in a glass-covered shrine which can still be viewed at the Eastland County courthouse. To this day people still argue over whether the toad was really alive when it was removed from the cornerstone, or whether a fraud was perpetuated. Such is the stuff of local legends. Fortunately, folklorists do not have to prove whether something is true or not, only that people talk about it.

Legends differ from Märchen in a number of ways. While Märchen are set in a world of fantasy with make-believe characters, legends are set in the real world with real human beings. This does not mean there are no evil spirits or supernatural creatures in legends; the difference is that a legend character, such as a ghost, is *believed* to be real, at least from the perspective of some people. (See also Chapter 6 **Folk Beliefs.**)

Moreover, Märchen characters are flat and stereotypical, whereas legend characters are more realistic. In a Märchen, when Cinderella's sister cuts off her toes to try to make the glass slipper fit, we see no blood spurting because the characters are two-dimensional. However, legend characters are more like us; they bleed, and they affect our emotions and heighten our fears. Märchen are told primarily to entertain; legends are told primarily to inform, to advise, to enlighten, to warn. Of course, in any given performance situation, both Märchen and legends may have other functions as well. Märchen deal with hopes and dreams; legends deal with our deepest anxieties.

Personal Narratives

A personal narrative is a first-person account about a personal experience. Unlike myths, folktales and legends, the personal narrative is not **traditional** in content. It is instead a *unique* story about an event that has occurred in the narrator's life (though narrators *may* borrow elements from the common store of oral narrative techniques, themes or symbols when constructing their accounts).

By repeating the story over time, the narrator becomes identified with it and comes to *own* the story. That is, no one else will tell the story if the original narrator is present, and others may even request the story from him or her. Even though the story is told primarily by one person, it qualifies as folklore because it is performed over and over again and because no two performances will ever be alike.

The story may become more elaborate with each telling, or it may be abbreviated over time. Additionally, the story may be tailored to a particular audience at any given telling. Another source of story change is the changing perspective of the teller, who may see the events narrated in a new light as she or he matures. Gradually, as the story is told and retold, it is shaped to more artistically express the ethical values of the teller or to heighten comic or dramatic effect.

A woman in West Texas often tells the story of being bitten on the arm by a rattlesnake while she was on the floor straightening carpet. After the accident, she calmly applied first aid, called the hospital to tell them she was coming in, changed into clean clothing, and drove herself to the emergency room. While most people who hear the story are

amazed that she would stop to change her clothing in such a life-threatening situation, the story expresses the value the woman places in maintaining a good public image, being able to stay cool in a crisis, and practicing self-reliance. Most personal narratives will contain some such illustration of the teller's personal values.

Community values are also reflected in personal narratives. For instance, in some communities personal narratives may focus on miraculous healings and religious conversions, while in others, they might deal more commonly with feats of bravado and *beating the system*. Each community will have its own sets of values that show up in stories.

Some popular themes of personal narratives include embarrassing situations, courtship stories, crime-victim stories, close calls, encounters with famous people, and family stories (see Stahl 1979, 1983, 1989).

COLLECTION STRATEGIES

When you are collecting oral narratives, keep your tape recorder running all the time, from the moment you walk into a situation until after you leave. Once you have placed the recorder on a table or other surface, ignore it, except to turn the tape over or put new tape in. The best way to collect narratives is to *listen* enthusiastically. However, if the conversation is slow, or if people are not yet relaxed enough to tell stories comfortably, it is perfectly acceptable for you to tell a narrative yourself in order to stimulate reactions and the telling of other narratives. Or, you can ask a question, such as: "Have you heard the story of the House of Blue Lights?" If the response is positive, simply say, "Tell me about it."

Once a narrative session has begun, do not hasten to fill every silent spot in the conversation. Everyone feels as much need as you do to fill the silent pause, and often the most interesting stories emerge as a narrator fills this pause for you. You must follow your instincts, of course, but as a rule, try to talk less rather than more. It is frustrating to listen to a tape-recording and discover that a person was just about to tell you a promising story before you interrupted her or him and told your own story (and of course, in the meantime, the other person's story was forgotten).

Be sure to note what events occurred before, during, and after the storytelling session. Were you washing dishes? Returning from a funeral? Riding in a car on the way to a golf tournament? Make a note of the names and addresses of every person present. At some point, you should also collect background information from your informants including name, age, place of birth, education, religion, ethnicity, occupation, etc. Because a series of questions might interrupt the natural flow of conversation, you will want to interview participants individually after the session or perhaps within the next day or so.

It's also a good idea to review your taped materials before conducting subsequent interviews. You will want to keep a mental or written note of the stories your narrator shared with you and the issues they bring up for you. Some questions you may wish to ask *yourself* are: Why did the person tell a particular story? What is the connection between the conversation or activity preceding the telling of the narrative itself? What cultural values does this story contain? What things would an audience need to know to understand the point of the story? Is there a recognizable pattern among the stories I have collected?

Background material that you will need to gather from the narrator him/herself includes: When and where did the person first hear the story and what is the typical setting for such a story? Is the story told *only* on certain occasions? What *kind* of person is the narrator and his/her usual audience——what kind of work do they do? Where do they come from? What major historical events have affected them? What is important to them?

If you are conducting a community-based project, you will need to find out how one narrator's stories fit into the community's repertoire. Does the story contain themes or ideas common to other forms of folklore performed in this area or among this group? Does it reflect a community aesthetic for storytelling? What is the narrator's relationship to others in his/her community? Is the narrator recognized as a local authority, an equal, a marginal member of the community?

You will also want to collect oral literary criticism from your narrator and/or his/her audience. Oral literary criticism constitutes the narrator/audience's interpretation of the meaning of the story (Dundes 1966). Not many narrators, however, are likely to engage in spontaneous interpretation, since they will assume that the story's message or purpose is clear from the telling. For instance, if you ask a teenager why he tells the urban legend, "The Hook," he will probably say because it is amusing. If you ask another person why the joke she tells is funny, you will probably receive a look of puzzled amazement. In order to collect good oral literary criticism, you must ask perceptive questions that demonstrate an understanding of the story's basic appeal. You might ask a narrator to comment on what she thinks the real point of the story is. You might ask if the story he

tells reflects something about his life. Beyond these general questions, you'll need to focus on the particular details of a story. With the legend, "The Hook," for example, you may want to ask if the narrator sees the hook as a symbol for something else. While you may not always agree with the interpretation your narrator offers, you can still enrich your analysis by gathering his or her oral literary criticism.

As you can see from the variety of questions suggested above, the amount of potentially useful background material for oral narratives is infinite. Therefore, your secondary interviews will be more successful if you plan ahead. Review the materials you've collected; think about what issues or connections you are most interested in exploring; develop your own set of questions; and direct your secondary interviews in such a way that you gather the information you'll need later on when you sit down to interpret your data. You may still not get all the information you would like to have ideally, but you will have something manageable to work with. Depending on the kinds of narratives you are interested in collecting, there are some additional issues and strategies that you should keep in mind.

Myths. You will not be able to walk up to people and say, "Please tell me some myths," because the word *myth* is often understood to mean *lie* or *foolish belief*. Since myths are sacred narratives, regarded reverently by the people who tell and believe them, you will want to be sure that your attitude conveys respect for your informants' beliefs. Attending religious services with your informant is a good way to begin to learn the sacred stories. You could also ask a person specific questions, such as, "According to your religion, how did the earth come to be? How were human beings created?"

It is also important to collect information about the context of a story so that you can understand its nature. One culture's fantasy tale might be another culture's sacred myth. You should try to find out what the narrator's intent was in telling the story.

Legends. When you collect supernatural legends, it is important for you to look for or help create a *legend climate*. You probably will not be able to collect a great many supernatural legends on a bright sunny morning outdoors on a tennis court. People who tell and listen to supernatural legends are usually psychologically prepared to be "scared to death." Therefore, you might want to invite several people to a midnight gathering, to a seance, to an all-night party, to a camping trip, or to an evening picnic at the lake. Many dormitories arrange for ghost-telling sessions on Halloween, complete with candle-lit jack-o-lanterns, and you might attend one of these. Or you might want to arrange for a visit to a haunted house or some other local legendary landmark. If you take a trip in a car to a local site, be sure to have your tape recorder running all the time in the car.

Urban Legends. These can be collected wherever people gather for conversation, such as around the kitchen table or at the coffee station at work. It is best to have several people present so that they can interact with each other. Legends are often told in fragments, with several people contributing parts of the story. Therefore it is best not to try to collect legends during an interview with one person, but in a social situation that is as close to natural as possible. As you collect legends, do not challenge people's beliefs if they differ from your own. A folklorist respects all people's beliefs.

Personal Narratives. Your family is one of the best sources for personal narratives. Grandparents, aunts, uncles, parents, and siblings all have stocks of stories which they tell over and over. A family gathering is a good time to ask these relatives to retell the stories for you. Try to have at least one person present who has never heard the story before, since storytellers may tend to abridge stories that they feel everyone has already heard. Specific suggestions can start the flow of stories. For instance, you might ask, "Tell us about that time you almost fell out of an airplane."

Your friends will also have many personal narratives. Leading suggestions can help elicit the flow of these stories, such as, "Tell us about one of your most embarrassing moments." "Tell us about a narrow escape." "What was the worst injustice you ever suffered?" "How did you meet your spouse?"

Although your family and friends are excellent sources of personal narratives, you may also have success collecting anywhere where people gather to socialize and swap stories—from your local beauty parlor to the county fair.

ANALYSIS AND INTERPRETATION OF DATA

The most important part of your collection project will be to analyze and interpret the meaning of your data. This part is the hardest. There is no set prescription or formula for analyzing data, because each new act of analysis is individual and depends on a person's abilities to see patterns that may not have been noticed before. As Clifford Geertz puts it, analysis is guessing at meanings (1973). You should look at yourself as contributing to a conversation about your data. You have not had the first word on the subject, nor will you have the last.

In order to contribute intelligently to this conversa-tion, you may want to find out what other scholars have said about the subject you are studying. Then, as you look at your own data, you can see how your ideas might correspond to or vary from past interpre-tations. To see what other scholars have done, you can look up your topic in the several indexes which are listed in the bibliography to this article. The *Centennial Index* of the *Journal of American Folklore* is a good place to start. You can also look in the tale type and motif indexes to see how your material might have changed over the years. You may want to review the collections and interpretations you have been reading in your folklore class to gather ideas about how to approach your data.

The most important step towards analysis, however, is to *study* the material that you yourself have collect-ed. Here are some general ideas about projects you might consider. In analyzing and interpreting myths, you might want to see how the myths actually influ-ence the day-to-day decisions that people make. You may want to see how they relate to other aspects of life, such as food production. Since legends frequent-ly deal with our fears, one task might be to find out what these masked fears and anxieties are. In analyz-ing personal narratives, you may want to see how the story functions to establish a bond between teller and listener. For example, a new daughter-in-law may realize that she has been completely accepted into her new family when the mother-in-law shares a personal narrative with her.

Folklorists have developed several approaches to analyzing oral prose narratives. One approach looks at how the narrative is constructed, and is therefore called the structural approach. Just as a house has a particular structure, with a porch, say, a front door, staircase, rooms and roof, so do narratives. You may decide you want to look at the various parts that make up your narrative and see how they fit together. For instance, does the order of events related in the narrative correspond to the order in which the events narrated would be experienced in real life, or has the narrator reworked the time sequence in some way? What effect does this have on the telling? If you are comparing more than one narrative, can you establish a structural pattern common to them all?

Another approach looks at how narratives function in society. Here you might look at the *activity* of storytelling and its purpose: to entertain, build group solidarity, provide an outlet for personal expression, or transform the social relations of performer and audience in some way. Alternately, you may look at the content of the narratives. Do they counsel conformity to the status quo or question received

attitudes and stereotypes? Do they pass on knowledge of some sort?

A third approach looks at the actual context of
storytelling and how this affects the stories themselves. Are there specific uses to which a story is put
in a particular situation? For instance, a mother tells
her disobedient child a story about her own youthful
mischievousness and its dire consequences. Later, she
tells the same story to friends at a cocktail party.
The story remains basically the same, but its message
changes in these two different contexts.

Psychological and/or psychoanalytic approaches
attempt to account for the ways individuals use
narratives to symbolically express deep-seated feelings,
such as repressed sexuality or homophobia. A semiotics approach focuses on the way oral prose narratives
and other forms of folklore are used as systems of
signs to communicate something. In an anthropological approach, one can also study narratives to find out
about the narrator him/herself. What kinds of values
does this person embrace? What does he/she approve
or disapprove of? How does the narrator express
him/herself? What aspects of his/her life are reflected
in the stories he/she tells?

All of these approaches culminate in the most
current approach—performance theory. Here one
tries to determine the nature of the performance, cues
to performance, patterns within a performance and
the emergent uniqueness of a performance (Bauman
1977). One might focus on the performer's additions
to or embellishments of a traditional story, or on the
role of the audience in shaping the performance by
their responses. This approach calls for extensive
ethnographic study.

None of these approaches is mutually exclusive.
Indeed, they often overlap. And researchers are
constantly refining existing approaches and trying out
new ones. Perhaps as you become involved in your
project, you will be able to contribute ideas of your
own to our current scholarly conversation about
folklore.

Acknowledgements

I am indebted to Linda Dégh, Hasan El-Shamy, John W. Johnson,
Kenneth Davis, Warren Walker, Donald Rude, Greg Schrempp,
John McDowell, Beverly Stoeltje, Sandra Stahl, and Richard
Bauman for their teachings. I am also grateful to Katie Borland for
editorial improvements to this chapter.

Selected Annotated Bibliography

The following bibliography lists important works on oral prose
narratives but should not be considered comprehensive.

I) **Indexes and Resources**

Aarne, Antti and Stith Thompson. 1964. *The Types of the Folktale:
A Classification and Bibliography.* Translated and enlarged by
Stith Thompson. 2d rev. ed. Helsinki: Suomalainen Tiedeaka-
temia, Academia Scientiarum Fennica.
Classifies tales from various countries according to type.
Contains subject index. Serves as a starting point for locating
folktale variants.

Abstracts of Folklore Studies. Austin: American Folklore Society.
Vol 1-13. 1963-1975.
Lists and summarizes articles from various folklore journals but
was discontinued in 1975.

Azzolina, David S. 1987. *Tale Type- and Motif-Indexes: An
Annotated Bibliography.* New York and London: Garland Publish-
ing, Inc.
Guides users to indexes in several countries.

Baughman, Ernest W. 1966. *Type and Motif Index of the Folktales
of England and North America.* The Hague: Mouton and Company.
Contains the most recent motif numbers but has no subject index
(users needing a subject index must first consult the Aarne--
Thompson tale type index or the Thompson motif index for
appropriate numbers and then proceed to Baughman's work).

Boggs, Ralph S. 1930. *Index of Spanish Folktales: Classified
According to Antti Aarne's Types of the Folktale, Translated and
Enlarged by Stith Thompson in FF Communications, no. 74.*
Dissertation, University of Chicago. *FFC* 90. Helsinki: Suomalai-
nen Tiedeakatemia.
Focuses mainly on European texts.

Briggs, Katharine. 1970-71. *A Dictionary of British Folktales in the
English Language.* 4 vols. Bloomington: Indiana University Press.
Presents tale texts and/or summaries with extensive bibliographical
notes.

Brunvand, Jan Harold. 1976. *Folklore: A Study and Research Guide.*
New York: St. Martin's Press.
Outlines the history of folkloristics and lists all the major folklore
reference tools (complete with library call numbers). Includes a
sample research paper for beginning folklore students.

Christensen, Reidar Th. 1958. The Migratory Legends. *FFC* 175.
Offers a universal classification system of legends; lists type
numbers for Norwegian legends, divided into eight categories
such as 3030-3080, Witches and Witchcraft.

Dundes, Alan. 1976. *Folklore Theses and Dissertations in the United
States.* Austin: University of Texas Press.
Includes indexes for year, author, subject, and academic institu-
tion.

Jackson, Bruce, Michael Taft, and Harvey S. Axlerod, eds. 1988. *The Centennial Index: One Hundred Years of the Journal of American Folklore.* Washington, D.C.: The American Folklore Society.
Guides users to every article ever printed in the leading folklore journal in the U.S. Contains listings in chronological order as well as by author, subject, and title. Also contains biographical information about each editor of the journal.

Modern Language Association. 1921- . *MLA International Bibliography of Books and Articles on the Modern Language and Literatures.* New York: University Press.
Has a separate section on folklore (beginning with 1970 edition); classified by genre as well as by area.

Perkal, Joan Ruman. 1969. *Western Folklore and California Folklore Quarterly: Twenty-Five Year Index.* Berkeley: University of California Press.

Randolph, Vance. 1987. *Ozark Folklore: An Annotated Bibliography.* Vol. 1. Columbia: University of Missouri Press.

_____., and Gordon McCann. 1987. *Ozark Folklore: An Annotated Bibliography.* Vol. 2. Columbia: University of Missouri Press.

Robe, Stanley Linn. 1973. *Index of Mexican Folktales, Including Narrative Texts from Mexico, Central American and the Hispanic United States.* University of California Folklore Studies, no. 26. Berkeley: University of California Press.
Supplements the work of Boggs.

Simmons, Merle E. *Folklore Bibliography.* 1975-1976. Bloomington: Indiana University Folklore Institute, monograph Series vols. 28-29.
Picks up for two years where the *Southern Folklore Quarterly* bibliography left off.

Southern Folklore Quarterly. University of Florida: South Atlantic Modern Language Association, 1937-1972.
Emphasizes Latin America.

Taft, Michael. 1989. Supplement to the Centennial Index. *Journal of American Folklore* 102:299-314.
Updates and corrects the Centennial Index (see Jackson et al entry above).

Thompson, Stith. 1955. *Motif-Index of Folk-Literature.* 6 vols. Bloomington: Indiana University Press.
Lists thousands of motifs and resources; has its own subject index in Vol. 6.

Woods, Barbara Allen. 1959. *The Devil in Dog Form: A Partial Type-Index of Devil Legends.* Berkeley: University of California Folklore Studies, no. 11.
Lists devil legends of Western Europe and includes analyses.

II) **General Works**
Abrahams, Roger D. 1970. *Deep Down in the Jungle: Negro Narrative Folklore from the Streets of Philadelphia.* Chicago: Aldine.
Shows how the folklore of urban black men is integrally related to their lifestyles and identities.

Bascom, William. 1965. The Forms of Folklore: Prose Narratives. *Journal of American Folklore* 78:3-20.
Distinguishes myths, legends, and folktales.

Bauman, Richard. 1972. The La Have Island General Store: Sociability and Verbal Art in a Nova Scotia Community. *Journal of American Folklore* 85:330-343.
Discusses the complex interplay between individual narrative performances and the aesthetic dimensions of particular social situations.

_____. 1977. *Verbal Art as Performance.* Prospect Heights, Ill.: Waveland Press, Inc.
Argues for an approach to the study of folklore based on performance theory; discusses the nature, keying, patterning, and emergent qualities of performance.

_____. 1986. *Story, Performance, and Event: Contextual Studies of Oral Narrative.* New York: Cambridge University Press.
Analyzes oral narratives in light of the poetics of performance, the social context, and form-function interrelationships.

Bauman, Richard and Roger D. Abrahams, eds. 1981. "*And Other Neighborly Names*": Social Process and Cultural Image in Texas Folklore. Austin: University of Texas Press.
Presents essays which analyze particular forms of folklore in their living context and in terms of their social ramifications.

Bauman, Richard and Joel Sherzer, eds. 1989[1974]. *Explorations in the Ethnography of Speaking.* Cambridge: Cambridge University Press.
Presents ethnographic case studies which examine ways of speaking in particular communities; emphasizes the emergent nature of performance in the ongoing dynamic constitution of social life.

Bennett, Gillian. 1986. Narrative as Expository Discourse. *Journal of American Folklore* 99:415-434.

Briggs, Charles L. 1088. *Competence in Performance: The Creativity of Tradition in Mexicano Verbal Art.* Philadelphia: University of Pennsylvania Press.
Presents an ethnographic study of the verbal art of Spanish speakers in New Mexico; emphasizes sociolinguistic analysis.

Brunvand, Jan Harold. 1986[1968]. *The Study of American Folklore: An Introduction.* 3d ed. New York: W.W. Norton and Company.
Introduces the beginner to American genres of folklore; contains bibliographical summaries at the end of each chapter.

Crowley, Daniel J. 1966. *I Could Talk Old-Story Good: Creativity in Bahamian Folklore.* Berkeley and Los Angeles: University of California Press.

Dégh, Linda. 1972. Folk Narrative. IN *Folklore and Folklife: An Introduction*, ed. Richard M. Dorson, pp. 53-83. Chicago: University of Chicago Press.
Describes the basic narrative genres and includes an annotated bibliography.

_____. 1979. Biology of Storytelling. *Folklore Preprint Series* 7:3.
Discusses the history of an attitude in which the entire social context of tales are analyzed to determine their meanings; calls for a greater emphasis on fieldwork.

Dundes, Alan. 1965. *The Study of Folklore*. Englewood Cliffs, N.J.: Prentice-Hall, Inc.
Contains historically important essays on the nature of folklore, such as Axel Olrik's "Epic Laws of Folk Narrative."

_____. 1975. *Analytic Essays in Folklore*. The Hague: Mouton.
Emphasizes folklore analysis based on structural and psychoanalytic approaches. Includes articles on latrinalia, elephant jokes, and the number three, among others.

_____. 1980. *Interpreting Folklore*. Bloomington: Indiana University Press.
Based mainly on psychoanalytic analyses; includes the controversial article which asserts that football is a manifestation of homosexual tendencies.

Dorson, Richard M. 1971. *American Folklore and the Historian*. Chicago: University of Chicago Press.
Argues for grounding the study of American folklore in the study of American history, and vice-versa.

_____. 1977[1959]. *American Folklore*. Chicago and London: University of Chicago Press.
Traces American folklore from colonial to modern times.

Georges, Robert A. 1969. Toward an Understanding of Storytelling Events. *Journal of American Folklore* 82:313-328.
Argues for a holistic study of storytelling; discusses the uniqueness of each storytelling event.

Hymes, Dell. 1975. Folklore's Nature and the Sun's Myth. *Journal of American Folklore* 88:345-369.
Emphasizes an ethnographic approach in the study of patterns and meaning of folklore.

Jolles, Andre. 1965[1930]. *Einfache Formen*. Halle: Max Niemeyer.
Discusses nine "simple forms" of oral folklore, including legend, myth, joke, and Märchen.

Kiefer, Emma Emily. 1940. *Albert Wesselski and Recent Folktale Theories*. Ph.D. dissertation, Indiana University.
Provides a concise history of early folktale scholars.

Labov, William. 1972. *Language in the Inner City: Studies in the Black English Vernacular*. Philadelphia: University of Pennsylvania Press.
See particularly Chapter 9, entitled "The Transformation of Experience in Narrative Syntax." Defines the qualities and features of narratives.

Labov, William and Joshua Waletzky. 1967. Narrative Analysis: Oral Versions of Personal Experience. IN *Essays in the Visual Arts*, ed. June Helm, pp. 12-44. Seattle: University of Washington Press.
Defines a narrative as containing "temporal juncture," such that a temporal sequence of sentences cannot be rearranged without affecting the original meaning.

McGlathery, James M., ed. et al. 1988. *The Brothers Grimm and Folktale*. Urbana and Chicago: University of Illinois Press.
Presents essays which explore various factors operating in the transmission of folklore.

Propp, Vladimir. 1968. *Morphology of the Folktale*. Translated by Laurence Scott. 2d revised edition. Austin and London: University of Texas Press.
Analyzes the surface structure of tales in terms of the actions of the main characters; shows that the number of these actions is limited and that the actions always occur in a particular sequence.

Sydow, Carl Wilhelm von. 1948. *Selected Papers on Folklore*. Copenhagen: Rosenkilde and Bagger.
Emphasizes the need for collecting folklore in context; defines various narrative genres in "The Categories of Prose Tradition."

III) **Folktale**
   A) **Märchen Theory**
Bettelheim, Bruno. 1976. *The Uses of Enchantment: The Meaning and Importance of Fairy Tales*. New York: Knopf.

Bottigheimer, Ruth B., ed. 1986. *Fairy Tales and Society: Illusion, Allusion and Paradigm*. Philadelphia: University of Pennsylvania Press.

Dégh, Linda. 1969. *Folktales and Society: Story-Telling in a Hungarian Peasant Community*. Bloomington: Indiana University Press.
Remains an exemplary model of how to study oral narrative through ethnography; shows the interrelationship between storytelling and the social, political, historical and economic realities in a particular transplanted Hungarian community; presents in-depth information on the lifestyles of individual narrators.

_____. 1988. What Did the Grimm Brothers Give to and Take from the Folk? IN *The Brothers Grimm and Folktale*, ed. James M. McGlathery, pp. 66-90. Urbana and Chicago: University of Illinois Press.
Emphasizes that literary publication is part of the process of oral transmission of folktales.

Dégh, Linda and Andrew Vazsonyi. 1979. Magic for Sale: Märchen and Legend in TV Advertising. *Fabula* 20:47-68.
Shows that although the Märchen has declined in America, it thrives in television commercials.

Dundes, Alan, ed. 1983. *Cinderella: A Casebook*. New York: Wildman Press.

_____. 1989. *Little Red Riding Hood: A Casebook*. Madison: The University of Wisconsin Press.

Lüthi, Max. 1969. Aspects of the Märchen and the Legend. *Genre* 2:162-178.
Outlines features of the Märchen as contrasted with features of the legend.

_____. 1976[1970]. *Once Upon a Time: On the Nature of Fairy Tales*. Bloomington: Indiana University Press.

_____. 1982. *The European Folktale: Form and Nature*. Translated by John D. Niles. Bloomington and Indianapolis: Indiana University Press.

_____. 1984[1975]. *The Fairytale As Art Form and Portrait of Man*. Bloomington: Indiana University Press.

Stone, Kay. 1981. Märchen to Fairy Tales: An Unmagical Transformation. *Western Folklore* 40:232-244.

Tatar, Maria M. 1987. *The Hard Facts of the Grimms' Fairy Tales*. Princeton: Princeton University Press.
Examines the violent aspects of Grimm tales.

Thompson, Stith. 1946. *The Folktale*. New York: Dryden Press.
Discusses Indo-European and Asiatic folktales. Outdated now but an important historical reference.

B) Folktale Collections
(A good collection of folktale texts is contained in the Folktales of the World Series published by the University of Chicago Press. Countries represented by this series include: India, England, Norway, Hungary, Germany, China, Egypt, France, Israel, Greece, Ireland, Chile, Mexico, and Japan. Richard Dorson was the general editor of this series.)

Briggs, Katharine. 1970. *British Folktales*. New York: Pantheon Books.

Chase, Richard. 1943. *The Jack Tales*. Cambridge: Houghton Mifflin.

Dorson, Richard M. 1946. *Jonathan Draws the Long Bow: New England Popular Tales and Legends*. Cambridge: Harvard University Press.

_____. 1952. *Bloodstoppers & Bearwalkers: Folk Traditions of the Upper Peninsula*. Cambridge: Harvard University Press.

_____. 1967. *American Negro Folktales*. New York: Fawcett.

Finnegan, Ruth. 1967. *Limba Stories and Story-Telling*. Oxford: Clarendon Press.

Glassie, Henry. 1985. *Irish Folk Tales*. New York: Pantheon Books.

Hurston, Zora Neale. 1963[1935]. *Mules and Men*. Bloomington: Indiana University Press.

Magoun, Francis P. Jr. and Alexander H. Krappe, translators. 1960. *The Grimms' German Folk Tales*. Carbondale and Edwardsville: Southern Illinois University Press.

Randolph, Vance. 1951. *We Always Lie to Strangers: Tall Tales from the Ozarks*. New York: Columbia University Press.

_____. 1976. *Pissing in the Snow and Other Ozark Folktales*. Urbana: University of Illinois Press.

Roberts, Leonard W. 1955. *South From Hell-fer-Sartin*. Lexington: University of Kentucky Press.

Seitel, Peter. 1980. *See So That We May See: Performances and Interpretations of Traditional Tales from Tanzania*. Bloomington and London: Indiana University Press.

Thompson, Stith. 1966. *Tales of the North American Indians*. Bloomington and London: Indiana University Press.

Walker, Barbara K. and Warren S. Walker, eds. 1980 [1961]. *Nigerian Folk Tales*. 2d ed. Hamden, Conn.: Archon Books.

Walker, Warren S. and Ahmet E. Uysal. 1966. *Tales Alive in Turkey*. Cambridge: Harvard University Press.

Zong, In-sob, ed. and trans.. 1979 [1952]. *Folk Tales From Korea*. New York: Grove Press, Inc.

C) Jokes
See chapter on Folk Humor.

IV) Legend
A) Legend Theory
Bennett, Gillian, Paul Smith, and J.D.A. Widdowson, eds. 1987. *Perspectives on Contemporary Legend*. Vol. 2. Sheffield, England: Sheffield Academic Press.
Presents various papers resulting from a conference on contemporary legend held in 1983 at the University of Sheffield. Sections are devoted to collection, transcription and analysis; varieties of legend; psychology of legend; and offspring of legends (jokes and photocopy lore). A sequel to Smith (see below).

Brunvand, Jan Harold. 1981. *The Vanishing Hitchhiker: American Urban Legends and Their Meanings*. New York: W.W. Norton and Company.
Traces the history of the most popular current urban legends and analyzes their meanings. Sequels in 1984 and 1986 listed below.

_____. 1984. *The Choking Doberman and Other New Urban Legends*. New York: W.W. Norton and Company.

_____. 1986. *The Mexican Pet: More "New" Urban Legends and Some Old Favorites*. New York: W.W. Norton and Company.

_____. 1986. The Baby-Roast Story as a "New American Urban Legend." IN *The Study of American Folklore: An Introduction*. 3d ed. New York: W.W. Norton and Company.

Dégh, Linda. 1965. Processes of Legend Formation. *Laographia* 23:77-87.

_____. 1969. The Roommate's Death and Related Dormitory Stories. *Indiana Folklore* 2.2:55-74.

_____. 1976. Symbiosis of Joke and Legend: A Case of Conversational Folklore. IN *Readings in American Folklore*, ed. Jan Harold Brunvand, pp. 236-259. New York: W.W. Norton & Company.
Shows how as woman's supernatural stories and her husband's jokes reinforce each other in their narrative performance.

_____. ed., 1978. *East European Folk Narrative Studies*. Bloomington and Austin: American Folklore Society and Indiana University Folklore Monograph Series.

_____. ed., 1980. *Indiana Folklore: A Reader*. Bloomington: Indiana University Press.
Contains analyses such as "The Hatchet Man," by Sylvia Grider; "The House of Blue Lights" by Linda Dégh; as well as analyses of several Indiana ghost stories.

Dégh, Linda and Andrew Vazsonyi. 1971. Legend and Belief. *Genre* 4.3:281-304.
Demonstrates that the question of objective truth is not relevant to the definition of legend or to its transmission.

_____. 1973. The Dialectics of the Legend. *Folklore Preprint Series* 1.6:1-65.
Discusses the legend as the manifestation of a *debate* on the truth value of the legend's content.

_____. 1974. The Memorate and the Proto Memorate. *Journal of American Folklore* 87:225-239.
Questions Von Sydow's definition of memorate by asking, "Is there any scholarly need to determine which is the memorate and which is the fabulate with the same excited joy as newborn babes are distinguished according to sex?"

_____. 1975. Hypothesis of Multi-Conduit Transmission in Folklore. IN *Folklore: Performance and Communication*, ed. Dan Ben-Amos and Kenneth S. Goldstein, pp. 207-52. The Hauge: Mouton.
Discusses the nature of legend transmission; in stressing the voluntary nature of transmission, suggests that certain kinds of personalities are more likely to pass along certain kinds of stories.

Dorson, Richard. 1968. Legends and Tall Tales. IN *Our Living Traditions: An Introduction to American Folklore*, ed. Tristram Potter Coffin, pp. 154-169. New York: Basic Books..

_____. 1973. *American in Legend: Folklore from the Colonial Period to the Present*. New York: Pantheon Books.
Presents American history through its folklore.

Fine, Gary Alan. 1980. The Kentucky Fried Rat: Legends and Modern Society. *Journal of the Folklore Institute* 17:222-243.

Grider, Sylvia. 1976. *The Supernatural Narratives of Children*. Ph.D. dissertation, Indiana University.

Hand, Wayland D. 1965. Status of European and American Legend Study. *Current Anthropology* 6:439-446.
Outdated now but provides historical perspectives to legend study.

_____. 1971. *American Folk Legend*. Berkeley: University of California Press.
Contains articles from the proceedings of the UCLA Conference on American Folk Legend in 1969, written by the top legend scholars in the U.S.

Lee, Hector. 1949. *The Three Nephites: The Substance and Significance of the Legend in Folklore*. Albuquerque: University of New Mexico Publications in Language and Literature, no. 2.

Pentikainen, Juha. 1973. Belief, Memorate, and Legend. *Folklore Forum* 6:217-241.
Historically sorts out various conflicting legend terminologies.

Smith, Paul, ed. 1984. *Perspectives on Contemporary Legend*. Proceedings of the Conference on Contemporary Legend, Sheffield, July 1982. University of Sheffield: The Centre for English Cultural Tradition and Language.
Contains articles presented at the 1982 Perspective on Contemporary Legend seminar at the University of Sheffield.

B) Legend Collections

Baker, Ronald L. 1982. *Hoosier Folk Legends*. Bloomington: Indiana University Press.

Dorson, Richard M. 1962. *Folk Legends of Japan*. Rutland, Vermont and Tokyo: Charles E. Tuttle Company.

_____. ed., 1964. *Buying the Wind: Regional Folklore in the United States*. Chicago: University of Chicago Press.

Jones, Louis C. 1959. *Things That Go Bump in the Night*. New York: Hill and Wang.

Montell, William Lynwood. 1975. *Ghosts Along the Cumberland: Deathlore in the Kentucky Foothills*. Knoxville: University of Tennessee Press.

Musick, Ruth Ann. 1965. *The Telltale Lilac Bush and Other West Virginia Ghost Tales*. Lexington: University of Kentucky Press.

Scott, Beth and Michael Norman. 1985. *Haunted Heartland*. Madison, Wis.: Stanton and Lee Publishers, Inc.

Ward, Donald, ed. and trans. 1981. *The German Legends of the Brothers Grimm*. 2 vols. Philadelphia: Institute for the Study of Human Issues.

V) Myth

Dundes, Alan. 1964. The Morphology of North American Indian Folktales. *FFC* 195.
Looks at similarities of narrative plot structures among various Indian groups and presents a "grammar" of mythological tales.

_____. ed., 1984. *Sacred Narrative: Readings in the Theory of Myth*. Berkeley and Los Angeles: University of California Press.
Assembles historically important essays on the theory of myth.

_____. ed., 1988. *The Flood Myth*. Berkeley: University of California Press.
Brings together various analyses of the flood myth from around the world.

Sebeok, Thomas, ed. 1955. *Myth: A Symposium*. Bloomington: Indiana University Press.
Discusses basic questions on the nature and function of myths.

VI) Personal Narrative

Abrahams, Roger D. 1977. The Most Embarrassing Thing That Ever Happened: Conversational Stories in a Theory of Enactment. *Folklore Forum* 10.3:9-15.
Examines the patterns of expectation and formulas in embarrassment stories and suggests that such stories are a valid topic for folkloristic study.

Bausinger, Herman. 1987. The Structures of Everyday Narration. Translated by Mary Beth Stein with Regina Bendix. *Folklore Forum* 20:9-37. (Original: Strukturen des alltaglichen Erzahlens, *Fabula* 1:234-254, 1958.)
Draws analogies between personal narratives and Märchen; calls for folklorists to examine everyday stories.

Boatright, Mody. 1958. *The Family Saga and Other Phases of American Folklore*. Urbana: University of Illinois Press.
Argues that the family saga is an "important source of living folklore."

Brandes, Stanley H. 1975. Family Misfortune Stories in American Folklore. *Journal of the Folklore Institute* 12:5-17.
Discusses how family stories weld the family group together.

Clements, William. 1985. "I Once Was Lost": Oral Narratives of Born-Again Christians. *International Folklore Review* 2:105-111.
Examines the influence of pre-established patterns on narrators' accounts of personal experience.

Dorson, Richard M. 1981. *Land of the Millrats*. Cambridge, Mass.: Harvard University Press.
An ethnographic study which weaves texts of anecdotes and personal experiences with a discussion of the social context of the Calumet Region of northwest Indiana.

Graham, Joe. 1981. The "Caso": An Emic Genre of Folk Narrative. IN *"And Other Neighborly Names": Social Process and Cultural Image in Texas Folklore*, ed. Richard Bauman and Roger D. Abrahams, pp. 11-43. Austin: University of Texas Press.
Defines the "caso," a story of personal experience, which in many cases functions to validate folk belief.

Hufford, David J. 1982. *The Terror That Comes in the Night: An Experience-Centered Study of Supernatural Assault Traditions*. Philadelphia: University of Pennsylvania Press.
Discusses attacks variously known as "Mara attacks" and "The Old Hag," in which a person's sleep is interrupted by conscious paralysis, during which evil spirits perform various acts; shows how variations in the stories from culture to culture reflect local contexts, needs, and functions.

Kalcik, Susan. 1975. "Like Ann's gynecologist or the time I was almost raped": Personal Narratives in Women's Rap Groups. *Journal of American Folklore* 88:3-11.
Discusses "kernel stories," which are known to a group but not necessarily fully performed. Functions include showing moral support for a previous story just told, while providing a possible transition to the kernel story in question. Illustrates the conversational nature of personal narratives.

Robinson, John A. 1981. Personal Narratives Reconsidered. *Journal of American Folklore* 94:58-85.
Argues against Labov and Waletzky's (cf.) contention that an evaluative component is an essential ingredient of personal narrative; states that the explicit point of the story is often delegated to the listener.

Stahl, Sandra Dolby. 1975. The Local Character Anecdote. *Genre* 8:283-302.
Examines the nature of story cycles which are attached to a local individual; discusses pros and cons of classifying the local character anecdote as a distinct genre.

_____. 1977a. The Oral Personal Narrative in Its Generic Context. *Fabula* 18:18-39.
Defines personal narrative and distinguishes it from other closely related genres.

_____. 1977b. The Personal Narrative as Folklore. *Journal of the Folklore Institute* 14:9-30.
Discusses the traditional nature of personal narratives.

_____. 1979. Style in Oral and Written Narratives. *Southern Folklore Quarterly* 43:39-62.
Lists stylistic features of personal narratives.

_____. 1983. Personal Experience Stories. IN *Handbook of American Folklore*, ed. Richard M. Dorson, pp. 268-276. Bloomington: Indiana University Press.
Discusses how personal narratives function to create intimacy and to represent the teller's ethical values.

_____. 1985. A Literary Folkloristic Methodology for the Study of Meaning in Personal Narrative. *Journal of Folklore Research* 22:45-69.
Discusses the interpretation of personal narratives.

_____. 1989. *Literary Folkloristics and the Personal Narrative*. Bloomington: Indiana University Press.
Draws on reader-response theory to show how listeners participate in the giving of meaning to personal narratives.

Yocom, Margaret R. 1982. Family Folklore and Oral History Interviews: Strategies for Introducing a Project to One's Own Relatives. *Western Folklore* 41:251-174.

Wachs, Eleanor. 1982. The Crime-Victim Narrative as a Folkloric Genre. *Journal of the Folklore Institute* 19:17-30.

_____. 1988. *Crime-Victim Stories: New York City's Urban Folklore*. Bloomington: Indiana University Press.
Analyzes personal narratives of urban violence.

Zeitlin, Steven J. 1980. "An Alchemy of Mind:" The Family Courtship Story. *Western Folklore* 39:17-33.
Discusses how certain family stories become a family's way of expressively presenting itself; shows how story patterns can be picked up to shape other stories in other families; and suggests that stories function differently for different families.

CHAPTER 5
Folk Speech

Katherine Borland and Jennifer Livesay

INTRODUCTION

To embark on a project that deals with folk speech you will need a keen ear for language and a tape recorder. Later in this chapter we will offer some suggestions for developing an ear for language. You're on your own about the tape recorder.

Folk speech might be most broadly defined as non-standard language——those aspects of speech that are subject to variation. We can narrow this definition some by referring to the definition of folklore being used in this guide: *artistic communication in small groups.* Following this definition, folk speech is that aspect of language which is learned and performed in face to face situations, with attention given to the style as well as the content of that performance. It is used consciously or unconsciously in our everyday interactions with friends, family, coworkers, and strangers. Folk speech is *both* the information about ourselves that we express or give off by our particular way of talking *and* those stylistic elements that we can choose as resources for presenting ourselves.

In defining folk speech as variations from the standard, however, we need to caution that *the standard* (which in the United States would be Standard American English) is itself a problematic category. We tend to have an intuitive sense of the standard as what they tried to teach us in English class or the way network news broadcasters speak. But people often unconsciously consider their own speech as the standard against which other variations in speaking are to be measured. Thus, we hear as different those varieties of speech that are most noticeably different from our own, and do not hear as easily the differences in varieties that are closely related to our own. For a discussion of the problem of *the standard* see Trudgill (in Bibliography, pp. 161-166), and the entries under "Language Ideology" and "Language Varieties" in the *International Encyclopedia of Communications*.

LANGUAGE AND SPEECH

Speech is language in use. To speak correctly we need to know more than just the vocabulary and grammatical rules of our language; we also need to know the social rules for appropriately speaking. For instance, we need to know how to take turns in a conversation, or when and with whom it's appropriate to tell a long story or a dirty joke. We adjust our style of speaking according to the situation——is it a job interview, a discussion section, or hanging out with friends? Obviously, to successfully participate in each of these settings calls for very different uses of speech.

Additionally, when we speak we communicate on three levels at once: the *linguistic*, which includes vocabulary, pronunciation, and grammar; the *paralinguistic*, which includes such features as tone of voice and the loudness and speed of our talk; and the *kinesic*, which includes facial expressions and gestures.

MULTIPLE FUNCTIONS OF SPEECH

We are most inclined to think of speaking, when we think about it at all, as a way of referring to things in the world for the purpose of communicating something about those things to others. This is known as the referential function of speech, that is, what the words *mean* in their dictionary sense. But there are many other levels of communication besides the referential. The focus of any item of speech may be on the object that the speech is referring to on the person who is speaking, the person being spoken to, the relationship between the two speakers, or the form of the message itself. The ability of speech to point our attention to, and convey meanings on many different levels is what Roman Jakobson called the *multifunctionality* of speech. Let's look at what these functions can mean in practice.

Speech can give us information about the speaker's identity, such as where he or she is from: does the speaker have a foreign accent, or a dialect from a different region of the country? Often the way a person speaks can give us clues as to that person's occupation, level of education, socioeconomic class, age, and gender. A person's speech can convey other information, as well. Does he sound angry, happy, sad? Does it sound like she means what she's saying, or is she being sarcastic, or is she lying? These bits of information are conveyed not just by *what* is being said, but by *how* it is said, the tone of voice, loudness, rapidity, as well as by accompanying gestures and facial expression. We are generally quite good at picking up many different levels of information about speakers, just from hearing and watching them speak; but we don't always know what it was that tipped us off.

Speaking can also help us to create or maintain a level of intimacy, or a sense of community. Consider that much of our everyday talk does not convey essential information, but does establish a connection between the conversants. This function of speaking is the one that's involved when we say "Hi, how are you?" to the bank teller, or engage in *small talk* about the weather or sports with coworkers. Here it is not the content of what we are saying that is important, but the fact that we are using conventional forms of polite talk to establish a connection in which some other transaction can take place. We use talk in this way to create or maintain a relationship, however transitory.

Speech is also a resource we can use to express conflict and competition. For instance, children and adolescents often engage in verbal dueling or ritualized insults, and competitive joke telling and riddling sessions (see Chapter 8 **Jokes and Practical Jokes** and Chapter 17 **Collecting Children's Folklore**). Many young city-dwellers engage in formalized verbal dueling such as *playing the dozens*; this genre has been particularly well documented among African American youths (see Chapter 15 **African American Folklore**). Courtrooms, college classrooms, and political campaigns are other places where people often attempt to gain prestige or win battles by virtue of their speaking abilities. In all of these cases, attention is often directed to the form of the message itself and to how well the speaker manipulates verbal resources. This brings us to the next point we want to make about the relevance of the functions of speech. That is,

speaking can be artistic. As speakers and listeners, we can attend to the way words sound and to the images they conjure up. This function is at the root of folk speech and of all of the oral genres of folklore (discussed in several chapters in this guide). It is also central to such speech situations as political, legal, and religious *oratory*.

Our attention to the sounds of words can be playful as well as serious. Playful usage can include the familiar response to people whose words inadvertently rhyme: "You're a poet and don't know it!" Other playful examples are *puns*, *Spoonerisms* (switching the initial sounds of two words, such as "an asp in the grass"), *Wellerisms* (parody proverbs in quotation form, such as "'I see,' said the blind man as he picked up his hammer and saw"), and *malapropisms* (comical misuses of words; for example, a woman of our acquaintance tells the story of a little girl who, when the minister comes to the door to speak to her mother, tells him she's "upstairs prostituted [for prostrated] on the bed").

Now that we have an idea of the things that speech can do, let's look in greater detail at some specific examples of variation in speech: dialect, registers and slang, secret languages, and family codes.

Dialect

A *dialect* is a variety of a language that differs from other varieties on three levels: pronunciation, vocabulary, and grammar. Dialects develop out of the tendency for language to change in different ways in different communities, especially when these communities are at least partially isolated from each other. There are two types of dialect: regional and social.

Regional dialect has provided the material for many studies of folk speech in folkloristics. The tendency toward regional variation meets with an opposing tendency in the modern world—the move toward standardization in the way language is taught in the schools and used in the mass media. Thus, for folklorists, the initial interest in studying dialect came from their view of dialect as a survival from an earlier time, spoken in *pockets* of the society less influenced by modern communication technologies. The belief was that dialects would die out in the face of standardization. However, the effect that education and the mass media have had on dialects is still unclear. A quick trip around the United States would show us that regional variation in vocabulary, grammar, and pronunciation is still alive and well.

Some people have suggested that standardization might even encourage dialects, as people strive to assert their regional identity vis a vis the other regions of the nation. This phenomenon shows us that it is possible to have passive knowledge of a number of dialects, and to make choices about which are put to active use. Exposure to other dialects, including the *standard*, might make a speaker more emphatic in his or her use of the home dialect. A particular speaker may choose to approximate the standard in some situations, and to use her or his own dialect in others. For a fascinating look at American regional dialects and their uses, we recommend the videotape program *American Tongues*, available in the media centers of many college libraries.

The other form of dialect is based on social class. Some years ago, a sociolinguist named William Labov conducted a study in which he determined that the pronunciation of postvocalic [r] (an [r] following a vowel, as in *car*) is closely correlated with socioeconomic class among New York City dwellers. That is, the higher up the scale toward upper class, the more likely people are to pronounce the [r] in *car*. This distinction is between people who live in the same area and come into contact with each other on a daily basis, yet are separated from each other by social differences. One explanation for this is that children grow up learning to speak amidst their own families, in their own neighborhoods, and thus learn to speak differently from children of other neighborhoods.

These two forms, social and regional dialect, are not mutually exclusive. Regional dialects often carry positive or negative social value. This fact was brought home to one of this chapter's writers when I left my home state of New York to attend school in Texas. One day while I was listening to the radio, I heard an ad in which one of the speakers had a strong southern accent. I realized as I listened to this ad that I was expecting there to be some reason for this accent, that the ad was using it to imply the speaker was not *cultured* or well-educated. I quickly realized that no such characterization was being made by the ad, but rather that I was listening through my own prejudices. A southern accent did not have the same set of meanings in the South that it had in the North. Those of you who are going to school in a region far from the one you grew up in may have had a similar experience, either in the way you reacted to other people's speech or in the way others reacted to your speech. This sort of experience could provide the basis for a good collection project, as we will explain later. College towns are often places where regional dialect overlaps with social dialect. It is often the case that local people, who are employed in secretarial, custodial, and other support services for the school, speak in the local dialect, while the professors and most of the students do not. In communities where there are town/gown tensions, dialect may be very important as a sign of identity.

Registers, Jargon, Slang, and Taboo Words

Registers are ways of speaking that are peculiar to certain professions, activities, or social groups. For instance, when computer scientists get together to talk shop, they speak in a very different way than any one of them would to a non-computer person. They use special words, abbreviations, and acronyms (such as RAM and ROM). Common words may have special meanings for them. The same is true for doctors, English professors, fire fighters, and so on. College students have registers, as well, of both official and folk varieties. In addition to learning how to speak, read, and write *academese*, students develop their own ways of speaking to address the experiences they share. Some phrases are recognized by most American students, while others are peculiar to a single campus, or to the campuses in a certain region. At one university in upstate New York, incoming students learn expressions such as *face time* (time spent in public to see or be seen by potential romantic interests) and *gorge out* (to commit suicide by jumping into the gorge). Some of these students decide to major in *architorture*, while others become *enginerds*. At this and perhaps other schools, many students are required to take a course in *sadistics* (statistics). Along with this general college-student register, students also learn one particular to their field. This may include parodies on the names of required classes, professional organizations or important people in the field. Thus college students are learning the official registers of academe and of their future professions, as well as the folk registers of students in general, and their major in particular.

The term *jargon* is used to mean the specialized terminology used in a register, although it is sometimes used as a synonym for *register*. Jargon is often used critically to mean that someone is deliberately using esoteric or *fancy* words in order to mislead others. *Slang* is closely related to *jargon*, but many people distinguish between the two by defining as *slang* words which are no longer limited to use within a register, but have entered into more general usage. *Taboo* words (four-letter words and many derogatory terms) are likewise often words which have been removed from their original contexts and misapplied for effect. Both slang and taboo words are more likely to be used in folk speech than in either writing or formal speech (with the exception of quoting). Another distinguishing characteristic of slang words is that they pass quickly in and out of vogue. While using slang properly produces social benefits for the speaker, generally these benefits accrue *only* when the slang still has a newness about it.

SECRET LANGUAGE, RITUAL LANGUAGE, PLAY LANGUAGE

Under this heading we are including both the playful and the serious, as well as those languages for which there is a solution, or translation, and those for which there is not. Children often make use of secret languages, such as Pig Latin (or Igpay Atinlay), either strictly as play languages, or to keep younger siblings from understanding them. Some children make up their own special secret languages; identical twins have been known to speak exclusively in their own made-up language during early childhood.

Ritual language is language which is used in religious and ritual contexts. Ritual language may be a register or a true language; it may be secret or known to all participants. *Glossolalia*, or speaking in tongues, is considered here as a ritual language because it is often considered as such by members of religious groups who practice it. That is, many participants in these practices consider glossolalia a true language, the meaning of which is potentially discoverable (see also Chapter 7 **Folklore and Religion**). The Latin used in Latin Mass is a ritual language which might also be considered a secret language for worshippers who don't understand it but find it more satisfying than vernacular mass.

Finally, families often have special languages, although not usually as highly developed as the case of twinspeak mentioned above. Family language can include nicknames and special names for places and things, *secret codes* for private communication in public, special meanings for common phrases, endearing grammatical mistakes borrowed from the baby, and so on. You can probably think of a number of examples of this kind of special language use from your own family. Since families spend so much of their time in *small group* communication, they are an ideal place for folk speech to flourish. You may be interested in doing a collection project on your family's special language use (or on another family's), in which case you should study both this chapter and the one on Family Folklore later in this guide.

Bilingualism

In many parts of the country, particularly in big cities and the Southwest, bilingualism is an important phenomenon. If this is true in your area, you might want to examine *code-switching* between, for example, English and Spanish. This might be a resource for speech play or group identification. You might want to ask yourself during your research: When groups are using two languages at once, are there different uses for each language? What are people's attitudes toward the two languages, within the group and in the larger community? How might the two languages be adding to and changing each other? Is one language ever used as a *secret language* in front of people who only speak the other?

CONVERSATIONAL GENRES

We have already been discussing some of the *conversational genres*, so now it's time to define what is meant by this term. Conversational genres are small, relatively fixed and traditional forms of expression used in everyday conversation. These include local conventions for naming people, places, and things; jargon and slang; special languages; taboo words; and *intensifiers* (like "dead as a doornail"). These conversational genres are very short, often only a word or brief phrase inserted in discourse to *spice it up*, thereby increasing its impact or persuasive power. Other conversational genres are longer and more formalized, and include traditional greetings and leave-takings (like "see you later, alligator"); proverbs ("A rolling stone gathers no moss," etc.) and proverbial phrases (abbreviations or allusions to proverbs, such as "You know what they say about the squeaky wheel!"); and curses and charms. (The folklorist who coined the term *conversational genres*, Roger Abrahams, makes a distinction between these and the *play genres* in which he includes jokes and riddles, because these are often performed in special joking and riddling sessions, and don't always come up naturally in conversation.)

Conversational genres are often rooted in a particular dialect or register. That is, conventional expressions or names often vary according to region, class, social group, or occupation. As just one example of the regional nature of an expression, Jan Brunvand talks about non-Mormons in Utah saying "He took off like a Mormon on a mission!" to describe someone leaving in a hurry. This expression, an intensifier, would not be as likely to be used in a region where the L.D.S. Church is less well known.

Studying Conversation

So far we have examined folk speech from the perspectives of *sociolinguistics*, or how social *work* is accomplished through speech, and *performance*, or how people demonstrate artfulness in their talk. We have seen that a verbal message involves many levels of meaning beyond that of simply communicating an idea in words. A person's dialect, his or her choice of vocabulary, etc., and the way he or she takes on the role of speaker in conversation will all be understood to communicate something about the speaker, whether the speaker intends to convey these impressions or not. The verbal context for folk speech is, of course, conversation. Thus we see the close interconnection between folk speech and conversational genres. But conversation also constitutes the natural context for a number of other folklore genres as well. Going up a step in complexity, we find that many folk narrative genres are embedded in ordinary conversation as well. Legends, for example, may be exchanged within the course of a conversation over coffee with friends. Likewise, jokes, tall tales, and personal narratives are rooted in ordinary conversation. Nonverbal folklore forms such as beliefs, folk custom and practices, and even folk crafts, may be talked about and described in conversation. Thus, understanding how conversation works, even if you are not specifically interested in collecting folk speech, will provide you with a foundation for recognizing and interpreting any number of folklore genres.

Of course, you are already very familiar with conversations, having engaged in countless verbal exchanges with different kinds of people over the course of your lifetime. Studying conversation as a folklorist, however, involves listening to people's talk in a new way. You need to recognize not only *what* people are communicating through their talk, but also alert yourself to and actively take note of *how* people express themselves with style and creativity, and how they make use of the traditional store of verbal resources for conversation. You'll need to ask yourself what features of a person's talk are determined by his/her individual personality, by his/her particular audience, by his/her membership in a particular folk group. At the beginning of this chapter we promised to try to help you develop an ear for artful verbal communication. Here are some concrete suggestions for activities that will help you do this.

Keeping a folk speech diary. If you are a student at a college far from your native region, this will be a relatively easy task. Buy a small notebook and carry it with you wherever you go. When you hear a word, phrase, or expression that you find unfamiliar or puzzling, write it down. Note the conversational context in which the speech occurred. Later, you may even want to ask people native to the area to give you a definition of the folk speech and explain when it would be used (by whom, to whom, under what circumstances, to express what kind of idea). You may even wish to translate the expression into your own dialect. At the end of the semester you should have a healthy list of regional (and other) folk expressions.

Another way you can use your folk speech diary is to record conventional conversational expressions. Greetings and leavetakings are two common and highly noticeable conversational elements that you might start with. Spend a week listening to the ways in which people open and close conversations. You can use your own conversations for this exercise or those of people around you. After each conversation, write down the exact words people used to greet and depart from one another. You might also want to note your impressions of the social relationships operating between the participants. That is, are they close friends, relatives, acquaintances, professor and student, etc.? See whether this relates in any way to variations in how people initiate and end their conversations.

Another use for your diary is listening for quoted speech. There is a saying among folklore students that our mouths are filled with the words of others. And certainly, if you listen closely to almost any conversation, you will find evidence of the frequency of quoted speech (Bakhtin 1981). One interesting phenomenon is that today, when so many of us spend our free time watching movies and tv shows, we often memorize and perform bits of movie dialogue in our everyday conversations. A few years ago, a beginning folklore student at Indiana University reported that residents on her dormitory floor frequently used dialogue from *The Wizard of Oz* when they discussed their college experiences. For instance, when two female freshmen got lost on their way to class, one said to the other, "Toto, I have a feeling we're not in Kansas anymore." Try listening for instances of quoted speech in your informal conversations. Write down the phrases used and the conversational context in which they came up. Note whether the speaker is quoting a movie, book, or other media source, or quoting someone of his or her acquaintance. Did he or she change tone of voice, put on a different dialect? Does the way the speaker spoke while quoting give you an idea of how he or she feels about the source being quoted? Try to identify what in their speech gave you that idea.

Taping from the radio. To get an idea of the structure of different kinds of specialized discourse try taping sermons, call-in talk shows, newscasts, and other spoken programs you find on the radio. Once you have collected two or three examples of one kind of program, you can begin to analyze the conventions specific to it. How does the speaker address his/her absent audience? How is the program different from ordinary conversation? In what ways is the radio broadcaster's speech different, or more *poetic* than normal talk? Listen for the repetition of sounds, like vowels and consonants, or of the same grammatical construction (as in "I came, I saw, I conquered.") Since radio talk cannot rely on visual channels such as gesture and facial expression, you will find that its *verbal* stylistic devices are more concentrated or marked than ordinary face-to-face conversation.

Taping conversations. This exercise has a dual purpose. First, it provides you with an opportunity to practice your technical skills in using a tape recorder to get good, clear recordings. Second, it allows you to focus on the unspoken but observable rules of ordinary conversation. Try getting into the habit of switching on your tape-recorder when you attend informal gatherings of friends, coworkers, or family members. Of course, it is *absolutely essential* that everyone participating in such a gathering *knows* that you are recording and *agrees* to being tape-recorded (see Chapter 2 **Ethics and the Student Fieldworker**). You will generally find, however, that the tape-recorder, once introduced, will be quickly forgotten unless you call attention to it yourself. Keep a list of the participants in each conversation you record. Once you have some conversations to analyze, try to determine what rules the participants are following. Who gets to speak, when, how often, and how do they manage to get the floor? What makes for an appropriate interruption? Are there special phrases or attitudes people adopt when they begin to speak? How do people change the subject? Are there differences in participation level that you can trace to differences in the gender, age, or social standing of the participants? In this exercise you will be looking at conversation as a rule-governed activity that reflects the power relations operating among a group of speakers.

Analyzing Communication Roadblocks. Another way to discover the underlying conventions of conversation is to look at what happens when things go wrong. As we have shown, verbal communication is a complex, multi-faceted activity. Therefore, it is not surprising that people often misread or mishear one another. The results of such miscommunication can be amusing, or potentially violent. They may involve elaborate negotiations by the parties involved, or even by a third party, to clarify what has happened. You might attend to instances in your daily life when conversation breaks down, and carefully note what led to the misunderstanding and what the consequences for the participants were. How does a speaker respond to a listener's inappropriate response? How does a confused listener ask for clarification? Once a conversation is derailed, how do the participants get it back on track? Can an instance of miscommunication be traced to the speaker's and listener's membership in different folk groups?

Doing experimental folklore. Another way of getting at conversational conventions is to create a situation yourself that draws attention to conversational etiquette. Choose a proverb that you are familiar with and, during the course of a week, try dropping the proverb into ongoing conversations at a point you take to be *inappropriate*. For example, let's use the proverb, *There's no use crying over spilt milk.* We can imagine that the *appropriate* use for this proverb would be when you want to tell someone that they shouldn't regret a mistake they've already made, that the best thing, in such an instance, is to do what one can to correct the error and then put the whole incident behind them. Now, use this proverb at any time when such advice is not appropriate to the conversation, and observe what happens. Does your remark stop the conversation? Do other participants acknowledge the inappropriateness of the proverb, and reprimand or make fun of you? Or do they attempt to make sense of the proverb in its inappropriate context? Does anyone offer a more appropriate proverb? Does the conversation turn in on itself as people attempt to *backtrack* to understand what went wrong? After the conversation, write up a description of what happened and see if you can account for the participants' responses.

These seven, easily performed exercises will polish your skill in recognizing the strategic and artful qualities of conversation, a skill that you will need as a folklore fieldworker, regardless of the kind of folklore you decide to collect. What if you decide to do a project on folk speech? What kinds of collection projects might you design? Keep in mind that comparative studies of folk speech require a large data sample that you may not have the time or facilities to collect in one semester. For instance, tracing changes in dialect or speech patterns over time, or differences in speech patterns across the country, are interesting and valuable projects. However, studies of this kind will not be possible if you record the speech of only one or two or even ten informants.

Likewise, recording variations in dialect pronunciation *in writing* will be difficult, since pronunciation is an oral paralinguistic phenomenon. If you try to indicate through nonstandard spelling the dialect variations that you hear, you run the risk of creating an imprecise record. For instance, if you come from an area of the country where the postvocalic [r] sound is muted, and you record an informant who emphasizes the postvocalic [r], you might double the [r] in spelling the word car (carr). This approach to transcribing the sound qualities of speech, however, will not effectively communicate those qualities to a reader who does not share *your* base-dialect. While linguists have developed a special phonetic alphabet to encode differences in pronunciation accurately, using this special alphabet requires training that you may not have. We suggest you discuss transcription strategies with your instructor, and always provide him or her with a taped record of your research data.

When planning your project, then, you'll need to keep in mind not only the topics that interest you but also the limitations you are working with, including time, access to informants, and your own abilities. Below is a list of suggestions for projects that you can successfully complete in the course of one semester. These are only suggestions. You may come up with very different ideas and approaches. These suggestions should give you an idea of the possibilities.

Working with one person. Suppose you would like to examine the speech of just one person. You've done a few interviews with your subject and you are reviewing your tapes. One project you might do would be to look closely at a section of your interview conversation that you identify as artistically heightened or rich. For instance, suppose you're listening to the taped conversation. Things are going along nicely, you're asking questions, your informant is responding actively, and then he or she begins to tell you a story. All of a sudden, you notice that the conversation has changed into a performance. Instead of you directing the conversation with questions, your informant has taken over. Note the point at which the conversation changes and then identify artistic

features of the performance. How does your interviewee's speech style change between the question-and-answer segment and the story? Does the vocabulary change? Are certain words repeated? What happens to the tone of voice? Loudness? Facial expressions and gestures? (Note: since these do not come across on the tape recorder, you should take notes during the interview to remind yourself of important visual cues, as well as any noise that may be unidentifiable later.) Take note of the speed of delivery, and also pay attention to pauses. You should also look at the conversation surrounding this artistic verbal performance to see how the performance is anchored in your general discussion. Was there any transitional moment between ordinary conversation and the story? What precipitated the story? What could have motivated your informant to tell that particular story at that particular time? (If your interest is in the content and meaning of the story itself, see Chapter 4 **Folk Narrative**.)

Another possible project would involve looking at the social meanings of one person's speech. Maybe you're interested in dialects and have observed that your collaborator's vocabulary and pronunciation differ markedly from your own. You may then want to identify instances of these differences in your taped conversation and explore their possible origins. Is the unusual (to you) pronunciation or word use an individual speech variation or can it be traced to the speaking conventions of your informant's home community, work community, or other folk group? Did your informant's dialect get stronger or weaker when he or she spoke to you, as opposed to someone else present? Can you identify intentional messages being conveyed by your informant's marked use of dialect or jargon?

The two above projects are two different kinds of study that your can do with the same item of folklore, one focusing on language used artistically, the other on language used to convey social identity. (For an idea of how you might identify the artistic features of an oral performance, see **Figure 1**.)

Working with groups. Alternatively, you may chose to study the speech of a group of people. You might, for instance, locate an occupational group (firefighters, factory workers, restaurant service people, college professors) and observe how and why they use a particular register. You might record people speaking together in their workplace or arrange to do a recording of a social occasion outside work, or both. Identify the characteristic words, phrases, and speech styles that you can identify as work-related language.

Below is a fragment of a story that one of the writers of this article collected during a conversation with her grandmother. It is transcribed so as to indicate *paralinguistic* features important to the artistry of the performance. There are many available models for marking these features, and, if you are interested, you can follow one of these models or develop your own system (see, for example, the works of Dennis Tedlock and Elizabeth Fine). The narrative shown below has been arranged in lines to indicate differences in the *speed of delivery*. Short lines are spoken more slowly than normal conversation, while longer lines are spoken at regular speed. *Pauses* are indicated by various forms of standard punctuation. Underlined words indicate those that were strongly *stressed* in the actual performance. By marking these features a folklorist attempts to give his or her reader an idea of the rhythm and cadence of the spoken words. Try reading this story aloud to yourself to see whether you can catch the general rhythm of the performance.

```
 1  Well in our town, uh,
 2                          there was a couple:
 3  Bertha-
 4        and Gilbert:
 5  It starts
 6          with them.
 7  And Gilbert is...a very individual person- he's not like other people-
 8  And Bertha is not like other women!
 9  Gilbert...is very talented plumber.  He can do anything with your broken down water pipes,
10      or sinks, or...anything.
11  If you can get him!
12  But he works only when he wants to.
13  So you always tried to be on the good side of Gilbert so if something happens- he will
14      come!  Otherwise you can wait six months!  And every time you see'im you can say
15      "Gilbert when are you coming to fix my furnace,"
16      "Ohh-I'll be there; I'll be there, someday...I'll get ova there." (loud, sing-song)
17      and you can never pin 'im down-see, well anyway that's Gilbert.
18  Bertha- I have no idea where she ever came from.  She was not a native of Brooks.  She
19      looked as though she might have come from (lilting) Puerto Rico- or South America-
20      she was a very flaming personality, uh heh she was gaunt.  And had flashing black eyes.
21      And her teeth needed...attention.  [audience laughter]  And she had loonnggstringy black
22      hair.  But she was very vital, and very alive.
23  Somehow or other
24                          she and Gilbert got together and they
25                                                      got married.
26  Time went by and they had a little girl, named Thelma, and
27  Then-
28  Things
29          got
30              boring
31                  I suppose.
```

Now let's look at the artistic qualities evident in the linguistic choices the speaker made. *Repetition* of whole phrases appears in lines 7 and 8, and in line 16. The narrative is also marked by several kinds of sound repetitions: In line 13, the words *tried* and *side* are an example of *rhyme*. *Alliteration*, the repetition of word initial consonant sounds appears in fix/furnace (l. 15) and flaming/flashing (l. 20.) *Consonance*, the repetition of consonant sounds within words, occurs in loon*nggstri*ngy (l. 21) and *v*ital/a*li*ve (l. 22). *Assonance*, the repetition of vowel sounds within words occurs in c*o*me/m*o*nths (l. 14) and, in the dialect pronunciation of the speaker, in id*ea*/*wh*ere (l. 18). Try to see if you can tease out for yourself the variations in the use of a small number of repeated sounds in lines 23-25.

The narrator also uses very colorful adjectives, particularly when she describes Bertha (*gaunt, flaming, flashing, lonnggstringy*). And she uses quotation (l. 16), with an appropriate moderation of voice quality, to convey Gilbert's personality. One can also see the artistic qualities of this performance in the way in which the narrative is structured. The beginning of the tale is clearly marked on a number of levels simultaneously (speed, emphasis, word meaning), and is followed by an introduction of each of the major characters who are involved in a series of *episodes* that make up the whole story. We can see that the author is directing our expectations for narrative developments in the *way* she tells the story as well. For example, right away we know that the story is not concerned with Bertha and Gilbert's courtship, because this aspect of the characters' experience is prefaced by the qualifier, someone or other.

Moving away from the artistic features of the speech in this narrative, you might use the same text to explore the social or cultural understandings that it conveys. Here you would be doing a content analysis of the underlying assumptions operating in the story. Notice, for instance, that while the portrait of Gilbert focuses on his occupation (what he *does*), Bertha's portrait focuses much more strongly on her appearance (who she *is*). Moreover, the emphasis placed on Bertha's foreign origin reflects the attitude of townspeople whose families have resided in the area for a long time toward those who are more recent arrivals. Questions of gender, ethnic identity, community or religious values, and socioeconomic distinctions will all be operating in the items of folklore you collect. (For more on content analysis, see Chapter 4 **Folk Narrative**.)

Figure 1. Artistic qualities of speech.

Does the group use jargon to exclude outsider participation? To exclude you? Do group members have stories about the origin of a particular example of jargon? Do they use jargon metaphorically to apply to subjects or things outside the work environment? Do they talk about people misusing their jargon, and, if so, what attitudes do they express towards incompetent jargon users?

You might also try examining the characteristic ways of speaking that other kinds of folk groups, besides occupational groups, develop. For example, you might want to visit a nursing home for the elderly to see if the residents have developed a particular kind of speaking pattern. You might choose to work with a religious group to see whether they employ special language styles when they get together for devotional and church-related social events.

Working in public places. Another possibility for a folk speech project would be to look at the kinds of messages that are *given off* by people merely by the way they speak. In this kind of project you would need to choose a public place—a local establishment like a diner, gas station, or hardware store, for example—and request the permission and collaboration of the person in charge for your field project. Take two of three afternoons to hang around the site, making notes of who comes in and what they say. Then ask the person(s) working in the establishment to describe what their impressions of the client are, based on the way he or she speaks. For instance, can your collaborators determine whether the person is a local resident or a foreigner? Rich, middle class, or poor? Ethnic-american? Business person, homemaker, professor? Ask your collaborators what in the person's speech made them arrive at their conclusions. In this project you will be looking at stereotypes people hold and assumptions people make about others based on their patterns of speech.

In a similar type of project you might use yourself as a subject and collect instances of words and phrases that are unfamiliar to you but common to the community in which you are living. As you collect community dialect, record your own impressions of these items. Then, consult with a number of long--time residents of the community to find out what these items mean to them, what kinds of people use them, in what situations, and what associations native speakers make between the items and the social identity of the speaker using them.

Experimental project. Our last suggestion involves a form of experimental folklore. In this kind of project you set up an unnatural situation that allows you to provoke the kind of performance you are interested in studying. To see how people change the way they speak when they are purposefully attending to their own speaking, for instance, you need to record their ordinary speaking style as a baseline for analysis. For this project, arrange to interview just one person. Explain to your volunteer that you are generally interested in collecting his or her folklore and ask for permission to do so. Then, start the interview by asking him or her to tell you about family upbringing, roots, etc. After you have talked generally for a while, announce that you are interested in collecting items of folk speech. Direct your interviewee to instances of folk speech you have observed in your preceding conversation, and ask her to comment on her own language use. When you review your taped interview, look for observable differences in the way your collaborator spoke before and after you announced your specific interest in language. Did his or her dialect become stronger or less distinct? Did the level of formality in speaking change? What did your collaborator have to say about his or her own dialect?

These are a few suggestions we have thought up to get you going. You may wish to try one, or to devise your own fieldwork strategy. Keep in mind what you can do in the time you have with the tools you have. Remember also that, as in any fieldwork project, you are asking people to share with you something of themselves. Since language use is tied up with a person's identity, you'll want to respect the language of others at all times and be aware of topics that your collaborators may find overly sensitive. Your task as a folklorist is to understand the diversity of language uses and language styles and promote that understanding among others.

A WORD OR TWO ABOUT GRAFFITI

Graffiti is a written genre of folklore that is difficult to categorize. Like folk speech, it is often verbal, but it has neither the oral nor the face-to-face dimensions of speaking. Since it often involves stylized script and may even be pictorial, it shares some of the features of folk art as well (see Chapter 12 **Folklife and Material Culture**). However we choose to categorize it, graffiti is definitely a potent vehicle for the expression of individual or group convictions, protest, advice, aggression, humor, and poetry. Among groups of *writers*, for whom graffiti writing is a central activity, it may also operate as a secret language or mark off territorial boundaries. You probably already have a good working knowledge of the variety of messages conveyed through graffiti: from *JESUS SAVES* on the highway overpass to _____*SUCKS* (fill in a proper noun) on a bathroom wall.

Though some may think that graffiti is a relatively modern occurrence, people have been writing or carving on walls, sidewalks, desks, park benches, national monuments and other public places for centuries. People have been complaining about graffiti for just as long. A common anecdote in introductory Latin textbooks tells of the graffiti found in a public bath in ancient Pompeii: *Fools' names and fools' faces always appear in public places.* Today graffiti is generally regarded as an act of vandalism, punishable by law. Yet, in the late 1970s New York City art galleries were selling canvases spray painted by local graffiti *artists* for upwards of a thousand dollars a piece.

One of the central characteristics of most graffiti is its anonymity. While it can be used to express ownership, as when a gang marks off its territory, the graffiti itself is not typically owned by anyone. We can distinguish graffiti from paintings or murals, for example, by the fact that it is not signed or claimed by a particular person. Ironically, though, one of the most common subjects of graffiti is the personal name. Here you might think of the traditional carving of two linked names surrounded by a heart. More recently, a group of New York City graffiti writers identified one of their goals as *going all-city*, which means getting their name on every subway line.

While much graffiti is anonymous to the outsider, among certain groups it constitutes a secret language. That is, those in the group recognize the characteristic mark of each *writer*, while outsiders do not. This is the case among gangs in various parts of the country and among *writers* who have developed a complex social network around graffiti writing. In New York City, for example, *writers* work in teams to *bomb* subway cars (a particularly elaborate form of spray paint graffiti). They also have a particular meeting place in the subway, called the *writers' bench*, where they gather to trade designs, talk about their work, and discuss strategies for dealing with hostile outsiders.

Political uses of graffiti are also highly evident in some parts of the country. Sometimes graffiti is used politically to get a message out that would be censored in other communication media. For instance, one of the writers of this article participated in a feminist group in college. A number of rapes had been committed in our community, and one of the group's major concerns was to have the statistics for attacks on women published so that others would be aware of the danger. College administrators with whom we talked, however, were unwilling to take prompt action, fearing that the publicity would negatively affect the school's image. When negotiations between the two groups broke down, my group decided to pool our own knowledge of where and when the attacks had occurred and plan a covert action. One morning, the bright red message *A Woman Was Raped Here* appeared on sidewalks and walls throughout the neighborhood. Thus, graffiti got our message out in an informal and highly dramatic way.

Graffiti can also take on the form of a conversation. For instance, in the Indiana University library, people take time out from studying to contribute to a silent existential running dialogue in the stacks. *Latrinalia*, or bathroom graffiti, often mimics conversation as well. Often, these conversations deal with topics that appear to be particularly personal or sensitive, things that people might not want to admit about themselves in their face-to-face interactions with others. For instance, in one lavatory we visited, a woman wrote: *Help! I'm about to graduate, and I'm still a virgin.* This message elicited a number of responses that offered advice or consolation from a variety of perspectives. In this case, then, we might view graffiti as a form of social work.

Another characteristic of graffiti is that it doesn't last long. It may survive a few days or even weeks, but eventually it gets scrubbed or sanded off by a diligent janitorial staff, or written over by an equally diligent graffiti writer. Sometimes graffiti is even linked to a specific event, and therefore becomes particularly topical. For instance, at Indiana University, the Little 500 bicycle race is accompanied each year by at outpouring of Little 500-related graffiti.

Finally, graffiti can be viewed as artistic communication. Like folk speech, graffiti exhibits stylistic features on a number of levels. The script style is often an artistic choice. For instance, the New York city subway *writers* have developed elaborate script styles involving *bubble letters, 3-D images* and *wild style*, or distorted letters. The placement of the message on a surface can also involve artistic choice. Sometimes words are even used pictorially as in the Art School bathroom we observed recently. The *writer* had written a careful text in small letters at the space where the ceiling meets the wall. The text proceeded halfway around the room at this altitude and then descended across the wall to about waist level, went out the door and continued for several yards down the hallway. Though the writing was too high and too small in the bathroom to be read

The Emergence of Folklore in Everyday Life

without standing on a chair, the visual effect was impressive.

The *language* of graffiti can be artistic as well, demonstrating repetition, rhyme, alliteration, assonance, consonance, etc. For instance, the following poem was found in the Folklore Institute's bathroom at Indiana University a while back: *They painted the walls to discourage my pen, but the shithouse poet has struck again.* You might also think about the color and medium used to make the message. Graffiti comes in all colors and may be penciled, penned, crayoned, magic markered, chalked, taped, stenciled, painted, spray painted, carved etched, or chiselled.

Let's consider how color might be used for effect. In Bloomington, a graffiti campaign of sorts took root, targeting banks, business establishments and the IRS office. Messages like *Poverty is Violence* were spray-painted in large letters with hazard orange paint. If the same message had been written in blue, let's say, its impact would probably not have been as great. A different artistic choice is evident in the graffiti appended to a black-lettered sign that read: *Cornell University.* The graffiti writer added *Supports Racism* in black paint. When you examine the materials of graffiti, you'll need to ask yourself whether they add to the verbal message in any way or simply reflect the available tools at hand.

To summarize, graffiti can be a fascinating topic for cultural analysis. On one hand it performs several social and artistic functions among a group of *writers* who know each other. On the other, it provides a special avenue for communication among *anonymous* writers and readers who communicate *only* through writing. It conveys messages that, through repetition over the years, have acquired a traditional form, messages that are highly idiosyncratic and personalized, and messages of social protest or commentary.

Here are some ideas that we've thought up for interesting collection projects:

Examine the graffiti of a particular location. In every community there is a wall or other public surface that forms a target for graffiti writing. Take a look at this graffiti bulletin board and examine *either* the layout and content of the graffiti at one particular time (*synchronic analysis*) or the transformations that occur over a period of weeks (*diachronic analysis*). You'll want to take a photograph or make a diagram of the graffiti location each time you visit.

Examine a form. If you notice a particular form of graffiti that is common in your area, you might trace that form across locations. Try to determine what it is communicating, why it appears in certain locations and not others, and whether the message varies depending upon its context or setting.

Compare graffiti of one area to that of another. Often the graffiti in one classroom or one university building will express the particular concerns of the people occupying/using that space. To get an idea of different groups in your area and their different concerns, try comparing the graffiti common to one area with that common to another. You might also want to explore the gender-specific qualities of graffiti in men's and women's lavatories as a key to cultural differences between the sexes.

Look at a group of "writers". Although groups of graffiti writers are difficult to identify, since they remain anonymous to outsiders, if you are involved or know someone involved in one of these groups, you might do a folklore collection project on the group. How did the individuals become involved in this activity? What do they consider the purpose of graffiti writing to be? How do they distinguish good graffiti from bad? You might also look at the esoteric/exoteric dimensions of their experience.

Explore event-related graffiti. If you observe graffiti related to an event (competition or festival) on your campus or in your community, you might want to study the links between the activity and the graffiti. We have already mentioned the example of the Little 500 at Indiana University. Another example is the Cornell campus festival *Green Dragon Day* which provokes a lot of graffiti, mostly from those students who are putting on the event. Graffiti is used to announce the arrival of Green Dragon Day in a number of ways. Campus symbols are painted green (one year students painted the presidents' statues; another, they painted a traffic control booth), and green dragon footprints appear on walkways across campus. The disobedience reflected in this graffiti-writing is linked to other forms of disobedience indulged in the festival. But to fully understand this event-related graffiti, one would need to understand the symbolism and significance of the festival itself. On your campus such graffiti may not be as highly elaborated, but you may find some interesting and potentially illuminating connections between festival activities and the written signs that accompany them (see Chapter 9 **Cultural Performances: Public Display Events and Festival**).

Acknowledgements

We would like to acknowledge a general debt to Richard Bauman and John McDowell, as well as to the work of Dell Hymes, Erving Goffman, and Roger Abrahams. We also want to thank Vickie West for her help and encouragement.

References Cited

Bakhtin, Mikhail M. 1981. Discourse in the Novel. IN *The Dialogic Imagination: Four Essays*, tr. Caryl Emerson and Michael Holquist. Austin: University of Texas Press.

Brunvand, Jan Harold. 1983. Regional Folk Speech and Sayings. IN *Handbook of American Folklore*, ed. Richard M. Dorson. Bloomington: Indiana University Press.

Jakobson, Roman. 1960. Concluding Statement: Linguistics and Poetics. IN *Style in Language*, ed. Thomas Sebeok. Cambridge, MA: M.I.T. Press.

Labov, William. 1966. *The Social Stratification of English in New York City*. Washington, D.C.: Center for Applied Linguistics.

Selected Annotated Bibliography

There is a wealth of literature in a number of disciplines dealing with issues related to Folk Speech. Here we present a small sample of the ones we feel are most accessible to a general audience.

1) **General Works**

Abrahams, Roger D. 1983. *The Man of Words in the West Indies: Performance and the Emergence of Creole Culture*. Baltimore: Johns Hopkins University Press.
Looks at the artfulness of speech forms. See especially chapter on "Folklore and Communication on St. Vincent" for a discussion of the relationship between folklore and other kinds of speech communication.

_____. 1970. *Deep Down in the Jungle*. Revised ed. Chicago: Aldine Publishing Co.
Another study of the performance of artful speech forms in urban African American folklore, with a focus on ritual insults and other forms of speech play. Contains texts of playing the dozens and toasts.

Bauman, Richard. 1986. *Story, Performance, and Event*. New York: Cambridge University Press.
Four studies of the contexts of storytelling. Conversation is considered both as the medium of storytelling and as it is represented in stories. Theoretical, fairly challenging reading.

_____. 1977. *Verbal Art as Performance*. Prospect Heights, IL: Waveland Press.
An important early work delineating the *performance* approach to artistic speech, which focuses on the process of communication more than on the formal features of the text or piece of spoken art itself.

Dundes, Alan. 1980. Texture, Text, and Context. IN *Interpreting Folklore*. Bloomington: Indiana University Press.
Discusses three levels of analysis and the need to pursue all three in interpreting folklore. Includes some discussion of conversational genres.

Goffman, Erving. 1983[1981]. *Forms of Talk*. Philadelphia: University of Pennsylvania Press.
A detailed look at the strategies involved in a number of different speech situations common in the modern United States and England. Fairly technical but accessible to most readers.

International Encyclopedia of Communications. 4 vols. 1989. New York: Oxford University Press.
A very useful reference tool for any number of studies. See especially the following entries: Roger D. Abrahams, "Insult"; Alessandro Duranti, "Oratory"; Thomas A. Green, "Riddle"; Galit Hasan-Rokem, "Proverb"; Shirley Brice Heath, "Language Ideology"; John Holmes McDowell, "Speech Play"; Susan Romaine, "Language Variation"; and Joel Sherzer, "Speaking, Ethnography of."

Kirshenblatt-Gimblett, Barbara, ed. 1976. *Speech Play: Research and Resources for the Study of Linguistic Creativity*. Philadelphia: University of Pennsylvania Press.
A collection of articles on play languages, riddles, children's languages, verbal dueling, and other aspects of speech play; with a large bibliography and bibliographic survey.

Sherzer, Joel. 1983. *Kuna Ways of Speaking*. Austin: University of Texas Press.
A look at the roles that different styles of speaking play in a Central American Indian culture. Looks at the relationship between everyday and artistic styles, adaptation and tradition, and other issues of language use.

Trudgill, Peter. 1983. *Sociolinguistics: An Introduction to Language and Society*. New York: Penguin Books.
A very readable introduction to sociolinguistics "that part of linguistics which is concerned with language as a social and cultural phenomenon." Looks at, among other things, the ways in which language use identifies our social class, ethnicity, gender. Recommended for beginners.

2) **Dialect**

American Speech: A Quarterly of Linguistic Usage. 1925-.
Articles range from popular to highly theoretical. Recent issues contain such features as "New Words" in British and American English, an article on the use of "like" in American English, and many more.

"American Tongues" [videorecording]. 1986. Andrew Kolker and Louis Alvarez. The Center for New American Media. New York: International Production Center.
An interesting look at dialect in the United States. Looks at regional, social, and ethnic differences and attitudes toward these differences.

Brunvand, Jan Harold. 1983. Regional Folk Speech and Sayings. IN *Handbook of American Folklore*, ed. Richard M. Dorson. Bloomington: Indiana University Press.
A good look at some of the regional differences in dialect and folk sayings, which encourages the fieldworker to take history, culture, and local geography into account when studying these elements of language.

Publications of the American Dialect Society. (various formats and topics)

Richmond, W. Edson. 1972. Folk Speech. IN *Folklore and Folklife: An Introduction*, ed. Richard M. Dorson. Chicago: University of Chicago Press.
Concentrates on regional dialect and contains philological discussion of the origin of some peculiarities of American regional dialects. For instance, he traces a folk speech phrase common in parts of Pennsylvania and Ohio back to its Old English roots.

3) **Conversational Genres**
  a) **general**
Abrahams, Roger D. 1976. The Complex Relations of Simple Forms. IN *Folklore Genres*, ed, Dan Ben-Amos. Austin: University of Texas Press.
Discusses the relationship between the conversational genres and other genres of verbal folklore. Fairly theoretical.

_____. 1968. A Rhetoric of Everyday Life: Traditional Conversational Genres. *Southern Folklore Quarterly* 32:44-59.
One of Abrahams' first attempts at defining and discussing conversational genres.

Yercovitch, Sally. 1983. Conversational Genres. IN *Handbook of American Folklore*, ed. Richard M. Dorson. Bloomington: Indiana University Press.
Brief but useful discussion of the conversational genres and of conversation as the basis for many of the longer forms of oral folklore.

  b) **proverbs and proverbial phrases**
Abrahams, Roger D. 1972. Proverbs and Proverbial Expressions. IN *Folklore and Folklife: An Introduction*, ed. Richard M. Dorson. Bloomington: Indiana University Press.
A good introduction to the subject, discusses and distinguishes proverbs and proverbial expressions; contains an annotated bibliography for further reading.

Holbek, Bengt. 1970. Proverb Style. *Proverbium* 15:470-472.
Discusses formal features of proverbs such as alliteration, rhyme, rhythm, and parallelism. etc.

McDowell, John H. 1985. The Poetic Rites of Conversation. *Journal of Folklore Research* 22:113-132.
Looks at the use of a proverbial expression in a conversation to apologize for a social gaffe. A good example of what you can do with conversational analysis if you pay close attention to what's going on.

Mieder, Wolfgang. 1982. *International Proverb Scholarship: An Annotated Bibliography*. Garland Folklore Bibliographies, vol. 3, ed. Alan Dundes. New York: Garland Publishing, Inc.
Useful for anyone planning an extended project on the proverb.

Taylor, Archer. 1962[1931]. *The Proverb and an Index to the Proverb*. Hatboro, PA: Folklore Associates.
Large, early work on the origins, content, and style of the proverb, also discusses proverbial phrases.

_____. 1950. "Proverbs,""Proverbial Phrases," and "Wellerisms" IN *Funk and Wagnalls Standard Dictionary of Folklore, Mythology, and Legend*, ed. Maria Leach. New York: Funk and Wagnalls.
Good, brief definitions, discussion and examples included.

  c) **mnemonic devices**
Backhouse, Anthony E. 1976. How to Remember Numbers in Japanese. IN *Speech Play*, ed. Barbara Kirshenblatt-Gimblett. Philadelphia: University of Pennsylvania Press.
An examination of the way in which the structure of a language can provide resources for mnemonic devices.

Brakeley, Theresa. 1950. "Mnemonic Device." IN *Funk and Wagnalls Standard Dictionary of Folklore, Mythology, and Legend*, ed. Maria Leach. New York: Funk and Wagnalls.
Provides a definition plus a large number of examples of mnemonic devices.

Dundes, Alan. 1961. Mnemonic Devices. *Midwest Folklore* 11:139-147.
An examination of mnemonics both *in* verbal folklore and *as* verbal folklore, calls for further study into mnemonic devices as folkloric phenomena.

  d) **miscellaneous**
Opie, Iona and Moira Tatem. 1989. *A Dictionary of Superstitions*. New York: Oxford University Press.
Contains "divinations, spells, cures, charms," and other, nonconversational, expressions of "superstition."

Sherzer, Joel. 1978. "Oh! That's a pun and I didn't mean it." *Semiotica* 22:335-350.
For more advanced readers, a good look at the sociolinguistics of punning.

4) **Fieldwork, Collecting, and Transcribing Techniques**
Fine, Elizabeth C. 1984. *The Folklore Text: From Performance to Print*. Bloomington: Indiana University Press.
Discusses methods of transcribing and presenting the text of a folkloric performance. Points out that the method chosen has a close relationship to the theories with which the folklorist is working.

Ives, Edward D. 1974. *The Tape-Recorded Interview: A Manual for Fieldworkers in Folklore and Oral History*. Knoxville: University of Tennessee Press.
Contains a wealth of practical and reassuring advice for students embarking on an interviewing project. Divided into three parts: 1) How a Tape Recorder Works; 2) Interviewing; 3) Processing. Although the advice on tape-recorders is now somewhat dated, most of the information in the book remains valid.

Preston, Dennis R. 1982. 'Ritin' Fowklower Daun 'Rong: Folklorists' Failures in Phonology. *Journal of American Folklore* 95:304-326.
Critiques folklorists' early attempts to represent dialect with phonetic spellings, suggests alternatives.

Tedlock, Dennis. 1972. On the Translation of Style in Oral Narrative. IN *Toward New Perspectives in Folklore*, eds. Americo Paredes and Richard Bauman. Austin: University of Texas Press.
A critical examination of the translation of American Indian tales which argues that a good transcription and translation must attend to and notate the performance style, including pause structure and loudness, as well as the performance context.

CHAPTER 6
Folk Beliefs

Kenneth D. Pimple

INTRODUCTION

The challenge in studying folk beliefs is not so much finding them as recognizing them. People can express and act on their folk beliefs at any time, in any setting, and in a great number of ways. We are so surrounded by folk beliefs and the effects of folk beliefs that we tend not to notice them, like the air we breathe.

The first thing to understand when setting off to collect folk beliefs is that it can't be done—that is, you can't collect beliefs. Beliefs exist only in people's heads; all we can collect are *expressions* of beliefs. Expressions can take either verbal or behavioral form, and they often take both. Sometimes the most interesting aspect of studying folk beliefs is observing the ways that verbal and behavioral expressions of folk beliefs match up or fail to match up. In other words, in what ways does a person *act* as if she believes what she *says* she believes?

BELIEFS

A *belief* is a conviction or an acceptance that something is true. Let me dwell for a moment on two parts of this definition. First, notice that "conviction or acceptance" can have both an intellectual and an emotional component. I can *think* something is true and I can also *feel* something is true. Presumably when I think something is true I can come up with reasons for thinking so, but often when I feel something is true it is harder to explain why. There are many things that I think are true and that I have good reasons for thinking are true, but which have an emotional importance to me that predominates over the abstract or rational significance.

The second part of this definition I want to expand upon is the word *something*. It can be useful to think of three kinds of *somethings* that people can believe are true, namely *facts*, *categories* or *systems of categori-*

zation, and what I'll call *theories*. (These three sometimes overlap.)

Facts are ideas about the world which can be stated in the form "x is y," and such a statement can be evaluated to be true or false. For example, "My eyes are blue" is a statement of fact; "Sit down!" is a statement, but since it can't rightly be understood to be either true or false, it is not factual. It is also important to note that statements of fact can be false; thus, "My eyes are brown" is a statement of fact, but, when spoken by the author of this chapter, it is false. There are also many statements of fact which are not empirically verifiable—such as, "My grandmother is a saint in heaven." It makes sense to consider whether this is true or false (in contrast to "Sit down!"), but it can't be *proven* to be either true or false.

Along with beliefs about facts, people have many beliefs about how the world should be *categorized* or *classified*. For example, what falls into the category of food? Americans and Europeans think of cheese as food, but the Chinese find cheese disgusting—after all, it's milk gone bad. And you and your parents might have quite different ideas about what constitutes a good meal or who is good to date.

Finally, by *theories* I mean ideas about cause and effect. How does a woman get pregnant—or avoid getting pregnant? Why was my cousin born mentally retarded? What can I do to improve my grades, my batting average, my success in love? These are the kinds of questions that theories, ideas about cause and effect relationships, are used to answer.

FOLK BELIEFS

So *beliefs* are convictions about what is in the world (facts), how the world is best understood (categories), and what makes things happen (theories). What, then, is a folk belief? To me, it is not very useful to think of the study of folk belief as the study of a certain *kind* of belief (as the study of the blues is the study of a certain *kind* of music). Rather, the study of folk belief is a *perspective* or a *point of view* taken when studying beliefs. I'll try to make this clear by discussing some possible definitions of folk belief and showing that these definitions don't really distinguish one kind of belief from other kinds of beliefs. Then I will try to show that, taken as *perspectives*, some of these are worthwhile ways to study beliefs.

Here, then, are a few possible definitions of *folk belief*:

(1) Folk beliefs are beliefs that are false.
(2) Folk beliefs are beliefs that have not been demonstrated to be true.
(3) Folk beliefs are beliefs that are held uncritically, are taken for granted, or are never examined very closely by their believers.
(4) Folk beliefs are beliefs that members of a (folk) group hold because they are members of that group.
(5) Folk beliefs are *traditional* beliefs; that is, they are beliefs that are circulated by word of mouth or by observation and imitation and, as a result of this circulation, undergo change.

These are easily divided into two categories: #1 and #2 focus on the relationship between the beliefs and the world, whereas #3, #4, and #5 focus on the relationship between the beliefs and the believer.

As you can see, #1 and #2 imply that folk beliefs provide a mistaken or wrong picture of the world. These definitions also have the unfortunate effect of implying that people who have folk beliefs are irrational, uncritical, or stupid. This is simply not the case. While it is true that irrational, uncritical, and stupid people have folk beliefs, it is also the case with rational, critical, and brilliant people (and everyone else). If your interest is in the mistakes people make, #1 and #2 might be useful; but if that is the case, you might as well be accurate and say you are studying *mistaken beliefs* rather than *folk beliefs*. Besides, there are many things about beliefs that are much more interesting than whether they happen to be true or not. In addition, there are very many beliefs that simply can't be proven to be true or false scientifically or otherwise; as a mundane example, consider the expression "He who hesitates is lost."

On the other hand, #3, #4, and #5 emphasize (respectively) the attitude of the believer toward folk beliefs; the social, shared nature of folk beliefs; and the ways folk beliefs are circulated. I think that these

are more useful, but they, too, fail to distinguish folk beliefs as a certain *kind* of belief. Let me give an example. If there is any kind of belief that is *not* a folk belief, then the germ theory of disease is a belief of this kind, being a product of science—of institutionalized, elite culture, promulgated by highly educated, trained professionals. Now, very few Americans have ever seen a germ or any real proof of the theory, but still the vast majority of Americans believe that many diseases are spread by germs. Even so, it can be described as a folk belief under #3 (most Americans aren't critical about the theory), #4 (Americans as a group tend to hold this belief), and, not quite so neatly, #5 (we learn about the theory when our mothers admonish us, "Cover your mouth when you sneeze!", etc.).

The concept of *folk belief* derives its usefulness from context. I would say, for example, that the germ theory of disease is a folk belief (from perspective #3—it's held uncritically) for most 20th-century Americans, but what makes this a useful insight is considering the influence that scientific authority has on most Americans, or contrasting 20th-century Americans with, say, 18th-century Americans, who had quite a different idea of what caused disease. Likewise, the germ theory of disease is *not* a folk belief from perspective #3 for physicians and nurses because they have plenty of good evidence for the theory, but it *is* a folk belief for physicians and nurses in contrast to, say, folklorists (from perspective #4—folk group), because medical practitioners derive a sense of identity from the theory and their stance towards it that folklorists do not share. The notion of folk belief is productive, then, not due to the *kind* of belief it points to, but because of the kinds of concerns it raises—because of the perspectives it encourages us to take.

Next I'll discuss a couple of kinds of belief that are certainly folk beliefs (though they don't cover all instances of folk beliefs), and then I'll give some advice on how to collect and analyze folk beliefs.

TWO SUB-CATEGORIES OF BELIEFS
World View

A *world view* is the system of beliefs that provides a person's fundamental understanding of the way the world works. It is derived from the totality of our many different experiences, from aspects of our life including familial upbringing, education, religious, socio-economic, cultural, and political influences. *World view* is closely related to what we call *common sense*. Many aspects of our own world view seem so self-evident to us that it seems absurd to question them, or even to comment on them. One aspect of American world view is our belief that ordinarily individuals are responsible for their actions. Americans take a lot of convincing (usually by high-priced psychiatrists) that someone is insane and therefore not responsible for his actions, and we take even more convincing that someone is possessed by an evil spirit. But in former times and in other cultures, some people believed that a person's actions could be controlled by such things as fate, God, the gods, or demons.

By definition, a culture's world view includes beliefs that people of that culture take for granted and ideas about the world that they see as inarguably true, and therefore, as *natural*. But not everything that we take for granted *is* natural, and not every element of our world view is shared by all people. For example, there has been an ongoing debate in our culture for more than a century between evolutionists and creationists. The debate has been over whether the world and the animals in it have been slowly changing (evolving) through time, or whether the world and its creatures were brought into being pretty much as they are now all at once at the moment of creation. For some people, the belief that human beings evolved from ape-like creatures is not consistent with how they perceive the world and the place of human beings in the cosmos—it is not part of their world view. For others, the related ideas of evolution and of progress are integral to how they believe the world works. The way a person acts and interacts in the world will be directly influenced by such a belief as part of her world view.

A world view is built up of many different fundamental beliefs all working together to give the people who hold it a more-or-less coherent picture of the world. As I've implied in my discussion above, the notion of world view is usually applied to groups of people (like Americans or peasants) rather than individuals. Certainly every individual has a world view, but people who have studied world view have tended to be interested in the basic *shared* perception of the world of given peoples.

Superstitions

Another interesting kind of belief is the superstition, which can be called a folk belief from any of the five perspectives. Superstition has been defined in many ways, but I think the following is a useful definition: A *superstition* is a belief, usually about luck or concerned with the successful completion of a specific task, often associated with ritual behaviors,

that the believer recognizes is probably not valid, but continues to hold anyway. For example, consider the belief expressed by the saying "It's unlucky to walk under ladders." A person who believes this might well admit (when pressed) that walking under a ladder doesn't have anything to do with luck, but will continue to avoid walking under ladders (ritual behavior). Many people admit that they are superstitious and recognize their superstitions as false beliefs, but they continue to be emotionally attached to them, perhaps saying that they knock on wood or avoid walking under ladders "just in case."

The existence of superstitions points to the fact that people can believe contradictory things; usually, however, people manage to compartmentalize their beliefs so that contradictory beliefs don't come into conflict with each other. Imagine Sam: In most settings, Sam is convinced that there is no such thing as "luck," let alone any way to ensure good or bad luck, and yet Sam goes out of his way to avoid walking under ladders. How can he really be *convinced* that there's no such thing as luck *and* be convinced that walking under a ladder will bring him bad luck? People have different levels of conviction about their beliefs, and in this case Sam's disbelief in luck is much stronger (in most settings) than his belief in the danger of walking under ladders. But when he's near a ladder, his superstition is the stronger. This causes no problems unless something forces Sam to think about his disbelief in luck as he's walking toward a ladder; then the conflict is likely to cause Sam a degree of emotional distress.

THE SOCIAL BASE OF BELIEFS

Beliefs can be completely idiosyncratic (that is, held by only one person) or widely shared. The beliefs a given person holds are influenced by unique events in that person's life and character, and they are also influenced by factors which affect many of the people around her.

A good example of beliefs influenced by social surroundings is racism. I grew up in a white working-class neighborhood in Denver, Colorado, and whenever I heard the word "Mexican" in my youth it was spoken like a curse. I now know that the ethnic stereotypes I learned about Mexicans and Mexican-Americans when I was a child have no basis in reality, but when I hear the word "Mexican" (even in a phrase like "I love Mexican food"), I sometimes still cringe as if I've heard a bad word.

There is nothing intrinsically wrong with the word "Mexican," just as there is nothing intrinsically wrong with being Mexican or Mexican-American, but due to the way the word was used when I was growing up it triggers certain associations in me. The *social* meaning the word had, the meaning understood by my family and neighbors, remains with me no matter how hard I try to get rid of it and is in some ways stronger than the literal meaning of the word.

The social base of shared beliefs can be along lines of race, ethnicity, economic class, geographical region, age, religion, political persuasion (conservative, liberal, radical), sexual orientation, occupation, gender—any group a person belongs to might have its own fund of shared beliefs.

People of different ages and in different life-situations tend to have their own overriding interests and their own folk beliefs. Teenagers have plenty of beliefs about contraception and courting; pre-teens tend to wrestle with ideas about just what sex is; college seniors have loads of superstitions about job interviews; and parents have their own theories about what makes their offspring tick.

COLLECTING EXPRESSIONS OF FOLK BELIEFS

How, then, to go about collecting folk beliefs? Expressions of folk beliefs are easy to collect informally—that is, by just keeping your eyes and ears open. Watch what people do and listen to what they say, and when you have observed something that seems to stem from a folk belief, ask the person about it—"Why did you say/do that?" You can also go about the task of doing fieldwork in a formal setting, that is, by performing an interview.

Superstitions. Superstitions are often associated with luck, and, as Bronislaw Malinowski observed years ago, people feel the greatest need for luck when they are performing tasks over which they have limited control, especially when the tasks are dangerous. For this reason, athletes often have lucky items of clothing or follow set routines (rituals) before big games, such as eating only certain foods, dressing in a prescribed order, avoiding certain practices, and so on. Perhaps you know someone who is in a high-risk occupation, like steel construction work, who has superstitions and takes precautions before going on the job. Many different folk expressions emerge from any group involved in high-risk activities. The risk need not be physical well-being; actors and musicians face uncontrollable factors which threaten them with failure or embarrassment every time they perform in public, and so they are likely to have little rituals intended to bring them luck. I don't mean to suggest that athletes, actors, and musicians are more superstitious than everyone else, but rather that since competing in sporting events and performing on stage are by

their nature uncontrollable and unpredictable, those activities lead to many superstitions. (The same can be said of test-taking.)

A word of warning, however: Although superstitions are easy to collect, it is generally quite difficult to come up with anything interesting or original to say about them. If your assignment has an emphasis on interpretation or analysis, you'd be well advised to go lightly on superstitions.

Folk medicine. Another area where one is likely to have limited control is health. Folk beliefs about diseases that doctors can now cure have tended to fade away, but many people have folk cures for those pesky, ubiquitous conditions that defy science, like hiccups, hangovers, warts, and the common cold. Folk medicines derived from herbs and organic compounds are common in many rural areas and have been passed down through the generations by families living in the area.

Rivaling health is, of course, love; beliefs about attracting a potential sexual partner range from superstitions (love charms and the like) to fairly compelling ideas of how one should act, dress, speak, and so on, to be attractive. Advertisers are very skilled at playing on these ideas and promoting some of them.

Divination. Associated with the idea of love are various beliefs on the means by which one chooses a mate, either on one's own or through a matchmaker as is still practiced in some cultures. Once couples have married, there are beliefs surrounding pregnancy and being able to predict the sex of the baby. You may have heard that if the mother spits into a can of Drano, you can usually predict the sex of the baby by what color the Drano turns. It's kind of like a folk litmus test. A general term for these sorts of activities is *divination*.

Another form of divination is dowsing or water witching. In dowsing, the goal is to try and locate a water table with the least amount of expense and inconvenience for the purpose of drilling a well (See Figure 1). If you live in a rural community you may know of someone who is a water witch and you could probably obtain a good interview on the art of dowsing. In fact, you might not have to look to rural areas to study dowsing; I've seen maintenance workers at Indiana University searching for buried water lines by carrying two rods across a field and waiting for the rods to cross.

If you live in an urban center, there may be people you know who read palms or Tarot cards or tell fortunes in various ways. These are ancient practices which still have currency across America.

Figure 1. Linzey Neal, a Well Witcher. Brown County, Indiana, 1936. Hohenberger Collection, courtesy of Indiana University Foundation and Lilly Manuscript Library.

Belief in the Supernatural. Americans also have a variety of folk beliefs about the supernatural; you yourself might know a legend (see Chapter 4 **Folk Narrative**) about a haunted house, bridge, or tunnel, or about a specific person returning from the dead. The Ouija board is a particularly interesting example because it is so common in the United States and so complex. People have differing views not only on whether Ouija boards work, but how Ouija boards work; that is, when you say that your Ouija board works, do you mean that you can use it to contact ghosts? or demons? or to tap your own psychic powers? Your understanding of how it works will have a considerable effect on your attitude toward it.

Proverbs. It is useful, when looking for folk beliefs, to be attuned to proverbs. Not all proverbs express folk beliefs, but many do. *Proverbs* are short, pithy, traditional sayings that sum up an argument or a point of view; I've already mentioned one: "He who hesitates is lost." Another well-known English

proverb is "Look before you leap." As you can see, proverbs often contradict each other, yet it is perfectly possible to believe that both of these proverbs contain good advice. The interesting question to pursue is not which of these is true, but rather under what circumstances each proverb holds. We all know that there are some circumstances in which hesitation doesn't pay and some in which caution is advisable. You might ask of a specific person which attitude holds in certain risky situations—like merging onto a freeway or asking a stranger for a date—to gain insights into that individual's personality.

INTERPRETING EXPRESSIONS OF FOLK BELIEFS

Once you have figured out that someone holds certain beliefs, how can you study them as folk beliefs? The trick is to ask yourself (and probably the believer) a few questions about each belief to see if it reveals something interesting about the believer or the circumstances under which you observed the belief being expressed. Consider these questions:

1) What does this belief do for the believer?
2) How does this belief fit with beliefs held by the larger society?
3) How does this belief fit with the life experiences, economic condition, level of education, occupation, religion, ethnicity, age, gender, etc., of the believer? Do any of these factors "explain" the belief, or do any of them seem to clash with the belief?
4) Does it seem likely that the believer would be threatened by a challenge to this belief, or believes it so strongly that he simply can't think about it critically? (Perspective #3.)
5) How does this belief fit with beliefs held by a smaller group of which the believer is a member? Does it seem to be something shared by the members but not by the larger society? (Perspective #4.)
6) How did this person learn this belief, and does that have a strong influence on why she continues to believe it? (Perspective #5.)

All of these, of course, have to do not only with collecting expressions of beliefs, but with interpreting them as well. If you can thoroughly answer one or more of these questions with regard to a belief, you will have gone a long way towards a useful analysis.

One problem that I mentioned above is the relationship of a belief to its expression. This is a problem that you can make as difficult or as easy as you please. The simple fact is that we have access only to expressions of beliefs, and never to the beliefs themselves. You should not make the mistake of confusing the two, for that would be like saying George Washington's portrait is George Washington. Some people argue that the separation between a belief and its expression is so great that we can't really talk about beliefs at all, but only about expressions. It's true that people can lie and that they can even deceive themselves, but I hold that we can often infer beliefs from their expressions. One rule of thumb is to consider both a person's verbal and behavioral expressions; it often helps to observe both over a period of time.

It does happen at times, though, that even a person's expressions don't seem to hold together—he might seem to act in one way and say something contradictory. What, in such a case, does he really believe? Sometimes the evidence just isn't sufficient to come to a conclusion; but sometimes those are the most interesting cases, as long as you can make a clear statement as to why you can't tell.

Acknowledgement

I would like to thank William F. Guinee, Martha K. Griesheimer, Jennifer Livesay, and especially Patricia E. Sawin for helpful comments on an earlier draft. I would also like to acknowledge that most of my ideas about folk beliefs have developed under the influence of Roger L. Janelli. None of these good scholars should be held responsible for the positions put forth here.

Selected Annotated Bibliography

Baker, Ronald L. 1979. "Hogs are Playing with Sticks—Bound to be Bad Weather": Folk Belief or Proverb? IN Jan Harold Brunvand, ed., *Readings in American Folklore*, pp. 199-202. New York: W. W. Norton and Company.
A very short, amusing piece on the relationship between folk belief and proverb, and also a very good example of why contextual data is important.

Cannon, Walter B. 1979 [1942]. "Voodoo" Death. IN Lessa and Vogt, pp. 367-373.
A classic article on one kind of magic that actually works, but only on people who really believe in it.

de Caro, F. A. 1986. Riddles and Proverbs. IN Elliott Oring, ed., *Folk Groups and Folklore Genres: An Introduction*, pp. 175-197. Logan, UT: Utah State University Press.
A good discussion of these two related forms; discusses many interesting insights of past scholarship.

Dubisch, Jill. 1979. You Are What You Eat: Religious Aspects of the Health Food Movement. IN Elliott Oring, ed., *Folk Groups and Folklore Genres: A Reader*, pp. 124-135. Logan, UT: Utah State University Press.
A look at the world view implied in the health food movement which began in the late 1960s.

Dundes, Alan. 1972. Folk Ideas as Units of World View. IN Américo Paredes and Richard Bauman, eds., *Toward New Perspectives in Folklore*, pp. 93-103. Austin: University of Texas Press.
An interesting discussion of the building blocks of world view; includes several examples of what Dundes takes to be American folk ideas.

_____. 1980. *Interpreting Folklore*. Bloomington, IN: Indiana University Press.
Includes several essays on American folk beliefs and world view, including "Thinking Ahead: A Folkloristic Reflection of the Future Orientation in American Worldview;" "Seeing is Believing;" and "The Number Three in American Culture."

Evans-Pritchard, E. E. 1979 [1937]. Witchcraft Explains Unfortunate Events. IN Lessa and Vogt, pp. 362-366.
An excellent description of Zande witch beliefs; excerpted from Evans-Pritchard's study of African witchcraft, *Witchcraft, Oracles and Magic among the Azande*. Shows clearly that false beliefs can still be formed into a logical system.

Foster, George M. 1965. Peasant Society and the Images of Limited Good. *American Anthropologist* 67:293-315.
An important essay on what Foster takes to be a central aspect of peasant world view.

Frazer, James G. 1979 [1911-1915]. Sympathetic Magic. IN Lessa and Vogt, pp. 337-352.
Frazer's classic theory of magic, highly abridged from his 13-volume work, *The Golden Bough: A Study in Magic and Religion*. Frazer's theory, like Malinowski's (below), is still very useful in studying beliefs and superstitions.

Gmelch, George. 1971. Baseball Magic. IN Spradley and Rynkiewich, pp. 348-352.
An application of Malinowski's theory of magic to professional baseball.

Graebner, Alan. 1975. Growing Up Female. IN Spradley and Rynkiewich, pp. 23-29.
A provocative essay on how Americans are taught to be female.

Gruss, Edmond C., with John G. Hotchkiss. 1975. *The Ouija Board: Doorway to the Occult*. Chicago: Moody Press.
Gruss is an evangelical Christian minister who believes that using the Ouija board can lead to demonic possession. This is *not* a scholarly work; it reveals at least as much about Gruss's beliefs as it does about the Ouija board.

Hand, Wayland D., ed. 1964. *Popular Beliefs and Superstitions from North Carolina*. Durham, NC: Duke University Press. From *The Frank C. Brown Collection of North Carolina Folklore*, Volume 7, Newman Ivey White, general editor.
A massive collection of American folk beliefs and superstitions. If you want to see if a belief is traditional, this is a good place to start.

_____., ed. 1980. *American Folk Medicine: A Symposium*. Berkeley: University of California Press.
A collection of essays by several scholars on a wide variety of topics, including warts, marking unborn babies, and amputated limbs. More analytical than the Brown collection (Hand 1964).

Hufford, David J. 1982. *The Terror that Comes in the Night: An Experience-Centered Study of Supernatural Assault Traditions.* Philadelphia: University of Pennsylvania Press.
Probably the best recent work on a specific folk belief, known as "the Old Hag" or nightmare. Fascinating, but don't read it in bed! For a shortened version of the argument, see Hufford's essay in Hand 1980.

Jahoda, Gustav. 1969. *The Psychology of Superstition.* London: Allen Lane the Penguin Press.
Jahoda's definition of superstition differs from mine. A thorough examination of the subject.

Jansen, Wm. Hugh. 1965. The Esoteric-Exoteric Factor in Folklore. IN Alan Dundes, ed., *The Study of Folklore*, pp. 43-51. Englewood Cliffs, NJ: Prentice-Hall, Inc.
A truly classic essay concerning beliefs groups of people have about themselves and about other groups; has much to say about the social base of folk beliefs.

Kearney, Michael. 1975. World View Theory and Study. *Annual Review of Anthropology* 4:247-270.
Not an easy read, but if you're interested in the topic of world view, you'll find a very extensive bibliography here.

Langlois, Janet. 1980. "Mary Whales, I Believe In You." IN Linda Dégh, ed., *Indiana Folklore: A Reader*, pp. 196-224. Bloomington: Indiana University Press.
Langlois discusses several issues, including the relationship of myth and ritual (belief and practice). The Mary Whales of the title is a ghost who can be summoned in a divinatory game usually played by pre-teenagers.

Leary, James P. 1989. "The Land Won't Burn": An Esoteric American Proverb And Its Significance. IN Elliott Oring, ed., *Folk Groups and Folklore Genres: A Reader*, pp. 302-307. Logan, UT: Utah State University Press.
A very good short essay on a saying traditional in one family and what that saying expressed to them and about them.

Lessa, William A. and Evon Z. Vogt, eds. 1979. *Reader in Comparative Religion: An Anthropological Approach.* New York: Harper and Row. 4th edition.
Contains a number of extremely interesting and useful essays on religion, magic, divination, and belief, including several classics, many of them cited in this bibliography. Definitely worth looking through.

Malinowski, Bronislaw. 1984 [1954]. *Magic, Science and Religion and Other Essays.* Westport, CT: Greenwood Press.
Malinowski's title essay is a pleasantly readable statement of his theory that magic functions to relieve anxiety, a theory that can still be used fruitfully. See also his essay in Lessa and Vogt.

Miner, Horace. 1975. Body Ritual Among the Nacirema. IN Spradley and Rynkiewich, pp. 10-13.
An interesting depiction of some medical beliefs and practices of an exotic people.

Moore, Omar Khayyam. 1979 [1957]. Divination—A New Perspective. IN Lessa and Vogt, pp. 376-379.
A short article which postulates that some forms of divination actually work, but not for the reasons that people who believe in them would assert.

Moyle, Natalie K. 1989. Spacey Soviets and the Russian Attitude Toward Territorial Passage. IN Elliott Oring, ed., *Folk Groups and Folklore Genres: A Reader*, pp. 87-97. Logan, UT: Utah State University Press.
An intriguing look at one aspect of Russian world view contrasted with the corresponding aspect of American world view.

Mullen, Patrick B. 1978. *I Heard the Old Fishermen Say: Folklore of the Texas Gulf Coast.* Logan, UT: Utah State University Press.
Includes description and analysis of many folk beliefs.

Paredes, Américo. 1977. On Ethnographic Work Among Minority Groups: A Folklorist's Perspective. *New Scholar* 6:1-32.
This essay has many things to recommend it, including a short discussion of the Mexican-American perception of the germ theory of disease.

_____. 1989. Folk Medicine and the Intercultural Jest. IN Elliott Oring, ed., *Folk Groups and Folklore Genres: A Reader*, pp. 63-77. Logan, UT: Utah State University Press.
An outstanding essay examining intertwining concerns of folk beliefs about medicine and healers, the use of jests to make a point, and reactions to cultural change. The jests were collected in Spanish on the Texas-Mexican border.

Poggie, John J., Jr., and Carl Gersuny. 1989. Risk and Ritual: An Interpretation of Fishermen's Folklore in a New England Community. IN Elliott Oring, ed., *Folk Groups and Folklore Genres: A Reader*, pp. 137-145. Logan, UT: Utah State University Press.
A test of Malinowski's theory of magic. See also Mullen 1988.

Radcliffe-Brown, A. R. 1979 [1939]. Taboo. IN Lessa and Vogt, pp. 46-56.
Radcliffe-Brown challenges Malinowski's theory of magic, asserting that magic sometimes creates or raises anxiety, rather than relieving it. Another classic.

Rickels, Patricia K. 1979. Some Accounts of Witch Riding. IN Jan Harold Brunvand, ed., *Readings in American Folklore*, pp. 53-63. New York: W. W. Norton and Company.
Some recent accounts of witch riding along with historical information on the belief.

Spradley, James P., and Michael A. Rynkiewich, eds. 1975. *The Nacirema: Readings on American Culture.* Boston: Little, Brown and Company.
A collection of essays on many aspects of American culture, including a wealth of views on American values, beliefs, and world view. I've referred to some of the essays in this bibliography, but the whole book is worth looking through.

Vogt, Evon Z., and Ray Hyman. 1979. *Water Witching U.S.A.* 2nd edition. Chicago: The University of Chicago Press.
A good study of dowsing. The original research was done in 1959, but the 1979 edition has a new preface, as well as a postscript on "urban dowsers" who use rods or pendulums to find things other than water.

Zumwalt, Rosemary. 1979. Plain and Fancy: A Content Analysis of Children's Jokes Dealing with Adult Sexuality. IN Jan Harold Brunvand, ed., *Readings in American Folklore*, pp. 344-354. New York: W. W. Norton and Company.
Provides and analyzes several jokes that reveal ideas that children have about adult sexuality.

CHAPTER 7
Folklore and Religion:
Approaches to Folklore Fieldwork

George H. Schoemaker

INTRODUCTION

There are few topics of conversation that are more sensitive and controversial than religion and politics. The reason for this is that religion and politics are more *ideological* and personal in nature than any other subject. By *ideology*, I mean the belief system or pattern of ideas peculiar to a specific culture group. The term has been used synonymously with worldview. You should also know that there is a distinction between folk or unofficial ideology and official ideology. For example, Catholics have an official ideology that is contained in an official document called the Credo. Official Catholic ideology might be characterized in the following manner: belief in the trinity (God the Father, God the Son, and God the Holy Spirit), belief in the absolute infallibility and authority of the Pope as the mouthpiece of God, an adherence to the seven sacraments of the church, a belief in the Bible (Old and New Testaments) as the word of God, certain symbols that have special meaning to Catholics, and so forth. By contrast, folk ideology or unofficial ideology is based on the unofficial beliefs and practices of the people, usually performed in face-to-face interaction, and which makes up what is called the folklore of religion.

In this chapter I want to address how folklorists approach religion and how you, the student, can engage in meaningful fieldwork in this area. However, in order to understand how religion and folklore are conceptualized as dimensions of culture, it is necessary to explore the nature of the sacred and profane.

THE NATURE OF THE SACRED AND THE PROFANE

The notion of the sacred and profane relates to qualities of culture. These qualities of culture are based on differences that are not scientifically verifiable. The distinctions made between the sacred and the profane are primarily a modern, patriarchal, westernized notion, superimposed on the *other*. In this model, the profane refers to the quality of our experience in the everyday world, while the sacred refers to a heightened transformed state of consciousness that takes us out of everyday reality. While this model should not be considered universal, it provides a useful way of looking at religion as a quality of experience, different and distinct from other types of everyday experience.

The sacred is manifested as a discontinuity with the normal and the everyday. It is manifested by means of certain signs. Signs indicating sacred behavior might include silence or reverence (or noise and chanting), expressions of belief through prayer and ritual, displays of emotion and spirituality, the preparation and consumption of certain foods, the adoption of different modes of dress, and so forth.

Moreover, the sacred is marked off spatially and temporally from everyday experience. Most likely, you have entered a Cathedral during your lifetime and became aware that you had entered sacred space. The stained glass, the sculpture, the paintings, all were visual signs that you had crossed the threshold of the secular or profane and entered another mode of experience. Interestingly, during the medieval and renaissance eras, the Cathedral was the center of religious and secular learning in Christian Europe. The sculpture, statues, and stained glass made the cathedral an encyclopedia of medieval faith and learning. There were representations of every aspect of the medieval world including signs of the zodiac, contemporary and historical figures, christian legends, the vices and virtues, the times of the season, the philosophers, and the seven liberal arts (i.e. grammar, rhetoric, dialectic, arithmetic, geometry, astronomy, and music). It was also during this period that the cult of the Virgin Mary came into full bloom. Almost every cathedral built during this time was dedicated to Mary.

Later in late eighteenth-century Europe, the Enlightenment thinkers used science and logic to explain things that happened in the world, and the split between science and religion became more evident. The separation between the sacred and the profane became institutionalized in two separate forms: the church and the academy.

Religion as a Dimension of Culture

In the same way that folklore is a category of culture, so too is religion. *Religion* can be defined in terms of sacred experience. It is the organization of life around this kind of experience, however varied in form or content. It includes a system of beliefs, a set of patterns of behavior, or a set of rituals, pertaining to a deity of some kind. The organization of religious experience leads to the formation of religious communities—communities that are set apart from the rest of society. This separation is observed in the numerous churches all over United States and also in small homogeneous ethnic/religious communities like the Amish, the Mennonites, and the Hutterites.

Individuals are also set apart from society for religious purposes. These are usually religious or ritual specialists of some kind including: shamans, soothsayers, witch doctors, medicine men, or witches. Occasionally groups may form which have a belief system centered upon an entity or a person other than a deity. These are called *cults*. Specialists of cults perform rituals and practice certain beliefs just as would be done in a religion.

Characteristics of Religion

Religion has several characteristics—I am sure that you can think of many based upon your own experience. For our purposes, however, we will draw upon the work of Winston L. King and his analysis of religion (1987:282-293).

Tradition. In this book we have defined tradition as a continuity over time and space of some aspect of culture. I have also said that tradition can represent symbolic links of an aspect of culture in the present to the past. Tradition is a vital characteristic of religion because established religious denominations usually claim some kind of divine lineage or link themselves with a divine, primordial origin. King says "Present modes of religious activity always seem to look backward for origins, precedents, and standards. As cultures become more complex and literate, these traditions of ancient thought and practice become more elaborate and stylized." The link or continuity with the past is reinforced by myths and legends.

Myths and Symbols. As explained earlier in this book, myths are sacred narratives associated with ritual and which explain sacred origins. They are considered to be true and are revered by most adherents of a religious culture. Legends are considered true and factual accounts of occurrences in the recent or historical past. These narratives are the cornerstones of many religious cultures. They establish the authority and validity of religious practices, the divine calling of individual founders, sacred writings, cultural history, and maintain the overall worldview and ideology of the religious culture.

Expressions of an emotional and spiritual nature regarding the transcendent realities—realities about god, eternal salvation, the sanctity of sacred teachings, and so forth—are often ineffable, that is, they are unable to be espressed in words. For this purpose, *symbols* are used to communicate and express that which transcends natural reality. King writes that "Symbol is the language of myth." A cross, a star of David, bread and wine, and so forth, all have a meaning other than what they are. These things are symbols for something else. They are made sacred, endowed with power, and infused with ideological meaning by the culture that holds them to be sacred.

Concepts of Salvation. Every religious culture has some concept of salvation—ideas which answer major questions about where we came from, why we are on the earth, and where we are going after death? Answers to these questions provide meaning in the lives of individuals and fulfill their needs and desires within a religious culture. Concepts of salvation are an essential part of the ideology of a culture, and as such, can contribute to feelings of ethnocentrism—a feeling that one's own culture is right—especially if the ideology maintains that only certain people are privileged to participate in saving ordinances.

Sacred places and objects. Almost every religion has places and objects which are considered to be sacred. While tradition maintains or establishes links with the past, places and objects provide powerful symbols to maintain traditional practices in the present. These places and objects operate at different levels of inclusiveness. For instance, the Vatican is the center of the universe or the *axis mundi* for devout Roman Catholics. However, individual churches, mountains, tabernacles, mosques, temples, etc. are all places where the sacred is manifested and is separated from the profane. Objects of a sacred nature are endowed with symbolic significance; the ark of the covenant, the menorah, holy candles, holy water, and so on, are a few examples of sacred objects.

Rituals. Concepts of salvation require sacred actions, or rituals performed by ritual specialists. A *ritual* is a category of symbolic behavior occasionally associated but not necessarily dependent on religious myth. The meaning of rituals is complex and ambiguous because of the use of symbols. It is best to consider ritual meaning in terms of many levels of meaning. Baptism, sacrament, confession, circumcision, marriage, last rites, etc. are a few rituals in Judeo-Christian tradition. Other rituals are performed by religious specialists in order to exorcise evil, heal the sick, speak in tongues (called *glossolalia*), or even to separate *undesirables* from the culture through excommunication.

Sacred writings. Links with the past are often based upon the sacred writings of a religious founder. Buddha, Christ, Confucius, Mohammed, and Moses, to name a few, have had their words and teachings canonized or made official, and these writings have provided their religious cultures with scriptures. Scriptures or sacred writings are central to the formation of official religious ideology. Examples of sacred writings might include the Bible, the Torah, the Koran, the Book of Mormon, the Mahabharata, the Upanishads, the Tao Teh Ching, and so forth.

Sacred community. Communitas or a sense of community and fellowship are desired goals of most religious cultures. Individuals assemble to participate in ritual, to hear sacred words, experience the sacred, and ultimately, become transformed and assimilated into a unified community. These individuals are bound together by similar backgrounds, experiences, goals, and expectations. Each person has had to endure rites of initiation in order to receive full fellowship in a community, and because of this, there is a clear and strong sense of social identity and social solidarity among individuals of a religious group.

Sacred experience. Experiences of a spiritual and transcendent nature become a prerequisite for some religious cultures. It is also important to recognize, though, that these may vary from religion to religion and that both men and women experience the sacred in different and relative ways.

All these characteristics of religion are found in various forms and in varying degrees within most religious cultures. An argument could also be made supporting the idea of secular religion—sports, motivational marketing, fad-diets, get-rich-quick schemes, are some examples. The rhetoric, symbols, shared peak experiences, and shared community among these groups are similar in nature to those of many religious cultures.

On Magic and Religion

The distinction between magic and religion is vague. This is because magical and religious occurrences are both experienced in the realm of the supernatural—the realm beyond the natural. Magic and religion can be distinguished by the ways supernatural powers are evoked. In religion, a specialist of a religious community solicits, begs, and pleads for aid from the supernatural or from the gods. On the other hand, in magic an individual attempts to influence or control supernatural conditions through some kind of ritual. Magic cannot really be taken as an independent system of beliefs. It is usually associated with other aspects of religious beliefs and other religious practices.

According to Sir James G. Frazer, the nineteenth-century British anthropologist, magic was an early form of religion and science. According to Frazer, magic, religion, and early science were very much tied to the way nature, the elements, and human beings all interacted with and acted upon each other. Frazer's tripartite evolutionary model is similar to the model of culture that Edward B. Tylor proposed. You remember that Tylor viewed culture in terms of stages of social development from *savagery* to *barbarism* to *civilization*. By the same token, Frazer saw *magic* and *religion* as earlier stages of *science* in the intellectual and social development of society.

Today, this kind of thinking is viewed as ethnocentric, westernized, and seriously flawed. It does not hold much relevance in folklore scholarship; however, one important aspect of Frazer's study of magic still remains. According to Frazer, there are two basic kinds of magic: homeopathic and contagious. *Homeopathic or sympathetic magic* operates on the principle that things that are alike will produce or experience the same effect. An example of homeopathic magic is the voodoo doll. It has the likeness of another person and when certain actions are done towards the doll, the actions are supposed to produce the same kinds of experiences in the person. The other kind of magic is called *contagious magic or the magic of touch*. The operating principle in this kind of magic is that things never lose contact or their natural tie. For example, if you are able to obtain a lock of hair from your lover, you will be able to have control over that individual. This kind of magic employs hair, nail parings, personal items, or old clothing.

While it is difficult to find magic practiced in modern mainstream American culture, you can find examples in some religious cultures, among Native-American cultures, or among some ethnic groups. It can even be argued that advertising operates on the principle of homeopathic magic. For example, many car ads depict a beautiful shapely car with a beautiful shapely woman. The implicit message of the advertisement directed towards men is that if you buy and possess this car, you will possess the woman or a woman like her. In other words, like produces like. (Of course, if you are a female, the ad's message to you is more complex.) Cigarette and beer ads operate the same way. You will never see fat, unshaven, bums depicted in these kinds of ads. Instead they usually show young, rich, carefree, handsome or beautiful people. (See Chapter 6 **Folk Beliefs**)

CONCEPTUALIZING FOLKLORE AND RELIGION

There are several approaches that folklorists have taken towards religion. Many of these are contained in an influential article by Don Yoder entitled "Toward a Definition of Folk Religion" (1974:2-15).

Folk Religion. One way of understanding folklore and religion is to conceptualize them as an informal organization, independent of institutional religious structures—a *folk religion*. This approach is influenced by Robert Redfield's work on folk culture. To Redfield, folk culture was "small, isolated, nonliterate, and homogeneous, with a strong sense of group solidarity . . . " A folk religion would exhibit these characteristics, and in addition, its adherents would focus their worship and adoration upon a particular deity or person. Implicit in this approach to religion is the idea that folk religion is somehow a deviation from official religion. In fact, Yoder points out that a major characteristic of folklore and religion is the tension which exists between official and unofficial (folk), between *great* and *little* traditions.

Another approach views *folk religion* as comprising survivals of ancient, primitive religious cultures. This idea is based on the work of the British School of Anthropology of the nineteenth century. *Folk religion* is seen in two ways—evolutionary or devolutionary. The evolutionary approach to religion regards *folk religion* as the survivals of *primitive* religions, of earlier stages of cultural development. Implicit in this notion is the idea that religious culture is evolving into a more civilized form of culture. The devolutionary premise views *folk religion* as survivals of an ancient golden age when religion was in its pristine and most

pure form. Another approach views folk religion as that part of a former high religion that has trickled down to and been preserved among the *backwards* people of a culture. This view is influenced by earlier German scholars notion of *gesunkenes Kulturgut*, meaning sunken culture. This notion refers to the sinking of culture from the elite to the peasant strata.

The problem with these particular approaches is that the analytical focus is not clearly defined. For example, if you were to focus on Protestantism, it could be a *folk religion* because it was a protest movement against Catholicism and hence represents survivals from an earlier stage of development. The Catholics will say devolutionary, while Protestants will say evolutionary. Whether it is evolutionary or devolutionary depends on whose perspective you side with. Either way, to call them folk religions would not be accurate.

Syncretism and Acculturation. Another way to define folk religion is to view it as a mixture of different traditions—either through **syncretism** or **acculturation**. **Syncretism** occurs when one culture imposes itself onto another and culture traits are blended or mixed. An example of this process occurred when Catholicism was introduced or imposed upon Native-American cultures in the United States by missionaries during the eighteenth and nineteenth centuries. Many Native American cultures adopted aspects of the *new* religion while still maintaining their old belief systems. There was a mixing of two religious and cultural traditions.

Folk interpretations of religion. Another way to conceptualize folk religion is to view it as the entire body of attitudes, beliefs, and concerns that the folk or unofficial stratum of culture have of a religion.

Unofficial aspects of an Institutionalized Religion. Similar in many respects to the above formulation, is Yoder's approach which defines folk religion as those aspects of religious culture that are unofficial, and unsanctioned, but observed and practiced by many people as part of their religious experience. For example, I once had a student who was Jewish. She and her family observed all the prescribed ways of preparing and eating food including using special plates for meat and dairy products. But on occasion when it was too much of a bother to go across town to obtain kosher food, my student's parents would purchase food at the store around the corner and eat it (the unkosher food) on paper plates, thereby obeying the letter of the law, but still being permitted to have the food in the house. The perceptions, attitudes, and practices that people have alongside the strictly official practices of an institutionalized religion constitute the folk-cultural dimension of religion. Implicit in Yoder's idea is the notion of a tension between official and unofficial strata of culture. The boundaries between the strata, however, are vague.

Religious Folklore. When religion is the subject or topic of cultural expressions, this constitutes *religious folklore.* The context of such expressions may or may not have any relation to any particular religion. For example, you may be at a party and someone initiates a joke-telling session. During the course of the joke-telling session, the subjects of the jokes range from ethnicity, to sex, to women, to sports, to religion, and so forth. Jokes, narratives, folk songs, and other forms of cultural expression that take religion as their subject may involve cultural **stereotypes.**

A *stereotype* is a preconceived idea, image, or attitude that an individual or group has about another person or group. *Stereotypes* are not based on experience but are learned as part of our socialization process. You should also remember that the esoteric/exoteric factor will influence the meaning and interpretation of religious folklore. For example, jokes told about Jews by non-Jews mean something different and can be interpreted differently from jokes told be Jews about Jews and Jewish culture.

These are some of the ways folklore and religion are conceptualized. These approaches were presented only to help you realize that there are numerous perspectives that can be used to look at expressive forms of religious groups. You might keep these in mind as you decide to focus on a particular religious group for your field project.

Doing Fieldwork in a Religious Culture
Religious Culture Groups in America

You may belong to or you may have a friend who belongs to a religious culture group in United States or Canada. Historically, United States and Canada have represented a *land of promise* for those who did not experience religious freedom in the *old country.* The constitution of the United States permits freedom of religion. As a result, there are several hundred practicing religious groups in North America.

Some of the more predominant religious culture groups in America are rooted in Judeo-Christian tradition. These would include: *Jews,* who have a very long and rich religious and ethnic heritage; *Catholics*; *Mormons*; various Protestant religions such as *Pentecostals, Baptists, Quakers*; ethnic/religious groups like *Amish, Mennonites,* and *Hutterites*; African American (such as the African Methodist Episcopal church),

Native American (each culture has its own distinct religion), or other *syncretic religious traditions*; or various *cults* devoted to the worship of a particular person. Demonic cults or cults practicing witchcraft can also be an interesting subject for fieldwork.

Many ethnic groups who immigrated to the United States brought many aspects of their *old world* culture with them. Religion was often one of the community's strongest ties, and as such, constituted a significant part of social, ethnic, and cultural identity. (See Chapter 14 **Ethnic and Immigrant Folklore**)

Preliminary Strategies and Preparation

There are three ways to enter into a religious culture. The first way is to go in *naked.* I don't mean *naked* in the literal sense, but rather to go in without any prior knowledge or contacts. This strategy would not yield very good data because you would spend most of your time trying to establish rapport with people, choosing informants who were reliable, and so forth.

The second way is to have a contact before you begin your fieldwork. Most likely this would be a friend who could introduce you into the culture with more ease and effectiveness than if you went in *naked.* Your friend could fill you in on the ideology of the religious group, introduce you to good informants—the ones who know the stories, make the best quilts, cook the best food, and so on.

The third way to enter a religious culture is probably the most effective, that is, to already be a member of the group. You know the good informants, are fairly versed in the ideology, know the proper mode of communication, the taboos, etc. The only disadvantage to this particular strategy is that your ability or inability to distance yourself from your own culture of study will need to be taken into consideration as you write up your notes, analyze your data, and make interpretations.

Since religion is a very personal and controversial topic, it is likely that many people will not appreciate their beliefs being brought under scrutiny. The conclusions you make may not be flattering or complimentary to the people you work with. How will you deal with this if it happens? Remember, you have a responsibility to your informants, the culture group, the religion, your academic community, and yourself. If you are dealing with personal narratives or memorates involving experience with the supernatural, be considerate with what people have shared with you. If they ask you not to use any portion of the data you have obtained from them, then it is your responsibility to respect their wishes.

Since religious meetings are of a sacred nature, if you decide you would like to tape-record portions of the meeting, you will need to obtain permission from the presiding authority. If you are straightforward about what you plan to do, then there should not be any objections. If you are not allowed to record the meeting, then take notes on a notepad. When you perform interviews, make sure you have a skeleton of questions ready as a guide for your informant. When you meet with your informant, give him or her some kind of overview of what you will be doing.

Discovering Religious Ideology

One of your goals in doing a field project will be to discover or assess religious ideology. There are a few ways to do this. You could go to the library and get a *textbook-version* of what ideology is for a particular religious group. The only problem is that reality rarely conforms to what is written in textbooks. Another way is to ask people about their own religious ideology. This may be an interesting exercise because you will probably get a wide range and variety of answers. Each person has aspects of his/her religion that he/she considers to be more important than others. From the fragments you obtain in interviews you might be able to paint an interesting picture of what religious ideology is for a particular religious group. The fragments will also communicate something about the unofficial beliefs, attitudes, values, fears, and concerns of the folk within an official institutionalized religion.

Another way to assess ideology is to visit a religious meeting and be a participant observer. Using this approach, you would pay particular attention to what is said, how it is said, what symbols are present in the meeting, how people are dressed, the presence or absence of children, the structure of the meeting, the arrangement of space, the physical boundaries demarcating sacred and profane space, the presence or absence of music, ritual, sacred writings, and so forth. Let me give you an example from my own fieldwork.

Assessing Quaker Ideology

I read an announcement in a local newspaper that spoke of a silent gathering to share community and to *wait upon the Light within every person.* The announcement was sponsored by the Bloomington Religious Society of Friends—the Quakers. My primary reaction to the word *Quaker* conjured up images of quaint, simple, peasants dressed in black. These were stereotypes.

Sunday came and I began making preparations to attend the meeting. I became extremely self-conscious of the fact that I would probably stick out like a sore thumb. I didn't want to be conspicuous but what else could I do, since I was a stranger. I arrived at the meeting place fifteen minutes early and wrote down some initial thoughts and feelings. I went into the reception area. In terms of defining space, the reception area functions as a threshold between the outer and inner world—between the profane and the sacred. Before entering the meeting room, I read a sign on the wall:

> Enter the room quietly and sit in any of the vacant seats. Meeting for worship lasts about one hour; but most of the children leave for First Day School at the end of fifteen minutes. Our meeting begins as soon as friends sit down together and become quiet.
>
> The way is open to any person present to speak. The words of one may assist the search of others; yet one does not lightly break the silence. When any attender feels that his thoughts may be helpful to others, or if he feels a prompting from within, he should speak. One cannot know in advance whom one may help by one's words. So we do not prepare talks in advance but follow the leading of the spirit. A few heartfelt words are generally more effective than a long discourse.

I proceeded to enter the meeting room and was immediately struck by the arrangement and utilization of space. The benches were set in three rows arranged in a square facing the middle. The corners of the square had chairs facing the middle and enough room for the people to go in and out of the benches. This spacial arrangement communicated a great deal to me about Quaker ideology. The arrangement of the benches and chairs in this manner eliminated any kind of hierarchical structure. All people were considered equals, there was no head of the room from which one person presided as in most Christian meeting places. This arrangement also made it extremely intimate and highly conducive to *sharing community.*

I noticed the absence of any kind of keyboard instrument—piano or organ. I learned later by talking to members that music, ritual (sacrament of communion), and prayer did not play a part in the this particular Quaker service. Silence and economy of discourse were valued over displays of praise and adoration through music and prayer.

The interior of the meeting room was simple and plain. There was a conscious lack of visual symbol, ornamentation, and decoration. Lining the walls were bookcases filled with books on various topics from religion to biographies. I noticed a number of books authored by George Fox. I assumed that this man must be the founder and spiritual leader of Quaker religion. Based on the subjects of the tracts on display, I concluded that Quakers were extremely active in political affairs and human rights.

People began to assemble and I took a seat. Complete silence filled the room and I quickly became self-conscious of every sound I was making—from the clearing of my throat, to the growling of my stomach. But I wanted to understand something about the meeting and about the folk ideology. The only way to do this was to forget about myself and become involved in the flow of the experience.

I began to meditate and fifteen minutes later the children arose and left the room reverently. Ten minutes later an elderly woman arose and shared some words of wisdom and consolation. Fifteen minutes later a gentleman arose and spoke of Tolstoy. This kind of action occurred twice more during the span of an hour and fifteen minutes. There was no apparent expression of ideology in what the people said, but it was certain that silence was prized over platitudes and diatribes.

Simple observation can uncover much about another culture. From this very short religious experience I was able to come to some conclusions regarding folk ideology of Quakers. If I were to do a more extensive field project on Quaker ideology, I would do follow-up interviews with members of the congregation. Questions I would ask might focus on why silence is so important, how the church is organized, who determines leadership positions if there are any, what beliefs are important, how is social conduct and behavior enforced, and so forth. These and other questions would help me in formulating a picture of what Quaker ideology might be.

GENRES, ANALYSIS, AND INTERPRETING RELIGIOUS FOLKLORE

If you belong to a religious culture that you know well, you may want to do *participant observation* since you already know what the ideology is. You need to determine whether your religious culture is fruitful for performing folklore fieldwork. If it is, then perhaps you should decide on a particular genre of folklore to focus your attention on. You are likely to know instances of when that genre will be performed and can be prepared to record the performance of artistic communication through tape-recorder, note taking, and follow-up interviews.

Verbal Art

The Sermon. Expressions of belief are communicated and performed in numerous verbal art forms. For example, if you are in the congregation during your service, perhaps your preacher (bishop, priest, minister, rabbi, whatever) will present a sermon to the congregation. You can record the performance of the sermon, while taking notes on the contextual information, the style, the texture, the gestural techniques used by the preacher, and the general reactions of the audience (see Chapter 1 **Introduction: Basic Concepts of Folkloristics**). Afterwards, you may be able to detect whether genres of folklore may have been used to artistically communicate didactic messages that could not be done in any other manner. For example, genres employed in a sermon might include the memorate, fable (an animal tale with a moral), myth, religious legend, personal narrative, joke, poetry, or proverb. These genres of verbal art are good vehicles for religious ideology. People in the congregation can easily relate to them since there is a kind of universality about the forms of cultural expression. How these genres are performed (texture) is important too. Did the preacher's voice become, higher or lower, louder or softer, faster or slower? Did changes in the loudness and swiftness occur gradually or abruptly? Were the genres of verbal art couched in an exhortation of some kind? Were the genres of verbal art used to support or maintain a dogma, doctrine, a religious principle? How did it function in this particular context? Did the preacher obtain the desired result? What was the reaction of the audience? You may have to perform follow-up interviews to obtain answers to some of these questions.

Legend. If there is a certain legend that you are familiar with, a legend that is peculiar to your religious culture, you may wish to interview several people about this legend and obtain several different versions of the same legend. The discontinuities and variation you discover will communicate certain attitudes, beliefs, and concerns about individuals towards the subject matter in the legend, or about the culture as a whole. Remember though, the *context of a performance is extremely important.*

Memorate. Experiences which are first-hand accounts of supernatural experiences are called memorates. Among the Pentecostals it is common to share experiences involving the conversion of individuals to Jesus Christ, and ultimately, direct experience with the Holy Ghost. A field study done by James Peacock, "A Pentecostal Account of Spiritual Quest" (1988), among Pentecostal in North Carolina provides an excellent model for this kind of study. In his study, Peacock describes the spiritual quest of a pastor. He begins by asking "Will you tell us the history of how you came to be a member of the church?" (192).

Among Pentecostals the experience with the Holy Ghost, either in public or private, is an important part of their belief system. Manifestations of experience with the Holy Ghost include: *glossolalia* or speaking in tongues, and being in the rapture which is characterized as shouting, convulsive movements of the body, and even rolling on the floor. Members are not accepted into full fellowship until a *baptism of the Holy Ghost* experience occurs. Therefore, every person has his/her own experience to share with whoever is willing to listen. An interesting study might focus on the great variety of this type of memorate, comparing them with one another to determine the unofficial folk beliefs within the official church doctrines——what concerns, and attitudes people have regarding salvation, spirituality, sin, outsiders, the word of God, and so forth.

Joke. Jokes told about one's own religion or those told about an exoteric group may reveal certain attitudes, values, and beliefs. Esoteric jokes may undermine and contradict official religious ideology. The joke is a very aggressive form of artistic communication and is an expressive form of tension either from inside or outside the culture. It is an opportunity to turn the structure of the official hierarchy on its head and to poke fun at it in a culturally sanctioned manner. More often than not, jokes are told about leaders of the official church culture.

On the other hand, exoteric jokes can mock or poke fun at other religious groups, while maintaining the notion that one's own religion is superior to another. Jokes have many meanings and many functions. It will be up to you to determine what jokes mean and how they function within a particular context. (See Chapter 8 **Jokes and Practical Jokes**)

Myth. Myths are told to explain and reinforce a cultural practice. For example, the stories of the Bible are sacred myths in the Christian world. To some devout Christians, the story of the tower of babel explains why there are diverse languages and cultures in the world. Myths can also explain the beginnings of religious cultures, especially when they focus on the actions and teachings of a particular founder. Myths are considered to be true by most followers of a religion and explain the origins of humanity, rituals, sacred places, practices, and other aspects of culture. If you choose to do fieldwork in a religious culture, are there myths told by members to explain why certain practices and beliefs are held today? Are there myths associated with the performance of certain rituals? Are there myths about the founders, saints, or religious leaders of a religion?

Festivals and Celebrations

Religious festivals and celebrations are occasions for a religious culture to put itself on display for members of the community, as well as for outsiders. Festivals are full-blown displays of culture and multiple expressions of artistic communication (see Chapter 9 **Cultural Performances: Public Display Events and Festival**). Numerous genres are performed by individuals or groups, all at the same time and in the same space. If you plan on doing fieldwork at a festival, you will need to prepare yourself well in advance because everything will be going on at once.

Celebrations are important rites of passage for members of the family. Baptism, communion, marriage, death and other similar kinds of celebrations are performed in many different ways and can provide a good topic for fieldwork. Other family celebrations center on seasonal or calendrical periods including Thanksgiving, Christmas, Easter, Ash Wednesday, Hanukkah, the Day of Feasts, and so on.

Ceremony and ritual are also feasible topics. A good example of a cross-cultural study of funerary ceremonies among the Mormon, Zuni, and Navajo cultures has been done by Keith Cunningham in New Mexico (1989:197-215). In his study, Cunningham attempts to make sense of three different approaches to performing funerals at two neighboring cemeteries in New Mexico. He discovers three cultural world views, and three conceptions of the afterlife that motivate the funerary practices. During his study he attended funerary ceremonies of all three culture groups, noted the direction and placement of the graves relative to the rest of the cemetery, documented gravemarkers used on the grave site in terms of their informational, aesthetic, and symbolic significance, and made conclusions based on what all these factors communicated to him within the larger social, cultural, and historical contexts of these three culture groups. Field studies of this nature are interesting, and because of their comparative nature, yield multiple insights and perspectives.

Foodways

Associated with festivals and celebrations is the preparation and consumption of special religious food items. Food items have strong ties to ethnic, religious, and familial identities. Food and food preparation can have deep religious significance. For example, in Judaism each item of food prepared for Passover seder has some kind of symbolic significance. In your study of religious folklore you might ask: Are there special foods prepared and served for particular celebrations? How are they prepared, is there a certain ritual involved in making it? Does your family deviate at all from these traditional practices?

Material Culture

Material culture covers a large range of things including: folk architecture, folk arts and crafts, costume, and tools. Some aspects of material culture have religious significance. Most often religious symbols can be found permeating architectural edifices. The Salt Lake Temple of the Mormon culture

glass, paintings, and furniture. For Mormons of the Great Basin region, the beehive, the all-seeing eye, the square and compass, the sun, moon and stars, and the handclasp, all have special symbolic significance and are found on many kinds of material culture. Since religious culture is defined in terms of experience with the sacred, it follows that each religious group would express the ineffable—that which is impossible to be expressed in words—through symbols and other visual icons.

The Amish by contrast, have relatively few pictorial

Figure 1. Cloudstones, moonstones, and stars on the Salt Lake Temple representing the Mormon cosmos. (Photograph courtesy of Matthew Heiss)

Figure 2. Mormon tombstone in Brigham City, Utah with depiction of an all-seeing eye. (Photograph by George Schoemaker)

is the center of the universe for devout Mormons. It too is an encyclopedia into Mormon cosmology, as was the Cathedral of Chartres for medieval Roman Catholics, and as such, it is replete with visual symbols and icons (see Figure 1). The symbols depicted on Mormon temples and tabernacles influence other aspects of Mormon material culture such as arts and crafts like quilts, tombstones (see Figure 2), stained

symbols and icons in their material culture. Their symbol of social identity is *clothing* and it can communicate much about Amish ideology. In his book *Amish Society*, John Hostetler writes about the significance of Amish clothing as a language of protest (1980:231-248).

The Amish operate under a very strict code of conduct called the *ordnung*. The *ordnung* helps the

Amish maintain their separateness from the world, a world that they perceive as being a constant threat to their beliefs and their way of life. The *ordnung* also helps prevent them from becoming too proud and worldly. Accordingly, Amish dress customs are very plain and simple to reflect this ideal of humility. However, what may appear to reflect humility can also be a language of protest.

Men's dress consists of "a full beard; black simple clothing with no outside or hip pockets; suspenders; and black hats with a three-inch brim." The men also wear a *mutze*—a special coat with a split tail. The shirts and trousers are fastened with buttons while the vests and coat fasten with hooks and eyes. In the more progressive communities zippers are permitted.

The women, on the other hand, are permitted to wear clothes which are more colorful but that are modest: "For the women there must be no silk, showy, form-fitting garments; dresses must be within eight inches of the floor; and must remain uncut . . . Aprons, shawls, and bonnets of proper size and color must be worn at the appropriate time." (Proper color denotes solids and not patterns.) Women wear a *halsduch* over the bodice which is similar to a cape. Married women wear colored capes and aprons which match the color of the dress. Single women must wear a white *halsduch*. All women must wear a head cap called a *kapp*. Girls from age 12 until marriage wear a black head cap to Sunday services and a white one while they are at home. A white *kapp* is worn at all times after marriage. Pleats and seams are ironed into the *kapp* and have several variations depending on what community the Amish woman comes from. Hostetler says that the "width of the pleats and seams is a sacred symbol of the community."

The basic dress described above reflects the most conservative of the Amish communities. Interestingly, the language of protest and fragmentation is the same for all Amish, that is, through dress. Whenever a schism occurs among the Amish, whether it is precipitated by a doctrinal dispute or a debate over the *ordnung*, it is very likely that it will be noticeably reflected in the dress styles. Hostetler says "Where tunes are sung more slowly, the dresses of the women are longer, the hair of the men longer and the men's hat brims wider." This is indicative of a more conservative, traditional group of Amish. Depending on their cultural diversity, a community of Amish will abstract one particular element from their dress and endow it with cultural significance. This dress feature then becomes the sign or marker of that community. An example of this is the suspender. Hostetler

continues "The Old Amish School in Pennsylvania do not wear suspenders, another group wears a single suspender over one shoulder, and another group wear suspenders over both shoulders. . . . Some Amish groups were more opposed to changes than other." The style and color of women's bonnets may vary, the color of men's shirts, the use of zippers, buttons, sweaters, collarless coats, ties, print dresses, hair length, all are cultural signs of entering a more liberal Amish group.

Amish clothing, then, has symbolic significance and can communicate much about Amish social and cultural life, and Amish ideology. Interpretations of Amish clothing can be as numerous as their different styles. Amish clothing can reinforce cultural values, beliefs, concerns, and attitudes, or it can undermine the *ordnung* and be a language of protest and disassociation with a more orthodox group.

Conclusion. These are just a few of the genres of folklore that you might collect. To exhaust the possibilities would require a separate book. Consult with your instructor or someone who is experienced about the kinds of things you would like to do for a field project. Read the other chapters that deal with the individual categories and genres of folklore in more detail.

CONCLUSION

The analysis and interpretation of your data will depend very much on what you would like to accomplish. For the most part, you will probably write about the functional and symbolic aspects of certain items of folklore in a particular context, as with the above example on Amish clothing. You may want to analyze the form and content of the items of religious folklore to determine patterns of speech, the discontinuities and deviations from culturally accepted ways of speaking and what these things tell you about either the individual informant or the culture as a whole. Issues relating to the performance of items by different genders, whether certain aspects of material culture are gender specific and why, or why not? The possibilities are numerous.

Another point to consider is the perspective or conceptualization of folklore and religion you are taking. Is the religious culture considered a folk religion? Are the items of folklore part of the unofficial practices of an institutionalized religion? Is the folklore religious in theme, content, or subject? Is the folklore emerging as a result of syncretism or a mixing of cultures? Does the folklore express folk interpretations of an established religious ideology? Are there ways you can assess the religious ideology of a religious culture group? What genres of folklore are performed by a particular religious culture? How are they performed, what textural features are used, and in what contexts are they performed? How do they function within a particular context? These are only some of the numerous questions that you should be thinking about as you engage in your folklore fieldwork on religious cultures.

Acknowledgements

I would like to acknowledge the influence of several people in the writing of this chapter including: William A. Wilson, Richard C. Poulsen, Hasan El-Shamy, Richard Bauman, and Roger Janelli. I also want to thank Phillip McArthur, Bob Walls, Katherine Borland, and Guntis Šmidchens for reading and commenting on earlier versions of this chapter.

Selected Annotated Bibliography

1) **GENERAL THEORETICAL WORKS**—Some of these works were influential in the formulation and the writing of this chapter.
Danielson, Larry. 1986. Religious Folklore. IN *Folk Groups and Folklore Genres: An Introduction*, ed. Elliott Oring, pp. 45-69. Logan, UT: Utah State Univeristy Press.
Good, basic introductory essay on the topic of folklore with religion as its topic.

Dorson, Richard M., ed. 1983. *Handbook of American Folklore*. Bloomington, IN: Indiana University Press.
This book contains a number of good essays on different aspects of religious folklore. See especially Clements, William. "The Folk Church: Institution, Event, Performance"; Wiggins, William. :The Black Folk Church"; and Wilson, William A. "Mormon Folklore" for introductions to the various topics.

Eliade, Mircea. 1961. *The Sacred and the Profane: The Nature of Religion*. Translated by William R. Trask. New York: Harper and Row.
Influencial work on the nature of religion as qualities of culture and behavior.

Frazer, James G. 1913-1922. *The Golden Bough: A Study in Magic and Religion*. 12 vols., 3d. ed., rev. and enl. London: Macmillan.

Geertz, Clifford. 1973. Religion as a Cultural System. IN *The Interpretation of Cultures*, pp. 87-125. New York:Basic Books.

Goldstein, Diane E. 1983. The Language of Religious Experience and its Implications for Fieldwork. *Western Folklore* 42:105-113.

Hostetler, John A. 1980. *Amish Society*. Baltimore: Johns Hopkins University Press.
Excellent book describing Amish culture including history of the group, religion, material culture, customs, dress, esoteric/exoteric considerations, practices to maintain separateness, healing practices, and so forth.

Hufford, David J. 1985. Reason, Rhetoric, and Religion: Academic Ideology versus Folk Belief. *New York Folklore* 11:177-194.

King, Winston L. 1987. Religion. IN *The Encyclopedia of Religion*, ed. Mircea Eliade, vol. 12 pp. 282-293. New York: MacMillan Publishing Company.
Introductory essay on the concept of religion.

Malinowski, Bronislaw. 1954. *Magic, Science and Religion and Other Essays*. Garden City: Doubleday and Company.

Messenger, John C. 1972. Folk Religion. IN *Folklore and Folklife: An Introduction*, ed. Richard M. Dorson, pp. 217-232. Chicago: University of Chicago Press.
Messenger's study focuses on the folk religion of the Aran Islanders off the coast of Ireland. His view of folk religion is influenced by Anthony Wallace's work on religion from an anthropological perspective, and as such, views peseant or *primitive* religious traditions as folk religions.

Yoder, Don. 1974. Toward a Definition of Folk Religion. *Western Folklore* 33:2-15.
Seminal article attempting to define various approaches to folklore and religion. Contained in a special issue of *Western Folklore* that includes an Introductory Bibliography on Folk Religion by Yoder.

2) **RELIGIOUS FOLKLORE ACCORDING TO RELIGIOUS GROUP**—The following references are weighed heavily towards Judeo-Christian groups. The reason is simply because most students will have had exposure to these groups.
A. Catholic
Boeckman, Frances. 1987. Roman Catholic Wooden Churches in Mississippi: Charm with Simple Elegence. *Mississippi Folklore Register* 21(1/2):23-27.

Fish, Lydia. 1982. Ethnicity and Catholicism. *New York Folklore* 8:83-92.

Gaudet, Marcia. 1984. Tales from the Levee: The Folklore of St. John the Baptist Parish. *Center for Louisiana Studies, Univeristy of Southwestern Louisiana*. (Louisiana Folklife Series #1)

Griffith, James S. 1975. The Folk-Catholic Chapels of the Papaguria. *Pioneer America* 7:2.

Hufford, David J. 1985. Ste. Anne de Beaupré: Roman Catholic Pilgrimage and Healing. *Western Folklore* 44:194-207.

Krasniewicz, Louise. 1986. Growing Up Catholic and American: The Oral Tradition of Catholic School Students. *New York Folklore* 12(3/4):51-68.
This essay is concerned with the personal narratives told by student's of Catholic school systems about Catholic school systems.

Orsi, Robert A. 1985. *The Madonna of 115th Street: Faith and Community in Italian Harlem, 1880-1950*. New Haven: Yale University Press.

Santino, Jack. 1982. Catholic Folklore and Folk Catholicism. *New York Folklore* 8(3/4):93-106.

Turner, Kay., and Suzanne Serif. 1987. "Giving an Altar": The Ideology of Reproduction in a St. Joseph's Day Feast. *Journal of American Folklore* 100:446-460.

Wilson, Stephen. 1983. *Saints and Their Cults: Studies in Religious Sociology, Folklore and History*. Cambridge: Cambridge University Press.

B. Protestant

Bauman, Richard. 1983. *Let your words be few: Symbolism of Speaking and Silence Among Seventeenth-century Quakers*. Cambridge: Cambridge University Press.
Using the ethnography of speaking, symbolic anthropology, and the sociology of religion, Bauman investigates the use of speaking and silence in the shaping of Quaker belief and practice.

Bruce, Dickson D. 1974. *And They All Sang Hallelujah: Plain-Folk Camp-Meeting Religion, 1800-1845*. Knoxville: University of Tennessee Press.

Clements, William M. 1981. Ritual Expectation in Pentecostal Healing Experience. *Western Folklore* 40:139-148.

Hall, Robert L. and Carol B. Stack., eds. 1982. *Holding On to the Land and the Lord: Kinship, Ritual, Land Tenure, and Social Policy in the Rural South*. Athens: University of Georgia Press.

Harding, Susan F. 1987. Convicted by the Holy Spirit: The Rhetoric of Fundamental Baptist Conversion. *American Ethnologist* 14:167-181.

Larlham, Peter. 1981. Festivals of the Nazareth Baptist Church. *The Drama Review* 25(4):59-74.

Lawless, Elaine J. 1980. Making a Joyful Noise: An Ethnography of Communication in the Pentecostal Religious Service. *Southern Folklore Quarterly* 44:1-21.

_____. 1983. Brothers and Sisters: Pentecostals as a Religious Folk Group. *Western Folklore* 42:85-104. Also printed in *Folk Groups and Folklore Genres: A Reader*, ed. Elliott Oring, pp. 99-113. Logan, UT: Utah State University Press.
This essay describes how Pentecostals maintain a sense of separateness and social identity through cultural expressions including dress, language, ritual and comportment. The persecution and ridicule that members receive because of these cultural expressions help them to reinforce their sense of separateness.

_____. 1983a. Shouting for the Lord: The Power of Women's Speech in the Pentecostal Religious Service. *Journal of American Folklore* 96:434-459.

_____. 1986. "Your Hair is Your Glory:" Public and Private Symbology of Long Hair for Pentecostal Women. *New York Folklore* 12(3/4):33-50.

_____. 1987. Piety and Motherhood: Reproductive Images and Maternal Strategies of the Womam Preacher. *Journal of American Folklore* 100:469-478.

_____. 1988. The Night I Got the Holy Ghost . . .: Holy Ghost Narratives and the Pentecostal Conversion Process. *Western Folklore* 47:1-19.

Milspaw, Yvonne J. 1986. Protestant Home Shrines: Icon and Image. *New York Folklore* 12(3/4):119-136.
Examination and analysis of eclectic home shrines combining Roman Catholic, Protestant, Methodist, and Pennsylvania Dutch motifs.

Scholfield, Mary Anne. 1987. 'Womens Speaking Justified': The Feminine Quaker Voice, 1662-1797. *Tulsa Studies in Women's Literature* 6:61-77.

Titon, Jeff Todd. 1988. *Powerhouse For God: Speech, Chant, and Song in an Appalachian Baptist Church*. Austin, TX: University of Texas Press.

Tyson, Ruel W. James L. Peacock, and Daniel W. Patterson., eds. 1988. *Diversities of Gifts: Field Studies in Southern Religion*. Urbana: University of Illinois Press.
This collection of essays focusses on fieldwork done among Southern independent Protestant religious groups in North Carolina. A variety of genres are explored within their performance contexts, these include: sermons, prayers, testimonies, songs, and ceremonies. The religious groups represented include: Baptists, Quakers, Pentecostals, and African American churches. The essayists take a number of different perspectives.

C. Mormon—Most of the following citations deal with verbal or customary lore, with some citations dealing with material culture. Mormon folklore has quite an extensive bibliography and is, by no means, fully represented below.

Brady, Margaret P. 1987. Transformations of Power: Mormon Women's Visionary Narratives. *Journal of American Folklore* 100:461-468.

Brunvand, Jan Harold. 1968. Folklore of the Great Basin. *Northwest Folklore* 3:17-32.

_____. 1970. As the saints go marching by: Mormon Jokelore About Mormons. *Journal of American Folklore* 83:53-60.

_____. 1971. Modern Legends of Mormondom, or Supernaturalism is Alive and Well in Salt Lake City. IN *American Folk Legend: A Symposium*, ed. Wayland D. Hand, pp. 185-202. Berkeley: University of California Press.
This essay examines types of Mormon legend including: three nephite, evil spirits, return-from-the-dead stories, other spiritual visitations, religious duties and regulations, ancient American archaeology, and famous church members.

_____. 1971a. *A Guide for Collectors of Folklore in Utah*. Salt Lake City, UT: University of Utah Press.
This fieldguide has a good introduction to folklore and the study of folklore materials. It then suggests the range of folk groups found in Utah, the kinds of materials that can be collected in Utah, and how to document the material for an archive.

Burt, Olive W. 1959. Murder Ballads of Mormondom. *Western Folklore* 18:141-156.

Hand, Wayland D. and Jeannine E Talley., eds. 1984 *Popular Beliefs and Superstitions from Utah*. Collected by Anthon S. Cannon. Salt Lake City, UT: University of Utah Press.
Collection of folk beliefs in Utah ranging from folk medicine, to witchcraft, and weather lore.

Carter, Thomas Robert. 1984. Building Zion: Folk Architecture in the Mormon Settlements of Utah's Sanpete Valley, 1850-1890. Ph.D. Dissertation, Indiana University.

_____, and Carl Fleischhauer. *The Grouse Creek Cultural Survey: Integrating Folklife and Historic Preservation Field Research.* Washington, D.C.: Library of Congress.

Cheney, Thomas E., ed. 1971. *Lore of Faith and Folly.* Salt Lake City, UT: University of Utah Press.
Compilation of essays on Mormon folklore in Utah including family history and family folklore, polygamy, indians, cultural heroes, folkways, superstitions, and folk medicine.

_____. 1973. *The Golden Legacy: A Folk History of J. Golden Kimball.* Salt Lake City: Peregrin-Smith, Inc.
Compilation of annecdotes by or about J. Golden Kimball, a Mormon folk hero of the nineteenth century.

_____. 1981[1968]. *Mormon Songs from the Rocky Mountains: A Compilation of Mormon Folksong.* Salt Lake City: University of Utah Press.
Over a thousand songs collected from Mormons by Cheney in order to reveal historical and social values of Mormon people in the Great Basin region.

Coates, Lawrence. 1985. The Mormons and the Ghost Dance. *Dialogue: A Journal of Mormon Thought* 18(4):89-111.

Fife, Austin E. The Legend of the Three Nephites Among the Mormons. *Journal of American Folklore* 53:1-49.

_____., and Alta Fife. 1956. *Saints of Sage and Saddle: Folklore Among Mormons.* Bloomington, IN Indiana University Press.

_____. 1988. *Exploring Western Americana.* Ann Arbor: UMI Research Press.
Numerous essays on Western folklife, especially in Utah. Focus on architecture, gravestones, and Mormon culture.

Hand, Wayland D. 1938. The Three Nephites in Popular Tradition. *Southern Folklore Quarterly* 2:123-29.

Heeron, John, Donald B. Lindsay, and Marylee Mason. 1984. The Mormon Concept of Mother in Heaven: A Sociological Account of its Origin and Development. *Journal for the Scientific Study of Religion* 23:396-411.

Hill, Marvin S. 1984. Money-Digging Folklore and the Beginnings of Mormonism: An Interpretive Suggestion. *Brigham Young University Studies* 24:473-488.

Lawless, Elaine J. 1984. "I Know If I Don't Bear My Testimony, I'll Lose It": Why Mormon Women Bother To Speak at All. *Kentucky Folklore Record* 30:79-96.

Lee, David, R. and Hector H. Lee. 1981. Thatched Cowsheds of the Mormon Country. *Western Folklore* 40:171-187.

Lee, Hector H. 1949. *The Three Nephites: The Substance and Significance of the Legend in Folklore.* Albuquerque: University of New Mexico Press.

Lundahl, Craig R. 1983. Near-Death Experiences of Mormons. IN *A Collection of Near-Death Research Readings.* Chicago: Nelson-Hall.

McHale, Ellen E. 1985. "Witnessing for Christ": The Hill Cumorah Pageant of Palmyra, New York. *Western Folklore* 44:34-40.

Poulsen, Richard C. 1977. This is the Place: Myth and Mormondom. *Western Folklore* 36:246-252.

_____. 1978. Fate and the Persecutors of Joseph Smith: Transformations of an American Myth. *Dialogue: A Journal of Mormon Thought* 11:63-70.

_____. 1979. Bosom Serpentry Among Puritans and Mormons. *Journal of the Folklore Institute* 16:176-189.

_____. 1982. *The Pure Experience of Order: Essays on the Symbolic in the Folk Material Culture of Western America.* Albuquerque: University of New Mexico Press.
An interpretive study of architecture, gravestones, and Mormon folk culture in Utah and the American Southwest.

_____. 1988. *Misbegotten Muses: History and Anti-History.* New York: Peter Lang.
Collection of essays on various aspects of Mormon culture and history.

Riches, Suzanne Volmar. 1987. Threads Through a Patchwork Quilt: The Wedding Shower as a Communicative Tirual and Rite of Passage for the Mormon Women. Ph.D. dissertation, University of Utah.

Schoemaker, George H. 1989. Made in Heaven: Marriage Confirmation Narratives Among Mormons. *Northwest Folklore* 7(2):38-53.

_____. 1989. The Shift From Artist to Consumer: Changes in Mormon Tombstone Art in Utah. IN *The Old Traditional Way of Life: Essays in Honor of Warren E. Roberts,* eds. Robert E. Walls and George H. Schoemaker, pp. 130-145. Bloomington, IN: Trickster Press.

Wilson, William A. 1973. Folklore and History: Fact Amid Legends. *Utah Historical Quarterly* 41:40-58.

_____. 1976. The Paradox of Mormon Folklore. *Brigham Young University Studies* 17:40-58.
Addresses how Mormon folklore can function to reinforce church dogma, sanction forms of behavior, and give people a sense of stability in an unstable world. At the same time, Mormon folklore undermines and challenges the official structure of the church, hence the paradox.

_____., ed. 1976a. *Utah Historical Quarterly* 44(4):317-418.
This special issue of the *Utah Historical Quarterly* contains five essays on Mormon folklore including: "The Legend of Jessie Evans Smith," Linda W. Harris; "The Martyrdom of Joseph Smith: An Archetypal Study," Clifton Holt Jolley; "The Great and Dreadful Day: Mormon Folklore and the Apocalypse," Susan Peterson; "Some Botanical Cures in Mormon Folk Medicine: An Analysis," Richard C. Poulsen; "The Study of Mormon Folklore," William A. Wilson; and a bibliography of studies in Mormon folklore by Wilson.

_____. 1982. On Being Human: The Folklore of Mormon Missionaries. *New York Folklore* 8:5-28.

_____. 1983. Trickster Tales and the Location of Cultural Boundaries: A Mormon Example. *Journal of Folklore Research* 20:55-66.

_____. 1985. We Did Everything Together: Farming Customs of the Mountainwest. *Northwest Folklore* 4:23-30.

_____. 1988. Dealing with Organizational Stress: Lessons from the Folklore of Mormon Missionaries. IN *Inside Organizations: Understanding the Human Dimensions*, eds. Michael Owen Jones, Michael Dane Moore, and Richard Christopher Snyder, pp. 271-279. Newbury Park, CA: Sage Publications.

_____. 1988. Freeways, Parking Lots and Ice Cream Stands: The Three Nephites in Contemporary Mormon Culture. *Dialogue: A Journal of Mormon Thought* 21:13-26.

D. Jewish
Deshen, Shlomo A. 1972. Ethnicity and Citizenship in the Ritual of an Israeli Synagogue. *Southwestern Journal of Anthropology* 28:69-82. Also excerpted in *Folk Groups and Folklore Genres: A Reader*, ed. Elliott Oring, pp. 114-123. Logan, UT: Utah State University Press.

Kleeblatt, Norman L., and Gerard C. Wertkin. 1984. *The Jewish Heritage in American Folk Art*. New York: Universe Books.

Lehrhaupt, Linda. 1986. The Organizational Seder in American Jewish Life. *Western Folklore* 45:186-202.

Patai, Raphael. 1983. *On Jewish Folklore*. Detroit: Wayne State University Press.
Contains a number of essays of hebrew mythology, the goddess cult in Jewish religion, verbal and customary folklore, and some syncretic traditions.

Scheiber, Alexander. 1985. *Essays on Jewish Folklore and Comparative Literature*. Budapest: Akadémiai Kiado.

Schwarzbaum, Haim. 1968. *Studies in Jewish and World Folklore*. Berlin: Walter de Gruyter & Co.
Contains essays on verbal genres. Includes tale-type index and table of narrative motifs.

Singer, Merrill. 1980. The Use of Folklore in Religious Conversion: The Chassidic Case. *Review of Religious Research* 22:170-185.

E. African-American (See Chapter 15 **African American Folklore** for further references to African American religion.)

Baklanoff, Joy Driskell. 1987. The Celebration of a Feast: Music, Dance, and Possession Trance in the Black Primitive Baptist Footwashing Ritual. *Ethnomusicology* 31:381-394.

Davis, Gerald L. 1985. *I Got the Word in Me and I Can Sing It, You Know: A Study of the Performed African-American Sermon*. Philadelphia: University of Pennsylvania Press.

Glazier, Stephen D. 1985. Syncretism and Separation: Ritual Change in an Afro-Caribbean Faith. *Journal of American Folklore* 98:49-62.

Overton, Betty J. Black Women Preachers: A Literary View. *The Southern Quarterly: A Journal of the Arts in the South* 23(3):157-166.

Rosenberg, Bruce A. 1988. *Can These Bones Live? The Art of the American Folk Preacher*. Urbana and Chicago: University of Illinois Press.
Rosenberg's book applies the Parry-Lord oral-formulaic theory to the sermons of Southern preachers.

F. Native-American (See Chapter 19 **Contemporary Native American Folklore** for further references on Native American folk-religion.
Brady, Margaret K. 1984. *"Some Kind of Power": Navajo Children's Skinwalker Narratives*. Salt Lake City: University of Utah Press.
An analysis of navajo children's skinwalker narratives.

Cunningham, Keith. 1989. Navajo, Mormon, Zuni Graves: Navajo, Mormon, Zuni Ways. IN *Cemeteries and Gravemarkers: Voices of American Culture*, ed. Richard E. Meyer, pp. 197-215. Ann Arbor: UMI Research Press.

DeMallie, Raymond J. and Douglas R. Parks., eds. 1987. *Sioux Indian Religion: Tradition and Innovation*. Norman: University of Oklahoma Press.

Witherspoon, Gary. 1977. *Language and Art in the Navajo Universe*. Ann Arbor: The University of Michigan Press.

G. Other
Dubisch, Jill. 1981. You Are What You Eat: Religious Aspects of the Health Food Movement. *The American Dimension: Cultural Myths and Social Realities*, 2d ed., ed. Susan P. Montague and W. Arens, pp. 115-127. Palo, Alto: Alfred Publishing Co. Also reprinted in *Folk Groups and Folklore Genres: A Reader*, ed. Elliott Oring, pp. 124-135. Logan, UT: Utah State University Press.
Health Food movements as secular religion or religious behavior is the focus of this essay.

Guinee, William. 1987. Satanism in Yellowwood Forest: The Interdependence of Antagonistic Worldviews. *Indiana Folklore and Oral History*. 16(1):1-30.

Starhawk. 1979. *The Spiral Dance: A Rebirth of the Ancient Religion of the Great Goddess*. San Francisco: Harper and Row.

_____. 1988. *Dreaming the Dark: Magic, Sex and Politics*. Boston: Beacon Press.

Stevens, Phillips, Jr. 1982. Some Implications of Urban Witchcraft Belief. *New York Folklore* 8:29-46.

The Emergence of Folklore in Everyday Life

CHAPTER 8
Jokes and Practical Jokes

Moira Smith

Humor occurs in many folklore forms and in the folklore of many different groups. There are humorous folk tales, tall tales, and personal narratives. Some of the most popular folk songs amongst college students are humorous, notably fraternity and sorority songs. Both adults and children enjoy creating and performing humorous parodies of songs, poems, and advertising slogans. This chapter covers fixed form jokes and practical jokes.

Fixed form jokes are those that may be told in more or less the same way in different situations. In modern American society jokes most often take the form of narratives or riddles. *Narrative jokes* are short narratives that end in a *punchline*:

(1)   There was this man who was an exhibitionist. And he was going to take a trip on this airplane. And there was this stewardess who was waiting at the top of the stairs that go onto the plane, and she was collecting tickets. So when this man got to the top of the stairs, he opened his coat and exposed himself. And the stewardess said, "I'm sorry sir. You have to show your ticket here, not your stub" (Mitchell 1977:310-311).

The punchline is what the audience is waiting for, and the narrative exists mainly to set up the punchline. No matter how well you tell the rest of the story, if you forget the punchline or garble it, the whole joke is ruined.

The *riddle joke* uses a question and answer format. Unlike real questions, in riddles the person asking the question already knows the answer, and assumes that the person being asked does not know it. In true riddling, people may make serious efforts to guess the answer, but in riddle jokes they are more likely to simply ask for it. The question exists so the teller will be invited to reveal the answer, and thus the joke. (For true riddling, see Chapter 17 **Collecting Children's Folklore**.)

(2)   How do Jewish couples have sex doggie style?
—He sits up and begs; she rolls over and plays dead.

(3)   What's the first thing a sorority girl does in the morning?
—Gets dressed and goes home.

(4)   Did you hear they are making a movie about Dan Quayle's war service?
—It's called *Full Dinner Jacket*.

Both narrative and riddle jokes cover a wide variety of topics, including sexual jokes, ethnic jokes, religious and political jokes. In addition, cycles of jokes sharing a similar subject and form have wide popularity for short periods of time. These include light-bulb jokes, dead baby jokes, and some AIDS jokes (see illustration). Joke cycles establish well-known formats that encourage people to play with them and invent variations. For example light bulb jokes use the format, How many [insert name of group] does it take to change a lightbulb? People not only repeat these jokes but constantly invent new ones to add to the cycle.

COLLECTING JOKES

You cannot collect jokes by simply going up to your friends and demanding, "Tell me some jokes!" That approach is guaranteed to turn people's minds blank. Jokes, like other folklore forms, are not performed 'cold.' They occur in appropriate situations, usually when people are relaxing and enjoying themselves, and usually when and where other jokes are being told as well.

One collecting method is to take your tape recorder or notebook to a party or a bar or any other place where people you know are likely to tell jokes. You can get the ball rolling by telling some jokes yourself, or if you do not fancy yourself as a good joke teller you can simply ask people to tell some jokes. One method is to remind someone of a joke that they told some other time. If the situation is right, one joke

AIDS UPDATE REPORT

FLASH! NEW STRAINS TO CREATE FURTHER MISCONCEPTIONS & HYSTERIA

- If you catch it from a cocktail waitress, it's now BARMAIDS.
- If you get it from a virgin, you have FIRST AIDS.
- If you've been infected by Jack Lemmon, they call it LEMONAIDS.
- If you catch it at school, it's now GRAIDS.
- If you contract it from a follower of Jim Jones, it's KOOL AIDS.
- If you get it in Florida, it's called GATORAIDS.
- If it's spread by cockroaches, it's RAIDS.
- If you're lucky enough to have gotten it from Bo Derek, it's BRAIDS.
- If you catch it while marching, you have PARAIDS.
- If you get it from touching an air freshener, you've got GLAIDS.
- If you give it back to someone who infected you, it's now called TRAIDS.
- If you catch it in France, you have PAR LE VOUZ FRANCAIDS.
- If you've been digging with a gang member, you'll get SWITCHBLAIDS.
- If you get it from from a Black, it's now ZIPPITY DO DA DAIDS.
- If you're infected by Ronald Reagan, you have PRESIDENTIAL AIDS.
- If you catch it from Anthony Perkins dressed like an old lady, it's NORMAN BAID.
- If you've touched a pair of infected sunglasses, it's SHAIDS.
- If you get ill during the end of a work week, it's T.G.I. FRIDAIDS.
- If you get it playing party games, you've now got CHARAIDS.
- If you get it on Halloween, it's MASQUERAIDS.
- If you're sleeping with Gumby, you get GREEN CLAIDS.
- If you get it from a leather jacket, it's SUAIDS.
- If you have been using an infected dishwasher, you're likely to get CASCAIDS.
- If you've been fucking a Jamaican, you've gotten REGGAIDS.
- If you eat an infected chocolate bar, you could contract MILKY WAIDS.
- If you get it from a musician, it's BANDAIDS.
- If you get it from a pest control person, it's ORCAIDS.
- If you get it from the swamps of Florida, it's EVERGLAIDS.
- And now, the worst! Did you know that finally you can catch it all by yourself?   and that's called MASTERBAIDS

Figure 1. Xeroxlore is a popular medium for transmitting jokes, parodies, and cartoons in offices, businesses, and factories.

will lead to another and you the folklorist will be there to take them all down on tape or paper.

You may find yourself unexpectedly in a joke-telling situation. This is not a disaster. As soon as you can, write some notes on what just happened—what jokes were told, who told them, etc. Later you can go back to some of the people involved and ask them for an interview, in which they repeat the jokes and answer other questions.

Another technique is to *make your own* joke-telling situation, say by throwing a small party in your room and inviting friends. Set up the tape recorder and provide the appropriate refreshments, and ask people to tell jokes. You can prime the pump by telling some yourself or reminding people of jokes they once told. Many students have used this technique with great success.

You can also collect folk humor from *graffiti* and *xeroxlore* (see Figure. 1). Not only jokes, but also cartoons and parodies are transmitted through these written media. This indirect form of transmission allows humorists to be anonymous, they can safely get away with material that is more risque and taboo than that which they may use in face to face communication.

In order to analyze the jokes that you collect, you will need additional information about the situation in which they were told and about the people who tell and listen to them. You can gather some of this *contextual* information by observing and writing down everything that happens during the joke performances, and also by drawing on your general knowledge of the group involved and their joking practices in general. Another important method is to arrange *formal interviews* with the tellers and audiences of the jokes you collect.

The interview should follow the joke-telling session, preferably at a different time and with only one or two people present. It is not a good idea to ask your formal interview questions in the middle of a joking session. Not only will people think you are weird, they are also unlikely to give serious answers at such a time. People do not normally tell jokes in an interview, which is a strange and formal situation for both of you, but if you took good notes you can ask them to repeat the jokes they told at the party last night so you can get them on tape; and you can ask follow-up questions. The sections that follow describe some topics of analysis, the kinds of questions to ask, and what sort of things to look for.

What Does This Joke Mean / Why Is It Funny?

This question may seem too obvious to bother with, especially if you have collected jokes that you immediately understand and find funny. The truth is that the same joke has many different meanings depending on context, and even if several people laugh at a joke, they are probably laughing for different reasons.

For example, Carol Mitchell (1977) asked men and women to rate the humor of a sample of jokes, and to comment on why they found them funny or not funny. While most of the women rated the exhibitionist and stewardess joke (no. 1) very funny, most of the men found it only mildly funny, and some did not think it was humorous at all. The women identified with the stewardess and admired her calm and quick wit. Some women liked the fact that the she was not the stereotypical promiscuous stewardess. In contrast some men felt that her promiscuity was obvious because she was not shocked. While most of the women said the exhibitionist got what he deserved, none of the men felt that way, and many of them commented on the cruelty of belittling his penis size (an aspect of the joke that none of the women mentioned).

Since everyone interprets jokes differently and does not find them equally funny, you cannot rely solely on your own interpretation of the jokes that you collect. Instead you must set up interviews with joke tellers and listeners, and ask them to discuss their jokes, explain them, and comment on them. Take your notes about the jokes told, or your recording, and ask each person to rate each joke on a scale of 1 to 4, where 1 is very funny, 2 is funny, 3 is mildly funny, and 4 is not funny. Then ask them to comment on the joke:

1) What makes this joke funny (or not funny) to you?
2) What is the joke about?
3) Which of the characters in the joke do you like? Which do you dislike? Why?

Another method is to take a sample of jokes that are current in oral tradition in your area, and ask different people to rate and comment on them using the questions above. You can compare how different groups respond to the same jokes, for example men versus women (especially for sexual jokes); different age groups; liberals versus conservatives (especially for political jokes); or people of different ethnic origin (especially for ethnic jokes; do WASPs find Polack jokes funnier than Polish-Americans, etc.?).

Why Do People Tell Jokes?

People perform jokes not just to be amusing, but also to achieve particular social benefits. These are the *social functions* of jokes. As with other genres of folklore, performers receive certain payoffs. While telling jokes they are the center of attention. Good joke-tellers may win more esteem and popularity from their friends and associates. People who deal with the public may use jokes deliberately to win audiences over. This is why presidential candidates are coached in how to tell jokes during speeches. (For an example of someone who uses jokes deliberately in his speeches and teaching, see Bendix 1984 in the bibliography).

There may also be drawbacks to performing jokes. When you try to tell a joke there is always the risk that you will tell it badly, or that the audience will find the joke offensive. Also, someone who has the reputation of being a funny guy runs the risk of not being taken seriously. There is also the risk of being humorous in inappropriate situations. Anyone who uses jokes in social situations has to balance these potential benefits and drawbacks.

By analyzing a recording of a joke-telling session, you can see the risks and benefits of joke telling in action. What happens when someone performs a joke successfully, or when a joke fails? How do you know when a joke succeeds or not? How does the audience react to each joke? What happens when someone tells a joke on an inappropriate topic? Consider who the joke performers are. Do people fight to win audience attention for their joke? How do they win audience attention? Who tells the most jokes? Does anyone dominate the session? How and why? Does the session revolve around particular topics, and if so why? How did joking begin and end?

Folklorists know that the content and style of folklore performances, including joke performances, vary according to the time, the setting and occasion, and who is present. For example more explicit and aggressive sexual jokes might be expected in an all-male or all-female setting, rather than in a mixed-sex group. You can test this assumption for yourself by setting up joking sessions with all men, all women, and mixed groups, and comparing the recordings of each.

If you know people who use jokes a lot, you can discover the role of jokes in their lives by interviewing them. Questions to ask:

1) How many jokes do you know?

2) How often do you tell jokes? (These questions tell you how important joking is in the informant's life.)
3) When and where do you tell jokes?
4) Why do you tell them in these situations?
5) How do you rate yourself as a joke teller?
6) Do other people see you as a joker?
7) How does joke telling affect the way people see you?
8) How does joke telling affect your relationships with others?
9) I've noticed that you sometimes tell jokes in x situations. What are your reasons for doing that? (This question can also be asked about a specific joke told in a specific situation: why did you choose that particular joke to tell then? Did the joke work the way you wanted it to?)
10) How do you acquire new jokes? Where do you get them from?
11) What makes you decide to adopt a new joke?
12) What do you do to make sure you remember a new joke? (The above questions can also be asked about a specific joke that the informant has told before.)
13) About how many of the jokes that you try to remember do you actually succeed in remembering?
14) When you tell a new joke for the first time, do you pick a certain kind of situation to do it? Why? (The first time that a new joke is tried out might be an especially risky one—the teller can't be sure if it will work. What, if any, steps does he or she take to minimize the risk?)
15) What makes you decide to stop telling a particular joke? Tell me about a particular joke that you no longer tell, and why you no longer tell it.

Why Do People Tell The Particular Jokes That They Do?

The social benefits of telling jokes do not explain a joker's *choice* of jokes. Why does a particular person or group tell some jokes but not others? Even the most avid joke-tellers only remember and retell ten to twenty per cent of the many jokes that they come across. Why are some jokes selected and not others? What makes one or two jokes become a person's favorites?

If a joke is a person's favorite, or if she has several other jokes with the same theme, then it is likely that this choice of jokes is determined by her personality and personal experiences. For example, a woman could only remember one joke, but she told it often. The joke was about a man who kept asking the rabbi to grant him a divorce. The rabbi asked what was so bad about his wife that he wanted a divorce. The husband replied that she was such a slob that he couldn't stand it. "What do you mean, she's a slob?" "Well, everyone time I go to piss in the sink, it's always full of dirty dishes" (Legman 1968:17).

The reason why the woman was so attracted to this joke was that it reflected her own experience in an unhappy marriage to an abusive husband. By telling the joke, she was able to comment indirectly on her own situation. She may also have derived help in dealing psychologically with her problems. This is the *anxiety relief function* of jokes. By describing in the form of a joke the situation that causes fear or worry, you distance yourself from it, gain psychological control over it, and thus reduce feelings of anxiety or fear. The bad situation is made to seem absurd and laughable, rather than something to worry about.

This anxiety relief theory has been used to explain the popularity of disaster jokes, such as jokes about AIDS and about the *Challenger* explosion (e.g. What does NASA stand for?——Need another seven astronauts). However you should not assume that every joke that deals with a threatening topic must be relieving anxiety for everyone. In fact many people find AIDS jokes offensive because they laugh at the expense of people who are suffering.

In a folklore project, you have to prove that this function is applicable by studying some specific tellers and listeners of the joke concerned. Not every joke is chosen for personal reasons, but if the joke you have collected is the person's favorite, or one that she thinks is especially good, then there might be a personal connection. You can investigate this by asking her directly about her life history, her personal experiences, and her attitudes and feelings toward the topic of the joke, and by drawing on your own knowledge of her personality. An example of this method is Burns 1984 in the bibliography.

Are Jokes Aggressive?

(5) How many blacks does it take to pave a road?
    —Only one, if you slice him thin enough.
(6) What's the difference between a Jew and a pizza?
    —A pizza doesn't scream when you put it in the oven.

Jokes like these are likely to arouse hostility in some audiences, who find them offensive and racist. Many folklorists would agree, arguing that the humorous technique is only a disguise under which prejudices and hostile thoughts can be expressed. The

joke tellers on the other hand would probably say that they do not tell the jokes to be aggressive or offensive, but simply because they are funny. They are 'just jokes,' and they do not mean anything by them. Which side is right?

The 'just jokes' side argues that there is no connection between the content of jokes and the attitudes of those who enjoy them. They point out that ethnic jokes are generic——the same jokes are told about Polacks, Kentuckians, Aggies, Italians, and Irishmen. You can see this for yourself by looking in William Clements' book, *The Types of the Polack Joke* (see bibliography) for versions of any ethnic joke that you collect (not just those about Polacks). What's more, people sometimes tell ethnic jokes about their own groups, or about ethnic groups that they have never met; some people who tell Polack jokes have no idea that a *Polack* is a Polish-American. Finally, there are many more direct ways to express hostility and prejudice besides telling jokes.

On the other hand, there is evidence that some ethnic jokes do express prejudice and hostility toward outside groups. First, not all ethnic jokes are generic. Neither of the two jokes above (5 and 6) is likely to be told about any other group. Also, if ethnic jokes were completely generic, there would be no need to tie them to any group at all, yet they almost always are. Finally, many people definitely find these jokes offensive.

Folklorists are not concerned with whether the stereotypes contained in jokes are true or not; they want to know whether the joke expresses the true feelings and attitudes of the teller and audience. To investigate this you have to find out their attitudes, personality, and life experiences in direct interviews. For an example of this approach, see Paulette Cross 1973 in the bibliography. If the joke is a favorite of the teller, then it is more likely to reflect his real feelings. If the teller or group shares other folklore forms, such as legends, that express the same prejudices more directly, then you have evidence that their jokes are aggressive too. Finally, remember that different people see different meanings in the same joke, and that the same joke can be used in a hostile or amusing manner depending on the situation.

PRACTICAL JOKES

In this country April 1st (April Fool's Day) and October 31 (Halloween) are both traditionally accepted occasions for playing practical jokes and pranks. In addition, many *rites of passage* are marked by practical jokes. A rite of passage is a special occasion during which a person moves from one social stage into another, for example marriage, the first day on the job, and the initiation ceremonies of fraternities and sororities. People in any of these situations are the traditional targets of practical jokes. The modern legend called "The Fatal Fraternity Initiation" describes a practical joke played on a pledge that had fatal results. Many wedding night pranks use noise or mess to make the couple's bed unusable or to hinder their privacy; in some places this custom is called a *shivaree*. The newcomer on the job is likely to be sent on a fool's errand——i.e. sent to fetch some tool of the trade that does not actually exist, but the victim does not know this because of his ignorance of the new job and its jargon.

Practical jokes can also be played at any time, especially between friends, workmates, and family members. Children delight in playing telephone pranks. Students who live in dorms amuse themselves with *borassing*——that is, using various ingenious ways to booby-trap the rooms of friends and floor-mates.

COLLECTING PRACTICAL JOKES

Because they require secrecy, it is difficult to observe practical jokes as they happen, unless you are personally involved as either joker, accomplice, or target. However it is not hard to get people to talk about jokes that they have been involved in, especially as the story of a practical joke may be more enjoyable than the joke itself.

For a full understanding of practical jokes, you need to go beyond the joke itself. It is crucial to know about the people involved in the joke. Ask everyone involved to describe the joke and its aftermath. You can also interview people who witnessed the joke, and if you were involved you can ask the same questions of yourself. Find out why the joker decided to play this joke on this person; the relationships between the two sides before, during, and after the joke; how each side evaluated the success of the joke; and whether it was meant to be benevolent or aggressive.

How Practical Jokes Work

Practical jokers set up *fabrications* to fool their victims. A fabrication is a playful, unrealistic imitation of some portion of reality. Normally there are clues, called *play frames* or *joking frames*, that instruct observers that what they see is not one hundred percent real, and that they should not treat it seriously. In practical jokes and other deceptions these clues are deliberately hidden from the targets, so they are fooled into treating a fake as the real thing. As a result, the joke divides its participants into two sides, one of which is aware of the fabrication, while the other is kept in the dark.

Most——but not all——practical jokes end when the fabrication is discredited and the victims are let in on the true state of affairs. The discrediting may be gradual, when victims are simply left to gradually figure out that they have been fooled. Other jokes are brought to a sudden end, for instance when the joker bursts out laughing or announces, "April fool!" There is also the possibility that the target will spot the fabrication before the joker wanted him to, which gives her the opportunity to turn the joke around and turn the joker into the fool.

Because practical jokes divide their participants into two opposed sides, you should get the victim's account of what happened as well as the joker's. The two sides are likely to have different versions of what happened, as well as different emotional responses.

Reasons For Playing Practical Jokes

People play practical jokes not only for amusement——there are many far less risky forms of amusement——but also for a variety of very specific reasons. Many people play jokes on Halloween or April 1st simply because the date provides a license to joke, which makes this activity safer than it otherwise would be. Another common reason is to get even with someone who has previously played a joke on you.

I have found that people often play a particular joke on a particular person as a way of creating poetic justice or of indirectly criticizing their behavior. In one case a young man's office mates disapproved of his habit of hitting on young women:

> We try to stop it, given him lectures and all that, but that's been the tendency in the past. He had a note left on his office, when he was supposed to have been there. During his office hours. And it was in what looked like a woman's handwriting, and it was filthy. "Sorry I missed you, I had wanted to . . ." blankety blankety blank. All kinds of sexual stuff. Very very explicit. "I only wish I had the courage to come and face you again, it took all I had today. I'm sorry I missed you. Yours forever."
>
> He was going crazy. Had anybody seen her. Who was it. He was ragging everybody in the department about this thing. He just wouldn't stop. And finally somebody said they probably didn't exist. Finally he was probably thinking this was a practical joke, and who would do that.
>
> He wants this to be true so much; it really plays on his weakness. So that was a good one. I like that.

Many are jokes are tailor made like this one to play upon a particular weakness or interest of the target. Such jokes subtly call attention to that weakness, and the target's discomfiture is seen as his own fault. This young man's womanizing (and his failure to show up for his office hours) was punished by his being made a fool, but he brought the punishment on himself through his own actions. The indirect message is, you would not have been fooled if you were not excessively interested in chasing women. Ideally you would talk to the victim to find out whether he got the message.

Are Practical Jokes Funny Or Aggressive?

After the joke is revealed, joker and victim are likely to disagree about whether what happened was 'just a joke.' Unhappy victims might prefer to interpret the experience as cruelty or vandalism. Far from laughing, they may feel embarrassed and angry. Furthermore, many jokes, such as borassing, create messy or unpleasant situations for the victim to deal with even after the joke is over.

Many people refuse to see any humor at all in practical jokes, while others insist that they are only meant in fun, and that those who disagree must not have a sense of humor. Both sides of the argument have some truth; practical jokes combine humor and aggression. The usual term for the target of a practical joke is *victim*, which points to the mean side of all this fun.

Practical jokes can be either *benevolent* or *malevolent*, depending on the joker's intent, the social context in which they occur, and the effect that they have on the relationships between the two sides. These types are discussed below.

Benevolent practical jokes are those in which the joker wants the target to be able to laugh along too. Such jokes are inclusive rather than divisive, and are meant to strengthen the friendship between the two sides. To achieve these goals, the victim has to be persuaded to accept the joke in a spirit of fun. Therefore the jokers choose targets who are known to take a joke well; avoid topics that are sensitive to the target; make sure the fabrication is temporary and is discredited quickly; avoid permanent damage or serious harm (although the definition of serious harm is open to debate); and help to clean up the after effects of the joke.

Benevolent jokes are often reciprocal, in that the person who is a victim today can get even with the joker the next time. Reciprocity like this is a sign of a *joking relationship*. People in a joking relationship frequently play jokes on each other, as well as teasing each other, swapping joking insults, and doing other things that neither would tolerate from any other person. The relationship gives the members a license to joke, and they agree to interpret almost any prac-

tical joke as funny. Practical jokes are safer in the context of a joking relationship than in other contexts.

Malevolent practical jokes are meant to be divisive. They *exclude* their victims and keep them in the status of outsiders. Aggressive jokes are often aimed at people who are different, unpopular, or especially gullible. They are not reciprocal; the same person in a group may be the butt of practical jokes over and over again. Unlike benign practical jokes, the jokers in malevolent pranks do not try to ensure that the target can laugh along. Sometimes they actually prefer a negative response, as in most Halloween joking. Benevolent jokes avoid serious negative responses from victims by trying to keep the victims from getting too angry, but malevolent jokers avoid reprisals by remaining anonymous, or by choosing targets who cannot get back at them.

Initiation jokes are an intermediate category. Both benevolent and malevolent jokes try to keep the relationship between the participants unchanged, but initiation jokes are meant to alter the relationship between the two sides by bringing the target, who is an outsider, into the group. Sometimes full acceptance into the new group depends on whether or not the targets react well to the jokes played on them.

Acknowledgement

For discussing humor theory and providing me with jokes and references, I wish to thank Sean Galvin, Sabina Magliocco, Nancy Michael, and Gerry Wright.

Selected Annotated Bibliography

1) **Topical Joke Cycles**

Abrahams, Roger D. 1961. Ghastly Commands: The Cruel Joke Revisited. *Midwest Folklore* 11:235-246.
The cruel joke series has an unchanging form that invites people to experiment with possible variations. The cruelty of the jokes is a reaction against the excessive sincerity and sentimentality of our society.

Abrahams, Roger and Alan Dundes. 1987. Elephantasy and Elephanticide. IN *Cracking Jokes: Studies of Sick Humor Cycles and Stereotypes*, pp. 41-54. Berkeley: Ten Speed Press.
The elephant joke cycle that became popular in the 1960s appears to be simply absurd, but the authors argue that they are in fact a disguised expression of hostility toward blacks and especially toward the Civil Rights Movement.

Barrick, Mac E. 1980. The Helen Keller Joke Cycle. *Journal of American Folklore* 93:441-449.
Helen Keller jokes became popular after a movie about her and after disabled children were mainstreamed into schools. The jokes relieve the anxiety that these events caused, and erase resentment toward the disabled.

_____. 1964. The Shaggy Elephant Riddle. *Southern Folklore Quarterly* 28:266-290.
Collection of 245 elephant jokes in riddle format, collected in 1963, when this type of joke was sweeping the country. Argues that these jokes are meant to be nonsensical.

Dundes, Alan. 1987. *Cracking Jokes: Studies of Sick Humor Cycles and Stereotypes*. Berkeley: Ten Speed Press.
Contains several essays with texts and analysis of current jokes, including jokes about Polacks, elephants, light bulbs, and the Jewish American Princess. Dundes argues that jokes express aggression in a disguised form, but he does not ask any joke tellers or listeners what their interpretations of the joke are.

Fish, Lydia. 1980. Is the Pope Polish? Some Notes on the Polack Joke in Transition. *Journal of American Folklore* 93:450-454.
Pope jokes collected in 1978-79 use the characteristics usually attributed to Polacks in ethnic jokes. Argues that the jokes are an expression of ethnic pride.

Goodwin, Joseph P. 1989. Unprintable Reactions to All the News That's Fit to Print. *Southern Folklore* 46:15-39.
Some, but not all, topical events such as AIDS, disasters, and celebrity deaths generate jokes. Events involving blacks, gays, and Jews are most likely to be joked about. Discusses functions of AIDS jokes, and the change in AIDS jokes over time as the disease became too threatening even to joke about.

Kerman, Judith B. 1980. The Light-Bulb Jokes: Americans Look at Social Action Processes. *Journal of American Folklore* 93:454-458.
Light-bulb jokes and similar joke fads provide models from which people invent new variations. Light-bulb jokes are used to comment on the processes of the teller's own group.

Oring, Elliott. 1975. Everything is a Shade of Elephant: An Alternative to a Psychoanalysis of Humor. *New York Folklore* 1:149-159.
Not all jokes are aggressive; sometimes they are told simply for their playful and humorous function. Summarizes the incongruity theory and the objections to the aggression theory. Argues against Abrahams and Dundes' analysis of elephant jokes (see above).

_____. 1987. Jokes and the Discourse on Disaster. *Journal of American Folklore* 100:276-286.
The jokes about the *Challenger* disaster are not necessarily told to express cruelty or to deal with anxieties aroused by the disaster. Argues that jokes have a base meaning and a situational meaning.

Sutton-Smith, Brian. 1960. 'Shut Up and Keep Digging': The Cruel Joke Series. *Midwest Folklore* 10:11-22.
One hundred and fifty-five "cruel jokes" collected in 1958 from college students and school children. All disregard feelings that are normally sacrosanct, such as love for children. Most use a short dialogue format, and many are what are known as "Mommy Mommy" jokes.

2) **Ethnic Jokes**
Ben-Amos, Dan. 1973. The 'Myth' of Jewish Humor. *Western Folklore* 32:112-131.
Argues against the theory that Jewish humor is a form of self-ridicule. Although both teller and object of the joke may be Jews, the object of ridicule is always a group from which the teller disassociates himself.

Brunvand, Jan Harold. 1970. Some Thoughts on the Ethnic-Regional Riddle Jokes. *Indiana Folklore* 3:128:142.
Polack jokes are the most common ethnic riddle-jokes circulating—even among people who do not know any Polish-Americans. Argues that the Polack is simply a stereotyped ethnic character upon which riddle jokes can be hung, and a safer one.

Clements, William M. 1973. *The Types of the Polack Joke*. Bloomington: Folklore Forum Bibliographic and Special Series, 3.
Lists the types of ethnic jokes about Polacks found in the Indiana University Folklore Archives. The jokes are arranged by subject. Any ethnic joke about any group can be searched in this index, since the same jokes are often told about different groups.

_____. 1979. Cueing the Stereotype: The Verbal Strategy of the Ethnic Joke. *New York Folklore* 5:53-61.

_____. 1986. The Ethnic Joke as a Mirror of Culture. *New York Folklore* 12:87-97.
Ethnic jokes are as much about *us* as about *them*; groups use them not only to express aggression toward out-groups, but also to define themselves. The jokes hold up a mirror to culture by describing behavior that is the opposite of what proper behavior should be.

Cross, Paulette. 1973. Jokes and Black Consciousness: A Collection with Interviews. IN *Mother Wit From the Laughing Barrel*, ed. Alan Dundes, pp. 649-669. Englewood Cliffs, NJ: Prentice-Hall.
(First published in *Folklore Forum* 2 (1969):140-161.) The author wrote this article while she was an undergraduate student. She collected seven jokes from two informants and transcribed her interviews with them in which she asked them to comment on the jokes and about their attitudes relevant to the themes of the jokes.

Davies, Christie. 1982. Ethnic Jokes, Moral Values and Social Boundaries. *British Journal of Sociology* 33(3):383-403.
Each society tells jokes about different peripheral or subordinate groups that live nearby. The jokes confirm that these 'others' are different from us. The jokes are about stupidity and other values that are of concern in large industrial societies.

_____. 1988. Stupidity and Rationality: Jokes from the Iron Cage. IN *Humour in Society: Resistance and Control*, ed. Chris Powell and George E. C. Paton, pp. 1-32. New York: St. Martin's Press.
Jokes about stupidity or rationality taken to absurd lengths are more popular in industrialized societies than elsewhere. In the West, such jokes are told about outsiders (ethnic jokes), and in each country the same jokes are told about different outsiders. In Eastern Europe, such jokes are told about those with political power.

Dundes, Alan. 1975. Slurs International: Folk Comparisons of Ethnicity and National Character. *Southern Folklore Quarterly* 39:15-38.
Standard numskull stories and insults can be told about any group; such jokes tell us little about folk stereotypes about particular groups.

_____. 1971. A Study of Ethnic Slurs: The Jew and the Polack in the United States. *Journal of American Folklore* 84:186-203.
Ethnic slurs, which include names and proverbs as well as jokes, transmit stereotypes. Some traits in ethnic slurs are generic and are not attributed to one group alone; however some traits, including some stereotypes about Jews, are confined to slurs about a single group.

Ferris, William R. 1970. Racial Stereotypes in White Folklore. *Keystone Folklore Quarterly* 15:188-198.
Upper class whites tell jokes against poor whites which contain stereotypes similar to those held about blacks.

Greenberg, Andrea. 1972. Form and Function of the Ethnic Joke. *Keystone Folklore Quarterly* 17:144-161.
Discusses the psychological functions of Jewish and black jokes told by these groups themselves. While riddle jokes use interchangeable stereotypes, narrative jokes reveal more about the narrator's attitude to the joke subject.

Hurvitz, Nathan. 1974. Blacks and Jews in American Folklore. *Western Folklore* 33:301-325.
Jokes and legends about blacks and Jews reveal similarities in the stereotypes about these two groups.

Poulsen, Richard C. 1988. Violence and the Sacred: Mormon Jokes about Blacks. IN *Misbegotten Muses: History and Anti-History*, pp. 25-36. New York: Peter Lang.
Jokes about blacks in the Mormon church became popular among Mormons after the church leadership decided to admit blacks to the priesthood. The jokes express hostility, rebellion against the leadership, and have cognitive functions as well.

3) Sexual Jokes
Green, Rayna. 1976-77. Magnolias Grow in Dirt: The Bawdy Lore of Southern Women. *Southern Exposure* 4:29-33.
Southern women are not supposed to tell dirty jokes, but in private they do. Men and preachers are often the butt of these jokes, but women's jokes are not usually as derogatory or racist as those told by men.

Legman, Gershon. 1968. *Rationale of the Dirty Joke: An Analysis of Sexual Humor.* First Series. New York: Grove Press.

_____. 1975. *Rationale of the Dirty Joke: An Analysis of Sexual Humor.* Second Series. New York: Breaking Point.
These two books contain a large collection of sexual jokes, arranged under topics like "marriage" and "prostitution." Legman took the jokes from printed and oral sources, and offers his own interpretations of each.

Lyman, Peter. 1987. The Fraternal Bond as a Joking Relationship: A Case Study of the Role of Sexist Jokes in Male Group Bonding. IN *Changing Men, New Directions in Research on Men and Masculinity*, ed. Michael S. Kimmel, pp. 148-163. Newbury Park, CA: Sage.

Mitchell, Carol A. 1978. Hostility and Aggression Toward Males in Female Joke Telling. *Frontiers* 3:19-23.
Men and women tell different kinds of jokes. Most jokes told by females to females have men as the butt, especially jokes about penis size, sexual performance, and castration. Women sometimes tell the more aggressive jokes "to make men squirm"; they also tell obscene jokes to express sexual interest in a man.

_____. 1977. The Sexual Perspective in the Appreciation and Interpretation of Jokes. *Western Folklore* 36:303-330.
Mitchell asked 10 men and 10 women to rate a sample of sexual jokes from funny to not funny, and to say what they thought was significant about each one. Men and women often do not find the same jokes funny; even when they do laugh at the same jokes, they often have different reasons for laughing.

4) Jokes In Their Personal And Social Context
Bendix, Regina. 1984. Playing the Joker: Personal Biography and Attitudes in the Study of Joke Performance. *Folklore Forum* 17:209-219.
Discusses some jokes told by a British graduate student, his identity as a humorist, and his deliberate use of jokes as a tool in speeches, debating, and teaching.

Burns, Thomas A. 1984. Doing the Wash: Cycle Two. IN *Humor and the Individual*, ed. Elliott Oring, pp. 49-70. Los Angeles: California Folklore Society.
Case study of one joke teller and a particular joke. Shows the connections between the teller's personality, experience, and attitudes and his choice of a favorite joke, as well as his version and interpretation of the joke.

Dégh, Linda. 1979. Symbiosis of Joke and Legend: A Case of Conversational Folklore. IN *Readings in American Folklore*, ed. Jan Harold Brunvand, pp. 236-259. New York: Norton.
Describes a Hungarian-American couple; she is religious and tells supernatural stories and legends, while he is a skeptic and prefers to tell jokes, especially about the clergy. Dégh shows how these two support each other in conversational context.

Johnson, Robbie Davis. 1973. Folklore and Women: A Social Interactional Analysis of the Folklore of a Texas Madam. *Journal of American Folklore* 86:211-224.
A whorehouse madam uses jokes, in which men are the butts, and other verbal strategies to keep the upper hand in conversation, and to put down and control male customers who try to dominate her.

Kirshenblatt-Gimblett, Barbara. 1975. A Parable in Context: A Social Interactional Analysis of Storytelling Performance. IN *Folklore: Performance and Communication*, ed. Dan Ben-Amos and Kenneth S. Goldstein, pp. 105-130. The Hague: Mouton.
Study of the performance of a narrative joke in a particular context, where it was used to comment upon the poor behavior of one of the people present.

Limón, José E. 1977. Agringado Joking in Texas Mexican Society: Folklore and Differential Identity. *New Scholar* 1977: 33-50.
Study of jokes told as a form of social control. Agringados are Texas-Mexicans who act like Anglos and betray their ethnic heritage. Jokes about this behavior are used by friends and relatives to express disapproval of someone's agringado behavior, and sometimes encourage the person to change.

Oring, Elliott. 1984. Jokes and Their Relation to Sigmund Freud. IN *Humor and the Individual*, ed. Elliott Oring, pp. 37-48. Los Angeles: California Folklore Society.
Discusses the favorite jokes of Sigmund Freud and the aspects in his life and personality that explain why these jokes were his favorites.

Pocius, Gerald L. 1977-78. Frank Williams, Newfoundland Joke Teller. *Lore and Language* 2 no. 6:16-29; 2 no. 7:11-21; 2 no. 8:11-19; 2 no. 9:6-25.
Study of a single joke teller; his development as a joker, his position in the community, his joke repertoire, his method of remembering jokes, and social and psychological aspects of his performances.

Tannen, Holly and David Morris. 1989. AIDS Jokes: Punishment, Retribution and Regeneration. *Southern Folklore* 46:147-157.
AIDS jokes may be used like other humor to introduce a serious but difficult topic into conversation.

Walle, Alf H. 1976. Getting Picked Up Without Being Put Down: Jokes and the Bar Rush. *Journal of the Folklore Institute* 13:201-217.
Male customers in a bar use increasingly risky jokes, culminating in sexual jokes, to test the sexual availability of waitresses. If they laughed at one joke, that suggested that they were willing to interact on a more intimate level. The man could interpret a negative reaction as a rejection of the joke and not of him, thus saving face.

5) Practical Jokes

Bauman, Richard. 1986. "We Was Always Pulling Jokes": The Management of Point of View in Personal Experience Narratives. IN *Story, Performance, and Event: Contextual Studies of Oral Narrative*, pp. 33-53. New York: Cambridge University Press.
Discusses one man's personal experience stories about practical jokes. Outlines the structure of practical jokes and stories about them, and compares stories in which the narrator is the trickster to those in which he is the dupe.

Bowman, John Robert. 1982. On Getting Even: Notes on the Organization of Practical Jokes. IN *The Paradoxes of Play*, ed. John Loy, pp. 65-75. West Point, NY: Leisure Press.
Jokers have fun, but victims experience confusion, surprise, and sometimes anger. In benevolent jokes, victims are meant to accept jokes in a spirit of play, but this can be difficult. Discusses the precautions taken by jokers to "make sure it's play."

Leary, James P. 1979. Adolescent Pranks in Bloomington, Indiana. *Indiana Folklore* 12:55-64.
Study of two adolescent boys who play Halloween-style pranks on householders as a way to temporarily get back at the adults who normally wield power over them.

Morrison, Monica. 1974. Wedding Night Pranks in Western New Brunswick. *Southern Folklore Quarterly* 38:285-297.
Pranks played on the bride and groom on their wedding night all have the effect of inhibiting the sexual act through noise or mess.

Posen, I. S. 1974. Pranks and Practical Jokes at Children's Summer Camps. *Southern Folklore Quarterly* 38:299-309.

Santino, Jack. 1986. A Servant and a Man, A Hostess or a Woman: A Study of Expressive Culture in Two Transportation Occupations. *Journal of American Folklore* 99:304-319.
Reciprocal practical joking occurs between pilots and flight attendants, and expresses and relieves the tensions inherent in their job relationships. After work they are social equals, but at work flight attendants are subordinate. Black Pullman porters and white conductors did not have a practical joke tradition, because the social distance between them was too great.

Tallman, Richard. 1974. A Generic Approach to the Practical Joke. *Southern Folklore Quarterly* 38:259-274.
Introduction to a series of articles on practical jokes. Offers a definition and discusses the different types of practical joke, based on their effect on social relationships.

6) Other Sources

The journal *Humor* (1988 -) contains numerous articles on folk humor as well as other kinds.

Dundes, Alan and Carl R. Pagter. 1978. *Work Hard and You Shall be Rewarded: Folklore from the Paperwork Empire*. Bloomington: Indiana University Press.
A collection of American xeroxlore, with analysis of the modern anxieties and concerns expressed in them.

Smith, Moira. 1986. Walls Have Ears: A Contextual Approach to Graffiti. *International Folklore Review* 4:100-105.
When graffiti is analyzed in the context of all the other graffiti in the same location, it can be seen not as a solitary activity but a type of conversation, in which people can argue, perform verbal art including jokes, and take part in cooperative forms of humor and word play.

CHAPTER 9
Cultural Performances: Public Display Events and Festival

Rory Turner and Phillip H. McArthur

Folklore as a discipline has always had a strong interest in the shared artistic expressions of small groups. The interchanges, artistic forms, and customs that define and celebrate the identity of family, occupation, and friendships, have been rich ground for research in folklore studies. But there are other arenas of human expressive life that concern folklorists. One of the most exciting of these arenas is that of public display events and festival. Whether at a stock car race, the county fair, or a historical reenactment, the researcher is presented with forms that express, communicate and comment on our collective and individual identities. We find in public display events and festivals a grand intensification of experience, in which the symbolic and behavioral realms of life are most fully charged and elaborated.

How then does one go about studying such events? Our aim here is to give a beginning student some sense of what these events are, and how they are constituted. We also want you to think critically about what happens in public display events. This sort of reflection is essential to contemporary folkloristic inquiry. We want you to not only describe the events you see, to collect them on paper as it were, but to think about their meanings and functions. We will give you a game plan for conducting your research. We hope you will be provoked into fresh insights about these momentous occasions that punctuate and enrich our lives.

DEFINITIONS

Different scholars classify expressive occasions using different schemes. We offer a fairly simple framework that we hope will both clarify what these events are, and point to some of their significant dimensions.

Cultural Performance

When the anthropologist Milton Singer investigated the culture of India, his Indian colleagues and informants persuaded him that the way he could best find out about 'being Indian' was by attending events where Indian culture was on display, everything from lectures and music recitals to full blown religious festivals. Singer dubbed these events *cultural performances*. In cultural performances, the values, beliefs and identities of a people are put on display for themselves and others in some sort of bounded frame. Cultural performances occur within a time and space demarcated from ongoing social life where culture is encapsulated and communicated. Whether in a theater, a stadium, main street on a holiday, the county fairground, we know when we have entered into one of these *times out of time*. We know that we are seeing or participating in something a little different than normal daily life. They are reference points of identity, where what it means to be Indian or American, Southern or Yankee, Quebecois or Californian, wealthy or working class, Afro-American or Amish is comprehended by individuals and groups.

Public Display Event

Public display events are those cultural performances that are public and large scale. By calling them public, we contrast them with the range of cultural performances which are more private in scope, the thanksgiving dinner, the wedding, the party, and all those other performances which invisibly bleed off into the often unnoticed events of everyday routine and limited social arenas. Public display events are large scale; they make a splash in our lives and mobilize large numbers of people to participate. Football and basketball games, historical reenactments, auctions, political demonstrations, inaugurations and opening ceremonies, and graduations are some public display events.

Festivals

Festivals are those public display events that are calendrically scheduled. In societies which are based on an agricultural and pastoral economy, festivals were organized in terms of the agricultural and natural course of the year. Harvest festivals, fiestas, and spring celebrations punctuated the year and were occasions to celebrate and reconfirm social ties in the context of natural cycles. The county fair and the rodeo could be said to continue these festival motivations. Along with these festivals, major religions also had their celebrations, such as Mardi Gras carnival, and All Souls Day (our Halloween). Major historical events also, left their mark on the year; Guy Fawkes Day in England and July Fourth in the United States are examples. Some scholars argue that these pre-industrial types of gatherings are the only *genuine* festivals. With the coming of the modern age, and its changes in patterns of production, the agricultural year became less important, but the need to mark time and to communicate cultural values remained. Thus we have what some scholars call *fabricated festivals*, annual races like the Indianapolis 500, community celebrations of *the old ways*, or *folk festivals* that put traditional performers and material culture on display. All of these kinds of festivals exist today and respond to people's need to celebrate and experience themselves as part of a community. Often, it is hard to distinguish which of these categories a given event belongs to. A rodeo derives from a calendrical cattle culture economy, but might be held on July Fourth, allying it with a historic celebration.

Figure 1. A theme float in a Norwegian Constitution Day parade in Seattle, Washington. Norwegian-American traditions include foods, music, and dance. (Photograph courtesy of Robert Walls)

The Emergence of Folklore in Everyday Life

And if the rodeo was in Madison Square Garden, one could argue that it is a fabricated festival. Our concern is less with quibbling over a festival's provenance, as in seeing what that festival means and what it does for people who experience it now.

Dimensions

Public display events are characteristically active in terms of participation, and tend toward the use of multiple genres and activities. The genres and activities provide the context of participation. In some cultural performances the activities occur in a structured order of events: opening ceremony, main event, closing ceremony. Other kinds of events are more random with no clear linear structure. For example, in county fairs many activities occur simultaneously. Beverly Stoeltje provides six dimensions of genre and activity that should be identified and described (1989). To her list we add two more.

Opening Ceremony. Cultural performances will often open with some kind of ceremony which clearly indicates that the event has begun; a rodeo queen leads a procession through the arena, a large parade enters the stadium at a football game, a band plays the star spangled banner, a prayer is offered, names of participants announced. Beginning ceremonies reveal participant roles, such as judges, players, organizers and social identity in terms of gender, age, and status.

Ritual Activities that exhibit a religious quality may begin with prayer. Such an activity is a ritual. Other ritual acts may be recognition of former members of the community, the coronation of a rodeo queen, a reading of an organizational charter, throwing the first pitch at a baseball game, or giving away the key to the city.

Drama and Contest. Conflicts within the community often get expressed through drama and competitions. Dangerous acts, escapes, sports competitions, games of chance, parade floats contests, story telling competitions, dramatic reenactments, animal performances, and mask can all contribute to a highly charged environment. Drama and contest may distort or invert the everyday experience. These activities can reveal many tensions in social relationships, force realignments, or present new oppositions.

Food and Drink. At every cultural performance people consume large amounts of food and drink. Some foods and drink are only prepared for the specific performance. Such culinary items become expected by the participants, hot dogs and beer at a baseball game, beef and corn at a harvest festival, ethnic dishes at an Irish festival in downtown Chicago. Traditional food and drink can embody the identity of a group. This is especially the case with foods prepared for ethnic celebrations.

Dance and Music. Individuals and groups perform and often invite audience participation such as in sing alongs' or square dancing. Specialists may provide the music and drumming for dances. Both the emotional tone and content of the music and dance help set the pace of the event. Music is a very important factor in generating the shared experience and celebration so crucial to the success of the festival.

Crafts and Arts. Many kinds of material items put on display represent groups and their values. Tools, quilts and musical instruments are just some of the many material ways in which people express their tastes, skills, and lifestyle. Sometimes the items are judged and sold. Some materials are made just for the specific event such as parade floats and decorations.

Costuming. Clothing distinguishes the participants in their respective roles. Performers usually wear clothing which marks them off from other participants. The costumes of players, marching bands, auctioneers, magicians, ethnic groups, and dancers distinguishes them from other participants. Clothing may also identify to which group a person belongs. Sometimes costuming takes on bizarre forms such as masking and hair design. At sporting events one can see the San Diego Chicken or hair died the color of the representative team; at rodeos and parades clowns perform tricks behind masks; at civil war reenactments uniforms help create the impression that history has come alive. People will often dress in non-human costumes representing animals or comic figures that distort human shape.

Concluding Event. The conclusion of a cultural performance tends to be less structured than its opening event. The performance may end in a dramatic climax of noise, fireworks, intense competition, suspense or danger, or it may just fizzle out all together. In any case the conclusion tends to be more spontaneous with more liberties and privileges taken by both the performers and crowd.

All of the above dimensions may or may not be present at any one event. The field worker needs to identify which are part of the overall event and determine their role.

Functions

Cultural performances are certainly diverse and complex. A first step toward understanding what a cultural performance may mean is to pursue the question of its function. Function is the term used for what something does, what it accomplishes, the purpose it serves. To arrive at a functional explanation of a performance we need to know what it is that people are expressing.

A cultural performance can serve several purposes, but it is easiest to think about three general functions.

Sociological functions may reveal that the cultural performance either maintains or provides release of tension from existing social relationships. To access the social function the folklorist must determine the social relationships involved in the performance and how they are expressed. What does the performance tell us about the organization of the community, country, or family? Are there conflicts expressed? Is the traditional social structure reinforced? Are alternatives or new kinds of relationships being presented?

Psychological function tell us about what a performance is doing for the individuals who participate in it. Can we identify that deep emotions of contentment or frustration are being expressed? What are the personal and collective emotions expressed at the performance? Is the performance serving as a "steam valve", an outlet for human psychology?

Cultural functions reveal the role of the performance in its cultural context. What are the cultural traditions and innovations performed? What are the meaningful actions? What are the beliefs, ideas, attitudes, and feelings behind such actions? What cultural characteristics are displayed in the performance? What kinds of symbols are used in the performance and what do such symbols refer to for the members of the culture? Asking questions about cultural references tells us something of the cultural meanings used in the performance and in turn tells us something about how the performance functions to express, reinforce, and create culture.

These three primary functions, *sociological, psychological*, and *cultural*, are not mutually exclusive but may in fact overlap and all be present at any cultural performance. If you can identify just one of the functions you have moved closer to interpreting the event. But if you can identify more of its functions you will gain a clearer picture of its complex meaning. Because cultural performances are so complex, involving so many participants, genres, and events, several meanings can be expressed, and several interpretations of these meanings can be equally valid.

One way to examine how festivals function is to focus analysis on issues of identity. Existing identities may be reinforced, new ones created or negotiated, and old ones discarded. The following examples represent identity at several different levels: region (occupation), class, ethnicity, and individual. These

do not exhaust all of the possibilities, other identities such as gender, age, religion, also enter into many cultural performances. In any one performance several levels of identity may be involved. We have selected only four possibilities for demonstration.

Cowboy Rodeo

In a western cowboy rodeo, event structures are clear. The opening ceremony consists of a grand entrance of the rodeo queen and several riders carrying flags representative of different groups and organizations (see Figure 2). Following the opening ceremony and introductions of celebrities the actual rodeo competitions begin. These consists of several kinds of events such as bronc riding, barrel racing, calf roping, steer wrestling, culminating in the bull riding. Interspersed between each event are clown acts and other kinds of entertainment that highly involve the audience such as sing alongs or raffling tickets. These events have a clear linear structure and progression. Through the course of these events cowboys and spectators invert the normal relationship between a man and animal. Whereas livestock is usually part of the work and business experience of the community, in the rodeo the animals become instruments for play (Stoeltje 1987). While members of the ranching community play at the rodeo, they put on display their life style and social organization. Rodeo events not only represent an occupation or sport, but a region in which cattle ranching is a prominent part of its economic and social identity. This is made clear by the numerous events that surround the rodeo such as barbecues, square dances, memorial services and art and craft displays. The rodeo presents to its participants those things that symbolize the identity of the region.

Country Estate Auction

The participants at an estate auction are more communally based than regionally based. Estate auctions in Indiana usually occur after an older member of the agricultural community dies. Family members of the deceased sell his/her things, anything from tools, furniture, farm equipment, kitchen appliances and maybe even the house. The obvious center of attention is the auctioneer calling out the prices the participants bid on. Most of the people who attend the auctions are acquaintances of the deceased and his/her family. Many come to get good prices on used items. Good prices alone, however, are not what draw attendance because often the prices forced up by bidding are higher than what could be obtained at a store. People come to be entertained by the competi-

Figure 2. The Opening Ceremony consists of a grand entrance of several riders carrying flags representative of different clubs and organizations. (Photograph courtesy of Beverly J. Stoeltje)

tion and associate with community members. Also, at a symbolic level, the items represent the lower-middle class in America and are the means by which the class exercises some economic power outside of the larger capitalistic economy. The material items of a former member of the community also represent their values, their rural way of life, and their identity. At the auction people buy their heritage even if the items are old and prove useless. The bidding arena is not the only area of activity, however. Usually the auction affords time for members of the agricultural community to converse and reestablish ties. Women and men tend to split off into groups to talk of their concerns related to their gender roles (i.e. farming, livestock, recipes, child care). Women serve foods and background music is played. The auction is a time for buying up symbolic material culture, associating with fellow members of the community, and reinforcing community and traditional values.

Basque Festival

In the western states of Idaho, Nevada, Oregon and Washington are enclaves of Basque immigrants from Spain. The Basque people in America are most widely known for their sheep herding. But this stereotype greatly ignores their integration into their respective communities. Many Basque people today take pride in their success as prominent business people and politicians. In Boise, Idaho, a primary population center of the Basque people, a festival is held every July. Several Basque people from Spain, especially professional dancers and musicians, travel to attend this festival and join with family and friends in America. The festival begins with a parade which runs through the downtown streets of the city of Boise. The parade consists of musicians playing traditional music, dancers, clowns and jesters, all dressed in traditional costume, and an all Basque marching band. Most of the spectators are not Basque people themselves but come from the greater Boise area. After the parade the participants move to another site where Basque foods are prepared and served. These traditional foods include chorizos (sausages), bacalao (dried cod), tripacalos (tripe cooked in tomato sauce), lengue (fried tongue), roasted lamb, paella (rice fried with chicken), other meats, and omlettas potatas (potato omelets). The music and dancing continues for two more days interspersed with athletic competitions which are strictly Basque games. These games include hoisting 225 pound cylindrical weights, carrying 105 pound bell-shaped steel block weights as far as possible, throwing the bell weight, between the leg javelin throw and log chopping competitions while standing on the log (Munro 1985). Basque crafts and arts are also displayed and sold. Although the festival affords an opportunity for the Basque people of the region and their Spanish friends and family to associate, reinforce ties and share traditional culture, the majority of people who attend the festival are non-Basque. The festival can be viewed as providing the Basque people an opportunity to express their ethnic identity. They put on display for themselves and others what they consider their ethnic traditions and thus reinforce their ethnic identity within the community.

Civil War Reenactments

Nearly every weekend of the year, somewhere in the United States, people are reenacting the Civil War. These reenactments are portrayals of Civil War battles and life (see Figure 3). Participants create a highly realistic 19th century world which they inhabit and display for spectators. In these events identity is expressed and confirmed on many levels. All participants express to some degree their common alliance to American national values. For southern reenactors, this national identity can compliment or contrast with their expression of identity as rebels, as confederates. Also, by participating together in creating a Civil War world and fighting a Civil War battle, both challenging endeavors, reenactors feel bonds of camaraderie with each other. Not linked by anything other than an interest in the Civil War, reenactors *invent* a community, a community that becomes a meaningful and important part of their lives. On still another level, each reenactor uses reenacting to address personal agendas be it a farmer commemorating dead ancestors, a historian experiencing a tangible past, a disgruntled urbanite seeking value in a romanticized past. By participating in these events, reenactors explore the question, who am I? in personal occupational, regional, and national domains.

These four examples, a rodeo, an auction, an ethnic festival, and a historical reenactment represent only a fraction of the many cultural performances one can study.

People celebrate those aspects of their lives which are most relevant and meaningful to them. Whether centered around religion, occupation, sports, music, or any other valued part of human experience, cultural performances allow people to come together as communities and share in action that expresses their deepest concerns. In every region of North America one can find these cultural performances. How people celebrate, and what they celebrate in cultural performances deserves study.

GUIDE TO RESEARCH PRELIMINARIES

We suggest you begin your research by taking a look at the bibliography at the end of this chapter. The sources listed both elaborate and disagree with the orientations given here. They will stimulate your thinking and help you focus on an approach that interests you. They too have bibliographies which can guide you further in your explorations. Festival is also an entry in most libraries' subject card catalog and worth a look. You will also find in our bibliography some listings of North American public display events and festivals that might take place in your geographical area. Another place to look for events to research is the local newspaper. Since the events we are dealing with are public, often they are advertised or mentioned in feature articles. We also suggest you keep your ears open. Friends and acquaintances might know of or participate in these events. Those individuals can also become resources as you continue your study.

Once you have familiarized yourself somewhat with the scholarly literature and identified and event, get a file and use it to contain the information you collect. Try and find anything you can on the given event and any theoretical material you think will be useful. Before you go to the event you should have an orientation to work with. That is, your research on the event and in the scholarly literature should lead you to a certain issue that you will think important enough to pursue. Read what you can on that issue and develop a topic and a set of questions. If you were interested in ethnic identity for example, you might want to look first at how ethnic identity is expressed and next at how that identity is expressed in relation to American culture as a whole. In your fieldwork you would want to be sure to pay attention to the symbols of the ethnic group, its music, food, costume, and so on. You should also note how those symbols are deployed, especially in relationship to symbols of mainstream American culture.

Figure 3. Scene from the 125th anniversary Gettysburg Battle reenactment in 1988. (Photograph by Rory Turner)

As the event draws near, ready yourself for fieldwork. If at all possible identify and contact the event's organizers and arrange a time when you can talk to them. Get hold of a still camera (and also a video camera if possible), a tape recorder, and a notebook. Buy film, tapes, and other supplies in advance. If you can persuade some friends to work with you, its a big plus; a lot happens in a public display event and it is helpful to have more than one set of eyes and ears. Brief them on what you are trying to do and figure out a plan of action.

Fieldwork and Analysis

There are two main activities to do in this sort of fieldwork: observation and interviewing. The camera is a useful tool for observation. Use it to record performances and rituals, individuals you talk to, the layout of space, significant objects, incidents that strike you as significant. Some observations are better recorded on paper. Acquire or make a map of the

spatial layout of the site or sites. Record the sequence and time of events and any notes about those events you feel are significant. Little things that occur to you or that you overhear can be more significant that you realize. Record these too, they might prove to be compelling examples in your paper or orient your thinking in interesting directions.

Observation gives breadth to your fieldwork; interviews give depth. The hardest part of interviewing is mustering up the courage to approach someone you have never met and start asking them questions. Do it. You will probably be surprised how many people are willing to talk if you are interested in what they are saying and treat them politely. ALWAYS ask permission to tape, if you feel it is suitable to tape the person you approach. If it doesn't *feel right* to tape or if they refuse permission go ahead and talk with them and write down what you can remember as soon as possible.

What should you ask these people you have ap-

Figure 4. A Logging Festival in Washington State. Loggers participate in competitions based on historical and contemporary occupational skills. (Photograph courtesy of Robert Walls)

proached? You are trying to get information from them, but you are also trying to get insight. You want to develop some kind of rapport with them so they will tell you what they really think and not what they think you want to hear, so treat them with respect, and try to get comfortable with them. Be flexible, and think up some questions that are pertinent to your particular research topic. Here are some other questions you might want to ask. At some point, ask them their name. A good way to get a conversation going and to pick up some very useful information is to ask them to clarify things you observed or heard and didn't understand. If they are performers or active participants, ask them how they got involved in the event. Talk with them about their costume, their music, their sport, their animals or whatever is important to them. Ask them why they participate and why they think others participate. Ask them what the event or the subject of the event

means to them. If they are in some official capacity, ask them how the event is organized and structured. Find out who they are, what they do to make a living, where they are from, or what their ethnic background is if appropriate. Ask them about the history of the event if they seem to know a great deal about it. If there is something controversial that the event is expressing or commenting on, ask them their views on it. If they are really knowledgeable and you want to delve further, arrange to meet them at another time.

Basically, your fieldwork should accomplish two tasks. First you should be able to collect a rich description of the event. You should have a map of the event and a record of the sequence of actions. You should be able to answer the journalistic questions who, what, where, when, and how, both for the event as a whole, and for the particular segments or scenes within the event.

But this is not enough. As a student of folklore

and culture, you want to find out WHY. You must ask yourself questions about function and meaning, the reasons why people create and participate in cultural performances.

Before doing your fieldwork you should have some idea of what you want to find out, a topic that you are pursuing. If you have a good topic and conduct good fieldwork, you will probably get data that really says something about the event. Remember our hypothetical example of the expression of ethnicity in relationship to mainstream culture? Perhaps you found that there was an antagonistic relationship toward the broader culture. More likely, there would be some sort of compatible hierarchical affirmation, that "we are BOTH ethnic and American," but more one than the other. Perhaps, the bulk of the action expresses ethnicity and is highly participated in but the beginning and ending ceremonies use national symbols like flags, anthems, and bald eagles. From this sort of thing, one can make an interpretation. Why does this ethnic group engage in this festival? How does it function for them as a cultural expression of their ethnicity? Do they find it compatible and consistent with their identity as acculturated Americans?

You can go ahead and write up your paper. Present your interests and findings and the sources that you used to develop your ideas. Give some background information about the event and describe how it was structured. Present data that supports your interpretation. Explain how your data supports your interpretation and suggest some implications of your research for understanding cultural performances, or the groups and individuals who perform them.

Selected Annotated Bibliography

1) **Guides to Events**—These works will help you find an event to research.

Cohen, Hennig and Tristram Potter Coffin., eds. 1987. *The Folklore of American Holidays*. Detroit: Gale Research Company.
This reference work has a calendrically organized guide to over 100 American festivals and calendar custom with information on beliefs associated with them. Useful as a place to identify an event to study, its introduction is a thoughtful piece on the origin and current status of festival in America. Includes index.

Hill, Kathleen Thompson. 1988. *Festivals USA*. New York: John Wiley and Sons, Inc.
Arranged by state, has information on "the 1000 best festivals". Includes glossary, index, and an amusing foreword by Willard Scott, the TV weatherman.

Wasserman, Paul and Edmond L. Applebaum., eds. 1984. *Festivals Sourcebook*. Detroit: Gale Research Company.
A comprehensive reference to festivals and fairs organized by the topic of the festival. Contains name, geographic, subject, and chronological indexes.

2) **Theoretical Works**—These works will illuminate issues and approaches in the folkloristic study of festivals and public display events.

Abrahams, Roger D. 1981. Shouting Match at the Border: The Folklore of Display Events. IN *And Other Neighborly Names: Social Process and Cultural Image in Texas Folklore*. Richard Bauman and Roger D. Abrahams, eds, pp. 303-321. Austin: University of Texas Press.
This important article is foundational for an understanding of public display events. Abrahams focuses attention on display events which include "expositions and meets, games and carnivals and auctions." He discusses their role in the mediation of inter-group identity, dimensions of their setting, and issues concerning their variety in American culture, and relationship to the modern economy.

Falassi, Alessandro., ed. 1986. *Time Out of Time: Essays on the Festival*. Albuquerque: University of New Mexico Press.
A rich and wide ranging collection of articles on festivals. Includes many descriptive, literary pieces on festivals and also a number of more theoretical essays, most with a semiotic or structuralist orientation. Falassi's introduction and commentaries on the individual essays are especially useful. This book is a good bibliographic source.

Fernandez, James W. 1986. Convivial Attitudes: A Northern Spanish Kayak Festival in Its Historical Moment. IN *Persuasions and Performances: The Play of Tropes in Culture*, pp. 264-295 Bloomington: Indiana University Press.
An enjoyable, insightful example of an interpretation of a festival. Fernandez uses theories from studies of crowd behavior and symbolic anthropology with historical contextualization and detailed description of the festival's structure to understand the meaning and experience of this event.

Geertz, Clifford. 1973. Deep Play: Notes on the Balinese Cockfight. IN *The Interpretation of Cultures*, pp. 412-454. New York: Basic Books.
A seminal work in Geertz' interpretive anthropology. Geertz looks at Balinese cockfights as "a story they tell about themselves", which reveals underlying cultural themes that constitute tensions in Balinese identity.

MacAloon, John., ed. 1984. *Rite, Drama, Festival, Spectacle*. Philadelphia: Institute for the Study of Human Issues, Inc.
A collection of conference papers some of which address festival and public display events. Particularly useful in understanding public display events is MacAloon's article on the Olympic Games and his introduction.

Manning, Frank., ed. 1983. *The Celebration of Society*. Bowling Green, Ohio: Bowling Green University Popular Press.
A collection of articles on various cultural performances centering around their political aspects. Manning's introduction is clear and foundational, and the book has a useful bibliography.

Metraux, G.S., ed. 1976. *Cultures, Festivals, and Carnivals: The Major Traditions*. Special Issue on Festival of *Cultures* 3.
A special issue of Unesco's journal Cultures. Contains many articles on festivals worldwide.

Singer, Milton. 1977. On the Symbolic and Historic Structure of an American Identity. *Ethos*. pp. 431-455.
Here, Singer uses his idea of cultural performance in an American setting. He discusses the bicentennial historical reeenactments in a New England town, and suggests that these events help create and confirm a sense of American identity. Also see his When A Great Tradition Modernizes (1972) pp.70-75, for his initial working out of the meaning of cultural performance.

Smith, Robert J. 1972. Festivals and Celebrations. IN *Folklore and Folklife*, ed. Richard M. Dorson, pp.159-172. Chicago: University of Chicago Press.
A clear statement about varieties, structure, and function of festivals. Includes a short, useful bibliography of pre-1970 scholarship on festival.

_____. 1975. The Art of the Festival. *University of Kansas Publications in Anthropology #6*. Lawrence: University of Kansas Libraries.
An important book length treatment of a Peruvian Fiesta by a folklorist. Uses semiotic and anthropological theory to unpack this complex event.

Stoeltje, Beverly J. 1983. Festival in America. IN *Handbook of American Folklore*, ed. Richard M. Dorson, pp.239-246. Bloomington: Indiana University Press.
A lucid introduction to approaching festival in America. Offers a conceptual framework for studying festival which focuses on generic features, festival structures, and symbolic action. Includes a short but essential bibliography. See also her article in Falassi's *Time Out of Time* for an example of how her framework can be used.

_____. 1989. Festival. IN *International Encyclopedia of Communications*, ed. Erik Barnouw, pp. 161-166. London: Oxford University Press.
An article of definitions and formal characteristics of festivals. Clear presentation of festival structures and basic features common to many festivals.

Stoeltje, Beverly J. and Richard Bauman. 1988. The Semiotics of Folkloric Performance. IN *The Semiotic Web 1987*, eds. T.A. Sebeok and J. Umiker Sebeok, pp. 585-599. Berlin: Mouton de Gruyer.
An overview of folkloric approaches to performance, the section on cultural performance is clear and thought provoking, and provides a good sense of some elements to look at in interpreting cultural performances.

_____. 1989. Community Festival and the Enactment of Modernity. IN *The Old Traditional Way of Life: Essays in Honor of Warren E. Roberts*, eds. Robert E. Walls and George H. Schoemaker, pp. 159-171. Bloomington, IN: Trickster Press.
Discusses the Luling, Texas Watermelon Thump festival to explore how the festival deals expressively with the forces of modernity.

Turner, Victor W., ed. 1982. *Celebrations: Studies in Festivity and Ritual*. Washington, D.C.: Smithsonian Institution Press.
A companion book to a gallery exhibition on celebration, this book has excellent articles on different aspects and kinds of festive events, especially those by Dorson, Myerhoff, Abrahams, Turner and Turner, and MacAloon.

Selected Bibliography

Abrahams, Roger D. 1977. Toward Enactment-Centered Theory of Folklore. IN *Frontiers of Folklore*, ed. William R. Bascom, Boulder: Westview Press.

Abrahams, Roger D. and Richard Bauman. 1978. Ranges of Festival Behavior. IN *The Reversible World: Symbolic Inversions in Art and Society*, ed. Barbara Babcock, pp. 193-208. Ithaca: Cornell University Press.

Anderson, Jay. 1984. *Time Machines: The World of Living History*. Nashville: American Association for State and Local History.

Babcock, Barbara., ed. 1978. *The Reversible World: Symbolic Inversion in Art and Society*. Ithaca: Cornell University Press.

Bakhtin, Mikhail M. 1968. *Rabelais and His World*. Translated by Hélène Iswolsky. Bloomington, IN: Indiana University Press. (Original: *Tvorchestvo Fransua Rable*)

Byrne, Donald E. Jr. 1985. The Race of Saints: An Italian Religious Festival in Jessup, Pennsylvania. *Journal of Popular Culture* 19(3):119-130.

Coffin, Tristram P. and Hennig Cohen. 1966. Folk Drama and Folk Festival. IN *Folklore in America*, pp. 195-225. New York: Doubleday.

Cohen, Abner. 1982. A Polyethnic London Carnival as a Contested Cultural Performance. *Ethnic and Racial Studies* 5(1):1-22.

Cohn, William H. 1976. A National Celebration: The Fourth of July in American History. *Cultures* 3(2):141-156.

Cox, Harvey. 1969. *The Feast of Fools: A Theological Essay on Festivity and Fantasy*. Cambridge Mass.: Harvard University Press.

Dégh, Linda. 1977-1978. Grape-Harvest Festival of Strawberry Farmers: Folklore or Fake? *Ethnologia Europaea* 10(2):114-131.

Dorson, Ron. 1974. *The Indy 500: An American Institution Under Fire*. Newport Beach: Bond-Parkjurst Books.

Douglas, Mary T., ed. 1984. *Food in the Social Order: Studies of Food and Festivities in Three American Communities*. New York: Russell Sage Foundation.

Dundes, Alan and Alessandro Falassi. 1975. *La Terra in Piazza: An Interpretation of the Palio of Siena*. Berkeley: University of California Press.

Duvignaud, Jean. 1976. Festivals: A Sociological Approach. *Cultures* 3(1):13-28.

Errington, Fredrick. 1987. Reflexivity Deflected: The Festival of Nations as an American Cultural Performances. *American Ethnologist* 14(4):654-667.

The Emergence of Folklore in Everyday Life

Esman, Majorie R. 1982. Festival Change and Unity: The Celebration of Ethnic Identity Among Louisiana Cajuns. *Anthropological Quarterly* 55(4):199-210.

Gluckman, Max and Mary. 1977. On Drama and Games and Atheletic Contests. IN *Secular Ritual*, eds. Sally Falk Moore and Barbara G. Myerhoff. Amsterdam: Van Gorcum.

Green, Lewis. 1985. *Fairs and Festivals of the Pacific Northwest: A visual Journey through the Celebration of Washington, Oregon, and British Columbia.* Seattle: New Horizons Publishers.

Guiliano, Bruce. 1976. *Sacro o Profano? A consideration of four Italian-Canadian Religious Festivals.* Ottawa: National Museum of Canada.

Gutowski, John A. 1978. The Protofestival: Local Guide to American Folk Behavior. *Journal of the Folklore Institute* 15: 113-130.

Handler, Richard and William Saxton. 1988. Dyssimulation: Reflexivity, Narrative, and the Quest for Authenticity in "Living History". *Cultural Anthropology* 3(3):242-260.

Harrison-Brose, Phyllis. 1983. Community, Business and Play: The Country Sale as Symbolic Interaction. Dissertation, Indiana University.

Hill, D.R. and R. Abramson. 1979. West Indian Carnival in Brooklyn. *Natural History* 88(7):73-85.

Ivey, S.K. 1977. Ascribed Ethnicity and Ethnic Display Event: The Melungeons of Hancock County, Tennessee. *Western Folklore* 36:85-107.

James-Duguld, Charlene. 1985. Orofino Lumberjack Days. IN *Idaho Folklife: Homesteads to Headstones*, ed. Louie W. Attebery. pp. 81-90. Salt Lake City. University of Utah Press.

Lavenda, Robert H. 1988. Minnesota Queen Pageants: Play, Fun, and Dead Seriousness in a Festive Mode. *Journal of American Folklore* 101:168-175.

Ludwig, Jack Barry. 1976. *The Great American Spectaculars: The Kentucky Derby, Mardi Gras, and Other Days of Celebration.* Garden City: Doubleday.

Manning, Frank E. 1984. Carnival in Canada: The Politics of Celebration. IN *The Masks of Play*, eds. Brian Sutton-Smith and Diana Kelly-Byrne, pp. 24-33. New York: Leisure Press. Also printed in *Folk Groups and Folklore Genres: A Reader*, ed. Elliott Oring, pp. 78-86. Logan, Utah: Utah State University Press.

McNutt, James C. 1986. Folk Festivals and the Semiotics of Tourism in Texas. *Kentucky Folklore Record* 32(3-4):118-129.

Mesnil, Marianne. 1976. The Masked Festival: Disguise or Affirmation? *Cultures* 3(2):11-29.

Munro, Sarah Baker. 1985. Basque Celebrations in Eastern Oregon and Boise. IN *Idaho Folklife: Homesteads to Headstones*, ed. Louis W. Attebery, pp. 91-100. Salt Lake City: University of Utah Press.

Myerhoff, Barbara. 1986. The Los Angeles Jews' 'Walk for Solidarity': Parade, Festival, Pilgramage. IN *Symbolizing America*, ed. Herve Varenne, pp. 119-135. Lincoln: University of Nebraska Press.

Pirkova-Jakobson, Svatava. 1956. Harvest Festivals in America. IN *Slavic Folklore: A Symposium*, ed. Albert Bates Lord, pp. 68-82. Philadelphia: American Folklore Society Bibliographical and Special Series, 6.

Santino, Jack. 1983. Halloween in America: Contemporary Customs and Performances. *Western Folklore* 42:1-20.

Smith, Robert J. 1972. Licentious Behavior in Hispanic Festivals. *Western Folklore* 31:290-298.

Stoeltje, Beverly J. 1987. Riding, Roping and Reunion: Cowboy Festival. IN *Time Out of Time: Essays on the Festival*, ed. Alessandro Falassi, pp. 137-151. Albuquerque: University of New Mexico Press.

Turner, Victor W. 1969. The Ritual Process: Structure and Anti-Structure. Ithaca: Cornell University Press.

_____. 1982. *From Ritual to Theater: The Human Seriousness of Play.* New York: PAJ Publications.

Van Gennep, Arnold. 1960. *The Rites of Passage.* Translated by Monika B. Vizedom and Gabrielle L. Caffee. Chicago: University of Chicago Press.

Vaughn, Leroy F. 1956. *Parade and Float Guide.* Minneapolis: Denison

Vogt, Evon Z. 1955. A Study of the Southwestern Fiesta System as Exemplified by the Laguna Fiesta. *American Anthropologist* 57:820-839.

Wade, Melvin. 1981. 'Shining in Barrowed Plumage': Affirmation of Community in the Black Coronation Festivals of New England (c. 1750–c. 1850). *Western Folklore* 40(3):211-231.

Wiggins, William H. Jr. 1975. "Lift Every Voice": A Study of Afro-American Emancipation Celebrations. IN *Discovering Afro-America*, eds. Roger D. Abrahams and John Szwed, pp. 46-57. Leiden: E.J. Brill.

_____. 1979. Janurary 1: The Afro-Americans' "Day of Days". *Prospects* 5:331-345.

_____. 1989. Juneteenth: Afro-American Customs of the Emmnacipation. IN *The Old Traditional Way of Life: Essays in Honor of Warren E. Roberts*, eds. Robert E. Walls and George H. Schoemaker, pp. 146-158. Bloomington, IN: Trickster Press.

CHAPTER 10
Ethnomusicology and Musical Collecting Techniques

Michael Largey

This chapter is an introduction to the field of ethnomusicology and musical collecting techniques for students in an introductory world music course. Our goals are 1) to give the student some working vocabulary to talk about music from an analytical perspective and 2) to outline the steps necessary for writing a *musical observation* paper. The successful application of this *formula* for writing a paper assumes that the student is in contact with his/her instructor. Each instructor will have different ideas about what should go into a final paper, but this guide should answer some of the more frequently asked questions about how to get started on a musical observation.

WHAT IS ETHNOMUSICOLOGY?

Ethnomusicologists study music, but their primary aim is to understand how music works within a given culture or society. They not only listen to the way music is performed, but they look at the environment or *context* in which music is made. This double vision that ethnomusicologists develop, simultaneously looking at music and culture, is what makes ethnomusicolgical research interesting and difficult.

Since everyone is exposed to some kind of music, you will bring your own expertise to the musical observation project. We all observe music to some degree in our daily lives. However, in this musical observation paper, you will be called upon to listen critically to music and observe behavior associated with musical performance in a way that demands different techniques and ideas.

Before discussing some of the different techniques that ethnomusicologists use to study music, we need a working definition for ethnomusicology. We define *ethnomusicology* as the study of music in its cultural and social contexts. The cultural context is where we look to determine the meanings that people assign to music. Different cultures have different ways of categorizing what English-speaking Americans call *music*. Although all cultures practice what we call music, not all cultures have special words for music, nor do they use the word music the same way English speakers do. For example, in Arabic speaking countries, the word *musiqa*, which is linguistically similar to "music," refers only to instrumental music.

The social context of musical performance refers to the situations in which music is performed: the people who make music, listen to music and participate in non-musical ways in a music event all play important parts in the musical performance. While a culture might have generally accepted ideas about the definition of music (like in the case of Islamic countries), different groups within a single culture can perform very different kinds of music.

THE MUSICAL OBSERVATION

The musical observation is a form of research which combines two activities: observation and analysis. *Observation* will refer to the careful collection or documentation of events and materials as they occur in performance. Rather than attend an event and simply absorb the music, researchers listen to music with a heightened awareness of their surroundings, noticing and taking notes on not only the sounds, but also the sights, surroundings and even the smells and tastes of the performance.

Where and when do I do my musical observation?

Since we are looking at so many aspects of musical performance, we need to limit the scope of the musical observation to a manageable size. The observation paper should be about a single music event. For our purposes, we will define a *music event* as observable sound and behavior in a specific place and time. With such a broad definition, we can use nearly any event that has music in it as the subject for a musical observation. Popular topics for observation papers have included events which feature music prominently, such as: rock concerts, opera performances, bar bands, elementary school music classes, orchestra concerts, fraternity/sorority parties with "live" music, and student recitals.

Music does not have to be the most important aspect of a music event. In fact, music might account for only a small part of the total behavior you observe. Events in which music plays auxiliary role include: sporting events which have marching or "pep" bands, family gatherings, religious services, and parades.

The music event you observe should take place during the semester you are enrolled in a world music survey course. Many students ask, "why can't I write my paper about a concert I saw this past summer? I remember everything that happened during the show." You may remember many details about a concert that took place several months ago, but if you did not take detailed notes either during or immediately after the performance, you will not remember enough to write a successful musical observation. Most ethnomusicologists find that they can store details about a performance in their memory for about 24 hours. If they wait more than a day to write up their observations, more than half the details have been forgotten. After you complete your observation, try to write a rough draft immediately.

What do I look for in a music event?

Since the music event consists of both sound and behavior, there are many aspects we can use as the basis of our musical observation. Some of the categories that ethnomusicologists pay special attention to during a music event include: the participants in the event, musical instruments used, how the boundaries of the event are measured, and the use of movement and space.

Participants include the musicians involved in the music event, but depending on the situation, there can be a variety of other participants too. Spectators are important participants in many music events and can have profound effects on the performance. For example, in a football game, the spectators are often enlisted by the band to participate in cheers, songs and other musical activities as a way to build team spirit. Also, in blues concerts, the interaction be-

tween the crowd and audience affects the quality of the musician's performance.

Instruments can also play important roles in a music event. Besides their obvious musical contributions to a music event, instruments can bring a visual dimension to performance, as in the use of brightly shined cymbals in a marching band. In other cultures, some instruments are believed to have supernatural spirits associated with them. In Haiti, for example, drums used in *vodou* services must be ritually baptized before they can be used in a ceremony. Drums are both musical instruments and spiritual participants in *vodou* ceremonies. Depending on your musical event, you might be able to comment on some of the different ways instruments are put to use.

Boundaries within a music event are useful for breaking the event into manageable units. We isolate the music event in time with *markers* which signal the beginning and end of an event. Common beginning markers include the tuning of a symphony orchestra, raising the stage curtain, and dimming of the lights before a rock band enters the auditorium. Markers which signal the end of a performance include applause, bowing by performers, rasing the lights in an auditorium, or a marching band filing off a football field.

Cues mark the boundaries between different sections within the same musical piece. Cues can be visual in the case of a symphony conductor who communicates with the orchestra with a baton. Cues can also be audible as when a performer shouts "one more time" to signal the repeat of a musical phrase. Many observation papers begin with a hypothesis about the presence or absence of cues.

The use of body movement, or *kinesics* in a music event is another behavioral aspect warranting attention. *Kinesics* includes but is not limited to dance. (see Chapter 11 **Movement and Dance** for instruction on observing dance.) Other types of body movement include gestures, like shaking hands, rolling the eyes, shrugging the shoulders, arm waving and winking.

Kinesic features that warrant attention include the *body attitude* and *articulation*. A person's body attitude refers to the way the body is held and can be erect or slouched, rigid or loose. Articulation refers to where the body is bent; for example, at the neck, waist, knees, or elbows.

The use of space by participants, or *proxemics* of an event can give you plenty of material for a good observation project. It is often a good idea to draw a map of the area where your music event will take place and note arrangement of the fixed or immovable features of the performance space, such as the stage, walls, booths, etc. Also note the unfixed or movable features like tables and chairs, musical equipment, and other items which are not nailed down. One student wrote a paper about the use of space in a local bar and hypothesized that the fixed features of the bar made dancing difficult. She drew a map of the performance space, described the event and concluded that the problems she identified in the layout of the performance space affected the quality of the performance.

THE OBSERVATION PAPER

The work for the musical observation paper should be divided into three separate parts: the proposal, the fieldwork and the written paper. Your instructor may have different instructions for each of these parts, but the following description should answer some of the more commonly asked questions about the project.

The Paper Proposal

The paper proposal is the first step in the paper writing process and should consist of two parts: the topic and the hypothesis. When you choose a topic to study, make sure to include the following information in your proposal.

1) where the event will take place
2) who will participate
3) when will it take place
4) how will the observation be made (methods, equipment)

This will require you to do some looking around for a suitable event to observe before the paper proposal is due. Although most instructors give students freedom to choose a music event to study, the vast majority of students pick music events they have attended in the past, like parties, rock concerts, etc. Some fine papers come out of these topics, but most people who choose such familiar topics tend to miss some of their obvious features. It is easy to take some behavioral aspects for granted if you are already very familiar with a particular performance style. If at all possible, try to observe something that you have never experienced before.

Next, you should state your *hypothesis* for your musical observation. The *hypothesis* is a question you will ask about the music event you observe. Since the proposal will be completed before the actual music observation takes place, the *hypothesis* can be a rough guess. Nevertheless, try to formulate as specific a question as possible *before* you attend your music event. Even if you decide at a later date to change your *hypothesis*, you have already begun the process of thinking critically about the music event.

Doing Fieldwork

The fieldwork for the observation paper refers to the research that you do at the event itself. As a fieldworker, you will have to set up your *fieldsite* or location and prepare to carry out your observation.

First, you will have selected a place for your observation in your proposal. Although it may seem obvious, make sure to check beforehand to see that you can actually *do* the observing you proposed. Some students of mine once proposed to do fieldwork at a local bar where a blues musician was playing. They forgot to tell me that they were under the legal drinking age and were prevented from entering the bar by the bouncer at the door. Don't engage in any illegal activities to do your musical observation.

After the site is selected, you need to begin gathering information or data for your paper. The most important tool of the fieldworker is his/her notebook. Make sure to bring along a notebook and pencil for making notes during the performance. Take notes on the behavioral aspects mentioned above, details that relate to your *hypothesis* and any thoughts or questions that occur to you during the performance. Sometimes, these stray thoughts can be used as the basis of a new hypothesis. For example, one student who observed an indoor concert of his university's marching band noticed that the tubas in the band were polished so well that they reflected light throughout the auditorium. When he thought about this detail later, combined with the detailed notes he took during the performance, he realized that all of the movement during the band performance gave the impression that the band was doing one of their half-time shows despite the fact that the entire band was seated on a stage.

Many ethnomusicologists use tape recorders and cameras to record the music events they observe. With photos and tapes, it is possible to review the music event later to check the accuracy of your notes. Tapes and photos are only research aids, they are not substitutes for notetaking and observation during the music event. While most musical observation projects will not require you to make tape recordings, they can help you collect material in several different ways. First, if you are doing an observation paper on a small group of musicians or a single musician, you could interview them and collect information about their ideas of the music they perform. Interviews can help you refine your hypothesis since the musician's point of view often gives you unique insights to performance. Second, if you are doing a musical observation of friends or members of your family, you might want to collect information on family musical traditions and when and where music is performed in the home.

Doing an Interview

If you decide to interview the musicians you observe, you should take a few preparatory steps to make the most of your interview time.

First, get a tape cassette and tape recorder, preferably one with an external microphone. Familiarize yourself with its operation and make a test interview tape with a friend. This will help you decide where to place the recorder during your interview for the best possible recording.

Second, be sure to bring plenty of batteries and blank tape since both have been known to fail during interviews. Label your tapes with the date, name of your *informant* (the person to be interviewed) and announce the date, name and location of the recording on the beginning of the tape. If you misplace the tape and find it later, you can identify it easily.

Third, prepare some questions for your interview beforehand. You might not use all of your questions, but you will have a way of keeping the interview flowing if your informant is reserved. Last, if your informants are talkative, try not to interrupt them. Instead, have questions ready to lead them back to subjects that you want to hear more about. Once they get used to the idea of being tape recorded, most people lose their initial inhibitions and ignore the tape recorder. Since interviews will be about the music that your informants perform, they are *experts* and will probably have plenty to tell you about their art.

While sonic and visual records of performances are useful for remembering details of the event, you should exercise caution when using a recording device. Never record a musical performance or interview without the permission of the performers. There are laws protecting most public performances and you might be subject to legal action. Making secretive recordings not only threatens your relationship with your informants, but also makes it difficult for other researchers to gain their informant's trust in the future. When you are not sure whether to make a recording, *don't*.

Finally, you will notice that while you are observing your music event, you may be called upon to participate in the event. This is called **participant** *observation* and is a common research strategy used in ethnomusicology. Participant observation can allow you to experience the event as more than just a passive observer and can sometimes give you insights into the performance that would not otherwise occur to you. If you are attending a music event where people are dancing, you might dance a few times yourself to see if some significant behavior missed your attention. For one musical observation, a student studied an elementary school music class and learned the children's songs along with the class. She noticed that the students each had their own ways of participating in the learning process. Some students danced and moved their arms with the music, some concentrated on the teacher's example and others were not actively involved in the learning process at all. She then wrote her paper on the learning styles she observed in the classroom.

Participant observation is a useful tool for gaining insight to the motives and actions of participants, but you should be careful to allow enough time for observing if you decide to participate. If are singing, dancing or just listening to an event, make sure to balance the time spent participating with time devoted to taking notes. If your project involves observing music in a bar or party where alcohol is served, make sure to limit your consumption. In my research in Haiti, I am often called upon by my informants to drink shots of local rum when conducting interviews. After two rums, I have neither the ability nor the inclination to conduct a good interview. If I must drink during an event, I make sure to make one drink last as long as possible.

Writing the Observation Paper

When all of the research has been completed, you should start writing the paper as soon as possible. The paper should have three parts: introduction, body and conclusion.

The *introduction* should be a brief statement of the hypothesis of the paper and should not be more than a paragraph. In it, you should state the problem you will address in the paper. This gives the reader an idea of what to look for when you describe the event.

The *body* of the paper should contain detailed description of the music event. Introduce your description with a paragraph on where and when the event takes place and who is being studied. Sixty to seventy percent of your paper should be description of the event. You should mention behavioral aspects as they appear (like cues, markers, kinesics) but do not stop to analyze them in the body of the paper. Save your analysis for the conclusion.

You should also select a *voice* for your paper. Your topic might lend itself to a more conversational style of description rather than a formal, analytical one. In one observation paper, a student describes the use of space in a local bar. In her description section, she takes the reader on a walking tour of the bar, pointing out the prominent proxemic features. Her informal style was well suited for her paper and made it easier for the reader to imagine the use of space in the bar.

The *conclusion* should be an analysis of the event with particular attention to the original hypothesis. Did the hypothesis work or not? Did you discover a new question to address? In one observation of a blues band performance, a student hypothesized that the body movement of the blues performers would correspond to the mood of the music. In other words, she expected that fast music would be accompanied by fast body movement on the part of the musicians and slower music would be have correspondingly slower body movement and a relaxed body attitude. After a detailed description in the body of her paper, she concluded that her initial hypothesis was incorrect: the musicians held a rigid, disciplined body attitude throughout the concert, regardless of the speed of the songs played. Although her *hypothesis* did not produce the results she anticipated, the student was able to write a good paper due to the quality of her description and the flexibility of her conclusions.

CONCLUSION

From my experience, most students who take the introduction to world music course cite the observation paper as one of the more enjoyable and valuable parts of the course. If done with care, the paper can help you develop techniques for listening critically to music. Our hope is that students will continue to develop their critical listening skills after they leave the course. We also hope that in their exposure to different ways of thinking about music in the world music course, students will be able to appreciate different styles of music from around the world. (See Appendix C for example of Musical Observation Paper)

Acknowledgement

I have based this musical observation paper description on a similar assignment devised by Dr. Ruth M. Stone of Indiana University. I gratefully acknowledge her influence on this chapter. However, any errors or omissions are my responsibility alone.

Selected Annotated Bibliography

Berliner, Paul. 1981. *The Soul of Mbira*. Berkeley, CA: University of California Press.
Excellent ethnography of Shona people of Zimbabwe. Berliner uses the *mbira* (a hand-held musical instrument) as the focal point of his analysis of musical life among the Shona. Includes an appendix on how to build and play your own Shona *mbira*.

Blacking, John. 1973. *How Musical is Man?* Seattle: University of Washington Press.
A series of four essays which explore a wide range of musical and social issues. Blacking examines ideas about the biological and social origins of music.

Bohlman, Philip V. 1988. *The Study of Folk Music in the Modern World*. Bloomington, IN: Indiana University Press.
Bohlman argues that folk music is not a dying tradition, but rather a changing, modern phenomenon. Chapter Four, entitled "The Social Basis of Folk Music," discusses the importance of community and geographic location for the understanding of folk music. Chapter 5, "The Folk Musician," should be consulted by anyone writing a musical observations paper about an individual performer.

Denisoff, R. Serge and Peterson, Richard A., eds. 1972. *The Social Sounds of Change*. Chicago: Rand McNally.
A collection of essays exploring the music of social movements and its role in social change. Students observing rock concerts should consult this volume.

Herndon, Marcia and McLeod, Norma., eds. 1983. *Field Guide for Ethnomusicology*. Norwood, PA: Norwood Publications.
A detailed guide for ethnomusicological fieldwork. Important reading for students who wish to do a thorough musical observation paper.

Hood, Mantle. 1982. *The Ethnomusicologist*. 2nd. ed. Kent, Ohio: Kent State University Press.
An important book for anyone considering ethnomusicology as a career. Hood combines an insightful commentary on the discipline with a description of participant-observation as a field strategy. Includes information on microphone placement for recordings. See chapters on "Field Methods and the Human Equation, (197-246) and "Field Methods and the Technical Equation," (247-283).

May, Elizabeth., ed. 1981. *Musics of Many Cultures*. Berkeley: University of California Press.
Contains essays on music from around the world.

Merriam, Alan M. 1964. *The Anthropology of Music*. Evanston: Northwestern University Press.
One of the first books written for an undergraduate audience on the theories, methods and techniques of ethnomusicology. The first three chapters are especially interesting to students interested in ethnomusicological theory.

Nettl, Bruno. 1964. *Theory and Method in Ethnomusicology*. Glencoe, IL: The Free Press.
An advanced undergraduate textbook that explains how to conduct ethnomusicological fieldwork. Includes chapters on fieldwork, transcription of music, bibliography writing and use, musical instruments and some discussion of a few ethnomusicological theories.

_____. 1984. *The Study of Ethnomusicology*. Urbana, IL: University of Illinois Press.
A series of 29 short chapters on "issues and concepts" in ethnomusicology. Contains a bibliography of theoretical references and ethnographies about all types of music. A handy reference guide.

Reck, David. 1977. *Music of the Whole Earth*. New York: Scribner's.
An introductory text covering a wide range of topics. Reck includes instructions for making musical instruments from different cultures.

Stone, Ruth M. and Verlon L. 1979. Event, Feedback, and Analysis: Research Media in the Study of Music Events. *Ethnomusicology* 25(2):215-225.
For those interested in documenting their research with tape recorders, this article contains some helpful suggestions.

Titon, Jeff Todd, gen. ed. 1984. *Worlds of Music*, eds. James T. Koetting, David P. McAllester, David Reck and Mark Slobin. New York: G. Schirmer.
An introductory textbook for the study of world music. Chapters on Native American, African American, Eastern European, South Indian musics are written by ethnomusicological specialists. Some chapters include instructions for instrument building and performance. The final chapter describes ethnomusicological projects like the musical observation paper, musical journal and library research.

Wilson, William A. 1986. Documenting Folklore. IN *Folk Groups and Folklore Genres*, ed. Elliott Oring, pp. 225-254. Logan, UT: Utah State University Press.
Intended for collecting verbal folklore, but contains many helpful hints for recording written information and useful bibliographic citations.

CHAPTER 11
Movement and Dance: Non-verbal Clues About Culture and Worldview

Gail Matthews

MOVEMENT

In this guide you are learning that folklore involves artistic communication in groups. You have discovered that seemingly unimportant aspects of our culture such as jokes, games, and stories can reveal a great deal about human beings and their cultures. Yet there is another aspect of human behavior that we frequently overlook in our examination of expressive culture: human movement. We constantly communicate things about ourselves, our attitudes and our worldview without speaking a word; we frown, shake our heads, shrug, smile, and use our bodies to communicate often subtle information.

Because our culture does not stress the importance of non-verbal behavior, most Americans lack a sensitivity to the role that movement plays in everyday human communication—we usually only pay attention to movement when we watch a mime or a dancer. In order to get more out of our ethnographic observations, we need to practice looking specifically at human movement. Here is an exercise that will get you started. Try watching a television show with the volume turned down for five minutes and write down how the actors express their characters' personalities and advance the show plots with their movement (comedies are especially good for this exercise). Now turn the sound back up. In what ways does the communication that you observe hinge on timing, gestures, facial expressions, or physical events such as prat falls?

Our movements are not always in accordance with our words; all of us have had arguments with people who denied that they were angry, but whose tense and angry gestures belied their words. We often use movement to communicate information that contrasts with or contradicts what we are saying. Automobile ads may say you should buy their brand of car because their product has a superior engine, while the non-verbal cues tell you that you should buy this car because beautiful women will want to ride in it. Often times the non-verbal message is more accurate than the verbal one. We even have a proverb that states that *actions speak louder than words*.

As you can see, human movement is a vital part of our culture and should therefore be documented during our fieldwork. Just about any event that you examine will involve some movement: storytellers use hand and facial gestures, children's games entail jumping rope and hand play, festivals often include parades, religious rites involve sacred gestures such as crossing yourself, even the fabrication process of material culture involves specialized movements as things are hand made.

TRADITIONAL GESTURES

In addition to random or idiosyncratic motions in everyday life, we attach specific meanings to some motions that then become almost like words in their ability to communicate specific messages. Football referees signal penalties to on looking crowds without speaking a word, card players playing bridge give secret signals to their partners, Chicago stock market traders use hand gestures to communicate important transactions, and angered motorists sometimes *flip a bird*. These movements have been developed to communicate in situations where verbal communication is not feasible, where a secret code is important so that only in-group members will understand the message, or where the person doing the gesture does not want their (often socially unacceptable) message to be heard out loud.

You can make an inventory of American gestures

by watching people around you for several days. Pick a public place, such as a cafeteria, and watch for gestures. Be forewarned that human movement is difficult to write down on paper, but do not be afraid to try——you can enhance your descriptions by making simple drawings of the gestures that you see. If you own a video camera, have some friends over to your room for a party and set the camera in a corner where you can record some of the interaction. Then replay the tape and note each gesture that you see. With both of these exercises it is important to write down contextual information about who gestures to whom, and the nature of the setting.

This exercise must also include a summary of the gestures' meanings. First, write down what you think a gesture means, then ask the person who made the gesture what they were trying to communicate. Be as specific as you can——do not just say "she made a crazy sign to communicate that she thought he was crazy." Instead, give details, such as:

> Joan (18 year old college freshman) looks at Ken (her boyfriend, a 19 year old college freshman) and points to her left temple with her left index finger and circles the finger clockwise for two rotations. I thought that Joan was trying to tell Ken that he is crazy. When I questioned Joan, I discovered that she was in fact trying to tell Ken that all the pressure of mid-term testing is driving her crazy.

Your informants may have a difficult time explaining the meaning of their gestures because we do not often think about movement. Another problem that you might encounter is that many gestural meanings are difficult to put into words. Dancer Isadora Duncan reportedly once said, "If I could tell you what my dance means, then I wouldn't have to dance it!" Do not let these difficulties discourage you——you are an adventurous explorer navigating almost unchartered territory.

You can also collect a gestural repertoire that is unfamiliar to you. Talk with construction workers about how they communicate when working at a particularly noisy site, or ask a person who can speak and also knows sign language about how sign language differs from spoken language, or ask a priest about the meaning of gestures that they make while celebrating the mass.

Many of our gestures are culture specific. In other words, a gesture that might mean one thing to an American will mean something totally different to someone from another culture. For example, we think it is friendly to wave at people we know with our open palm facing outward in full view. If you wave this way at a person in Greece, they will proba-

bly become angry or hurt because for them this gesture is a vulgar insult that means "may you lose your five senses." You might want to work with someone from another culture and ask them about their gestures and compare how they differ from your own.

DANCE

Dance is perhaps the most artistic form of human movement; dancers can use their bodies to communicate abstract emotions or specific messages, but they also dance often just for the pleasure of physically experiencing motion. With the powerful image of Germans dancing on top of a crumbling Berlin Wall we discovered that dancers can effectively communicate emotions to an entire world that are too potent and complicated for words. Yet dance also plays an integral role in our immediate development of local community; little girls form cliques and perform line dances at 4th grade slumber parties, awkward adolescents grapple their way through the newness of dating while dancing at high school proms, sorority and fraternity members experience an exciting freedom from family surveillance at greek dances, and newlyweds symbolically say goodbye to their parents and hello to their new in-laws during wedding reception dances.

We learn how to dance in many contexts: from babysitters, older siblings and parents, at school, during slumber parties, at wedding receptions, at parties, in nightclubs, at square dances, and at home. For some people dance is a vital part of social life, for others dance is a very scary and often humiliating test of personal skill and competence. Some religious groups even believe that dance's physical sensuality is dangerous and forbid dancing. Dance involves a physical energy that has the power to evoke joy, embarrassment, and even disgust; surely something this powerful can tell us many interesting things about a group's or an individual's worldview.

Unlike gestures and everyday movement, dance usually only happens within a special event. The first step in studying dance is to find an event where dance usually occurs. Check around town——are there any dance clubs, square dances, aerobic dance classes, maypole dances, or upcoming weddings? You do not have to limit your study to only one kind of dance; sometimes we learn more about a culture when we compare it with another culture or our own culture. For instance, you could study the difference between dance at the reception after an Italian, Jewish or Polish wedding as opposed to the dance at a wedding where ethnicity or religiosity is not as important. Or, you might choose to study cheerleading, gymnastics,

Figure 1. At a small logging festival in western Washington, dancers perform a playful clogging routine for their audience. (Photograph courtesy of Robert Walls)

or military drills (e.g. ROTC), events that are closely related to dance, but are not defined as dance by our society. You might even try to look at the role of movement in an athletic event or music concert—do not forget that the audience is as much a part of the event as the cheerleader. For example, the audience may cheer or do a *wave* to celebrate a point score, or they might dance, flick lighters or play frisbee during a concert.

When you look at dance or any other movement, it is important to note more than just the surface details. Many studies of festivals, weddings, religious events, or parties are useless for dance ethnographers because they give detailed descriptions of the ceremony, the food, or the celebration, but when the dancing begins, they merely write "and then they danced." How did they dance? Were their steps light and delicate, or did they stomp their feet? Were their hand movements jerky or fluid? Did they dance in circles,

as individuals, or in straight lines? Did men and women dance together or separately? Your study of dance needs to provide answers to these kinds of questions or it will not make much sense to anybody who was not at the event. When you describe the dance, pretend that you are writing a letter to a martian who speaks English fluently, but has never been to the planet earth.

Dance ethnologist Judith Hanna developed a list of "relevant data categories" to help us remember often overlooked details about dance events.[1] Here are some of the things that Hanna thinks we should write about:

1) motive (e.g. the kind of occasion or reason for dancing)
2) setting (e.g. place, decorations, size of room)
3) season, day of week, time of day, sex and age of dancers

4) how many of the people at the gathering dance?
5) how do they learn to dance?
6) how much status or prestige good dancers have within the group?
7) how competitive the dance is?
8) how much individual creativity is allowed in the dance?
9) typical costume or clothes worn (do not forget the shoes)
10) typical music or instrumentation
11) tempo of the music
12) type of music
13) step names
14) importance of traditionality (or lack thereof)
15) duration of performance
16) dancer posture, and
17) repetition or variety of step.

Movements are often deceptive; they can look like one thing to the observer, but actually be another. It is therefore also important to try to do the dance. Experiencing a dance is often the only way that you can learn important details about how it is done and how it feels. Folklorists call this fieldwork technique *participant/observation*. Pay attention to the emotions that the dance evokes——is it playfully childlike or sexually provocative, militaristic and rule oriented or anarchic and free, mournfully sad or joyous? Double check your impressions of the dance with people who regularly do the dance——a movement that may seem sad to you might in fact be seductive for the culture group that actually does the dance. Make sure you interview some of the more talkative dancers and ask them what role this dance plays in their lives. Ask several dancers, because some people are very articulate about dance, while others have trouble verbalizing their knowledge and feelings.

All this information will be boring and pointless if you do not try to discover the meaning that the dance has for the people who do it. For example, several years ago I documented traditional dance in Western North Carolina. I used Hanna's "Relevant Data Categories" to note numerous details about the dance. This information has since proved useful to other dance scholars, but just gathering information would not have been enough for my project. I had to find out something about what the dance meant to the people in this region.

As I worked with the square dancers, I discovered that they were very upset about a new style of dance that had recently been introduced to the area. Their intense anger about the new dance style indicated to

me that the older style of dance had some special meaning that the local people did not want to lose. After interviewing the dancers I discovered that they objected to the new style of dance because they thought it was too rigid and squelched dancer creativity. I then went back to the detailed dance documentation that I had gathered and compared it with the opinions that dancers had expressed to me during my interviews. I concluded that the older style of dancing was important to local dancers because it combined two elements of individual freedom of movement and group cooperation to execute complicated figures, whereas the new style of dance had all dancers doing the same step at the same time, like the Radio City Music Hall Rockettes. The dancers liked their old style of dance because it provided a balance between individualism and community; this balance was perfectly suited to their farm lifestyle in which people needed to work both on their own and cooperate with each other working in groups. The new style of dance made them feel like cogs in a machine. I discovered that as these dancers argued about this new-fangled dance form they were in fact also processing their larger fears and anxieties about urbanization and rapidly changing lifestyles in what had traditionally been a rural farm community and wildlife preserve.

In order to find the meanings of a dance, you have to form questions in your mind, such as: Why do these people care so much about their dance? What is this dance doing for them that they cannot get by doing something else? or, What do the differences between these two dance traditions indicate about the different worldviews that these two groups have? If you can answer big, meaning-oriented questions like these, you will have really accomplished something significant.

Reference Cited

I would like to thank LeeEllen Friedland and Colin Quigley for their assistance in compiling this bibliography.

[1] For further reading, see Judith Lynne Hanna, Ethnic Dance Research Guide: Relevant Data Categories. *CORD NEWS* 1973:42-7.

Selected Bibliography

I have tried to provide a broad range of publication citations on dance styles that might interest the reader and basic writings about dance ethnography. Researchers may also want to consult local school or university audio/visual holdings for films and videotapes on traditional dance, festival, and other forms of movement.

Andrews, Edward D. 1940. *The Gift to be Simple: Songs, Dances, and Rituals of the American Shakers*. New York: J. J. Augustin.

Blacking, John. 1973. *How Musical is Man?* Seattle: University of Washington Press.

Buckland, Theresa. 1983. Definitions of Folk Dance—Some Explorations. *Folk Music* 4(4):315-332.

Dalsemer, Robert. 1982. *West Virginia Square Dances*. New York: Country Dance and Song Society.

Dart, Mary. 1987. Cuing in Contradance. *Folklore Forum* 20(1-2):85-107.

Dunin, Elsie Ivaicich. 1981. Change in South Slav-American Dance. *CORD Dance Research Journal* 14(1-2):59-61.

Friedland, LeeEllen. 1983. Disco: Afro-American Vernacular Performance. *CORD Dance Research Journal* 15(2):27-35.

_____. 1987. Square Dance. *International Encyclopedia of Dance*.

_____. 1985. 'Tanisn Is Lebn': Dancing in Eastern European Jewish Culture. *CORD Dance Research Journal* 17(2):77-81.

_____. 1986. Dance: Popular and Folk Dance. *The Encyclopedia of Religion*. Ed. Mircea Eliade, pp. 212-221.

Goines, Margaretta Bobo. 1971. African Retentions in the Dance of the Americas. *CORD Dance Research Monograph* I:207-229.

Halpert, Herbert. 1969. *Christmas Mumming in Newfoundland; Essays in Anthropology, Folklore, and History*. Toronto: University of Toronto Press.

Hanna, Judith Lynne. 1973. Ethnic Research Guide: Relevant Data Categories. *CORD News* VI(1):42-47.

_____. 1979. *To Dance Is Human: A Theory of Nonverbal Communication*. Chicago: University of Chicago Press.

Kaeppler, Adrienne. 1977. Polynesian Dance as 'Airport Art'. *CORD Dance Research Annual* VII:71-85.

Kligman, Gail. 1981. *Calus: Symbolic Transformation in Roumanian Ritual*. Chicago: University of Chicago Press.

Kealiinohomoku, Joann. 1972. Folk Dance. IN *Folklore and Folklife*. Ed. Richard M. Dorson, Chicago: University of Chicago Press.

_____. 1976. A Comparison of Dance as a Constellation of Motor Behaviors Among African and United States Negroes. *CORD Dance Research Annual* VII:15-181.

March, Stephen and David Holt. 1977. Chase That Rabbit. *Southern Exposure* 5:44-47.

Matthews, Gail. 1983. Cutting a Dido: A Dancer's-Eye View of Mountain Dance In Haywood County, N.C. Master's Thesis, Folklore Institute, Indiana University.

Quigley, Colin. 1985. *Close To the Floor*. St. John's, Newfoundland: Memorial University of Newfoundland.
_____. 1984. A Dance Event Ethnography: Roller Skating at Venice Beach. *UCLA Journal of Dance Ethnography* 8:21-33.

Royce, Anya Peterson. 1977. *The Anthropology of Dance*. Bloomington, IN: Indiana University Press.

Schneider, Gretchen Adel. 1969. *Pigeon Wings and Polkas: The Dance of the California Miners*. New York: Dance Perspectives Foundation.

Staub, Shalom. 1978. An Inquiry into the Nature of Yemenite Jewish Dance. *CORD Dance Research Annual* IX:157-169.

_____. 1985 Repertoire, Values, and Social Meaning in the Wedding Dances of a Yemenite Jewish Village in Israel. *CORD Dance Research Journal* 17(2):59-64.

Sweet, Jill. 1978. Space, Time and Festival: An Analysis of a San Juan Event. *CORD Dance Research Annual* IX:169-185.

_____. 1979. Play, Role Reversal and Humor: Symbolic Elements of a Tewa Pueblo Navaho Dance. *CORD Dance Research Journal* 12(1):3-13.

Waterman, Richard. 1960. *Focus on Dance*. Washington: National Dance Association of the American Alliance for Health, Physical Education and Recreation.

Zeitlin, Steven. 1982. The Wedding Dance. in *A Celebration of American Family Folklore*. New York: Pantheon, 213-221.

CHAPTER 12
Folklife and Material Culture

Robert E. Walls

All human societies must come to terms with the physical environment in which they live. In the process, societies have developed many variable strategies and methods to shape the natural world for their own ends. It is the transformation of natural resources to cultural artifacts that we commonly call *material culture*—those tangible creations that are based upon and incorporate human needs, ideas, values, and beliefs.

When folklorists look at material culture they see groups of people shaping, changing, and creating according to their needs and desires, guided by notions of tradition and what seems appropriate in a given setting. They see material culture for its functional value, its ability to serve a utilitarian purpose in everyday life. But they also see material culture as a communicative resource, used to transmit ideas which otherwise are difficult to express: a group's shared conception of beauty; a person's status in a community, or their resistance to authority or conformity; or someone's relationship to deity and all things sacred.

Folklorists are primarily concerned with three crucial aspects of the realm of material culture: product, process, and people. *Products* are the tangible results of people involved in the process of folk creation, ranging from something as small as an earring to something as all-encompassing as a regional landscape. *Process* involves the entire act of creating: from the realization of a need, to the planning and actual construction of an artifact, to the eventual evaluation of the artifact's suitability, as judged by both creator and audience. Inherent to this process is some notion of tradition or continuity. Tradition should *not* be viewed simply as old and unchanging ideas which are deeply rooted in time. Instead, tradition should be seen as a continuous process of creating meaning based on a group's shared experi-ences, a process that utilizes the old and the new to make things seem significant. (A handmade quilt can still be a folk artifact, even if century-old designs are replaced by sewn pictures of contemporary houses and events which are locally significant.) *People* are the individual workers, and the groups to which they belong—the *folk*—who actually create things. Understanding people means comprehending their every influence on both the product and the process, and their reasons for grasping tradition (and providing innovation) in the manner that they do.

It is the folkloric nature of product, process, and people that makes folk artifacts stand apart from mass-produced items so characteristic of our industri alized world. Understanding this, you will begin to notice why quilts and quilting are readily distinguish-able from Sears blankets and Saturday shopping, why Norwegian-American log buildings distinctly stand apart from prefabricated houses, and why a small Louisiana town's Cajun crawfish barbecue is far removed from a suburban family's visit to a neighbor-ing McDonalds.

IDENTIFYING MATERIAL FOLK CULTURE

Folklorists frequently break down material culture into separate categories. These categories, however, are usually artificial ones, imposed upon a particular set of objects for analytical reasons. They should by no means be seen as discrete or mutually exclusive, and often their boundaries seem to blur to such a degree that any attempt at categorization seems futile. But for the purposes of basic collection and analysis, some order may be gained by dividing material folk culture into the categories of folk architecture, folk art, folk craft, foodways, and clothing.

Folk architecture consists of artifacts—usually buildings—in a traditional context, with their forms and functions on a specific cultural landscape. Folk

107

architecture is based on traditional non-academic design, with construction techniques learned through oral communication or by imitation. Such architecture is built by *untrained* individuals or craftsmen utilizing materials which can be obtained locally. The form and layout of folk structures is generally based on tradition, and consequently some variation occurs as builders adapt the *mental template* to fit their own specific needs. Specific forms, layouts, and construction techniques are often limited in their geographical range, linked to a particular region or ethnic group. Folk architecture, then, is distinct from academic architecture, which is usually designed by trained architects, and from popular or vernacular architecture which is usually derived from blueprints or some sort of prefabricated plans.

Structures which can be considered as folk architecture often include hewn log houses, unhewn log cabins, some types of frame houses, barns, smokehouses, fences, walls, corrals, and so on. Once these structures are identified and described, the researcher can try to decipher how the physical environment and the region's and builder's cultural heritage has affected their construction, form, function, and use. They can then map their geographical distribution and diffusion through time in order to discover broad cultural patterns. The social aspects of folk housing (house or barn-raisings, uses of specific structures, reasons for remodeling, etc.) are all documented as well, including the nature of decorative or aesthetic characteristics.

Both *folk arts* and *folk crafts* employ traditional techniques, designs, and forms and use locally available materials. However, many folklorists might say that the only safe way to distinguish between the two is to note that in folk art aesthetic concerns generally override any need for practical functions, while in folk craft utilitarian concerns dominate. However, even this is a great oversimplification of the problem, and the dichotomy is rarely that easy to distinguish. If one *had* to distinguish between the two, on might focus on the creator's apparent or stated intentions. Folk art, then, could be defined as the manipulation of the material environment for the purpose of making an expressive or artistic statement, usually within the boundaries of the aesthetic conventions of a specific group of people (e.g., the decorative features which often adorn gravestones of a particular group, community, or region; or certain decorative arts such as Norwegian rosemaling or Ukrainian Easter eggs). Folk craft could be defined as the manipulation of the material environment for the purpose of creating an item that has significant

practical use in the activities of everyday life (e.g., furniture, fine leather saddles produced for cowboys, small wooden boats used by fishermen). Still, you will quickly notice that various items defy ready labeling: quilts, decorated ceramic containers, duck decoys, etc. Perhaps the most interesting way to identify a particular object is to ask the creator or the user——their answer may illuminate the entire process behind the item in question.

Foodways consist of a certain selection of foods, consumed on an everyday basis or only on special occasions, that are usually procured, prepared, and consumed in some traditional manner, unlike the consumption of mass-produced (*store-bought*) foods. The family, regional, ethnic, or religious group that shares in these foodways often feels some strong identification with the food and the process and events behind its eventual consumption.

Clothing serves obvious practical functions on the everyday level of existence. But clothes also communicate. What a person wears is an overt presentation of self to all those around them, marking that person as a member of one group or another, or marking their position within that group (e.g., gender, religion, ethnicity, occupation, class). What a folklorist might call folk costume is not necessarily homemade, but it is usually at least modified by the wearer and worn in some combination with other articles of clothing in such a manner (according to informal rules for dressing) as to make the wearer's group affiliation unmistakable. Folk costume must be distinguished from popular fashion; one will not see such clothing advertised for sale on T.V. or in magazines.

Finally, folklorists often use the term *folklife* when describing the totality of traditional life in a given area, rural or urban. Folklife encompasses *all* aspects of material folk culture, as well as all associated oral and customary traditions. Folklife studies describe the interconnectedness of a specific group's material, oral, and customary lore, be it in a small New York City neighborhood, the rolling hills and farmlands of southern Indiana, the bayous of Louisiana, the mountainous ranching country of the Far West, or the fishing communities of Puget Sound.

DESCRIBING THE CONTEXT OF YOUR STUDY

All cultural artifacts are embedded in a complex web of interrelationships, and it is of vital importance to learn about and understand those relationships before making assumptions and attempting interpretation. Proper documentation and comprehension of the social and cultural context in which the material object you are studying occurs will allow you to see why that object is deemed valuable, why it is significant, why it *makes sense* to the people who created it.

Description of **context** is more than just a simple who, what, when, where, why, and how. In order to thoroughly describe the relevant people, product, and process you must think about the different dimensions of context——the social, the cultural, the historical, the psychological, the economic, the ecological, the ideological. Try looking at the object of your research in light of the following three-way scheme: the immediate context; the historical context; and the context of the larger sphere of events in the modern world.

The *immediate context* includes the realm of social relationships and cultural significance that currently surrounds the object you are studying. Consider the individual creator and the widening spheres of influence on their activity: personal life, family, community, region, and society. How do their personal motivations, their personalities, their values and beliefs inform their work? How does the object fit into their life? What role does it play? How did they learn their skill, and do their individual tastes vary from others creating or doing the same thing? What forces affect the choices or compromises they must make in the act of creation? Does their family, the local community, or the region influence their work? How does modern mass culture or society affect their thinking? What do they think their role in life is?

Consider the group to which the specific tradition of creative activity seems to belong: family, community, region, religion, occupation, age, or gender. How does the individual fit into this group? Does the group seem to support the individual's activity? Why has the traditional activity developed in this particular group? How does the activity reflect the nature of the group——its beliefs, values, social relationships, etc.? What does the activity say about gender roles and relationships within the group? How does the group evaluate finished products? Why is the tradition important or significant in these peoples' eyes? Why does the tradition seem to be meaningful——is it because of religious beliefs, the sense of community gained through participation, or the tradition's ability to make a statement about the group to others? Does the individual and the group find that pleasure or meaning is derived from the product or the process, or both? Are there local oral or customary traditions associated with the material tradition?

The *historical context* includes information about change or continuity over long periods of time. What forces have created changes in the object and its social context? Why do some things remain unchanged? What does this say about the individual creator or the group and their place in the changing world? What does this say about social and cultural change in the family, the community, the region, or the nation?

The *context of the larger sphere of world events* addresses questions of why you, why folklorists, or why anyone would be interested in this particular aspect of material folk tradition. What does this tradition mean to us, as outsiders from the group——why are we interested? Why do Americans seem to appropriate the traditions of others, past and present? What needs are we satisfying? Why do we value the handmade over the mass produced, the rural made over the urban made? Why do we need to incorporate other peoples' traditional material things into our own lives in the form of souvenirs, even photographs? Why do material objects based on the traditions of others seem so necessary to *our* lives?

SOME EXAMPLES OF MATERIAL FOLK CULTURE IN CONTEXT

Norwegian-American Barn

Some architectural structures in rural areas of the United States are based on distinct Old World building traditions. The barn pictured in Figure 1 is a good example of this, as its form and construction closely follow a tradition of barn building in parts of Norway. This specific barn, however, is located in western Washington State in an area heavily populated by Norwegian immigrants and their descendants. Built in the late nineteenth century, this log barn is solidly constructed, with full-dovetail notching tightly securing the corners. It makes use of locally available materials, such as cedar and fir logs, and durable cedar shakes for the roof. The builder's decision to construct this type of barn was based on several practical reasons. He could take advantage of easily obtained local materials and do the work himself, thereby saving money. And the builder could use the mental template he had in his head, derived from Norwegian tradition, to construct a relatively small barn that would be useful in a hilly terrain and just large enough for the family's small number of livestock and the amount of hay needed for their upkeep. What truly makes the barn type unique in comparison to other log barns in America is the fact that it has no loft, only a *bridge* over the dirt floor, so that loose hay could be easily stacked without the use of

Figure 1. Norwegian-American barn in western Washington State. (Photograph by Robert E. Walls)

any mechanical devices and thrown down off the bridge for storage or for the animals underneath.

Aside from functional considerations, what else could one say about this barn? For one, it shows the builder's resistance to things American, or things modern. He made a decision not to build a barn like other types of barns already in the area, and chose not to use milled lumber for construction (which was certainly available at the time). This builder seemed to be tenaciously holding on to something of his Norwegian past. Today, the family continues to maintain the barn, even though they have less and less practical use for it as time goes on. But the barn remains an important subject of family memories, a reminder of family stories, a symbolic but tangible link to their Norwegian heritage.

Of course, there are plenty of other types of folk architecture to document, keeping in mind their functional attributes and what they reveal about the lives of their builders and users. One could look at the various types of smokehouses throughout the American South and what they reveal about the

continuity of foodways. Adobe construction has been used for centuries in the arid Southwest, and some interesting comparisons could be made between the ways in which Native Americans, Hispanics, and Anglos have tended to use it. Ranch gates and split-rail fences have always had much utilitarian value, but today they also serve other aesthetic and social purposes as well. One could consider changes in the history of individual folk houses, looking at the ways in which they were remodeled, and the reasons for doing so. (Was a building enlarged, sided, or changed in some way for practical reasons, or because the owners re-evaluated their status in the community? How were the rooms in a house organized and why?) Are there any recognizable patterns to the buildings on your local regional landscape? Can these buildings be connected in some way to regional identity?

Consider folk architecture in the sphere of wider events in the modern world. Today, log houses are often moved into the center of towns to serve as prominent public symbols of the area's pioneer heritage. Why is this happening? What does it say about our relationship to the past? Obviously, houses built today are much different from the past in terms of construction and the layout of rooms. But why are they different, and what social reasons could account for this? If owning a house is truly part of the *American dream*, then what does all this say about the American dream, past and present?

Tree-stump Tombstones

Tombstones and the material customs of cemeteries vary throughout the country. In the limestone belt of southern Indiana, a tradition of carving tree-stump tombstones arose among stone carvers during the last decades of the nineteenth century. (See Figure 2) Stone carvers generally were employed in local mills to carve work that later adorned buildings throughout the United States, but occasionally they found the time to carve things like tombstones on the side.

Whether these stone carvers could be called folk artists or folk craftsmen seems beside the point— they were definitely skilled individuals who applied their talents to create objects that were both functional and artistic. Consider the rich religious and regional symbolism that these tombstones exhibit. The broken-off tree stump represented an end to life, and frequently branches off the stump represented the number of children that were born to the individual

Figure 2. Tree-stump tombstone in southern Indiana. (Photograph by Robert E. Walls)

who was buried. Vines, doves, lilies, and Christmas ferns all have enduring symbolic significance in the Christian world. And Indiana's regional heritage is amply reflected in numerous carvings of spinning wheels, long rifles, hunting dogs, and axes, all of which are strongly symbolic of the domestic skills and backwoods abilities of the state's pioneers.

Hmong Story Cloths

Before the Vietnam War had disrupted their way of life, the Laotian Hmong had for centuries produced a traditional textile art form called *paj ntaub*, a colorful needlework that decorated Hmong clothing. The paj ntaub on a person's clothing served to identify the wearer's kinship relations and the region from which they came. However, after their exodus through Thai refugee camps and eventually into the United States, the Laotian Hmong developed a new variation on their traditional needlework, as they started making embroidered *story cloths*. (See Figure 3) These story cloths *tell*, in pictorial terms, a narrative of the Hmong's plight in recent years, from their existence as village farmers before the war, to their harrowing flight from attackers and escape across the Mekong River, to their internment in the Thai camps. Yet while the cloths tell the same general story, each varies somewhat according to the experiences of the individual needleworker. Some cloths tell other stories, like favorite folktales, or they pictorially represent the Hmong's conception of the zoological world as they knew it in Laos, a sort of ecological portrait with mammals, birds, insects, and plants. Today, Hmong-American men and women make a modest living creating and selling these cloths, but they also use them as ways to express their changing identity and their sense of historical consciousness, not only to Americans who see and purchase their art but also to their own children, born since the exodus from Southeast Asia.

Department Store Art

Some forms of folk art seem to emerge spontaneously, without any clearly evident basis in tradition, even in modern urban settings. Yet these forms certainly are traditional. To illustrate this, take the case of a specific example of decorative art that was used in a large department store in Seattle, Washington (see Figure 4). This particular piece of art was the inspired creation of three or four sales clerks who thought that a barren counter needed some color for an upcoming folkloric event,

Figure 3. A Laotian Hmong-American story cloth from Seattle. (Photograph by Robert E. Walls)

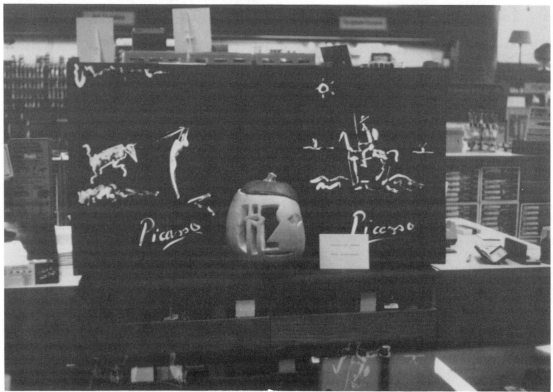

Figure 4. Department store art in Seattle. (Photograph by Robert E. Walls)

The Emergence of Folklore in Everyday Life

Halloween. Incorporating both aspects of folk tradition (a Halloween pumpkin) and *high* art (Picasso's *Don Quixote* and his cubist style), the clerks were able to produce a work that follows a long tradition in commercial stores: displays which are unique, artful, and aimed at a particular audience, in this case people who purchase art supplies. The display was fully functional in that it effectively attracted people and sold products. Yet, at the same time, the display served to poke fun at the more conventional, mass-produced forms of advertising. Even more importantly, the display demonstrated the creativity of sales clerks in their workplace——individuals who are not generally thought of as talented or creative.

There are so many more possible examples of folk art and craft that could be explored, from basketry to boat building, from unique lawn decorations to wooden chain carvings, from traditional American Indian textiles to the religious wood carvings of Hispanic santos, from the symbolic uses of beehives in Mormon material culture to the world of puppets as playful and often grotesque material representations of ourselves. So long as we bear in mind functional considerations, aesthetic choices, and the nature of the socio-cultural climate, we can see how an object as seemingly mundane as a quilt can serve as a practical household item, a family heirloom, a means to facilitate social interaction (as in quilting bees), and as a way to make an artistic statement.

Cajuns and Crawfish

Customary foodways and food-sharing events are often seen as expressions of community which reinforce local values, group affiliation, and status. For example, in southern Louisiana, Cajuns, a French-speaking minority, frequently enjoy crawfish——procured from local waters——as an addition to their meals. Now crawfish is not universally looked upon by Americans as a delicacy——many people in fact assert that crawfish are not fit for human consumption. Additionally, although you would not suspect it today with the widespread popularity of *Cajun* foods as restaurant fare, there has also been a good deal of prejudice against Cajuns, who are times stereotyped as crude, ignorant, backwoods-living people. Understandably, over time Cajuns have developed a certain sense of identity with crawfish due to their parallel low status in the eyes of the larger world. So by consuming crawfish——especially in group events such as family affairs and community festivals——Cajuns maintain a sense of group identity and solidarity. They are using the crawfish as a symbol of regional culture, and especially as a highly visible public symbol of their willingness to combat in a playful way the negative stereotype that outsiders have of Cajuns.

Many regions of the country, as well as ethnic and religious peoples dispersed throughout, have their own special food traditions. How might you document and analyze the cultural, historical, economic, ecological, ideological, and social elements of soul food consumption among African-Americans, or the use of salmon among Native and Euro-Americans in the Pacific Northwest, or the ways in which religious and ethnic groups maintain traditional foodways in non-traditional settings?

Bikers' Clothing

Clothes can be the most obvious and yet most subtle way of presenting our sense of *self* to others, our image of what we think we are or want to be. Take the motorcycle gang pictured in Figure 5, with their leather jackets and vests, flannel shirts, jeans, western boots, and numerous patches and insignia. Their attire certainly has practical aspects as durable clothing for outdoor wear. Yet is there any doubt that these individuals are members of an exclusive group, one that envisions itself as rough, tough, and potentially dangerous? The clothing is certainly not entirely *homemade*, but it is modified and worn in such a combination as to make the message clear. Of course this same pattern of dressing, with variations, is also followed by the many contemporary inner-city gangs in places such as Los Angeles, New York, and Chicago.

Other groups exhibit specific patterns of dress. Many loggers of the Pacific Northwest routinely wear in their work and even leisure time spiked boots called *corks*, *stagged* pants (with the bottom hem cut off as a safety precaution), suspenders, and a striped *hickory* shirt——all of which marks these individuals as members of an exclusive occupational group. Moreover, when you see someone wearing jeans, a wide belt buckle, western *cowboy* boots, a shirt with a bola, and a cowboy hat, could you make a reasonable guess as to what part of the country they might come from? What could you say about the attire of punk rockers, or religious groups such as the Amish in Pennsylvania or Hasidic Jews in New York City, or even students who modify their clothing according to the newest fads?

FOLKLIFE STUDIES

A general folklife study is perhaps the most difficult way to look at material folk culture. Such an approach normally requires extensive documentation and

Figure 5. Bikers in the Pacific Northwest. (Photograph by Robert E. Walls)

historical research, a total immersion into the folk environment to discover the patterns of material folk culture over time. This is a time-consuming process for even a small geographic area. Still, if you feel ambitious enough to undertake such a project, consult some of the works listed in the research bibliography to look at representative studies.

A few possible types of folklife study can be suggested. One could try to document the architecture, the arts and crafts, the foodways, and the clothing traditions of a rural farming or ranching area with which one is familiar. Or one could examine the material, customary, and oral traditions of a particular occupational group such as fishermen in Chesapeake Bay, or a religious group such as Mormons in the Far West, or an ethnic group such as Finns in the Upper Midwest or Germans in Missouri or southern Indiana. One could also document the material, customary, and oral traditions of an older inner-city neighborhood, looking at the ways people modify and name the places they live (inside and out), how they celebrate their sense of community and religious identity (e.g., festivals, religious events, the use of yard shrines), how they use any tradition to make their often crowded urban existence a more pleasant experience.

Throughout any of these kinds of projects you would want to keep in mind questions about what specifically makes this group of people or this region seem special or unique. How is the cultural landscape different from other locales? How does the area compare to other similar areas in the same city, or in another city? How does your area compare to other areas of the country? What do these traditions reveal about the area's sense of place? Why do we, as modern Americans, see certain rural or urban areas—such as Appalachia, the Far West, Texas, or the Bronx—as special, different, and unique compared to other similar areas of the country?

FINDING YOUR RESEARCH TOPIC

Obviously, preparation is the key to a successful project. Read through some of the relevant suggested literature beforehand and look at the photographs. By doing so, you'll have a more clear picture of precisely what you will be looking for, and some ideas of what to do when you find it. The more you know beforehand, the better your research will be, and little time will be wasted asking needless questions.

As the preceding examples amply demonstrate, material folk culture is all around us——we have only to open our eyes and carefully examine our local environment. Think of yourself as an investigative reporter. Look around when you walk or drive about the area in which you live. Examine people's houses from the street, watch what people wear, think about the foods that are locally available. Look for stories or leads in the newspaper. Read some local history books or look through the relevant files that may exist in your town or county library. Go to fairs, markets, or any place where people seem to engage in or sell the results of their creative activities. Check out some of the local cemeteries and inspect some of the older tombstones, and notice if there are any burial customs that seem folkloric.

Ask other people for information, starting with your friends, your neighbors, your family. Ask your professor for leads; someone else may have done a project previously that you could do better. Contact your local state or city folk arts council and explain to them your needs. Go to nearby museums, look at their collections of local things, and talk to the curators. Call up a local historian, someone who probably isn't an academic but surely knows the region and its people. Call up some local newspaper reporters, since they may know of relevant stories they have done in the past. (They may even want to do a story on your project!) Talking to people will not only provide valuable leads but also give you a name to use when you eventually introduce yourself to the people you'll be documenting——a common link to establish your credibility. When you do eventually find someone, call them before visiting to set up a convenient meeting time; you don't want to have to rush the occasion. However, don't necessarily latch on to the very first person or thing you find. Think carefully about the people, process, and product, and if your discovery is really a valid subject of inquiry as material *folk* culture. If your subject seems to be something of a *revival* (i.e. an older tradition that had more or less disappeared, but was recently revived by modern-day enthusiasts), then frame your investigation appropriately, asking questions that will get to the heart of the revival and its place in modern life. How is it different from the past? Why are people participating in the revival? Is the revival significant to a community of people?

DOCUMENTING YOUR RESEARCH TOPIC

Documentation of material folk culture can be done very poorly or very well, depending upon your skills, energy, and means available to you. At the very least, you should have a pencil and paper (preferably a blank sketch pad) so that you can take notes, make sketches, diagrams, and maps. It is also important (especially when documenting buildings) to have a tape measure, a compass, and a ruler or some recognizable object such as a pen for scale in photographs.

A camera is the next most important item. Instamatics will do in a pinch, providing you use a flash when necessary, and stand close enough to objects to get good clear pictures. (If finances are a problem, remember that they even have disposable cameras now, which certainly are better than no camera at all.) If at all possible, try to use a single lens reflex camera, preferably with a zoom lens (e.g., 35-135mm) that will give you wide angle perspectives and telephoto capacity. If the lens has a macro feature, use it for extreme close-ups of details; macros are particularly handy for on-the-spot copying of family photographs. Video cameras can also be excellent documentary tools, especially if you are investigating material folk culture in the context of social events such as a quilting bee or a puppet show, or food preparation and consumption at a local festival or family gathering.

If you have the money, take as many photographs as possible, especially if photographing something you may not have access to conveniently. Think about context when you photograph, and document as many aspects of people, product, and process as you can. Think about your photographic needs before purchasing your film: color print film is convenient for including prints with your paper; color slides will be essential for presentations; black and white film will give you the best range for shooting under variable lighting conditions, but it can be expensive to print.

A tape recorder is essential if you will be interviewing people over a long period of time, say for several hours. Be sure that you know how to use the machine prior to the interview, and always ask permission to tape record someone's comments. Large, bulky tape recorders tend to intimidate people who have never been interviewed, so try to use a small machine. When interviewing, talk to people like you would in any normal situation, but try to direct the conversation to the matters at hand. Be patient and listen. Talking about yourself for half the interview will not help you record the details you need to get. Have a list of questions to draw from so that you won't forget to ask about some crucial information. Think about the questions carefully, as they will enable you to eventually produce an accurate and complete portrait of your subject in context.

After the initial documentation is done, begin to assemble other sorts of contextual material, background data that will allow you to broaden your perspective and fill in missing gaps. Look for relevant information in local history books and library files. If you are investigating a specific building, contact your local county land office or a state historic preservation officer for assistance——they just might have a file with information on your building. And to place your work into the wider sphere of folklore scholarship, be sure to compare your documentation with the photographs and information available in books and articles which deal specifically with material folk culture, such as those listed in the following research bibliography.

Selected Annotated Bibliography

The following journals are important sources for articles on folklore and material culture: *Material Culture* (formerly *Pioneer America*), *Winterthur Portfolio*, *Pennsylvania Folklife*, *Vernacular Architecture Newsletter*, *Historical Archaeology*, *Foxfire*, *Journal of American Folklore*, *Western Folklore*, *Southern Folklore*. Many regional folklore and historical journals can be important sources as well.

1) Overviews of Material Culture

Bronner, Simon J. 1986. *Grasping Things: Folk Material Culture and Mass Society in America*. Lexington: University Press of Kentucky.
Very useful for understanding the place of art, craft, and architecture in modern American society.

Deetz, James. 1977. *In Small Things Forgotten: The Archeology of Early American Life*. Garden City, N.Y:Anchor Press.
Excellent introduction, with emphasis on New England and East Coast. Especially good for gravestones and architecture. Important for understanding the link between historical archaeology and folklife research.

Glassie, Henry. 1977. Meaningful Things and Appropriate Myths: The Artifact's Place in American Studies. *Prospects* 3:1-49.
A complex but rewarding essay that links artifact study to the study of humanities in general.

Hall, Patricia and Charlie Seemann, eds. 1987. *Folklife and Museums: Selected Readings*. Nashville: The American Association for State and Local History.
Many good essays on folk, ethnic, art, regional, and living history museums, and the interpretation of their artifacts.

Roberts, Warren E. 1972. Fieldwork: Recording Material Culture. IN *Folklore and Folklife: An Introduction*, ed. Richard M. Dorson, pp. 431-444. Chicago: University of Chicago Press.
Excellent introduction to the methods used in recording essential details.

St. George, Robert Blair, ed. 1988. *Material Life in America, 1600-1860*. Boston: Northeastern University Press.
A collection of articles on material culture studies in the Eastern U.S. Covers architecture, crafts, clothes, and foodways.

Schlereth, Thomas J., ed. 1985. *Material Culture: A Research Guide*. Lawrence: University Press of Kansas.
See especially the chapters by Bronner on folklife, Upton on vernacular architecture, and Lewis on landscape. An excellent resource for further sources.

2) Folklife Studies

Attebery, Louie W. 1985. A Contextual Survey of Selected Homestead Sites in Washington County. IN *Idaho Folklife: From Homesteads to Headstones*, ed. Louie W. Attebery, pp. 129-142. Salt Lake City: University of Utah Press.

Bronner, Simon J. 1985. Researching Material Folk Culture in the Modern American City. IN *American Material Culture And Folklife: A Prologue and Dialogue*, ed. Simon J. Bronner, pp. 221-244. Ann Arbor: UMI Research Press.
Excellent discussion of folk artifacts and community life in urban settings.

Carter, Thomas and Carl Fleischhauer. 1988. *The Grouse Creek Cultural Survey: Integrating Folklife and Historic Preservation Field Research*. Washington, D.C: Library of Congress.
The focus is a small Mormon ranching community in contemporary Utah. Excellent documentation of ranching, architecture, and foodways.

Clements, William M. and Frances M. Malpezzi. 1984. *Native American Folklore, 1879-1979: An Annotated Bibliography*. Athens, OH: Swallow Press.
A good reference for further sources on American Indian art, craft, and architecture.

Fife, Austin E. 1988. *Exploring Western Americana*. Ann Arbor: UMI Research Press.
Numerous essays on Western folklife, especially in Utah. Focus on architecture, gravestones, and Mormon culture.

Gilmore, Janet C. 1986. *The World of the Oregon Fishboat: A Study in Maritime Folklife*. Ann Arbor: UMI Research Press.
Excellent study of fishermen and their boats on the Oregon Coast.

Glassie, Henry. 1968. *Patterns in the Material Folk Culture of the Eastern United States*. Philadelphia: University of Pennsylvania Press.
Well-illustrated introduction to the patterns of folk art, craft, and architecture in the rural areas of the Appalachian Mountains, the Deep South, the Eastern Coast, and the Northeast.

Jordan, Terry G. and Matti Kaups. 1989. *The American Backwoods Frontier: An Ethnic and Ecological Interpretation.* Baltimore: Johns Hopkins University Press.
A historical-geographical explanation of the origins of American folk architecture and patterns of frontier living.

Kirshenblatt-Gimblett, Barbara. 1983. The Future of Folklore Studies in America: The Urban Frontier. *Folklore Forum* 16(2):175-234.
A suggestive folklife study of New York City and its built environment.

Marshall, Howard Wight and Richard E. Ahlborn. 1981. *Buckaroos in Paradise: Cowboy Life in Northern Nevada.* Lincoln: University of Nebraska Press.
Descriptive account of cowboys and ranching life, with plenty of photographs of work-related tools, crafts, and architecture.

Martin, Charles E. 1981. Head of Hollybush: Reconstructing Material Culture Through Oral History. *Pioneer America* 13(1):3-16.
Excellent treatment of rural Kentucky life in the past.

Miska, Maxine and I. Sheldon Posen. 1983. *Tradition and Community in the Urban Neighborhood: Making Brooklyn Home.* New York: Brooklyn Education and Cultural Alliance.
A brief but wonderful study of the folklife, built environment, and ethnic diversity of a New York City neighborhood.

Moonsammy, Rita Z.; David S. Cohen and Lorraine E. Williams. 1987. *Pinelands Folklife.* New Brunswick: Rutgers University Press.
Explores people and their material culture in the New Jersey Pine Barrens. Information on farming, fishing, hunting, local crafts, and architecture. Excellent essays on regionalism and sense of place.

Poulsen, Richard C. 1982. *The Pure Experience of Order: Essays on the Symbolic in the Folk Material Culture of Western America.* Albuquerque: University of New Mexico Press.
An interpretive study of architecture, gravestones, and Mormon folk culture in Utah and the American Southwest.

Rikoon, J. Sanford. 1988. *Threshing in the Midwest, 1820-1940: A Study of Traditional Culture and Technological Change.* Bloomington: Indiana University Press.

Roberts, Warren E. 1988. *Viewpoints on Folklife: Looking at the Overlooked.* Ann Arbor: UMI Research Press.
Many excellent essays on folk art, craft, and architecture, with a focus on Indiana and the Midwest.

Van Ravenswaay, Charles. 1977. *The Arts and Architecture of German Settlements in Missouri.* Columbia: University of Missouri Press.
Good descriptive study of German-American architecture and crafts, especially woodworking.

Weigle, Marta and Peter White. 1988. *The Lore of New Mexico.* Albuquerque: University of New Mexico Press.
The arts, crafts, and architecture of New Mexico. Especially fine study of the Southwest as a region and Mexican-American material culture. Many excellent historical photographs.

Yoder, Don. 1976. Folklife Studies in American Scholarship. IN *American Folklife*, ed. Don Yoder, pp. 3-18. Austin: University of Texas Press.
Summarizes the study of folklife in the U.S. and its roots in European scholarship.

3) **Folk Art**

Anderson, E.N. Jr. 1972. On the Folk Art of Landscaping. *Western Folklore* 31(3):179-88.
An approach to the how's and why's of decorating semi-public space, such as house lawns.

Babcock, Barbara A. and Guy and Doris Monthan. 1986. *The Pueblo Storyteller: Development of a Figurative Ceramic Tradition.* Tucson: University of Arizona Press.
Native American arts from the Southwest. An insightful look at the interrelationship between tradition, creativity, and a tourist market.

Briggs, Charles L. 1980. *The Wood Carvers of Córdova, New Mexico: Social Dimensions of an Artistic "Revival".* Knoxville: University of Tennessee Press.
Well-illustrated account of a Mexican-American art form.

Bronner, Simon J. 1984. *American Folk Art: A Guide to Sources.* New York: Garland.
An important reference to further sources.

_____. 1985. *Chain Carvers: Old Men Crafting Meaning.* Lexington: The University Press of Kentucky.
A study of woodcarving in Southern Indiana that looks at individual carvers and their life histories, and their motivations for carving.

Glassie, Henry. 1972. Folk Art. IN *Folklore and Folklife: An Introduction*, ed. Richard M. Dorson, pp. 253-280. Chicago: University of Chicago Press.

_____. 1989. *The Spirit of Folk Art.* New York: Harry N. Abrams, Inc.
A beautifully illustrated book, discussing folk art from around the world, with many fine examples from the American Southwest, the Upland South, and elsewhere around the world.

Graburn, Nelson H.H.,ed. 1979. *Ethnic and Tourist Arts: Cultural Expressions of the Fourth World.* Berkeley: University of California Press.
Many articles on folk arts and crafts from around the world, with a focus on those created for the tourist market. See especially the articles on contemporary Native American art forms in the Southwest.

Meyer, Richard E., ed. 1989. *Cemeteries and Gravemarkers: Voices of American Culture.* Ann Arbor: UMI Research Press.
Articles on material burial customs, including those of Northwest loggers, Mexican-, Afro-, and Native Americans, and people in the American South.

Peterson, Sally. 1988. Translating Experience and the Reading of a Story Cloth. *Journal of American Folklore* 101(399):6-22.
Looks at a contemporary Southeast Asian-American (Hmong) textile art form.

Roberts, Warren E. 1984. Investigating the Tree-Stump Tombstone in Indiana. IN *Folk Art and Art Worlds*, ed. John M. Vlach and Simon J. Bronner, pp. 135-153. Ann Arbor: UMI Research Press.

Sherzer, Dina and Joel Sherzer, eds. 1987. *Humor and Comedy in Puppetry: Celebration in Popular Culture*. Bowling Green, OH: Bowling Green State University Press.
See especially the introduction, the article by Proschan, and the article by Young on Native American puppetry.

Vlach, John Michael. 1988. *Plain Painters: Making Sense of American Folk Art*. Washington,D.C: Smithsonian Institution Press.
Looks at folk painting as an expression of popular art.

Sciorra, Joseph. 1989. Yard Shrines and Sidewalk Alters of New York's Italian-Americans. IN *Perspectives in Vernacular Architecture, III*, ed. Thomas Carter and Bernard L. Herman, pp. 185-198. Columbia: University of Missouri Press.
A well-illustrated account of how a form of folk art and vernacular architecture can enshrine community values of artfulness, religious belief, ethnic tradition, and family and neighborhood.

Wong, Hertha D. 1989. Pictographs as Autobiography: Plains Indian Sketchbooks of the Late Nineteenth and Early Twentieth Centuries. *American Literary History* 1(2):295-316.
Art which reveals culture conflict. Compare with Young (1988).

Young, M. Jane. 1988. *Signs From the Ancestors: Zuni Cultural Symbolism and Perceptions of Rock Art*. Albuquerque: University of New Mexico Press.
Looks at thousands of painted and carved rock art images in the context of one American Indian culture of the Southwest including their communicative functions in the world of contemporary tribal members.

4) Folk Craft

Carter, Thomas. 1989. Spindles and Spoon Racks: Local Style in Nineteenth-Century Mormon Furniture. IN *The Old Traditional Way of Life: Essays in Honor of Warren E. Roberts*, eds. Robert E. Walls and George H. Schoemaker, pp. 37-51. Bloomington: Trickster Press.
Particularly useful study of style, use, and religious values evident in early Mormon furniture in Utah.

Comeaux, Malcolm. 1985. Folk Boats of Louisiana. IN *Louisiana Folklife: A Guide to the State*, ed. Nicholas Spitzer, pp. 161-178. Baton Rouge: Louisiana Folklife Program.
Boats used for hunting, fishing, and general transportation.

Cooper, Patricia and Norma Bradley Buferd. 1977. *The Quilters: Women and Domestic Art*. Garden City, NY: Anchor Press.
A well-illustrated popular account which relies on oral history.

Johnson, Geraldine Niva. 1985. *Weaving Rag Rugs: A Woman's Craft in Western Maryland*. Knoxville: University of Tennessee Press.

Jones, Michael Owen. 1989. *Craftsman of the Cumberlands: Tradition and Creativity*. Lexington: The University Press of Kentucky.
An excellent treatment of an Appalachian folk craft—chairmaking—with a focus on one individual and the underlying motivations for creating the chairs which he makes.

McCarl, Robert S. 1974. The Production Welder: Product, Process and the Industrial Craftsman. *New York Folklore Quarterly* 30:243-53.
Crafts in a modern industrial setting.

Roach, Susan. 1985. The Kinship Quilt: An Ethnographic Semiotic Analysis of a Quilting Bee. IN *Women's Folklore, Women's Culture*, eds. Rosan A. Jordan and Susan J. Kalcik, pp. 54-64. Philadelphia: University of Pennsylvania Press.
Don't let the title throw you. This is a great article that looks at quilts in a communicative context, as a functional and artistic object, a means to facilitate social interaction, and an expression of beliefs and values.

Roberts, Warren E. 1972. Folk Crafts. IN *Folklore and Folklife: An Introduction*, ed. Richard M. Dorson, pp. 233-252. Chicago: University of Chicago Press.

_____. 1981. Turpin Chairs and the Turpin Family: Chairmaking in Southern Indiana. *Midwestern Journal of Language and Folklore* 7:55-106.
Also in Roberts' *Viewpoints on Folklife* (1988).

Sink, Susan. 1983. *Traditional Crafts and Craftmanship in America: A Selected Bibliography*. Washington, D.C: American Folklife Center.
An excellent reference for further sources.

Vennum, Thomas, Jr. 1982. *The Ojibwa Dance Drum: Its History and Construction*. (Smithsonian Folklife Studies, No. 2) Washington, D.C: Smithsonian Institution Press.
Documentation of a Native American craft.

Vlach, John Michael. 1978. *The Afro-American Tradition in Decorative Arts*. Cleveland: Cleveland Museum of Art.
Well-illustrated treatment of basketry, musical instruments, quilting, architecture, and graveyard decoration.

Zug, Charles G. III. 1986. *Turners and Burners: The Folk Potters of North Carolina*. Chapel Hill: University of North Carolina Press.

5) Folk Architecture

Barrick, Mac E. 1986. The Log House as Cultural Symbol. *Material Culture* 18(1):1-19.

Glassie, Henry. 1975. *Folk Housing in Middle Virginia: Structural Analysis of Historic Artifacts*. Knoxville: University of Tennessee Press.

Jordan, Terry G. 1978. *Texas Log Buildings: A Folk Architecture*. Austin: University of Texas Press.

Koskela, Alice. 1985. Finnish Log Homestead Buildings in Long Valley. IN *Idaho Folklife: From Homesteads to Headstones*, ed. Louie W. Attebery, pp. 29-36. Salt Lake City: University of Utah Press.
A good descriptive study of ethnic folk architecture in the American West.

Marshall, Howard Wight. 1981. *American Folk Architecture: A Selected Bibliography*. Washington, D.C: American Folklife Center.
An excellent reference to further sources.

_____. 1981. *Folk Architecture in Little Dixie: A Regional Culture in Missouri.* Columbia: University of Missouri Press.

Montell, William Lynwood and Michael Lynn Morse. 1976. *Kentucky Folk Architecture.* Lexington: University Press of Kentucky.

Nabokov, Peter and Robert Easton. 1989. *Native American Architecture.* New York: Oxford University Press.
Photographs of structures from all over North America, with discussion of their functional and spiritual significance.

Roberts, Warren E. 1972. Folk Architecture. IN *Folklore and Folklife: An Introduction*, ed. Richard M. Dorson, pp. 281-293. Chicago: University of Chicago Press.

_____. 1984. *Log Buildings of Southern Indiana.* Bloomington: Trickster Press.
An excellent model for the documentation of an area's folk architecture.

Upton, Dell, ed. 1986. *America's Architectural Roots: Ethnic Groups That Built America.* Washington, D.C: The Preservation Press.
Excellent descriptive guidebook, with plenty of photographs. Information on most ethnic peoples who settled in rural areas.

Upton, Dell and John Michael Vlach, eds. 1986. *Common Places: Readings in American Vernacular Architecture.* Athens: University of Georgia Press.
A collection of twenty-three readings addressing issues of construction, use, and intention.

Vlach, John Michael. 1976. The Shotgun House: An African Architectural Legacy. *Pioneer America* 8:47-70.
An Afro-American housing type in America. Also in Upton and Vlach (1986).

6) **Foodways**
Anderson, Jay. 1971. Special Food Issue. *Kentucky Folklore Quarterly* 16:153-214.
Focus is on specific groups such as Native Americans, Afro-Americans, and health food enthusiasts.

Brown, Linda Keller and Kay Mussell, eds. 1984. *Ethnic and Regional Foodways in the United States.* Knoxville: University of Tennessee Press.

Gutierrez, C. Paige. 1984. The Social and Symbolic Uses of Ethnic/Regional Foodways: Cajuns and Crawfish in South Louisiana. IN *Ethnic and Regional Foodways in the United States*, eds. Linda Keller Brown and Kay Mussell, pp. 169-182. Knoxville: University of Tennessee Press.

Humphrey, Theodore C. and Lin T. Humphrey, eds. 1988. *"We Gather Together": Food and Festival in American Life.* Ann Arbor: UMI Research Press.
Foodways and food-related celebrations in small groups such as families, work groups, and communities.

Jones, Michael Owen; Bruce Giuliano and Roberta Krell, eds. 1981. Foodways and Eating Habits: Directions for Research. *Western Folklore* Vol. 40 (Special Issue).
An interdisciplinary approach to the customs and trends in American foodways.

Yoder, Don. 1972. Folk Cookery. IN *Folklore and Folklife: An Introduction*, ed. Richard M. Dorson, pp. 325-350. Chicago: University of Chicago Press.

7) **Folk Costume**
Bogatyrev, Petr. 1971. *The Functions of Folk Costume in Moravian Slovakia.* The Hague: Mouton.
Although the focus is on an Old World region, this small book provides many useful insights to analyzing the clothing customs of any group.

Hebdige, Dick. 1979. *Subculture: The Meaning of Style.* London: Methuen.
Some fascinating discussion on the clothes styles of punk rockers and other youth groups. The focus is on style as communication.

Samuel, Cheryl. 1982. *The Chilkat Dancing Blanket.* Seattle: Pacific Search Press.
Documents a Northwest Coast Indian article of clothing that indicates wealth and prestige.

Yoder, Don. 1972. Folk Costume. IN *Folklore and Folklife: An Introduction*, ed. Richard M. Dorson, pp. 295-323. Chicago: University of Chicago Press.
A great introduction to the clothing patterns of religious, occupational, and regional groups.

CHAPTER 13
Occupational Folklore

Laura R. Marcus and Marianne T. Marcus

INTRODUCTION

Once you are familiar with the various kinds of folklore that you can collect, you may wonder where to start. Although occupational folklore has been an area of interest to folklorists for many years, especially where it relates to outdoor occupations such as logging and mining, it is enjoying increased attention from folklorists, as well as others, who have come to recognize the importance of this area of study.

Occupational folklore's rise in popularity is a sign of the times. This is in part due to the growing size of our country's work force, and by consequence, the increased amount of folklore that is performed in the workplace. Also, as folklorists have recently been reconsidering the boundaries of their discipline, they have been expanding their definitions beyond the realms of rural and oral models to include such items as xeroxlore (Dundes and Pagter 1975), and factory decoration (Nickerson 1983). Because the work environment is one where people are together regularly, often over an extended period of time, it is a place where individuals develop shared experiences. In the workplace, specialized language, ideas, customs, beliefs, symbols, tools, etc. are often created, used, and understood almost exclusively by those who are members of the occupational folk group. Collecting and reading about occupational folklore is both enjoyable and interesting because it highlights our everyday experiences, and gives us new insight into areas that are familiar to us. Occupational folklore provides valuable insights for educators, employers, and others who prepare or manage workers in a given field. Thus an understanding of occupational folklore can have real economic implications for managers who monitor the production and quality of goods and services in work settings (see Jones, Moore, Snyder 1988).

WHAT IS OCCUPATIONAL FOLKLORE?

Occupational folklore can take the shape of various genres such as narratives, songs and jokes performed both *in* and *about* the work environment, celebrations, and initiation rites (such as sending a new worker to get a *left-handed monkey-wrench*). Occupational folklore may often be more tangible, taking the shape of material objects that are actually created and/or sold in factories, workshops or studios, to items intended for the decorative enhancement or personalization of the workplace, and for the use of the workers themselves—for example clothing such as hats, uniforms, t-shirts, and so on (see Chapter 12 **Folklife and Material Culture**).

In adding to this expanding area of folklore study, several scholars have contributed to the growing body of literature on the socio-cultural dynamics of the workplace, that is, the interactions which take place in a working environment. At the end of this chapter, you will find an annotated bibliography containing related books and articles, which may be useful as you begin your own paper. It may be helpful for you to see what other people have done before you get started on your project. Be sure to consult the bibliographies of these sources to find further studies that may interest you.

GETTING STARTED: SELECTING A SITE

Many authors who have written about occupational folklore have suggested that it is best to begin in a place that is most familiar to you. For example, you might start with a project on student folklore (see Baker 1983). If you have had a summer job, or are working now, you might find your own work environment a good place to start, since you will already have a background in understanding how the place is run, how the organization is structured, and how the people there interact. Places where family or friends are employed might work just as well. The more you know about particular work environment, the better prepared you will be to perceive folkloric processes and to collect fieldwork data. Your familiarity with a job site will help you to ask more productive questions, and it may serve to lend an air of trust and confidentiality to your position as an interviewer. Also, since you will be stressing the context in which folklore is performed, your intimacy with a place and the people who work there will help you to interpret the dynamics of their folklore when you are preparing your conclusion.

COLLECTING, RECORDING AND ANALYZING DATA

You can approach your collection project in a number of different ways. You may choose to interview one or two individuals at length in order to get an in-depth profile of how a person relates to his or her job. Or, you might choose a certain genre, such as personal experience narrative, practical jokes, or job-related material objects, things people make and/or wear in order to enhance and personalize their work environment, and collect or document these items from a wide range of individuals. You may want to focus your study by concentrating on members of a particular age, gender or ethnic group. Another angle would be to choose members of a profession, such as nurses, postmasters/-mistresses, farmers, college professors and so on, and talk to a number of people who have the same job in a variety of settings. Your particular situation and your imagination will help you find the best solution for your project.

Although your first temptation may be to ask someone directly, "Do you know any initiation rites?" or "Have you created any artistic objects to beautify your working environment?" it is best to avoid such pointed questions. Quite often, people may respond to such a direct inquiry by genuinely racking their brains to find something to tell you, with the result that they may not be able to think of anything off hand. Also, it is best to recognize that in any field project, your ultimate goal in collecting folklore is to discover what people believe and express about themselves, and not to find out what you want to know about them. The unexpected and the unknown are two aspects of folklore fieldwork that make it such an enjoyable and enlightening enterprise! So, go into your project with an open mind, a tape recorder, a camera, a notepad, or whatever you need to record your field experience.

Regardless of the number of people you will be interviewing, it is often best to prepare a list of questions for your first interview or field session.

This is especially handy should you or your consultant be nervous because of the presence of the tape recorder, or just the unfamiliarity of the interview situation. You may be surprised to find that even if you are interviewing someone you have known for a while, for instance a relative or co-worker, one or both of you may be intimidated by the interview situation at first. This is a natural reaction, and you will probably find that it is only a matter of time before you and your consultant feel comfortable. It may help to downplay the presence of the tape recorder or whatever type of equipment you are using, and to discuss topics that are familiar and non-threatening to your consultant. Then again, you may find that your consultants are flattered and excited by the importance attributed to them by the interview setting, and that they may feel quite comfortable in front of a camera or tape recorder.

Conducting productive and ethical fieldwork entails a combination of common sense, courtesy, and perceptiveness. While most fieldwork is subject to similar guidelines, every situation will have its own individualized possibilities and limitations. Before you begin interviewing, be sure to explain to your consultant(s) who you are (if they do not already know you) and the purpose of your project. Be considerate: be sure to set up appointments that are convenient for them in terms of time and place. When collecting occupational folklore, it may be effective to interview people in their working environment, possibly even while they work. However, you may find that interviewees are not at ease discussing their job in front of other employees (or the boss!), or they may not have time to talk to you at work. If you are unable to conduct interviews in the workplace, perhaps you can schedule a time to tour your consultant's place of employment, so that you can have a better understanding of the nature of his/her working environment. Remember that consultants are doing you a favor by participating in your project, so be sure to let them know that you appreciate their taking time out to talk to you whenever it is possible for them.

When you are preparing your interview questions, you would do well to start with specific ones such as:

1. How did you come to work here?
2. How long have you been at this job?
3. Have you held other positions in this company?
4. What is going on here?
5. Who does what?
6. What is the goal of this work?
7. How did you learn to do this work?

Interviewees will often answer such questions and then spin off onto other topics. Though you may want to attempt to steer the interview in a certain direction, do not try to force consultants into talking about what you want to hear. If they are discussing a certain issue, they are doing so because it is an area of importance to them, and you should be attuned to their needs and interests. Let *them* tell *you*. Some beginning folklore students have complained that they have interviewed people who have *bossed them around* and told them what to ask. If this should happen, use it to your advantage. It is the consultants' way of revealing what they want you to know about them. Again, you may have to shift the emphasis of your paper as you proceed with your project. It may take you a few sessions with an individual or group before they begin to warm up to you and your project. Don't be discouraged: building a relationship of trust takes time, and is well worth any effort invested.

Do not try to be overly personal with your consultants right away. Quite often, as they feel comfortable with you, people may volunteer information of a more intimate nature. They may ask you who is going to read what you write, or ask you not to tell anyone what they have said, or to change their names when you write up your paper. It is important to respect their desire for privacy. Assure them that this is a class exercise, and that you will protect them and their reputation from harm. This is especially important in the case of occupational folklore where your consultant(s) may feel that their job could be affected by your interview. Be sensitive to their need for privacy and discretion.

Depending on the emphasis of your project, the kind of equipment you need will vary. For example, if you are working with a limestone carver or someone in a *visually* related field, you will want to document them and their work with a camera, or even a video-recorder, if one is available. If you are collecting narratives, then you will need a tape recorder. In most situations, you will probably want to have equipment to record both visual and verbal aspects of the person(s) with whom you are working. In all instances, you should be prepared to take notes. A journal in which you record impressions of your experiences, of your expectations, and how they may have been met or disappointed, is very important. Since your personal attitude will have direct bearing on the outcome of the project, you need to bear in mind the subjective factor of your work when you are preparing your interpretation.

Although you may be able to record everything a person does or says with audio-visual equipment, you need field notes to record contextual information. This includes such details as what a person was wearing, how concerned they seemed to be about their appearance, ie. is their job one where they are likely to get dirty, and thus dress down for work, or do they work in a place that requires a neat appearance? Look for markers of rank and status such as pins, buttons, stripes, uniform color, or more personal ones, such as the style of clothing worn to the workplace. Pay close attention to the workplace itself. If people work in a large area, such as a factory, do they have an office or small work area of their own? If so, how have they personalized this space? Calendars, posters, photographs, and plaques or posted slogans often reveal a good deal about peoples' attitudes about their jobs, or what other aspects of their lives they choose to bring into their work environment. Even the position of furniture and/or equipment can be informative. If possible, draw a map of a person's workplace, home or wherever you conduct your interviews; this may give you insight later on, when you go back over all your information.

Another area of contextual concern is interaction. Who else is present at the time of the interview? What is their relationship to the consultant? How might their presence affect the type of information your consultant chooses to share with you? How does your consultant seem to feel about you? Pay attention to body language, tone of voice, gestures, and so on. If you are uncomfortable taking notes in front of people, stop and write down as much as you can remember as soon as you leave the interview. I have often parked my car on the side of the road on my way home from conducting fieldwork to write notes while ideas are still fresh in my mind. Before you resume your fieldwork, read over your previous notes. This will help you develop new questions. It will also enable you to check your notes for accuracy and to notice any changes that may have taken place since the last time you were there. Contextual information, as a supplement to what you actually record the person saying and doing, will help you come out with a more rounded picture of your consultants and their jobs when you get ready to do your analysis.

It is always difficult to know when to stop collecting and start interpreting and writing up results. If you are working within the context of a folklore course, you will undoubtedly have a time limit. Remember you can always go back and collect more information after you have completed your project. It is impossible to get *everything*, so don't worry about leaving things out. You will need to choose a focus for your

Figure 1. Shown here at a quieter moment, Cow Canyon Trading Post is often the scene of much community activity. (Photograph by Laura Marcus)

project, and concentrate on that area as you write up your analysis, interpretation, and conclusion. To illustrate, we will provide two examples of collecting and interpreting field data with occupational groups.

TRADING ON THE NAVAJO RESERVATION:
A PRELIMINARY PERSPECTIVE   (Laura R. Marcus)

In preparing to do a larger project on traders on the Navajo Reservation, I combined contextual fieldwork with historical research in order to find a focus for my work. I lived and worked at Cow Canyon trading post in Bluff, Utah for a year, and then began to read about the history of trading on the Navajo reservation. Because there is such a great demand for Navajo rugs, both historically and in the present, I became interested in the influence traders have had on weaving designs, and on the rug market in general. In the past, traders have had to work hard to create a market that would satisfy customers in places as far from the Navajo reservation as New York, and to help the weavers, many of whom have never traveled far from the reservation, to make rugs that are aesthetically pleasing to buyers they will probably never see. In this light, traders can be seen as mediators between two very different cultural groups, as well as collaborators with the Navajo weavers.

Informed by recorded historical evidence, I am now looking at political and economical issues in my approach to fieldwork. At the time when the Navajo were forced to live on a reservation, to send their children to Anglo-American schools, and to participate in a cash economy, they were also encouraged to weave rugs that would be pleasing to an Anglo-American buying public. Out of economic necessity and convenience, the Navajo eventually gave up the practice of weaving blankets for their own use and for trade, and began to make rugs for "export." This shift put them in a relationship with traders that required continual communication about the rugs they were weaving, and the nature of the market. What was beautiful to rug buyers often had to do with their conception of who the Navajo were, and what looked most authentically *Navajo* or traditional to them. Weavers and traders worked together to develop rugs that would sell well in the market. Navajo rugs are still one of the most popular items for sale on the reservation, as well as in galleries around the country and the world. Thus, the trader continues to play an important role in mediating between weavers and the buying public.

In developing a project to deal with the present situation, I was interested in talking to a variety of traders, both young and old, and focusing on how they had been involved in helping the Navajo successfully connect with their audience. I also intend to interview the weavers themselves about their attitudes towards the situation, and possibly collect stories about the trading experiences of their ancestors, in order to round out the historical picture, which has mostly been drawn by Anglo-American traders and historians. Although I am just beginning my larger field project, I will be approaching my analysis from the perspective of political-economy (How have the political or *power* relationships among the Navajo weavers, traders, and consumers been informed by economic considerations, and vice versa?), and issues of aesthetics and authenticity (Who gets to decide what the public sees as *genuinely Navajo*? Whose taste is reflected in what is considered *beautiful*? How do traders, buyers, and weavers *communicate* through the rugs?)

Another field of inquiry dealing with traders would be to look at how they became involved with the business. Some people inherit their trading posts from parents and grandparents. Others see trading as a way to be involved with their interest in Navajo art and culture, while some are most interested in economic gain. These are some of the issues that I might consider when I begin to conduct my larger field project.

Because service industries are working environments where a great number of people interact, they are potentially rich sites for occupational folklore fieldwork. The approach discussed above could be modified to fit your particular project. For example, you could collect waitress narratives, or beliefs and amulets that waitresses use to attract high-tipping customers. The transportation industry would also be a fruitful place to search for occupational narratives, since employees in this area encounter a large and variable clientele. For sources on the transportation occupations, see references to Santino's work below. Postal workers, who consistently work with people from many sectors of society, may have insight into peoples' special communicative needs, especially at holiday times, such as Christmas, when stacks of brown parcels line the walls of post offices. Department store clerks, who are privy to peoples' more intimate and perhaps frivolous nature, might have narratives to share about regular customers, unusual requests, or favorite sales pitches. In the same vein, hair-dressers, who must be gifted conversationalists, have access to their customers' personal experience narratives, as well as their aesthetic inclinations. Dentists may have stories and strategies with which they ease the nerves of frightened patients. Have you ever wanted to ask your professors about the posters, photographs, slogans and so on that adorn their offices? Here is your chance!

Occupations which entail personal risk, such as factory work, fire-fighting (see McCarl 1986), fishing (see Mullen 1978), police work and more, may be especially good environments in which to collect lore that people in these dangerous professions may practice for their protection. The health profession is one where employees frequently deal with other peoples' life-threatening situations. In her discussion of surgical intensive care unit nursing below, Marianne will illustrate some of the strategies nurses devise in order to deal with the stress of their jobs.

SURGICAL INTENSIVE CARE NURSING WORK
(Marianne T. Marcus)

As a nurse educator I became interested in the perceived differences between the work that nurses are educated to perform and the *real world* or nursing as it occurs in a hospital setting. My study was motivated by practical concerns. With the current national shortage of nurses, it is imperative that nurse educators and nurse administrators know more precisely what it is that nurses do on the job and how they come to know what to do in any given work setting. All work groups establish rules, policies, and goals by which to govern the workplace. These formal rules are the structure and organization which underlie educational programs and job descriptions. But nurses, like other workers, develop less formal goals and behaviors to define the common reality of their work world. Hence, an understanding of these *real world* phenomena can provide valuable insights and a more realistic definition of the work.

DOING ETHNOGRAPHY
Describing the Work of ICU Nurses
I spent ten months investigating nursing work within the context of a surgical intensive care unit (a unit where complex care is given to critically ill patients after surgery), a prototype for care in the

modern hospital system. I then began with the broad question, "What is the work of nurses in this unit?" and eventually focused my inquiry on such questions as "How do nurses frame the work of the surgical intensive care unit?" and "How do nurses learn to do the work of the unit?"

I conducted intense observations, following individual nurses for complete work shifts and recording fieldnotes of everything that was said and done by the nurses. Each observation period was followed by a taped semi-structured debriefing interview. The interview began with questions such as "What were you doing (or thinking) when I saw you doing _____?" and "Why?" The second phase of the interview was structured around the following questions: "What is the general work of this unit?" "How do you set priorities?" "Who does what?" "How did you learn to do this work (education versus experience, other)?"

Analysis and Interpretation of Data

The study showed that the nurses' work was indeed in line with professional and institutional mandates, or rules, for providing care to critically ill patients in the immediate period following surgery. The universal goal of the unit is to sustain life, stabilize critically ill patients, and then transfer them out to make room for others. The nurses provide intense care for a relatively brief period as patients move through the hospital system toward recovery. They are troubleshooters at a time when patients' lives are at greatest risk. Their work is framed by the unstable physical condition of their patients. When stability is achieved, their work is completed for a given patient.

The work of sustaining life in surgical intensive care, though admittedly uncertain, is never haphazard. They attempt to establish routines, set priorities, and order their actions in the face of uncertainty. First, there are the *basics* or the general things, actions that are appropriate to all patients regardless of diagnosis. *Basics* have to do with the immediate threats to life —the ABCs—airway, breathing, and circulation.

Once these concerns are addressed, the nurses set priorities according to labels, or categories, which trigger a pattern of action. The categories provide a way of thinking about nursing work that is readily recognized from one nurse in the setting to the next. They provide shared meaning, or a short-hand, for conveying complex information in a simplified manner. For example, the terms used to describe the anatomical location of disease and/or surgery (*hearts*, *cranies*), identify a life-threatening symptom (*bleeders*) or connote an increase in the expected length of stay

in the unit (*chronics*). The categories, then, are *care plans in the head* which guide the direction of nursing work in the surgical intensive care unit under investigation. They are defined as follows:

Hearts   Patients who have had surgery to restore circulation. **Properties:** *Special* (the hospital is known for this type of surgery), predictable, documentable (machines monitor changes), routine, almost easy.

Cranies   Patients who have had surgical openings in the skull to relieve intracranial pressure. **Properties:** Unpredictable, *so little warning* (when their conditions change), uncertain, difficult to document.

Bleeders   Patients whose lives are threatened by loss of blood from some source within the gastrointestinal tract. **Properties:** Clear indicators (shock, obvious bleeding), *not difficult*, time consuming, require large amounts of valuable resources (blood, nursing time), temporary stability at best (they keep coming back).

Chronics   Patients who do not fit the norm of transience (cannot be stabilized and moved out within two days). **Properties:** Complex, multi-system failure, *twofers* (sometimes they have had *two* surgeries on the same day).

As you can see, the categories have become the shared body of knowledge for workers in the unit, a specialized manner of speaking which is peculiar to nurses. This is a kind of **folk speech** that is common to this group of people.

Another example of folklore revealed by this study concerned attitudes about death. Death is the obvious enemy in a setting where the common goal of the work is to sustain life. But death is always a threat in the surgical intensive care unit because the patients are gravely ill and, often, placed at greater risk because of the surgical procedure. The nurses in this setting have a euphemism for death. Patients who die have *gone to Chicago*. The phrase came into use after a patient, who was expected to be transferred to Chicago, died before the transfer could take place. When his bed was empty, the next shift asked if he had gone to Chicago as planned. "Yeah, he went to Chicago, all right" was the rueful response.

Since that time, patients are reported to be *Chicago bound*. They are said to have *bought a ticket* or *boarded the plane* depending upon the gravity of the situation. In this way, the particular experience of a few members of this work setting has been incorporated into a specialized communicative code, which allow surgical intensive care unit nurses to talk about this delicate and emotionally charged area. Having such a terminology may be especially helpful when nurses are in the position of discussing a patient's condition in front of other patients and their families. Recently I have discovered that the use of the euphemism also occurs in a nearby hospital in the same medical center. This is an interesting example of the process of folkloric diffusion.

My study of the work of nurses in a surgical intensive care unit also revealed an example of *material culture* unique to the setting. The nurses take patients' beds directly into the operating room where patients are transferred from operating table to bed when surgery is finished. The occupied bed is then returned to the intensive care unit. The technological devices which are connected to patients to monitor vital functions are located on the wall near the head of the bed. Occasionally, doctors and other workers in the operating room place patients without considering which end is the head of the bed and which the foot. If a patient returns to the surgical intensive care unit in the reverse position, vital time is lost while he or she is repositioned. When signs indicating *head of bed* and *foot of bed* did not remedy the problem, the nurses began to draw stick figures directly on the sheets! (See Figure 2.) This clear message is not disregarded. Thus in talking with surgical intensive care unit nurses about their work, I was able to discover how they personalize their work environment and how they have developed specialized modes of communication which make their jobs run more smoothly.

CONCLUSION

These two examples illustrate how you might prepare for your field project (L. Marcus), and how to interpret your material (M. Marcus). In the case of the trading post study, L. Marcus' familiarity with this area and her historical research provided a useful background from which to begin her fieldwork. The focus of any field project, however, should always be your actual interaction with field consultants, and your interpretation of this experience. A nurse herself, M. Marcus learned how a particular group of nurses developed specialized means of communication which

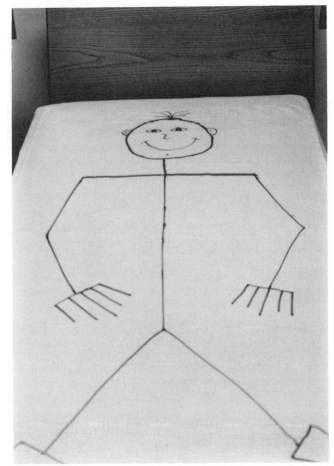

Figure 2. Stick figure drawn directly on sheets to indicate placement of head and feet.

enhanced the efficiency of the workplace, as well as personalized it. Terms like *hearts, cranies, Chicago bound*, as well as the stick figures drawn on a sheet, convey important messages among members of a work force.

Through attention to such specialized creations of a working environment, researchers can better understand the dynamics which emerge from peoples' interactions with their jobs. Such insight can facilitate a refined understanding of occupational phenomena, and can provide employers with a means of better communication with their employees, and inform them on how to meet workers' needs most effectively. Because folklore is an area where such sensitive and highly specialized communication occurs, folklorists are in a position to conduct valuable research whose results might be unobtainable in any other way. Regardless of the work environment you decide to study, you will undoubtedly discover a wealth of information that will give you insight into the way people cope with and enhance their jobs.

Acknowledgement

The authors would like to express their gratitude to Richard Bauman and to M. Jane Young for bibliographic suggestions. Thanks go also to Michael Owen Jones for sending information on occupational folklore. Lize Doran introduced Laura Marcus to the world of trading, and made valuable comments about the relationship between trader and weavers: *a'hehe' nad'aani*—"thanks chief." For his guidance and support, Marianne T. Marcus would like to thank Joseph P. Kotarba. She would also like to express her gratitude to the surgical intensive care unit nurses who shared their time and expertise.

References Cited

Baker, Ronald L. 1983. The Folklore of Students. IN *The Handbook of American Folklore*, ed. Richard Dorson, pp. 106-114. Bloomington, IN: Indiana University Press.

Dundes, Alan. 1983. Office Folklore. IN *The Handbook of American Folklore*, ed. Richard Dorson, pp. 115-120. Bloomington, IN: Indiana University Press.

Goffman, Erving. 1974. *Frame Analysis: An Essay on the Organization of Experience*. Cambridge, Mass: Harvard University Press.

Jones, Michael Owen., Moore, M. D., Snyder, R.C. (1988). *Inside Organizations: Understanding the Human Dimension*. Newberry Park, Ca.: Sage Publications.

McCarl, Robert. 1986. Occupational Folklore. IN *Folk Groups and Folk Genres: An Introduction*, ed. Elliott Oring, pp. Logan, Utah: Utah State University Press.

Marcus, Marianne T. 1989. *Surgical Intensive Care Nursing Work: A Phenomenological Study*. Unpublished Doctoral Dissertation, University of Houston, Houston, Texas.

Mullen, Patrick B. 1978. *I Heard the Old Fisherman Say*. Austin: University of Texas Press.

Nickerson, Bruce. 1983. Factory Folklore. IN *Handbook of American Folklore*, ed. Richard Dorson, pp. 121-127. Bloomington: Indiana University Press.

Santino, Jack. 1986. A Servant and a Man, A Hostess or a Woman; A Study of Expressive Culture in Two Transportation Occupations. *Journal of American Culture* 99:304-319.

Selected Annotated Bibliography

Adams, Ramon F. 1971. *The Cowman Says It Salty*. Tucson, Arizona: University of Arizona Press.
Adams presents the cowman's language in the context of anecdotes. The author collected this language in an attempt to presume this form of speech and ". . . to give the reader a deeper understanding of the man through his speech" (xiv). For other works by Adams on occupational language, see also: *Cowboy Lingo*. Boston: Houghton Mifflin Company (1936); *The Language of the Railroader*. Norman: University of Oklahoma Press (1977).

Baker, Margaret. 1977 *The Gardener's Folklore*. London: David and Charles.
The author presents a collection of beliefs and practices of gardeners who wish to maximize the success of their gardens. This book also includes information about seasonal and calendrical aspects of gardening, and on recipes and companion planting. See also *Folklore by the Sea*. London: David and Charles (1979).

Baker, Ronald L. 1983. The Folklore of Students. IN *The Handbook of American Folklore*, ed. Richard Dorson, pp. 106-114. Bloomington, IN: Indiana University Press.
Baker discusses a variety of folklore genres that are current among students. These include: narratives, songs, puns, rituals, graffiti, jokes. Although he focuses primarily on university-level folklore, Baker also mentions practices among the lower levels of academic experience as well. Exploring a range of themes which emerge in student folklore, Baker emphasizes the importance of an approach which will ". . . provide intensive analysis of the traditional life of students" (113).

Ballew, Stephen, and Joan Brooks, Dona Brotz, and Edward Ives. 1977. "Suthin (It's the opposite of nothin');" An Oral History of Grover Morrison's Woods Operation at Little Musquash Lake, 1945-1947. *Northeast Folklore* V:XVIII.
Inspired by a 54-stanza poem entitled *Suthin'*, which is a chronicle of a lumbering operation, Ives and three students conducted interviews with people whose names appeared in the poem. The result is an illustrated oral historical piece which relates the details of the lumbering operation.

Bartis, Peter, and Mary Hufford. 1980. *Maritime Folklife Resources: A Directory and Index*. Washington, D.C.: Publications of the American Folklife Center.
This is a valuable source of information for anyone interested in maritime folklife. This publication lists American Maritime museums and their holdings with listings under such categories as ships' equipment, art, songs, narratives, belief systems, rituals, music, and more. Institutions are also listed by state.

Bauman, Richard. 1981. "Any Man Who Keeps More'n One Hound'll Lie to You": Dog Trading and Storytelling at Canton, Texas. IN *"And Other Neighborly Names" Social Process and Cultural Image in Texas Folklore*, eds. Richard Bauman and Roger D. Abrahams, pp. Austin: University of Texas Press.
Bauman explores the "expressive lie" within the frame of tall tales told among hunters and dog traders at trading fairs. The focal event where this interaction occurs is First Monday at Canton, a monthly event in Canton, Texas, where traders and dealers come to trade and sell coon dogs. Although on the surface, First Monday is ostensibly a "business" realm, Bauman illustrates that, for the dog traders, the event is ". . . a form of play, a contest of wits and words" (82), where narrative is a significant element in this social sphere.

Beck, Earl C. 1948. *Lore of the Lumber Camps*. Menasha, Wisconsin: George Banta Publishing Company.
This collection contains songs, ballads, and tall tales which express the interests and concerns of mid-western lumber workers. The author collected the ballads, and has presented them thematically.

The Emergence of Folklore in Everyday Life

Bell, Michael J. 1983. *The World from Brown's Lounge; An Ethnography of Black Middle-Class Play*. Urbana: University of Illinois Press.
This is a study of black middle-class interaction at a neighborhood bar in Philadelphia. In the words of the author, this book focuses upon ". . . the aesthetics of ordinary experience" (9), highlighting the performative and artistic aspects of the social dynamics in this setting.

Boatright, Mody C. 1982. *Tall Tales From Texas Cow Camps*. Dallas: SMU Press.
First published in 1946, Boatright's collection of tall tales or "windies" illuminates popular themes among the cow camp workers who entertained each other with their narratives. Boatright has divided the book into such areas as "Wind and Weather," "By the Breadth of a Hair," "Adventures of Pecos Bill," and more. Boatright did several other studies of folklore among occupational groups. These include: (1945) *Gib Morgan: Minstrel of the Oil-fields*. Austin: Texas Folklore Society Publications, no. 20; (1963) *Folklore of the Oil Industry*. Dallas: SMU Press; (1970) with W.A. Owens, *Tales From the Derrick Floor: A People's History of the Oil Industry*. Garden City, N.Y.: Doubleday.

Botkin, Benjamin A., and Alvin F. Harlow. 1953. *A Treasury of Railroad Folklore; The Stories, Tall Tales, Ballads and Songs of the American Railroad Man*. New York: Bonanza Books.
In this book, the authors set out to ". . . give a picture of railroading as a way of life and of railroad folklore, as a way of looking at life" (xi). The collection contains a great deal of material including railroad songs, narratives about well-known railroad figures, folklore relating to historical eras and to geographical areas, and to relationships between railroad workers and passengers.

Boynton, Mia. 1988. Folklore in the Industrial Workplace. Special Issue *New York Folklore* 14(1/2).

Byington, Robert H., ed. 1978. *Western Folklore*, XXXVII, n. 3.
This is a special edition of *Western Folklore* devoted entirely to the subject of occupational folklore. This edition includes articles by Robert H. Byington, Robert S. McCarl, Roger D. Abrahams, Jack Santino, and Archie Green.

Cutting, Edith E. 1951. *Whistling Girls and Jumping Sheep*. Cooperstown, N.Y.: Farmers Museum and the New York Folklore Society.
This collection of beliefs, narratives, and rituals was amassed in rural New York from farmers. Topics include farming, livestock, weather lore and more.

Dobie, J. Frank. 1949. *A Vaquero of the Brush Country; Partly from the Reminiscences of John Young*. London: Hammond & Hammond, and Co., LTD.
This is a collection of reminiscences written from the collaboration of Dobie and Young. It is Young's autobiography, in which he presents his life's experiences as a vaquero in Texas and other areas in the American West.

Doerflinger, William M. 1951. *Songs of the Sailor and Lumberman*. New York: The Macmillan Company.
Doerflinger presents a collection of songs which he gathered from 1930 to 1950 in the eastern United States and in eastern Canada. The collection is thematically arranged, and is enhanced by contextual information about these occupations, as well as with illustrations.

Dorson, Richard M. 1949. The Folklore of Colleges. *American Mercury* 68:671-677.
Dorson provides a survey of college lore, including songs, narratives, pranks, rituals and beliefs. Such figures as professors, coaches, deans, lovers, and more are the subject of these timeless genres.

Dundes, Alan and Carl R. Pagter. 1975. *Urban Folklore from the Paperwork Empire*. Austin, Tx.: Publications of the American Folklore Society.
This compendium of American, urban corporate folklore offers the reader a variety of genres such as letters, memos, cartoons, applications and tests, and more. Most often satirical in nature, the folklore items collected here provide a valuable commentary on the American world of office work. See also: (1983) "Office Folklore," in *Handbook of American Folklore*, Richard Dorson, ed. Bloomington, Indiana: Indiana University Press, p 115-120.

Edison, Carol A. ed., 1985. *Cowboy Poetry from Utah; An Anthology*. Salt Lake City, Utah: Utah Folklife Center.
This collection contains biographical profiles of the cowboy poets, photographs of them, their poetry, and general information about cowboy poetry in Utah.

Fields, Mary C. 1974. The View from the Water Table. *Mid-South Folklore* VII:63-76.
Based on fieldwork among oilmen, the author presents their narratives within a body of contextual information. The article includes a glossary of oilfield terms.

Gelo, D. J. 1977. Material Culture of the Jersey Shore Lifeguards. *New Jersey Folklore* IX:6-11.
This article explores the social and occupational implications of the use of surf boats by Jersey Shore lifeguards, and includes narratives by the lifeguards.

Gillespie, Angus K. 1984. Narratives of the Jersey Shore Lifeguards. *New Jersey Folklore* IX:1-5.
Looking at the types of rescues inherent in this job, the author explores some of the less glamorous aspects of lifeguarding in a resort area. Gillespie draws on his fieldwork with lifeguards, and includes some of their narratives in the text of his article.

Goldstein, Kenneth S. 1964. *A Guide for Fieldworkers in Folklore*. Hatboro, Pennsylvania: The American Folklore Society.
This is a helpful guide for fieldworkers, old and new, with special insight into collecting occupational folklore (p. 70).

Gonzalez, Alicia M. 1981. 'Guess How Doughnuts Are Made': Verbal and Nonverbal Aspects of the Panadero and His Stereotype. IN *"And Other Neighborly Names"; Social Process and Cultural Image in Texas Folklore*, eds. Richard Bauman and Roger D. Abrahams, pp. 104-122. Austin: University of Texas Press.
The author did her fieldwork with panaderos or Mexican style bakers in Los Angeles, Austin, and in Mexico. In this article, she explores the ways in which stereotypes of panaderos are played out through narrative, song and gesture.

Green, Archie. 1972. *Only a Miner; Studies in Recorded Coal-Mining Songs*. Urbana: University of Illinois Press.
Drawing on a variety of sources, including archival materials and field recordings, Green explores ". . . sound recordings as cultural documents and communicative devices" (xii). The songs, appearing on disks issued between 1925 and 1970, are presented as case studies which illuminate the lives and values of American coal miners. See also (1987) "At the Hall, In the Stope: Who

Treasures Tales of Work?" in *Western Folklore* 46:153-170, in which the author advocates the study of occupational folklore.

Griffith, James S. 1983. The Cowboy Poetry of Everett Brisendine: A response to Cultural Change. *Western Folklore* 42:38-45.
Incorporating excerpts from Brisendine's narratives, as well as examples of his poetry, the author presents of Brisendine's expressive repertoire, which includes material culture as well as poetry and narrative. Griffith suggests that Brisendine is reacting to the process of cultural change, at the same time that he is celebrating the continuity of such values as ". . . love of the land and the lifestyle, respect for skill and hard work, love and respect for the old ways" (45).

Hand, Wayland D. 1946. The Folklore, Customs, and Traditions of the Butte Miner. *California Folklore Quarterly* 5:1-25.
Inspired by stories about this legendary mining town, the author has collected ". . . legends, customs, superstitions, and the jargon of this dangerous trade" (1) from members of this occupational community. Hand situates this body of folklore in its regional, historical and social context. See also: (1941) "Folklore from Utah's Silver Mining Camps" in *Journal of American Folklore* 54:132-161.

Ives, Edward D. 1971. *Lawrence Doyle: Farmer Poet of Prince Edward Island: A Study in Local Songmaking.* Orono: University of Maine Press.
Ives explores the various stages of rafting logs in Maine through the narratives of loggers. The book is illustrated with maps, photographs and diagrams, and is meant to be ". . . a contribution to our knowledge of the lumber industry in the New World and a tribute to the ingenuity and industry of the people of the Lower Penobscot Valley in the great state of Maine." See also: *Lawrence Doyle: Farmer-Poet of Prince Edward Island; A Study in Local Songmaking.* (Orono: University of Maine Press, 1971). In this work, Ives draws on interviews and correspondences, public records and historical documents, and newspapers to put together a picture of Lawrence Doyle. Doyle was a farmer, poet, and singer who described his world through the mediums of poetry and song, and whose compositions continue on in the repertoires of those who have lived on after him. Other works by Ives include: (1964) *Larry Gorman: The Man Who Made the Songs.* Bloomington: Indiana University Press; (1978) *Joe Scott, The Woodsman-Song-Maker.* Urbana: University of Illinois Press; (1986) Wilbur Day with Edward D. Ives, ed. *Wilbur Day, Hunter, Guide, and Poacher: An Autobiography.* Orono, Me: Northeast Folklore Society; (1988) *George Magoon and the Down East Game War: History, Folklore, and the Law.* Urbana: University of Illinois Press.

Jackson, Bruce. 1972. 'The Greatest Mathematician in the World': Norbert Wiener Stories. *Western Folklore* 31:1-22.
The M.I.T. mathematician, Norbert Wiener, best known for coining the word "cybernetics," was a figure who became the ". . . subject of dozens of professor tales, jokes, and representative and attributive anecdotes" (1). Jackson presents a variety of narratives about this illustrious professor, some based in reality, some in general professorial lore.

Jones, Michael Owen, D. M. Moore, and Snyder, R.C. 1988. *Inside Organizations; Understanding the Human Dimension.* Newbury Park, California: Sage Publications.
This collection of essays explores the symbolic dimension of organizational culture. "Using ethnographic techniques of documentation and analysis, authors describe real situations and actual behavior they have observed in order to derive principles about leadership, culture change, and the social and psychological functions of symbolic behavior" (11). Such genres as narrative, ritual and festival, and material culture are among the forms of folklore mentioned here. Jones has written extensively on occupational folklore. See also: (1981) "A Feeling for Form . . . As Illustrated by People at Work," in *Folklore on Two Continents: Essays in Honor of Linda Degh,* C. Lindahl and N. Burlakoff, eds. Bloomington, Indiana: Trickster Press; (1985) "Is Ethics the Issue?," in *Organizational Culture,* J. Frost, L.F. Moore, M.R. Louis, C.C. Lundberg, and J. Martin, eds. Beverly Hills, Ca.: Sage Publications; (1986) "Another America: Toward a Behavioral History Based on Folkloristics," in *Western Folklore,* 41, 43-51; (1987a) "Aesthetics at Work: Art and Ambience in an Organization," in *Exploring Folk Art: Twenty Years of Thought on Craft, Work, and Aesthetics.* Ann Arbor: UMI Research Press; (1987b) "Making Work Art and Art Work: The Aesthetic Impulse in Organizations and Education," in *Art in a Democracy,* D. Blandy and K. Congdon, eds. New York: Columbia Teachers College Press; (1990) "A Folklore Approach to Emotions in Work," in *American Behavioral Scientist,* 33, 278-286. This entire issue of *American Behavioral Scientist,* edited by Jones, is devoted to the topic, "Emotions in Work: A Folklore Approach."

Korson, George. 1926. *Songs and Ballads of the Anthracite Miner; A Seam of Folklore Which Once Ran Through Life in the Hard Coal Fields of Pennsylvania.* New York: The Grafton Press.
Korson has collected songs, ballads, and narratives from men and women who lived in mining communities in Pennsylvania. Having spent time with these people, Korson gained insight into the lives of the miners and their families. The songs and narratives present perspectives on strikes, accidents, individuals, and on the life of miners in general. Korson also authored several other works on the folklore of the mining industry. These are: (1938) *Minstrels of the Mine Patch; Songs and Stories of the Anthracite Industry.* Philadelphia: University of Pennsylvania Press; (1943) *Coal Dust on a Fiddle; Songs and Stories of the Bituminous Industry.* Philadelphia: University of Pennsylvania Press; (1960) *Black Rock Mining; Folklore of the Pennsylvania Dutch.* Baltimore: The Johns Hopkins Press.

Lloyd, Timothy C. and Patrick B. Mullen. 1990. *Lake Erie Fishermen; Work, Identity, and Tradition.* Urbana and Chicago: University of Illinois Press.
The authors present an ethnographic account of the experiences of Lake Erie Fishermen. The fishermen, who have witnessed vast changes in their occupational landscape, share their perspective through personal narrative.

Lomax, John A. and Alan Lomax. 1959. *Cowboy Songs and Other Frontier Ballads.* New York: Macmillan.
The Lomaxes recorded this collection of songs and ballads from the repertoire of singers throughout the American West. Covering a variety of categories, such as "Up the Trail," and "Campfire and Bunkhouse," the songs richly illustrate the details and themes of cowboy living.

McCarl, Robert. 1986. Occupational Folklore. IN *Folk Groups and Folk Genres: An Introduction,* ed. Elliott Oring, pp. 71-89. Logan, Utah: Utah State University Press.
The author illustrates the importance of "cultural scenes," wherein members of an occupational folk group may share their experiences, voice their opinions, and evaluate their own as well as others' work performances. McCarl illustrates his collection and interpretation techniques with examples from his own work with firefighters. For other work by the same author, see also:

"Occupational Folklife: A Theoretical Hypothesis," in *Working Americans: Contemporary Approaches to Occupational Folklife,* Robert H. Byington, ed. Smithsonian Folklife Studies No. 3 (Washington, D.C.: Smithsonian Institution Press, 1978); *Good Fire/Bad Night: A cultural Sketch of the District of Columbia Fire Fighters as Seen Through Their Occupational Folklife* (Washington, D.C.: D.C. Fire Fighters Association, Local 36); *The District of Columbia Fire Fighters' Project: A Case Study in Occupational Folklife,* Smithsonian Folklife Studies No. 4 (Washington, D. C.: Smithsonian Institution Press, 1985); "Fire and Dust: Ethnography at Work in Communities," in *Practicing Anthropology* 1-2: 21-22; "Accident Narratives," in *New York Folklore,* 14: 53-44; "The Folk as Occupational Group: From the Cow Camp to the Shop Floor," in *100 Years of American Folklore Studies: A Conceptual History,* William Clements, ed. with production editors David Stanley and Marta Weigle, p 40-43 (Washington, D.C.: The American Folklore Society, 1988); "Occupational Folklife in the Public Sector: A Case Study," in *Cultural Conservation: Folklorists & the Public Sector,* Burt Feintuch, ed. (Lexington: The University Press of Kentucky).

Marshall, Howard W. and Richard E. Ahlborn. 1980. *Buckaroos in Paradise; Cowboy Life in Northern Nevada.* Washington, D.C.: Library of Congress.
This publication is an exhibit catalogue, enhanced by good bibliography and an abundance of photographs. The focus of this intensive study is Paradise Valley, Nevada, where cowboy life prevails over the community. The catalogue presents a rich array of material culture, including quilts, tools, and other artifacts, as well as other intimate glimpses of this community.

Messenger, Betty. 1975. *Picking Up the Linen Threads: A Study in Industrial Folklore.* Austin: University of Texas Press.
Messenger interviewed men and women who worked in Northern Ireland's linen mills during the early decades of the 20th century onwards. While examining possible distinctions among the workers based on ". . . age, gender, personality, and religious differences, status distinctions, variant pay schemes, placement and type of equipment, . . . atmospheric conditions and noise levels," (224) and other variables in the linen mill environment, Messenger also presents her data in a way that represents the unique experience of the linen worker. Illustrating her book with photographs from the collections of her respondents, Messenger presents the oral, material, and behavioral traditions she encountered during her fieldwork.

Mitchell, Roger. 1983. Occupational Folklore: The Outdoor Industries. IN *Handbook of American Folklore,* ed. Richard Dorson, pp. 128-135. Bloomington: Indiana University Press.
This article is a survey of works on the folklore of the outdoor occupations, such as mining, lumbering, fishing, and more.

Mullen, Patrick B. 1978. *I Heard the Old Fisherman Say.* Austin: University of Texas Press.
This book is based on Mullen's extensive fieldwork with Gulf Coast fishermen. Mullen provides historical and geographical background to his analysis, which focuses on the functions and contexts of fishermen's folklore. The author also gives good insight into his fieldwork methodology. Songs, narratives, rituals, and beliefs are among the forms of folklore included in this work.

Murray, James. 1946. Sailors' Songs with California Significance. *California Folklore Quarterly* 5:143-152.
This article explores 19th century sailors' songs for their correlation with contemporary events in California.

Nickerson, Bruce E. 1983. Factory Folklore. IN *Handbook of American Folklore,* ed. Richard Dorson, pp. 121-127. Bloomington: Indiana University Press.
Nickerson's personal experience as a worker in a factory setting enhanced his perspective, and enabled him to carry out effective participant observation research. In this article, he explores such topics as narrative, ritual, dress, language and more. Nickerson presents this study as a means of exploring the parameters of the study of folklore, as well as a way for employers to better understand their employers. See also: "Is there a Folk in the Factory?" *Journal of American Folklore* 87(1974):134-139; "Antagonism at Work: Them and Us, A Widget Worldview," *American Behavioral Scientist* 33(1990):308-317.

Poggie, John J. Jr., and Carl Gersung. 1972. Risk and Ritual; An Interpretation of Fisherman's Folklore in a New England Community. *Journal of American Folklore* 85:66-72.
This article explores the use of ritual among members of occupational groups whose jobs entail a high degree of uncertainty. The authors make a distinction between ". . . ritual associated with production and ritual associated with protection of life and limb" (67). The authors argue that there is a higher degree of retention of rituals for mortal protection than those of production.

Rapp, Marvin A. 1965. *Canal Water and Whiskey; Tall Tales from the Erie Canal Country.* New York: Twayne Publishers, Inc.
The author actually worked along the canal, and in that context collected the tall tales presented here. These tales relate to the experience of "Canawlers," the Irish word for those who work the Erie Canal.

Raspa, Richard. 1989. Folkloric Expression in the Automobile Industry. *Southern Folklore* 46(1):71-78.
Fieldwork done among UAW workers at General Motors.

Santino, Jack. 1983. Miles of Smiles, Years of Struggle; The Negotiation of Black Occupational Identity Through Personal Experience Narrative. *Journal of American Folklore* 96:393-412.
In this analysis of one conversation among pullman porters, Santino sets his data against the larger frame of the world of pullman porters. The author's aim is to ". . . unveil deeper meanings and to reveal dynamics that are occurring within the narrative and the conversation," and he explores such themes as ". . . occupational subordination, stereotypes and job inequalities, and the porters responses to these conditions as these are presented in personal experience narrative" (394). For other works by Santino, see also "Characteristics of Occupational Narratives," *Western Folklore* 37(1978):199-212; "'Flew the Ocean in a Plane': An Investigation of Airline Occupational Narrative," *Journal of the Folklore Institute* 15(1978):183-202; "A Servant and a Man, A Hostess or a Woman; A Study of Expressive Culture in Two Transportation Occupations," *Journal of American Folklore* 99(1986):304-319; "The Outlaw Emotions: Narrative Expressions on the Rules and Roles of Occupational Identity," in *American Behavioral Scientist* 33(1990):318-329.

Seeger, Pete, and Bob Reiser. 1985. *Carry it On! A History in Song and Picture of the Working Men and Women of America.* New York: Simon & Schuster.
This is a musical and pictorial history of work in the United States. The songs and photographs collected here represent historical events, general occupational themes, and the experiences of various ethnic groups who have settled and worked in this country.

Smith, Patsy A. 1969. *The Folklore of the Australian Railwayman*. Melbourne, Australia: Macmillan.

Smith covers a range of topics about working on the railroad through the narratives of Australian railwaymen. She also includes tall stories, jokes and rhymes to illustrate the experience of this occupational group.

Stoeltje, Beverly J. 1981. Cowboys and Clowns: Rodeo Specialists and the Ideology of Work and Play. IN "*And Other Neighborly Names: Social Process and Cultural Image in Texas Folklore*, eds. Richard Bauman and Roger D. Abrahams, pp. 123-151. Austin: University of Texas Press.

In the multi-generic arena of festival, in this case, the Texas Cowboy Reunion held annually in Stamford, Texas, participants explore the various roles of the cowboy. In this article, Stoeltje illuminates ". . . the roles available, within the rodeo performance itself, for communicating the defining features of the cowboy as perceived in this locale" (123). The author examines the capacity of "cultural specialists" to negotiate their identity and position in the community in the context of this symbolic realm. For other works by Stoeltje on her work with rodeo, see also: The Rodeo Clown and the Semiotics of Metaphor. *Journal of Folklore Research* 22(1985):155-177; "Riding, Roping, and Reunion: Cowboy Festival" in *Time Out of Time: Essays on the Festival*, ed. Alessandro Falassi, Albuquerque: University of New Mexico Press (1987); Gender Representations in Performance: The Cowgirl and the Hostess. *Journal of Folklore Research* 25-(1988):219-241.

Swanson, Catherine and Phillip Nusbaum., eds. 1978. Occupational Folklore and the Folklore of Working. Special Issue *Folklore Forum* 11(1):1-65.

Seven articles in this special issue of *Folklore Forum* deal with various considerations of occupational folklore.

Toelken, Barre. 1979. *The Dynamics of Folklore*. Boston: Houghton Mifflin Co.

This folklore textbook is an excellent guide for beginning folklorists and fieldworkers. Toelken includes accounts of his fieldwork with loggers, who shared various forms of folklore, including narrative, belief, and ritual, with the author.

Walls, Robert E. 1987. Logger Poetry and the Expression of Worldview. *Northwest Folklore* 5:15-45.

Wall's presents logging poetry as a vehicle of personal and occupational identity, as well as a forum for the presentation of worldview to the public. The author suggests that logging may help to close the existing gap between loggers and outsiders, and to engender a more accurate and sympathetic attitude among the latter towards members of this occupational folk group.

Warner, William S. 1983. An Honest Woodsman; The Life and Opinions of Dave Priest—Maine Trapper, Guide and Game Warden. *Northeast Folklore* XXII.

In this oral historical profile, Warner interviews Priest about his life as a trapper, guide and game warden. Priest shares narratives about his experiences on the job relating to personal history, individuals, animals, seasons, and more.

Western Folklore 1984. 43:172-221. Special Section: Works of Art, Art as Work, and the Arts of Working.

With an introduction by Michael Owen Jones, this collection is the result of the 1982 conference, "Aesthetic Expression in the City: Art, Folk Art, and Popular Culture." The articles included here are: Marsha McDowell, "Insider vs. Outsider; Views of Art and Work" (178-192); C. Kurt Dewhurst, "The Arts of Working: Manipulating the Urban Environment" (192-202); Yvonne R. Lockwood, "The Joy of Labor" (202-211); Michael J. Bell, "Making Art Work" (211-221). MacDowell's article inludes some excellent examples of artistic enhancements of the work place, as well as artifacts made from materials available in the occupational environment.

CHAPTER 14
Immigrant and Ethnic Folklore

Guntis Šmidchens

When you ask an American or Canadian, "What nationality are you?", the answer may be as simple as, "I'm Korean," or as complex as, "My mother's half Polish, half Irish, and my father is a little bit of everything!" Many Americans are proud to belong to some ethnic group, a group of people who share by descent the same culture and history.

Ethnics usually share an ancestral homeland, the "old country" from which they, their parents, grandparents, or other ancestors originate. The homeland may be as distant as Japan, or as near as some region of North America. Members of an ethnic group often belong to the same religious denomination, and may sometimes speak a language or dialect other than American English. Many folklore traditions are shared in the ethnic community: ethnics usually eat the same foods, sing similar songs, tell similar stories, and celebrate the same holidays. These folk traditions create bonds among members of the group, and divide the world into *insiders* and *outsiders*——those who belong to the group, and those who do not.

Three American ethnic groups are discussed in detail elsewhere in this book. The Native American, African American, and various Hispanic cultures have existed alongside the mainstream of American culture for many centuries. For this reason, their histories and folklore are at times quite different from those of other ethnic groups, and must be examined in separate chapters.

IMMIGRANT FOLKLORE
Most Americans stem from *immigrants*, people who once chose to leave another country and live in America. Some wish to escape economic hardship in their homeland, and arrive in the "land of plenty," hoping to start a new life. Other immigrants arrive to escape political oppression in the old country. In a world plagued by wars and totalitarian governments, millions of people today have fled from their homelands to save their own lives. Thousands of these refugees are allowed to enter America each year.

Along with any suitcases, boxes, and bags that they might have, immigrants bring to America a large amount of cultural *baggage*——the customs, songs, stories, and other folklore which were a part of everyday life in the old country. The immigrants usually do not speak English, nor are they familiar with the life of the average American. To survive the traumatic experience of living in a foreign country, they often create small *cultural islands* in places and groups where they can feel at home. In their families and in larger communities, immigrants can speak the language and practice the traditions of their homeland.

TRANSITION FROM IMMIGRANT TO ETHNIC FOLKLORE
The language and folklore of the old country have few practical applications in America. When the children of immigrants enter the American schools, they begin to learn a new language, English, and all of the cultural knowledge and social skills needed for life in America. The language of their parents is of little use in the school or workplace, as is the old country folklore in the new world. Knowledge of food-making traditions in the homeland, for example, often cannot be adapted to the kinds of foods found in American supermarkets, and skills such as weaving and sewing are not really necessary when clothes can be purchased cheaply in discount department stores.

Immigrant children, along with all other children in school, wish to be like their peers. They are often ashamed of their parents and the non-American traditions kept at home. For this reason, most children of immigrants reject the language and folklore of their parents, in order to better adapt to American culture. The grandchildren of immigrants, however, have no emotional conflicts like their parents: they speak English very well, and have grown up like most other mainstream Americans. Members of this generation sometimes have an interest in their family's past, and look to earlier generations of their family or to the homeland of their ancestors, for ways to express their personal ethnic identity. They are no longer immigrants: their everyday life is like the life of mainstream Americans, and yet they maintain a sense of personal history, using folklore as a powerful symbol of their ethnic heritage.

The mittens of a Latvian family (Fig. 1) show the transition from immigrant to ethnic traditions in folk craft. Immigrants who arrived in the United States during the early 1950s knit mittens like those on the left. The worn and mended thumb and frayed edges show that these mittens were for practical, everyday use. Traditional mitten patterns of the homeland were often used, but improvised patterns (second from left) also appear. Most Latvian Americans today do not wear mittens like these in winter. Small, decorative mittens (third from left) may be pinned to Christmas cards to give them a special "Latvian" meaning. Ornate mittens (fourth from left) are valued for their ethnic symbolism and worn with folk costumes. Mittens are also sold at tourist shops in Latvia, and are brought back to America as souvenirs or symbols of sentimental attachment to the homeland (fifth from left).

Figure 1. Hand-knit mittens of a Latvian family.

Immigrants at first maintain the folklore of their homeland because they have no choice. They must use whatever knowledge they have learned in the old country to live and enjoy life. Immigrants go to great lengths, for example, to buy and prepare foods like the ones they ate before emigrating, since they like eating these foods the most. Traditional means of entertainment——narratives and songs in their own language, for example, are also kept as a part of their everyday life in America. As immigrants or their children learn English and gradually adapt to American foods and entertainment, the folklore of their homeland is used less and less. Folklore does, however, take on a new, symbolic meaning of sentimental attachment to the homeland, or solidarity with other members of the ethnic group. Traditional foods of the homeland are then prepared only on special holidays, and the language used only in special ceremonies.

Ethnic Americans often rely on contacts with their homeland to provide traditions which maintain ethnic identity. Friends and relatives in the old country send, among other things, songbooks, storybooks, religious icons, folk costumes, and written directions for folk dances or wedding customs. Ethnic businesses arise to supply specialty items produced in the homeland. The store in figure 2, for example, imports rice, tea, and other foods from China to provide for the everyday needs of Chinese Americans.

Figure 2. Imported traditional foods at a store in Chinatown, Philadelphia.

OLD WORLD FOLKLORE AND INNOVATIONS IN THE NEW WORLD

Folklorists formerly collected the folklore of immigrants and their descendants to learn more about the folklore of their homeland. A foreign folktale or song, for example, may have survived in an isolated part of America long after its variants have disappeared in the old country. These fragments of folklore may reveal much about the history of a certain folktale or song, but reveal little about the nature of folklore, a living tradition in the modern world. Recently folklorists have begun to study the new life that immigrant folklore, along with other folklore borrowed from foreign countries, takes on in America. What kinds of folklore survive the journey to the New World? How does this folklore continue to exist alongside American traditions? What changes take place in the folklore as immigrants or their descendants adapt and assimilate into American life? What new, unique forms of folklore arise out of the ethnic experience? Why do people today wish to maintain their ethnic identity? What kinds of folklore are used as symbols of ethnic identity? These are only a few general questions to keep in mind while reading this chapter.

THE ETHNIC GROUP AND INDIVIDUALS

Although an ethnic group is made up of people from a similar background, all members of the group are never identical. An ethnic group includes several generations. Older members of the group will have community traditions different from those of their descendants. Folklore of men and women will be different within each age group, as well. An ethnic group and its folklore may be divided by different religious denominations, by political ideology, by social class, and even by differences which go back to different regions of the same country from which the immigrants came. Outsiders are not likely to know, for example, that the people called *Italians* feel a strong attachment, not to Italy, but to different regions of the country: Sicilians from the island of Sicily, near the Western coast of Italy have traditions very different from those of Friulians, who come from a region in Northern Italy.

A fieldworker will therefore find that ethnic folklore and ethnic identity vary among different subgroups within the ethnic group. Ethnic folklore and identity are also expressed differently by each individual member of the group. Every person can maintain only a fraction of the group's traditions, and will choose from a wide variety of folklore only the folklore which suits the individual's own needs and tastes. Persons might even choose to identify with several different ethnic groups, changing their ethnic identity in different situations. What kinds of ethnic folklore do different individuals select to express ethnic identity? How does each individual affect the group traditions? Who are the leaders of the ethnic community, the people who maintain the group's community traditions? Folklorists have been studying problems like these for many years, to see the diversity that exists within ethnic groups.

INSIDERS, OUTSIDERS, AND FIELDWORK

Certain issues are important in planning fieldwork to study an ethnic group and its folklore. Should folklorists attempt to study the folklore of their own ethnic group? There are both advantages and disadvantages to being an insider. As an insider, you know who the leaders of a group are, and where group activities take place. You may also know the traditions important for the group. If you speak your group's language, you have access to a gold mine of information unavailable to most American scholars. Insiders may, however, make the mistake of thinking that they know everything about their own ethnic group, or of describing only what they like to see in their group. Fieldworkers must keep a distance between themselves and the people they study. An outsider, while not having many of the advantages of an insider, may often be better prepared to record all of the necessary information about a group, including things that an insider might think too obvious to mention, or the less positive aspects of ethnic activities. Both the insider's and the outsider's point of view can be useful in folklore fieldwork. The fieldworker should be aware of the strengths and weaknesses of the two approaches, and attempt to compensate for the weaknesses.

Whatever the relationship may be between the fieldworker and the ethnic community, other practical matters should also be considered before choosing a topic for fieldwork. What kinds of folklore should one look for? Where is the ethnic community located? How can one find people to talk to? A list of some common types of ethnic folklore, suggestions for research before fieldwork, and ways of finding people who can help you in your fieldwork are given below.

SOME FORMS OF ETHNIC FOLKLORE

Music, song, and dance are popular symbols used to celebrate ethnicity in American life. At many folk festivals we see dancers in colorful costumes on the stage, performing a wide array of dances, accompanied by unusual musical instruments and songs in foreign languages. From their performance, we can often learn much about the folklore of their ancestral homeland, but the performers reveal very little of their own lives. Who are the dancers in the group? How often do they practice these dances, and where? Who are the leaders of the group? Where have they learned the dances? Where do performers get their costumes? The same questions can be asked about the singers and musicians.

Musical instruments of the homeland often appear as symbols of ethnic identity, within an ethnic group as well as in representational events for outsiders. At the annual Ethnic Expo in Columbus, Indiana, for example, the organizers of the Japanese exhibit in 1989 prominently displayed the *koto*, a traditional stringed instrument of Japan (Figure 3).

Figure 3. The Koto, a Japanese musical instrument.

Much remains unknown about the history and activities of ethnic performing ensembles. Often the members themselves do not know when their group was founded, and few written records exist of group activities over the years. It may take many hours and days of patient detective work to trace back the history, for example, of a German *Liederkranz* (choral singing society), but the information you may find is well worth the effort. Why was the group originally founded? Has the group's membership and repertoire of songs changed over the years? Are performances different when the ensemble performs for its own ethnic group, or to the American public? An older member of the group may have collected the printed programs of concerts which can answer such questions. Ethnic concerts are often inexpensive, and provide a chance to look at the members of an ethnic group. Who comes to the ethnic concert? What is the average age of audience members? Do they speak a different language among themselves? Is the concert a simple musical performance, or is it also an occasion for members of the community to meet other members?

Along with the songs and dances performed by ensembles, ethnic communities maintain many musical traditions rarely seen by outsiders. In church, Poles, Ukrainians, Lithuanians, and many other ethnic groups sing songs in their own languages. At assemblies on national holidays, they rise to sing the national anthem or other patriotic songs of their homeland. At weddings and birthday parties, they sing traditional songs to wish health and happiness to the guests of honor, and dance waltzes and polkas to the music of an ethnic band. Late at night, as the party begins to wind down, a group of older men may begin to sing sentimental songs about the homeland or lost love.

Often these songs have been learned from printed songbooks. Others may have been passed on only by word of mouth. You should try to describe, not only the words to the songs, but the singing tradition itself. Do only certain members of the group sing? Is there a person leading the songs, and if so, how does that person lead the songs? How do people learn new songs? What songs are appropriate in various situations? Where do the ethnic bands learn the words and music for the songs they sing? Do they adapt their songs to different audiences? Similar questions can be asked about ethnic dance. Are the dances at ethnic parties the same as the dances performed on stage? How do ethnic song and dance, both on and off the stage, help people express their ethnic identity? (See Chapter 10 **Ethnomusicology**, and Chapter 11 **Dance and Movement**)

FOLK NARRATIVE

The stories people tell reveal much about their history, as well as their attitudes toward an ethnic group. Jokes and stories about personal experiences, to be discussed below, are two types of folk narrative found in nearly every ethnic community. (See Chapter 4 **Folk Narrative**)

Jokes may sometimes pass from generation to generation in immigrant families, but more often than not they grow out of the immigrant experience in America, and are passed from ethnic group to ethnic group. Immigrants in the New World are often the object of cruel ridicule from mainstream Americans. They can usually find jobs only at the bottom of the American economic ladder, and for this reason outsiders often imagine that all members of the immigrant group at hand are dirty, stupid, and lazy. Some jokes travel from group to group, and may be attached to any nationality that a person dislikes. Other jokes are more specific to certain ethnic groups, attacking the groups' religion, customs, or stereotypical physical characteristics (color of skin, for example), and using insulting names for members of a group. For example, *polak* in Polish means a Polish man, but in America, the name (usually spelled *Polack*) has been used by non-Polish people to make

The Emergence of Folklore in Everyday Life

fun of Poles. Ethnic jokes are often deeply insulting to members of an ethnic group, and great care should be taken not to offend the people you study. You may find, however, that the best collections of jokes about an ethnic group may come from members of that group. A Pole is likely to know more Polack jokes than anyone else, and the best narrators of Jewish jokes are often Jewish themselves.

Some ethnic jokes are clearly derogatory, and reveal the attitudes of outsiders toward an ethnic group. Other jokes are told by the members of a group about themselves, playing on ethnic stereotypes which the members of the group may consider to be negative or positive. Young men like to brag about the drinking abilities of their ethnic peers, for example, and tell jokes and riddles such as:

> What's the difference between a (Finnish, Latvian, or Polish) wedding and a (same group) funeral?
> —One less drunk!

or

> Wherever you find four (Finns, Latvians, Poles, etc.), there's bound to be a fifth! (Meaning a *fifth*—a bottle of liquor).

The same jokes may be told by outsiders who dislike drunken members of the group.

Ethnic jokes are easy to collect, since nearly everybody knows a few. You might ask several questions as you analyze the jokes you collect. Who are the tellers of ethnic jokes? Do the jokes reveal their actual feelings about the members of an ethnic group? What ethnic stereotypes appear in jokes? Where are the jokes told? Do all people present laugh when an ethnic joke is told? Do members of a group tell derogatory jokes about their own group? About other groups? Why? When told by either insiders or outsiders, do ethnic jokes contribute to solidarity among members of the group? (See Chapter 8 **Jokes and Practical Jokes**)

Narratives about personal experiences are an important part of every ethnic group's folklore. Families pass stories from generation to generation about ancestors who lived before the family emigrated from the homeland, about the voyage across the ocean to the New World, about humorous episodes at the border and in unfamiliar situations, about a new life in a strange and often hostile environment, and about adventures and success in America.

The immigrant *family saga*, all of the stories and memories that a family keeps about its immigrant past, begins with the immigrants themselves. You might choose to record an immigrant's *life story*, an oral autobiography. Good opening questions for a life story are, for example, "How did you decide to emigrate?," "What was life like in the old country?," or "Tell me about your family in the old country." It is best to let persons first tell you the story of their life without excessive interruptions or questions from you. In a later interview, you should fill in the details missed in the original narrative—the dates, names, and places that the narrator may have skipped over in the story. To help a narrator along, you might ask to see a photo album and record the descriptions and stories that go with each picture.

The life story provides information about an individual's history, and often includes detailed information about folklore in the life of an immigrant. A person might, for example, mention an old song or family custom, and tell you that "everything has changed nowadays." In a follow-up interview, you could use the person's own example to initiate a conversation about all of the songs or family customs that the immigrant remembers.

You should also keep in mind that the life story is itself a kind of folklore. Just like any other storyteller, the life story narrator chooses episodes from life and combines them to make a long story. What episodes have been chosen, and why? How are they linked together? Most immigrant life stories are structured around the great turning point in that person's life—the voyage to America. How does the immigrant portray life in the old country? Is the old country compared to America? How? Is there a difference in the subject matter of episodes before and after emigration?

The life story, like other folk narratives, is often passed from one generation to another. Does the immigrant tell the story or sections of it to his or her family? Has the immigrant written an autobiography for future generations? Were any members of the family at hand when you recorded the life story? You should, if possible, try to make the storytelling situation as natural as possible. Husbands and wives might enjoy telling their stories together. Other members of the family might also want to sit and listen, or interrupt with questions. Do not stop such conversations, but try to study them as you would any other storytelling event. Who are the members of the audience? How do they interact with the narrator? What are the narrator's goals in telling the story? Are members of the family familiar with certain parts of the life story? How do they react to these episodes?

An immigrant may never tell the entire story of her or his life to any children or grandchildren. Fragments of the life story are, however, often recounted to relatives. These stories enter the immigrant family saga. You might interview members of an ethnic group to see what kind of anecdotes have been passed from the immigrant generation. As in the life story interview, family stories might be elicited by looking at a family photo album and discussing the people and events shown in the pictures. How does an immigrant life story or family folklore affect an individual's ethnic identity when it is performed?

Verbal Art should also be considered. Up to this point, only a few of the more familiar forms of narrative have been discussed. These are not the only kinds of oral traditions important to the ethnic community. *Public speeches*, for example, are often read or spoken at assemblies on patriotic holidays. These and other speeches——sermons in church, congratulatory speeches at weddings and banquets, eulogies at funerals, and so on——all follow certain traditional rules of style and subject matter. Often these speeches and their contexts are very unlike the corresponding traditions in American mainstream culture. Oratory is intended to express the feelings of a group, or to influence the thoughts of others. How do orators use the language of the ethnic group to move their audience? What are the images used to evoke a feeling of ethnic unity? As with other kinds of folk narrative, you should also explore the relationship between narrator and audience. Who are the public speakers? Why have they been chosen to speak for the group? Who are the members of the audience? How do they react to the speaker's words?

FOLK CUSTOM

Many ethnic traditions revolve around celebrations of three important days in the human life cycle: birth, marriage, and death. Each group has unique customs that traditionally accompany the celebrations. Other important ceremonies in life also vary from group to group. Birthdays, for example, are celebrated in some ethnic cultures, and not in others. A second set of folk customs recur in cycles repeated each calendar year. Religious holidays such as Christmas and Hanukkah, and patriotic days such as Independence Day in the homeland, are marked by important folk traditions. (See Chapter 7 **Folklore and Religion**)

Certain types of ethnic traditions are not practiced by all members of the group, and yet for those who participate they are very important to group identity. Immigrants usually unite in organizations which resemble social groups of their homeland. Church congregations, Boy Scouts, ethnic schools, folk dance groups, and even some fraternities and sororities, all have been created to continue old-country traditions.

These groups will have their own customs that distinguish them from their American counterparts.

In your description and analysis of ethnic customs, you should keep in mind the relationships among tradition in the homeland, ethnic tradition in the new country, and the contemporary mainstream cultural traditions. How do the ethnic customs differ from customs practiced in the homeland? What American customs enter the ethnic life cycle and annual celebrations?

MATERIAL CULTURE

Beginning with the first European settlers in North America, all immigrants to the New World brought with them traditional knowledge of folk crafts: food preparation, home building, farming, and clothesmaking, to name a few. (See Chapter 12 **Folklife and Material Culture**)

The most important aspect of ethnic material culture cannot be described by objective methods. This is the subjective realm of meanings which people attach to things. American ethnics often use the traditional arts and crafts of their homeland as symbols of their ethnic identity. Because the meaning of the object is such an important part of ethnic material culture, you must take into account items that many folklorists would not consider to be folklore. Often it is not the items themselves, but rather their use in ethnic communities, which is the most important part of ethnic tradition. A look at the typical living room decorations of a family with roots in Eastern Europe, for example, shows many different kinds of objects, all a part of ethnic tradition in America. The mantelpiece, a place where Americans usually put family pictures and bowling trophies, is transformed into an ethnic shrine: decorative vases and wood carvings bought at tourist stores in the homeland, small tablecloths woven at the local ethnic arts and crafts meetings, along with religious icons, flags, and emblems of the homeland——all are placed in prominent view as symbols of the family's ethnic heritage. In public ceremonies as well, both performers and audience members may wear folk costumes and jewelry, or play traditional instruments of their homeland. Unlike older folk craft traditions, where items were created for practical everyday use, many of these objects have been made specifically for the tourist and ethnic market, and are bought and kept for no reason other than their ethnic symbolism. Swedish Dala horses (Figure 4), for example, were once carved by Swedish lumberjacks as toys for their children. Dala horse carving has been revived today with a different function. Many

Figure 4. Swedish Dala horses.

woodcarvers are employed today by the Swedish tourist industry, which sells the horses as international symbols of Sweden. Not only is the horse placed on the living room shelves of many Swedish Americans, but pictures of the horse appear on towels, aprons, cups, and even "Kiss Me, I'm Swedish" buttons. The symbolic meanings that ethnic groups attach to things, along with information about the processes of production, sale, purchase, and use of the items, should be studied during fieldwork.

THE FOLK FESTIVAL

Three kinds of festival are occasions for ethnic groups to display and celebrate their ethnicity. In-group festivals take place, for example, on religious holidays. As with other community customs described above, on these days the members of the group meet to express a feeling of solidarity with each other. Another type of festival again involves a single ethnic group, but outsiders are welcome as well. In Chicago, for example, Fiestas Patronales Puertoriqueñas in Humbolt Park, Chinatown Moon Festival, Midsomerfest in Swedish Andersonville, and many other festivals in ethnic neighborhoods are sponsored by local chambers of commerce with support from the Mayor's Office of Special Events. Such single-group festivals may sometimes be expanded to include several similar groups, for example, Swedes, Norwegians, and Danes may celebrate a "Scandinavian Festival." A third type of festival brings together representatives of as many ethnic groups as possible in "International Days" or "Folk Fairs" promoted by schools, universities, and city or state governments.

There are surely important political and economic reasons for government agencies to sponsor public ethnic festivals. This aspect of festival should not be ignored. Researchers of ethnic folklore are usually more interested, however, in the ethnic participants of these festivals. How do in-group festivals differ from those open to the public? How do American ethnics choose to represent themselves to a nonethnic audience? International forms of communication such as food, music, folk costume and dance, and folk art are the usual media of ethnic festivals. Many festivals include a parade, where a fieldworker can easily photograph important symbols of ethnicity, and discover what topics are important to the group.

Because the ethnic festival incorporates so many genres of folklore, it is a useful point of departure for any study of ethnicity and folklore in America. Here one can find some of the boundaries that separate the insiders of an ethnic group from the outsiders. Performers at these events provide *windows* into the ethnic community and its folklore: a folklorist should record everything that is offered here, and yet, fieldworkers should also explore the less visible side of ethnic display events. Here one can meet the individual active bearers of ethnic traditions in America. What are their personal goals as they perform their ethnicity to others? What effect do these performances have on the performers themselves? How has their ethnic identity been affected?

PREPARING FOR FIELDWORK IN AN ETHNIC GROUP

Once you have selected an ethnic group to study, you should find out everything you can about the history, social characteristics, and culture of that group before entering the community. You may plan to interview only one or two people, but knowledge about other group members is also important. Are the people you talk to average members of their ethnic group? Do they live in a large ethnic community? What can you find out about this ethnic group nationwide? What kinds of folklore have been studied in this ethnic group? The books and journals mentioned in this section and in the bibliography at the end of this chapter can be found in most university libraries. Each research project will, of course, require different kinds of sources.

A good starting point for library research is *The Harvard Encyclopedia of American Ethnic Groups*, edited by Stephan Thernstrom. It includes brief articles, arranged alphabetically, about nearly every group in the United States, for example, "Koreans," or "Germans from Russia." At the end of each article are references to other sources about the group. Books are also plentiful about the history of individual groups. Look for titles of books such as, for example, *The Italians in America, 1492-1972: a Chronology and Fact*

Italians in America, 1492-1972: a Chronology and Fact Book. This book and many others published in a series by Oceana Publications provide important facts and bibliographies for further reading. Other excellent books on ethnic groups and ethnicity have been published by Arno Press, Balch Institute Press, and the Canadian Centre for Folk Culture Studies (Mercury Series). Be on the lookout for histories published by the groups about themselves; these offer a wealth of information from the point of view of the group members.

Look for information on the social, economic, and geographical distribution of ethnic groups in the United States Census. Up to 1970, the census provides information about immigrants living in the USA, listed under "Detailed Population Characteristics" by country of origin. Remember to look both at the "United States Summary," as well as data from the state in which you will do fieldwork, to find the population statistics for major cities. In 1980, the census also included a special section on American ethnic groups, titled *Ancestry of the Population by State*. Both immigrants and their descendants are listed here, giving the first easily available national statistics about American-born ethnics. For groups with a nationwide population greater than 100,000, very detailed data are now available about language use, the number of families, the age of group members, and so on. For smaller ethnic groups, only the total number of persons in the group is given for each state.

The sources listed above will provide some information about the general characteristics and history of the group you wish to study, but give little data on folk traditions. For reliable information on the folklore of an ethnic community, you must look elsewhere. In addition to the articles and books listed in this chapter, *American and Canadian Immigrant and Ethnic Folklore: An Annotated Bibliography*, edited by Robert Georges and Stephen Stern, lists thousands of articles written about ethnic folklore, indexed by group and by subject matter. As you survey the work of folklore scholars on your topic, keep in mind that you may be the first person to study a specific kind of folklore in that specific community. You might have to use the methods of scholars who have studied similar traditions in other communities.

After researching the ethnic community's history, read all you can about the type of folklore you wish to collect. Read the chapter on folk narrative in this book, for example, if you will be collecting ethnic jokes, and combine analytic perspectives on narratives with questions derived from this chapter on ethnic folklore.

FINDING THE ETHNIC COMMUNITY AND PEOPLE TO INTERVIEW

Ethnic Information Sources of the United States, edited by Paul Wasserman, provides the addresses of many ethnic organizations that you can write to for information about coming events in the community, and about people who might be able to help you in your fieldwork. Look also in the local telephone book to find locations and phone numbers, for example, of the German-American Society, or Native American Folk Art Museum. For example, the Polish-American Cultural Center (Fig. 5) in Philadelphia houses displays of Polish folk arts and crafts, as well as historical information about Poles in America. In the lobby one can pick up various brochures and copies of the monthly English-language newspaper, *Polish American News*, to read about local organizations and community events, Polish-language radio broadcasts, and local ethnic business enterprises.

Local newspapers often carry stories about ethnic groups and their traditions; if an index to the newspaper is available, this quick (although not always reliable) source of information should be consulted. The local Chamber of Commerce, and the city or state Folk Arts Council, if your state has one, might be able to provide more information on local ethnic activities.

Once you know where and when a group meets, visit a few public events. These are not the only contexts for ethnic folklore. Try to discover other settings where members of the group communicate with each other. If the group lives in an ethnic

Figure 5. The Polish-American Cultural Center in Philadelphia, PA.

neighborhood, drive around to get an idea of the types of homes the people live in, the stores they go to, their churches, schools, and meeting halls. If other ethnic groups live close by, you might investigate the relations among the groups.

Contact community leaders through organizations which you have found. Trial and error is the only way of finding someone to show you around, and to lead you to people you can interview. Although your goal may be to describe only a single family's ethnic traditions, or to record one immigrant's life story, you should not limit yourself to talking with only one or two people. Ask the people you interview for suggestions as to other people you should meet.

As you meet the members of an ethnic community for the first time, or return to your own ethnic community with your new knowledge about ethnic folklore, take time to first observe the community before you pull out the tape recorder and camera. Does the type of folklore you wish to collect exist in the community at all? Are there other kinds of folk traditions, possibly more meaningful to members of the community? Don't ignore things that don't seem "ethnic" to you. Folklorists should record any folklore they find in an ethnic community to study the life of ethnic Americans. Some immigrants have been proud to adopt, for example, American Thanksgiving and Fourth of July as holidays to be celebrated in the "American" way.

CONCLUSION

Take notes on your first few visits and reread this chapter while deciding on the specific topic for your field research project. Stay flexible! Every ethnic group is unique, and maintains traditions different from all others. It is the fieldworker's job to identify which traditions are the most important, and to describe their special meaning for members of the community. The questions asked throughout this chapter provide analytical approaches to some of the folklore you wish to collect. You must decide how the information given here can be applied to the group you study.

Acknowledgements

I would like to thank Dr. Linda Dégh for introducing me to ethnic folklore research in courses she taught at Indiana University, 1985-1988. This chapter benefitted from careful readings and helpful comments by Zinta Šmidchens and Robert E. Walls.

Selected Annotated Bibliography

This bibliography is intended to be a general guide to research aids in the study of ethnic folklore. Many of the sources give further references for the study of particular ethnic groups or genres of folklore. Good introductory articles and exemplary case studies are marked with an asterisk (*).

1) **Ethnic Studies: History and Social Characteristics**
Journals: *Canadian Ethnic Studies* (1969-), *Ethnic Forum* (1980-), *Ethnicity* (1974-81), *Journal of American Ethnic History* (1981-), *Journal of Ethnic Studies* (1973-), *Journal of Multilingual and Multicultural Development* (1980-), *MELUS: The Journal of the Society for the Study of Multi-Ethnic Literature in the United States* (1974-), and *Polyphony*. See also regional journals and journals devoted to a single ethnic group, for example, *Pennsylvania Folklife* for articles on German-Americans in Pennsylvania; *Jewish Folklore and Ethnology Newsletter* (After 1987, *Jewish Folklore and Ethnology Review*) for information on Jewish traditions.

Byrne, David L., ed. 1983. *European Immigration and Ethnicity in the United States and Canada: A Historical Bibliography*. Santa Barbara, Calif: ABC-Clio Information Services.

Cole, Katherine. 1982. *Minority Organizations: A National Directory*. 2nd ed. Garrett Park, MD: Garrett Park Press.
Addresses of African, Hispanic, and Native American groups in various cities, found through a telephone book survey.

*Dinnerstein, Leonard, and David M. Reimers. 1982 [1975]. *Ethnic Americans: A History of Immigration and Assimilation*. 2nd. ed. New York: Harper & Row.
Good introduction to history of ethnics in America.

Ethnic Chronology Series. 1973-1981. 31 Vols. Dobbs Ferry, NY: Oceana Publications.
Each book in this series is devoted to a single ethnic group. For newer data on all ethnic groups in the series, see also George J. Lankevich. 1981. *Ethnic America 1978-1980: Updating the Ethnic Chronology Series*. London: Oceana Publications.

Ethnic Studies Information Guide Series. Detroit: Gale Research Co.
Consult these booklets on selected ethnic groups for a general view of the community.

Haines, David W., ed. 1985. *Refugees in the United States: A Reference Handbook*. Westport, CT: Greenwood Press.
General introduction to the study of refugees in America, with special attention to Chinese, Cubans, Haitians, Hmong, Khmer, Laotians, Salvadorans, Guatemalans, Soviet Jews, and Vietnamese.

*Thernstrom, Stephan, Ann Orlov, and Oscar Handlin, eds. 1980. *Harvard Encyclopedia of American Ethnic Groups*. Cambridge: Belknap Press.
Good source of basic information on most American ethnic groups.

U.S. Bureau of the Census. 1983. Census of the Population. Ancestry of the Population by State: 1980. Supplementary Report PC 80-S1-10.
Information on geographical distribution and size of ethnic groups; for groups larger than 100,000 nationwide, socioeconomic and demographic statistics are also given.

Wasserman, Paul. 1976. *Ethnic Information Sources of the United States*. Detroit: Gale Research Co.
Addresses of national ethnic organizations.

Wyman, Mark. 1989. *DP: Europe's Displaced Persons, 1945-1951*. Philadelphia: Balch Institute Press.

Wynar, L.R. 1975. *Encyclopedic Directory to Ethnic Newspapers and Periodicals in the United States*. Littleton, CO: Libraries Unlimited, Inc.
Lists addresses of organizations and various ethnic publications.

Wynar, L.R., and L. Buttlar. 1978. *Guide to Ethnic Museums, Libraries, and Archives in the United States*. Kent, OH: Program for the Study of Ethnic Publications, School of Library Science.

2) **Ethnic Folklore**
Abrahams, Roger D. 1980. Folklore. IN *Harvard Encyclopedia of American Ethnic Groups*, ed. Stephan Thernstrom, pp. 370-379. Cambridge: Belknap Press.

Bauman, Richard. 1971. Differential Identity and the Social Base of Folklore. *Journal of American Folklore* 84: 31-41.
Discussion of how difference can constitute the social base of folk identity.

Canadian Centre for Folk Culture Studies. Mercury Series. 59 Vols., 1972 -. Ottawa: National Museums of Man.
A large variety of ethnic folklore case studies.

Dégh, Linda. 1966. Approaches to Folklore Research among Immigrant Groups. *Journal of American Folklore* 79:553-556.

Dorson, Richard M. 1977 [1959]. Regional Folk Cultures; Immigrant Folklore. IN *American Folklore*, Second Printing with Revised Bibliographical Notes, pp. 74-134; 135-165. Chicago: University of Chicago Press.
See also bibliographical notes, pp. 294-302.

_____. 1980 [1977]. Hunting Folklore in the Armpit of America. IN *Folklore in the Calumet Region*, ed. Inta Gale Carpenter, pp. 97-106. New York: Arno Press.
Discussion of newer forms of folklore that arise in cities.

*Georges, Robert, and Stephen Stern. 1982. *American and Canadian Immigrant and Ethnic Folklore: An Annotated Bibliography*. New York: Garland Publishing.
Consult this book to find articles and books about specific ethnic groups. The index includes specific genres of ethnic folklore, for example, weddings, funerals, jokes, costume, etc.

Jansen, William Hugh. 1965 [1959]. The Esoteric-Exoteric Factor in Folklore Studies. IN *The Study of Folklore*, ed. Alan Dundes, pp. 43-51. Englewood Cliffs, N.J.: Prentice Hall, Inc.
Discussion of insiders and outsiders in folk tradition.

Journal of Folklore Research 21 (1982). Special issue: Culture, Tradition, Identity.

Kerst, Catherine Hiebert. 1986. *Ethnic Folklife Dissertations from the United States and Canada, 1960-1980; A Selected, Annotated Bibliography*. Publications of the American Folklife Center No. 12. Washington: Library of Congress.

Kirshenblatt-Gimblett, Barbara. 1983. Studying Immigrant and Ethnic Lore. IN *Handbook of American Folklore*, ed. Richard M. Dorson, pp. 39-47. Bloomington: Indiana University Press.

Klimasz, Robert B. 1973. From Immigrant to Ethnic Folklore: A Canadian View of Process and Transmission. *Journal of the Folklore Institute* 10:131-139.

*Oring, Elliott. 1986. Ethnic Groups and Ethnic Folklore. IN *Folk Groups and Folklore Genres: An Introduction*, ed. Elliott Oring, pp. 23-44. Logan, Utah: Utah State University Press.
Good introductory article.

_____., ed. 1989. Ethnic Groups and Ethnic Folklore. IN *Folk Groups and Folklore Genres: A Reader*, ed. Elliott Oring, pp. 53-97. Logan, Utah: Utah State University Press.
Four good articles on various aspects of ethnic folklore.

Stern, Steven. 1978 [1977]. Ethnic Folklore and the Folklore of Ethnicity. IN *Studies in Folklore and Ethnicity*, ed. Larry Danielson, pp. 7-32. Los Angeles: California Folklore Society. Reprint of Western Folklore 36.
Reviews scholarship on ethnic folklore. See also case studies of various ethnic groups in this volume.

Vowell, Faye Nell. 1981. Minorities in Popular Culture. IN *Handbook of American Popular Culture*, ed. M. Thomas Inge, pp. 205-229. Westport, Conn: Greenwood Press.
Discusses influence of Native Americans, African Americans, and Mexican Americans on American popular culture. Extensive bibliography.

3) **Folk Music, Song, and Dance**
*Erdely, Stephen. 1979. *Ethnic Music in the United States: An Overview*. Yearbook of the International Folk Music Council 11: 114-137.
Title of journal changed after 1981, to Yearbook for Traditional Music. A good introductory article.

Hopkins, Pandora. 1976. Individual Choice and the Control of Musical Change. *Journal of American Folklore* 89:449-462.
Discusses influence of the individual on stability or change in folk music, using examples from ethnic music.

McCulloh, Judith, ed. 1982. *Ethnic Recordings in America: A Neglected Heritage*. Washington, D.C.: American Folklife Center, Library of Congress.
See especially pp. 175-250 for a guide to resources.

Miller, Terry E. 1986. *Folk Music in America: A Reference Guide*. New York: Garland Publishing, Inc.
See Regional Studies, pp. 105-132; Afro American Music, pp. 292-355; Musics of Various Ethnic Traditions, pp. 356-394.

New York Folklore 14, 3-4 (1988). Special Issue: Folk and Traditional Music in New York State.
Articles on African American, Greek, Iroquois, Japanese, Chinese, Yiddish, Italian, Puerto Rican, and Haitian music in New York.

Porter, James. 1978. Introduction: The Traditional Music of Europeans in America. In *Selected Reports in Ethnomusicology*, Vol. 3, No. 1, ed. J. Porter, pp. 1-24. Los Angeles: Department of Music, University of California at Los Angeles.

In this volume, see also case studies of Louisiana French, Hungarian, Jewish, Serbian, and Latvian music in America.

4) Folk Narrative

Abrahams, Roger D. 1970. *Deep Down in the Jungle: Negro Narrative Folklore from the Streets of Philadelphia.* Rev. ed. Chicago: Aldine.
Describes oral tradition of an African American community.

*Asplund, Arvid. 1987. Via Dolorosa. *Folklife Annual 1986.* Washington: Library of Congress. Pp. 132-153.
Life story of the son of a Finnish immigrant. Followed by comments of seven folklorists, pp. 154-173.

Brednich, Rolf Wilhelm. 1981. *The Bible and the Plough: The Lives of a Hutterite Minister and a Mennonite Farmer.* Mercury Series. Canadian Centre for Folk Culture Studies Paper No. 37. Ottawa: National Museums of Man.
Two life stories and their relation to ethnic identity.

Clements, William M. 1979. Cueing the Stereotype: The Verbal Strategy of the Ethnic Joke. *New York Folklore* 5:53-61.
Discusses context and meaning of ethnic jokes to tellers and audiences.

*Davies, Christie, ed. 1990. *Ethnic Humor Around the World.* Bloomington: Indiana University Press.

Dégh, Linda. 1980 [1975]. *People in the Tobacco Belt: Four Lives.* New York: Arno Press.
Discusses immigrant life story as a genre of folklore.

_____. 1978. Two Letters from Home. *Journal of American Folklore* 91:808-822.
Discusses letters to and from the homeland as a form of folklore.

*Dorinson, Joseph, and Boskin, Joseph. 1988. Racial and Ethnic Humor. IN *Humor in America: A Research Guide to Genres and Topics*, ed. Lawrence E. Mintz, pp. 163-193. Westport, CT: Greenwood Press.
Good introductory article on ethnic jokes.

Dorson, Richard M. 1972 [1952]. *Bloodstoppers and Bearwalkers.* Cambridge: Harvard University Press.
Folk narratives collected in Upper Michigan.

*Dundes, Alan. 1975. Slurs International: Folk Comparison of Ethnicity and National Character. *Southern Folklore Quarterly* 39 (1975):15-38.
Includes discussion of riddles, proverbs, and jokes.

*Einarsson, Magnus, comp. 1984. *Nothing But Stars: Leaves from the Immigrant Saga.* Mercury Series. Canadian Centre for Folk Culture Studies Paper No. 51. Ottawa: National Museums of Man.
Ninety-three narratives about the immigrant experience. Includes index of traditional motifs.

Greenberg, Andrea. 1972. Form and Function of the Ethnic Joke. *Keystone Folklore Quarterly* 17:144-161.

*Morgan, Kathryn L. 1980. *Children of Strangers: The Stories of a Black Family.* Philadelphia: Temple University Press.
Case study describing effect of family stories on ethnic identity.

Myerhoff, Barbara. 1980. *Number Our Days.* New York: Simon and Schuster.
Case study of a Jewish community, using narratives as a source of information about the group.

Zenner, W.J. 1970. Joking and Ethnic Stereotyping. *Anthropological Quarterly* 43: 93-113.

5) Folk Religion, Folk Belief, Folk Medicine

Hand, Wayland D., ed. 1976. *American Folk Medicine: A Symposium.* Berkeley and Los Angeles: University of California Press.
See esp. articles by Graham, Granger, Yoder, Brandon.

_____. ed. 1980. *Magical Medicine: The Folkloric Component of Medicine in the Folk Belief, Custom, and Ritual of the Peoples of Europe and America.* Berkeley: University of California Press.

Jordan, Rosan A. 1975. Ethnic Identity and the Lore of the Supernatural. *Journal of American Folklore* 88:370-382.

Spicer, Edward H., ed. 1977. *Ethnic Medicine in the Southwest.* Tuscon: University of Arizona Press.

6) Material Culture

Deitch, Lewis I. 1977. The Impact of Tourism upon the Arts and Crafts of the Indians of the Southwestern United States. IN *Hosts and Guests: The Anthropology of Tourism*, ed. Valene L. Smith, pp. 173-184. Philadelphia: University of Pennsylvania Press.
Discusses the changes that traditional arts undergo to meet the demands of the market. Argues that revival strengthens ethnic identity.

Kalcik, Susan. 1984. Ethnic Foodways in America: Symbol and the Performance of Identity. IN *Ethnic and Regional Foodways in the United States: The Performance of Group Identity*, ed. Linda Keller Brown and Kay Mussell, pp. 37-65. Knoxville: University of Tennessee Press.
See also case studies of Italian, Russian, Jewish, Cajun, Mormon, and Hindu foodways in this volume.

Lockwood, Yvonne Hiipakka. 1987. Immigrant to Ethnic: Symbols of Identity Among Finnish-Americans. *Folklife Annual 1986.* Washington: Library of Congress. Pp. 92-107.
Using Finnish Americans as an example, this article describes various types of ethnic material culture.

Teske, Robert T. 1984. Ethnicity and Religion. IN *American Folk Art: A Guide to Sources*, ed. Simon J. Bronner. Pp. 139-168. NY: Garland Press.
Bibliography of articles about ethnic folk art, indexed by ethnic group.

_____. 1979. Living Room Furnishings, Ethnic Identity, and Acculturation Among Greek-Philadelphians. *New York Folklore* 5:21-31.
This case study is useful as a guide to studying ethnic living room decorations of any group.

Upton, Dell. 1986. *America's Architectural Roots: Ethnic Groups that Built America.* Washington, D.C.: Preservation Press.
See bibliography, pp. 169-176.

7) Folk Festival

Abrahams, Roger D. and Susan Kalcik. 1978. Folklore and
Cultural Pluralism. IN *Folklore in the Modern World*. Ed.
Richard M. Dorson. The Hague: Mouton. Pp. 223-236.
Discusses public display of ethnicity since the 1960s.

Dégh, Linda. 1977. Grape-Harvest Festival of Strawberry Farmers:
Folklore or Fake? *Ethnologia Europaea* 10:114-131.
This case study of a Hungarian-American festival raises
important questions about the study of ethnic folklore.

Errington, Fredrick. 1987. Reflexivity Deflected: The Festival of
Nations as an American Cultural Performance. *American
Ethnologist* 14:654-667.
Describes an interethnic festival in a small American town,
showing how the festival helps cool ethnic conflicts.

Gillespie, Angus K. 1987. Folk Festival and Festival Folk in
Twentieth-Century America. IN *Time out of Time: Essays on the
Festival*, ed. Alessandro Falassi, pp. 152-161. Albuquerque:
University of New Mexico Press.
Describes visitors at public folk festivals. Although the
description is done tongue-in-cheek, the article raises important
questions about the people who come to festivals and their
reasons for attending.

·Ivey, Saundra Keyes. 1978 [1977]. Ascribed Ethnicity and the
Ethnic Display Event. IN *Studies in Folklore and Ethnicity*, ed.
Larry Danielson, pp. 85-107. Los Angeles: California Folklore
Society.

CHAPTER 15
African American Folklore: Notes on Collection and Interpretation

Bill Stanford Pincheon

The study and collection of African American folklore materials begins with the study of African American culture and history. The student of African American folklore should immerse him- or herself into the study of the culture and history of Black people in the United States and the material, social and economic conditions which have influenced and shaped the development of Black Americans as a unique but inseparable entity within the fabric of the country. As such, this will necessitate a thorough understanding of American history since the arrival of Blacks on the North American continent predates the arrival of the English Mayflower (Bennett 1968:xii).

BLACK SOCIAL CULTURE AND HISTORY

Socially, African Americans are a diverse group with varying lifestyles, social affiliations, economic statuses and political agendas. Most African Americans are united because of a common history of shared oppression and because of a common, yet infinitely rich and multiplex culture. The roots of this culture can be found in older African cultures and its emergence can be distinctly traced to the forced arrival of millions of Africans to American shores at the advent of the Slave Trade. Its growth and pattern can be seen in the era of American slavery and in the post-independence years following Emancipation.

African American culture, then, is a product of the interaction between different peoples and different cultures, lifestyles, economic systems and social, political and religious institutions. It is the product of a people who have endured a common fate and who have existed or died under laws of servitude, and after slavery, laws designed to circumvent their development and survival even as their energies have

been appropriated to forge a nation (Pincheon 1989: 16).

GENRE AND STUDY

There are many genres available for study with the full range of Black expressive culture and folklore. Verbal genres include but are not limited to jokes, *toasts*, *dozens*, tales, personal narratives, songs (work songs, children's songs, *blues* or *rap songs*, etc.), musical forms and styles (such as jazz forms and idioms), the *sermons*, and religious and ritual drama. Whatever form or genre one wishes to study and where one will find the emergence of these types of genres in social life may depend upon the location and history of a particular Black community or of Blacks in a particular area or region. The Southern United States would be a fertile area for one who wishes to study the blues as social process and cultural transmission, as would, say, Chicago, where reside a large population of Blacks who are offspring of southern migrants or who themselves have migrated from the South. This migration of poor Blacks has, in turn, born an urban blues which has flourished, declined, and with worsening economic conditions, may perhaps once again become popular. Similarly, one might choose to study rap musical performance in a Northern urban area or the urban area of almost any large city. Or, given the increasing popularity of rap with increased commercialization, one could focus on how a music style forged in the inner city environs is now being transmitted via recording onto the lips of rural and suburban youth. In this instance, one would do well to consider the interchange and exchange between folk and *popular culture*—or how a recorded rap is repeated and altered when performed by unrecorded rappers.

Similarly, one might consider how oral rap performances contribute and feed recorded performances and the interchange this entails.

The successful collector of items of Black folklore would do well to become as familiar as possible with the particular informants or group that he or she wishes to study. These studies should be conducted *within context*—the social situation, environment and particular history of one's informants. One should always pay as much attention to the audience and the community in which they reside as to the items being collected, as these are inevitably connected. The historical frame of reference enters when one considers the history of the culture to which an individual or group belongs. One might consider the relationship between the people and their culture and the extent to which these influence or are dependent upon each other. Further, one should note the item(s) under study and its closeness to other forms of folklore from which it may have evolved or may have been influenced. If one studies New Orleans jazz, for instance, one would note its influence from ragtime blues and worksongs.

THE NARRATIVE IN BLACK CULTURE
The Role of the Fieldworker

For my own research, I chose to focus upon the folk narrative as an expressive cultural system. If there is a single expressive form which connects all of Black culture, it is the narrative. The narrative allows members of a group or individuals to communicate shared experiences which may recount historical collective and personal joys and triumphs or tragedies as well as everyday life experiences. The narrative form is often thought to be the voice of the poor, the subjugated or the powerless. But the truth is, that we all engage in narrative exchange in social discourse, whether oral or printed. In a society which values print and writing, it is those who lack access to social and political power, that is, capital, formal education, and print whose voices have been studied most in particular studies of the narrative. Thus the narrative may also be said to be an examination of relations of dominance and subordination, differing power relations or of inequalities. This said, the role of the fieldworker in the narrative process is very important. One must know one's role in that process and how one might influence the quality of data presented—or how the interviewing process itself may structure and shape the communicative exchange.

Early Fieldwork Collections

When we consider the earliest collected narratives from slaves and, after Emancipation, the freedmen and -women, one thing most striking about the field collection process is the extent to which the interviewers, many of whom were white, some African American, were not required to reveal much about their collection techniques or of themselves. We must call into question the role of the interviewer or field collector and how those processes may frame the narrative as much as the story does itself (Frank 1979:86). Nowhere is this lack of such questioning more apparent than in the slave narratives collected in the 18th and 19th centuries. Consider the following encounter related by a WPA worker in North Carolina:

> I got several whuppings for this, that, and t'other; but I 'spects that I needed them. Anyhow, we was raised right; we warn't allowed to sass nobody, and we old ones still knows that we is got to be polite to you white ladies. [Hurmence 1983:4]

In the above example, there is an interplay of power and dominance at work. Succinctly put, the slaves and ex-slaves were subjected to a form of interrogation. While I do believe that those who recounted or told of their experiences and stories (and a lot of other genres which are embedded within the texts as part of the narrative system) did so of their own volition, we cannot ignore that the lot of Black America during the Jim Crow, post-Reconstructionist 1920s remained close to that of slavery. Moreover, many of the informants spoke with the interviewers believing them to be government agents such as welfare workers who could provide some material benefit in exchange for their stories. The interviewer may also have been perceived to possess the power to in some way harm the informants.

PERSONAL NARRATIVES AMONG SURVIVORS OF PERSONAL DISASTERS

For my study of personal narratives among survivors of personal tragedies, I chose a group of informants that I knew from my participation in a rap and study group in Louisville, Kentucky and I looked at printed stories of personal abuse. I interviewed two persons from Bloomington, Indiana, one who have survived a near-fatal automobile accident and another who had lost a spouse.

The most difficult stories to collect were from the discussion group in Louisville, but because I knew most of them already from my days as an active participant while an undergraduate student, I felt it was less difficult to collect their stories than if I had not previously participated in their discussions. Even before my actual field collecting began, I felt that because I had been a participant in their group, they would more easily trust me and I did not think it would be difficult to obtain the data that I needed to complete my project.

I started the project with an interest in personal narrative research while enrolled in a seminar on the personal narrative. Some scholars that we read referred to such stories as *experiences of victimization* (Robinson 1981:63) and from my prior experience with the group I felt this concept was not entirely correct. I was familiar with an earlier study of women's rap group stories (Kalcik 1983), which helped me to prepare for my study. After preliminary thinking and planning, I entered the field with the hypothesis that such stories, far from being told or seen by the tellers as "experiences of victimization" were rather "stories of affirmation and empowerment." That is, my thesis was to determine whether these narratives served to empower the tellers (victims), to aid in their healing process, and to give them a sense of control and stability, since their sense of self had been violated by circumstances beyond their control.

Also by virtue of prior participation, I felt that I possessed a sensitivity which would not prevent people from speaking naturally and openly. I had heard many of the members speak of their experiences among themselves and I had also seen and heard them recount their experiences to new members who came to join the group (sometimes after wanting or needing to talk about rape, sometimes out of a willingness to provide support for others who had survived such circumstances, and sometimes simply out of curiosity and a sense of expressed injustice at the lack of better social policy in dealing with such issues in the political arena.) In obtaining my field data, I would have to use the knowledge of these things to my advantage so that I might effectively complete my project. I knew that simply knowing or being familiar with a focus group and their folklore did not necessarily mean that I would be able to collect the data that I wanted.

Ethically, I have felt responsible for the non-disclosure of most of the stories which I have collected and will not publish them as such. I am comfortable, on the other hand, with citing the stories and obtained express permission to do so. Conversely, I have not disclosed individual names, as the members of the group do not wish to do so.

My Louisville informants were diverse. I interviewed a group which consisted mostly of females, with only a few males. All of them were Black and were from different parts of the city. Some were university educated, some were high school educated, a couple were high school dropouts, some were professionals, and some were not gainfully employed. Some were heterosexual and some were homosexual. My study group reflects in some ways, the diversity of the Black community and also how these different people had similar experiences which were later shared within the context of narrative exchange and group discussion.

I used my ears, eyes, and a tape recorder to record the discourse—the personal narratives and the sounds of the interview. The tape recorder sat inconspicuously on the floor by my feet and I used long-playing cassettes so I would not have to fumble with the recorder while someone was talking. The group knew that it was recording—I had asked for permission prior to starting it—and it did not seem to inhibit their speech or actions nor did it add any extra encouragement for them to speak. In truth, they seemed to ignore it until we all heard the reminder that the tape needed to be turned over because it had recorded the length of one side.

As well, I relied on keen vision and attentiveness. I used a note-pad to jot things down every now and then, but the note-pad in my lap and pencil in my fingers often seemed out of place. I sensed that it seemed to make some people uncomfortable. They would glance at me and then at the note-pad, and therefore, I tried not to use it very much. Twenty or so minutes into the interview, I simply stopped using it altogether. Whereas the tape recorder sat generally unnoticed on the floor, the pencil and paper seemed intrusive, and a little disruptive, a little bit out of place.

So, from that moment forth, I made mental notes, recording changing emotions, sounds which were barely audible and physical expressions and touching (a handshake, a hug, a person handing a tissue to another, etc.) I felt that I had to use all my senses (are there just five?) in the observation process. Mostly, I used my sight to see and then my other senses to identify or better understand what the informants were saying or feeling. I know what it feels like to hurt or to cry or to laugh and so I empathized and tried to feel some of what that person felt. I used my mouth to speak and ask questions. I, like the others present, used my mouth to soothe, and every now and then, insert a gentle "hmmm." These small sounds, though perhaps incomprehensible outside the context of the group process, formed backdrop to the stories. They were the chorus to the narratives, the choir to the soloist.

FIELDWORK AND RESPONSIBILITY

Collecting fieldwork is never really easy, but it has many rewards. The good fieldworker is a good listener and a good note-taker. Usually, the good fieldworker is one who likes people and likes to be around them and is curious. The fieldworker is like a good writer: he or she questions because he or she wants to know and will find out by asking. But fieldworkers do not exist in a vacuum, and they know that their work, their words, their ideas have impact. Observations, fieldwork data, analysis and interpretation can easily be used for wrong purposes and in furthering suffering and dominance. Therefore, you should know that your primary responsibility in doing field research is to those with whom you have chosen to study——not to any outside group or organization, your teachers or colleagues, your school, any ideology or political or social institution——but to those who give of their time and words and allow the researcher to join in, observe, and participate.

References Cited

Portions of this chapter are revised from an unpublished manuscript, "Nonlegitimate Folk and Nonlegitimate Genres: Stories of Self-Affirmation", 1988, Bill Stanford Pincheon. Fieldwork was conducted in March and April of 1988 in Louisville, Kentucky and Bloomington, Indiana.

Bennett, Leronne. 1966[1962]. *They Came Before the Mayflower*. Baltimore: Penguin Publishing Co.

Hurmence, Belinda. 1984. *My Folks Don't Want Me to Talk About Slavery*. Winston-Salem: John F. Blair.

Kalcik, Susan. 1986[1975]. "Like Ann's Gynecologist—Or the Time I Was Almost Raped:" Personal narratives in Women's Rap Groups. IN *Women and Folklore: Images and Genres*, ed. Claire Farrer, pp. 3-11. Prospect heights: Waveland Press.

Pincheon, Bill S. 1989. Cultural Denial: Domination, Distortion and Black Culture Research. Manuscript.

_____. 1989. Deep Territory: Thinking Culture, Thinking Narrative, Thinking the Blues. Manuscript.

Robinson, John A. 1981. Personal Narratives Reconsidered. *Journal of American Folklore* 94:58-85.

Selected Annotated Bibliography

1) **The following works and authors' scholarship and thinking have helped immeasurably in guiding my own:**

Alabama Slave Narratives. 1973. Vol 1 in Slave Narrative series, orig. collected by Works Progress Administration—see introduction.

Balbus, Issac. 1987. *Marxism and Domination: A NeoHegelian, Feminist and Ecological Theory of Liberation*. Princeton: Yale University Press.

Bascom, William. 1954. Four Functions of Folklore. *Journal of American Folklore* 67:333-349. Also in *The Study of Folklore*, ed. Alan Dundes, pp. 279-298. Englewood Cliffs, NJ: Prentice-Hall, Inc.

Bass, Ellen and Thornton, Louise. 1983. *I Never Told Anyone: Writings by Women Survivors of Child Sexual Abuse*. New York: Harper and Rowe.

Brandes, Stanley H. 1975. Family Misfortune Stories in American Folklore. *Journal of the Folklore Institute* 12:5-17.

Fine, Gary Alan. 1984. Social Change and Folklore: The Interaction of Social Structure and Culture. *International Papers on Folk Narrative Research*.

Frank, Gelya. 1979. Finding the Common Denominator: A Phenomenological Critique of the Life History Method. *Ethos* 7:68-94.

Hurmence, Belinda. 1984. *My Folks Don't Want Me to Talk About Slavery*. Winston-Salem: John F. Blair.

Levine, Lawrence. 1977. *Black Culture and Black Consciousness*. New York: Oxford University Press.

Roberts, John M. and Forman, Michael L. 1972. Riddles: Expressive Models of Interrogation. IN *Directions in Sociolinquistics*, eds. John H. Gumperz and Dell Hymes, pp. 180-209. New York: Hold, Reinhart and Winston.

Russell, Diana E. H. 1975. *The Politics of Rape: The Victim's Perspective*. New York: Stein and Day.

Wachs, Eleanor. 1985. Crime-Victim Narratives as a Folklore Genre. *Journal of the Folklore Institute* 19:17-30.

2) **African American Folklore and Culture**
I. General Collections
Abrahams, Roger D. ed. 1986. *Afro-American Folktales: Stories from Black Traditions in the New World*. New York: Anthenaeum. Recent collection of selected items from Black traditions in the Americas and West Indies.

_____. 1970[1962]. *Deep Down in the Jungle: Negro Narrative Folklore from the Streets of Philadelphia*. Second Edition. Chicago: Aldine Press.
Useful discussion of Black male social organization and the "toasts".

Brewer, John Mason. 1949. Negro Preacher Tales from the Texas Brazos Bottoms. MA Thesis, Indiana University.
A collection from an early Afro-American folklore collector.

_____. 1963. *American Negro Folklore.* New York: Quadrangle/New York Times Book Co.
Another important collection by Brewer.

Dance, Daryl Cumber. 1987. *Shuckin' and Jivin': Folklore From Contemporary Black Americans.* Bloomington: Indiana University Press.
Impressive collection which draws upon traditions from many strata of Blacks in the United States.

Davis, Gerald L. 1985. *I Got the Word in Me and I can Sing It, You Know: A Study of the Performed African-American Sermon.* Philadelphia: University of Pennsylvania Press.
A very good study of the sermon as performance event; very good analysis.

Dorson, Richard M. 1967. *American Negro Folktales.* New York: Fawcett.
An important historical collection.

Dorson, Richard. 1972. *African Folklore.* Bloomington: Indiana University Press.
Contains many papers from a conference held at Indiana University, Bloomington in the early 1970s. Very insightful pieces.

Hughes, Langston and Bontemps, Arna. 1958. *The Book of Negro Folklore.* New York: Dodd, Mead and Company.
Some of the best stories and tales, anecdotes and jokes are found in this volume.

Hurston, Zora Neale. 1963. *Mules and Men.* Bloomington: Indiana University Press.
A classic work, from the field collection of Hurston in Etonville, Florida, her home town.

_____. 1938. *Tell My Horse.* New York: J. B. Lippincott Co.
Another collection by Hurston, from Jamaica and Haiti. Explores voodoo, culture and society, politics and government.

Lester, Julius. 1969. *Black Folktales.* New York: Grove Press.
Nice collection of tales by Lester.

Morgan, Kathryn. 1980. *Children of Strangers.* Philadelphia: Temple University Press.
Impressive collection of family folklore stories and recollections. Well written and researched.

II. Motif Indexes

Clark, Kenneth Wendell. 1957. Motif Index of Folktales of Culture Area V: West Africa. M.A. Thesis: Indiana University.

Thompson, Stith. 1932-36. *Motif Index of Folk Literature.* 6 vols. Bloomington: Indiana University Press.

III. Social and Cultural Studies

Abrahams, Roger D. 1976. *Talking Black.* Massachusetts: Newbury House.
A study of Black language styles and patterns within social and culture context.

Asante, Molefi Kete. 1987. *The Afrocentric Idea.* Philadelphia: Temple University Press.
An excellent theoretical work which is useful for establishing perspective and approaches to studies in Black culture and life.

Baldwin, James. 1963. *The Fire Next Time.* New York: Dell.
Penetrating essays on Black family relations, meaning in Black life and culture.

Beam, Joseph. 1986. *In The Life: A Black Gay Anthology.* Boston: Alyson Publications.
Useful study of homosexuality in African American society and culture, the struggle and hardships of Black men.

Boaz, Franz. 1940. *Race, Language and Culture.* New York: Free Press.
Useful for general social history and examining the intellectual climate which affected the development of race relations and social change. Generally useful in all historical studies of culture, race and language.

Davis, Angela. 1981. *Women, Race and Class: The Impact of Black Women on Race and Sex in America.* New York: Random House.
Examines the social and economic status of Black women from slavery to the present.

Du Bois, William Edward Burghardt. 1969. *The Souls of Black Folk.* New York: Signet Classics.
Classic reprint of Du Bois' pioneering essay on what it means to be Black and the social position of Blacks following reconstruction and slavery at the dawn of the Twentieth century.

Fanon, Franz. 1968[1963]. *The Wretched of the Earth.* New York: Grove Press. Orig. published as Les Dames de la Terre, Francois Maspero, editeur; Paris.

Foster, Herbert L. 1974. *Ribbin', Jivin' and Playin' the Dozens: The Unrecognized Dilemma of Inner City Schools.* Cambridge: Ballinger Publishing Co.
A useful study of language and social relations within an inner city urban enclave.

Georgia Writers Project. 1972. *Drums and Shadows: Survival Studies Among the Georgia Costal Negroes.* Garden City: Anchor, Doubleday.
Reprint of WPA project, material and verbal folklore and folklife.

Gwaltney, John Langston. 1980. *Drylongso: A Self-Portrait of Black America.* New York: Vintage Books.
Excellent work which gleans the wisdom and words from urban Black residents, former migrants from the South. "Drylongso" means ordinary, as the narratives are collected from "drylongso" Black people. Gwaltney utilizes an "insiders" approach to this anthropological study.

Hale, Janet E. 1982. *Black Children: Their Roots, Culture and Learning Styles.* Provo, Utah: Brigham Young University Press.
Excellent study of Black cultural knowledge as social process.

Hall, Robert L. and Stack, Carol B. 1982. Holding On to the Land and the Lord: Kinship, Ritual, Land Tenure and Social Policy in the Rural South. *Southern Anthropological Society, Proceedings* No. 15. Athens: University of Georgia Press.
This volume contains several essays which are useful to the student of Black culture, including articles on ritual conversion and experience in Black religion.

Herskovits, Melville. 1941. *The Myth of the Negro Past.* New York: Harper and Brothers.
Very important historical work which is one of the first social and cultural attempts to systematically document the links between African and African American culture.

Hull, Gloria T., et. al. 1982. *But Some of Us Are Brave: Black Women's Studies.* New York: The Feminist Press.
Explores various aspects of Black women in culture and society, in life and struggle.

Johnson, Guy B. 1930. *Folk Culture on St. Helena Island, South Carolina.* Chapel Hill: University of North Carolina.
Very good survey of the island culture and verbal folklore and language.

Kennedy, Theodore R. 1980. *You Gotta Deal With It: Black Family Relations in a Southern Community.* New York: Oxford University Press.
Very interesting and insightful study, especially the author's experience in attempting to collect field data and the "trials and tribulations" he encounters.

Locke, Alain. 1968. *The New Negro.* New York: Athenaeum.
Locke's collection of essay's heralded the rise of the "Talented Tenth" or the "Negro Genius" of the Harlem Renaissance. This was the first systematic scholarly collection of essays on various aspects of Black music and culture of the United States.

Myrdal, Gunnar. 1962. *An American Dilemma.* 2 Vols. New York: Harper and Row.
Important historical study of social and economic conditions, racial relations and discrimination in American society.

Washburn, Wilcomb E. 1983. The Noble and Ignoble Savage. IN *Handbook of American Folklore,* ed. Richard M. Dorson, pp. 60-66. Bloomington: Indiana University Press.
A useful study on racism and stereotypes in cultural studies and society.

Williams, John A. and Harris, Charles F. 1970. *Amistad: Writings on Black Culture and History.* New York: Vintage Books.
A "cultural manifesto" of the Black Studies Movement of the 1970s and approaches within the discipline.

IV. Historical Studies And Folklore
a. Historical Studies.

Blassingame, John W. 1962. *The Slave Community: Plantation Life in the Antebellum South.* New York: Oxford.
Useful for it's attempt to probe the day-to-day realities of slave life among themselves and in their social and cultural activity.

Genovese, Eugene. 1974. *Roll, Jordan, Roll: The World the Slaves Made.* New York: Random House.
Another well-written historical work on slave life.

Harding, Vincent. 1981. *There is a River: The Black Struggle for Freedom in America.* New York: Vintage Books.
This is one of the best written and well-evidenced histories written of African Americans. Harding's emphasis upon cultural understanding and perspective make this book easily one of the most invaluable of this decade.

Jordan, Winthrop. 1974[1968]. *White Man's Burden: Historical Origins of Racism in the United States.* New York: Oxford University Press. Orig. published as *White Over Black: American Attitudes Toward the Negro, 1550-1812,* University of North Carolina Press.
Excellent study of the image of Africa and darkness, dark skin, in the eyes of European religion and society and how this impacted upon the domination and colonization of Africa and slave trade. One of the most probing studies on racism. Highly recommended reading for anyone who would better understand racism in American society.

b. Folklore and Historical Perspectives

Crowley, Daniel J. 1977. *African Folklore in the New World.* Austin: University of Texas Press.
Explores African origins of African American folk culture and past debates over "survivals" in Black Culture.

Dorson, Richard. 1959. The Negro. IN *American Folklore.* Chicago, University of Chicago Press.
Useful for historical inquiry into the controversies and inconsistencies in the scholarly interpretation and reflection on Black culture and folklore.

Dundes, Alan. 1973. *Motherwit from the Laughing Barrel: Readings in the Interpretation of Afro-American Folklore.* Englewood Cliffs, NJ: Prentice Hall.
A very good source for a variety of topics and perspectives on African American folklore and culture interpretation.

Fry, Gladys-Marie. 1975. *Night Riders in Black Folk History.* Knoxville, University of Tennessee Press.
Thorough study of violence and folk history of Black Americans.

Harris, Trudier. 1984. *Exorcising Blackness: Historical and Literary Lynchings and Burning Rituals.* Bloomington: Indiana University Press.
This is a very good book focusing upon the history of ritual violence perpetuated against Blacks in American society and its incorporation into the literature of freedom written by African American men and women.

Levine, Lawrence. 1977. *Black Culture and Black Consciousness.* New York: Oxford University Press.
Excellent study of folklore in historical context and meaning. Gleans folk thought from a variety of sources.

_____. 1983. How to Interpret Folklore Historically. IN *Handbook of American Folklore,* ed. Richard M. Dorson, pp. 338-344. Bloomington: Indiana University Press.
Very useful for a historical approach to folklore interpretation in historical context and perspective.

Seward, Adrienne Lanier. 1983. The Legacy of Early Afro-American Folklore Scholarship. IN *Handbook of American Folklore,* ed. Richard M. Dorson, pp. 48-56. Bloomington: Indiana University Press.
Focuses upon the denial of African influence on African American culture and folklore in American folklore scholarship.

Wiggins, William H. Jr. 1983. The Black Folk Church. IN *Handbook of American Folklore*, ed. Richard M. Dorson, pp. 145-154. Bloomington: Indiana University Press.
Very good study of the Black folk church in American society and the traditions maintained therein, from slavery to contemporary.

_____. 1974. Free at Last: A Study of Afro-American Emancipation Day Celebrations. 2 Vols. Ph.D Dissertation, Indiana University.
Very important study, well researched and well focused.

V. Literature, Folklore and Narrative
a. Novels Which Draw Heavily From Black Folk Culture.
Baldwin, James. 1979. *Just Above My Head*. New York: Dial Press.
Utilizes blues and gospel them and motif to explore the meaning of the life of a gay blues-gospel singer from Harlem who travels throughout the country on Civil Rights engagements.

Chestnutt, Charles. 1969[1899]. *The Conjure Woman*. Michigan: Ann Arbor Paperbacks.
Profuse use of Black folk idiom, stories and tales in a collection of short stories.

Ellison, Ralph. 1952. *Invisible Man*. New York: Random House.
The journey of a young Black man from the South to the urban North. Uses the "mask" theme to delve into the social world of Blacks and through the maze of American racism.

Hurston, Zora Neale. 1978[1937]. *Their Eyes Were Watching God*. Urbana: University of Illinois Press.
Excellent novel by a brilliant folklorist and anthropologist. Draws heavily upon Southern Black folk speech and jokes.

Johnson, Charles. 1987. *Faith and the Good Thing*. New York: Athenaeum.
Emphasis upon the magical tradition of voodoo among Blacks.

Morrison, Toni. 1977. *Song of Solomon*. New York: Knopf.
Utilizes the theme of flight to explore relations in a Black community.

Morrison, Toni. 1981. *Tar Baby*. New York: Knopf.
Draws upon the Black "tar baby" story.

Southerland, Ellease. 1979. *Let the Lion Eat Straw*. New York: Scribner.
See especially for its use of folklife and culture.

Toomer, Jean. 1988[1923]. *Cane*. Norton Critical Edition, ed. Darwin Turner. New York: W. W. Norton and Co.

Walker, Alice. 1982. *The Color Purple*. New York: Washington Square Press.
A historical novel heavily profuse with Southern Black folk culture in the narrative of abuse and affirmative transformation of self.

b. Black Literature and Folklore Studies
Collier, Eugenia W. and Long, Richard A. 1985. *Afro-American Writing: An Anthology of Prose and Poetry*. 2nd and Enlarged edition. University Park, PA: Pennsylvania University Press.
Covers early Afro-American writings, essays, drama, fiction and poetry, until contemporary times (1970s).

Rowell, Charles H. 1974. Sterling A. Brown and the Afro-American Folk Tradition. *Studies in the Literary Imagination* 7/2:131-152.
Excellent essay on Brown's use of folklore in his poetry and art.

Southerland, Ellease. 1979. The Influence of Voodoo on the Fiction of Zora Neale Hurston. IN *Sturdy Black Bridges: Vision of Black Women in Literature*. Garden City: Doubleday. P. 172-183.
Examines the impact of voodoo experience upon Hurston's novels and writings. Very informative.

Stepto, Robert B. 1979. "I Rose and Found My Voice:" Narration, Authentication and Authorial Control in Four Slave Narratives. IN *From Behind the Veil: A Study of Afro-American Narrative*. Urbana: University of Illinois Press.
Wonderful study of slave narration and narratives in Black culture and life.

c. Historical Narratives
Douglass, Frederick. 1986[1845]. *The Narrative of Frederick Douglass, An American Slave*. New York: Penguin Classics. Orig. published by Anti-Slavery Office, 1845.
Douglass' informative and illuminating journey from slavery to freedom and the abolitionist movement in the United States.

Hurmence, Belinda. 1984. *My Folks Don't Want Me to Talk About Slavery*. Winston-Salem: John F. Blair.
A good collection of North Carolina slave narratives offering invaluable insight into the collection process and the minds of Southern ex-slaves.

Blockson, Charles L. 1987. *The Underground Railroad: First-Person Narratives of Escapes to Freedom in the North*. New York: Prentice Hall.
These are narratives of many slaves who became involved in the Underground Railroad, the flight from slavery and bondage to freedom, the North and Canada. Narratives of Harriet Tubman, Sojourner Truth, Frederick Douglass, John Brown, Lucretia Mott and many other important historical figures.

VI. Black Music Studies
a. Black Music History and Criticism, General
Southern, Eileen. 1983. *The Music of Black Americans: A History*. 2nd Edition. New York, Norton and Co.
Authoritative history of African American music development and scholarship, culls through primary and secondary sources, offering a concise and well-conceived analysis.

_____. 1971. *Readings in Black American Music*. New York: Norton and Co.
Various musicians, authors and commentators' reflections and views of Black music and musical development through time.

Cone, James H. 1972. *The Spirituals and the Blues: An Interpretation*. New York: Seabury Press.
One of the very best works on the relationship between gospel and blues and the social and historical conditions under which both functioned in Black life as a wellspring of affirmation and determination.

b. Sacred Music
Jackson, Mahalia. 1966. *Movin' on Up*. New York: Hawthorn.
An interesting autobiography of a pioneering gospel performer whose career begins while traveling as a performer with Thomas Dorsey.

Burnim, Mellonee. 1988. Functional Dimensions of Gospel Music Performance. *Western Journal of Black Studies* 12(2):112-121.
An excellent article which explores the functional aspects of Black music within the context of Black life and posits that gospel operates within a shared system of meaning.

Taylor, John E. 1975. Somethin' on My Mind: A Cultural and Historical Interpretation of Spiritual Texts. *Ethnomusicology* XIX(3):387-400.
Very good analysis, with well-conceived and supported arguments.

Williams-Jones, Pearl. 1975. Afro-American Gospel Music: A Crystallization of the Black Aesthetic. *Ethnomusicology* XIX(3):373-386.
Focus on the Black aesthetic as a cultural and conceptual approach to music making.

c. **Secular Music**

Charters, Samuel. 1981. *The Roots of the Blues: An African Search*. London: Quartet Books, Limited.
Interesting account of Charter's journey to West Africa in search of blues roots in West African traditional society.

Collier, James L. 1973. *Inside Jazz*. New York: Four Winds Press.
An "insiders" glimpse on the world of jazz music.

Ferris, William Jr. 1970. *Blues from the Delta*. London: Studio Vista.
One of the best studies of the performed blues.

Jones, Leroi (Amiri Baraka). 1967. *Black Music*. New York: William Morrow and Company.
A well-written book by a poet, cultural revolutionary and music scholar.

_____. 1963. *Blues People: The Negro Experience in White America and the Music That Developed From It*. New York: Morrow and Co.
Written during the cultural outpouring and interest in Black music which occurred during the 1960s and 70s. Penetrating and insightful analysis. Recommended.

McCutcheon, Lynn E. 1971. *Rhythm and Blues*. Arlington: R.W. Beatty, Limited.
A nice study, very nice bibliography.

Morse, David. 1971. *Motown and the Arrival of Black Music*. New York: MacMillan.
The impact of the recording industry and a Black recording company on American culture; the commercialization of Black music.

Schiffman, Jack. 1971. *Uptown: The Story of Harlem's Apollo Theatre*. New York: Cowles Book Company.
History of famed Apollo theatre where many bright young Black entertainers have made their debut and been spotted by agents and producers.

Spellman, A. B. 1970[1966]. *Black Music:Four Lives*. New York: Schocken Books.
Focuses on four talented Black musicians and their skill.

Toop, David. 1984. *The Rap Attack: African Jive to New York Hip Hop*. Boston: South End Press.
Very interesting analysis of rap music with plenty of photographs to enhance the text. Informative.

Williams, Martin. 1970. *The Jazz Tradition*. New York: Oxford University Press.
The development and flourishing of jazz as a musical style and genre.

d. **Dance**

Arvey, Verna. 1970. Negro Dance and its influence on Negro Music. IN *Reflections of Afro-American Music*, ed. Dominique-Rene de Lerma, pp. 79-92. Ohio: Kent State University Press.
Examines the exchange between body movement and music sound in Black culture, in the dance.

Emery, Lynne Fauley. 1980. *Black Dance in the United States, from 1619-1970*. New York: Books for Libraries.
Exhaustive and authoritative work on the history of Black dance and culture, from slavery to the contemporary.

VIII. **Black Material Culture Studies**

Phillips, Yvonne. 1963. The Shotgun House. *Louisiana Studies* 2:178-79.
Article on the "shot gun" style houses found in many cities throughout the United States.

Freeman, Roland and Long, Worth. 1975. Mississippi Black Folklife. *Southern Exposure* 3:84-87.
Very worthwhile read to get a "feel" of Southern Black folklife and culture.

Tullos, Allen. 1977. Graveyards and Afro-American Art. IN *Long Journey Home: Folklife in the South*. pp. 161-165. Chapel Hill: Southern Exposure.
The use of ornaments and objects to adorn grave sites, etc. Useful.

Ferris, William R. 1975. Vision in Afro-American Folk Art: The Sculpture of James Thomas. *Journal of American Folklore* 88:115-131.
Intensive study of musician and folk sculptor James Thomas. Recommended highly.

Vlach, John. 1978. *The Afro-American Tradition in Decorative Arts*. Cleveland: Cleveland Museum of Art.
Vlach has written extensively on the material culture tradition among Afro-Americans.

CHAPTER 16
Latino Folklore in the United States

Patricia E. Sawin

BACKGROUND INFORMATION

Latinos are people who trace their cultural and family background to the Spanish-speaking areas of the Western hemisphere. About 20 million Latinos live in the United States: some are descendants of original settlers whose lands were later incorporated into the U.S., while others have immigrated. Latinos as a whole comprise the second-largest U.S. minority group (at 8% of the total population, compared to African Americans' 12%) and are one of the fastest growing segments. Yet it would be a mistake to imagine that there is a single, homogeneous Latino culture in the U.S. Spanish-influenced cultures have been developing in the Americas for almost 500 years, ever since Columbus's Spanish-financed journey of exploration. These cultures share some common features because of their Spanish heritage, but have had plenty of time to diverge and develop unique characteristics under the influence of native peoples, other immigrants, geography, natural resources, and historical circumstances. U.S. Latinos come from all over South and Central America, Mexico, the Caribbean, and the Southwestern United States, and the culture and folklore they practice reflects the diversity of their backgrounds.

In Mexico and most of Central and South America the cultures reflect a mixing of Spanish and local native influences, with the native component more prominent among those of lower social class. In the Caribbean and the parts of Central and South America bordering the Caribbean, by contrast, local native cultures are hardly evident at all now, but there is a significant African influence because of the large number of Black slaves brought to those areas. The prominence of the African influence also varies according to region, urban or rural location, and class, with the wealthy more likely to emphasize the Spanish elements of their heritage. Mexicans and Central Americans have tended to settle more in the Southwestern United States, with significant resident populations increasing in areas like Illinois and Michigan to which people originally travelled for migrant agricultural labor. Caribbean immigrants have historically had easier access to Florida and the Eastern Seaboard of the United States, especially New York City. Finding out how and why a particular group ended up in a given part of the U.S. will help the researcher to fit them into this larger pattern of immigration.

A related issue that the researcher in Latino folklore will have to deal with early in the project is sorting out names: what do the people call themselves? how can one identify the same group when looking for comparative information in other studies? In speaking of the population as a whole, I chose the term *Latino* in order to emphasize that Spanish-speaking Americans come from all over Latin America, but it is rare for individuals to describe themselves as Latino; they usually prefer more specific self-ascriptions. Especially in California and the Western U.S. the term **Mexican-American** is probably most familiar to the non-Latino population, and the majority of Latinos in those areas do have Mexican ancestry. But, as suggested above, there are also many Latinos in the U.S. who have no link to Mexico. These include Cubans (especially in South Florida), Puerto Ricans (especially in New York City), and in urban areas all over the country increasing numbers of Salvadorans, Dominicans, Colombians, and immigrants from all the other Spanish-speaking nations of South and Central America and the Caribbean.

People of Mexican background may speak of themselves as Mexican-American or simply as **Mexican** or **Mexicano** even if they are long-time U.S. citizens. They may also describe themselves as **Chicano**, a self-ascription that emphasizes pride in the native as well as the Spanish background of their culture and serves as a rallying point for civil rights and political movements. Some residents of Northern New Mexico, in contrast, call themselves *Spanish-American, Hispanic,* or *Hispano* to emphasize links with European Spanish culture, since many of their ancestors moved to the region as early as the 1600s, before Mexico was politically independent or had developed a distinctive culture. The U.S. Census Bureau uses *Hispanic* (rather than Latino) as the general term, but researchers should be careful in applying it. To self-ascribed Chicanos, the term Hispanic may connote a person who denies the native component of his or her heritage and refuses to join in solidarity with other Mexican-Americans. To call a Chicano *Hispanic* could be taken as a reproach to his or her political commitment.

The researcher should also pay attention to people's strategic, situational use of names. A resident of South Texas whose ancestors settled in the area in the 1700s might call himself Mexicano in a conversation with a neighbor, Chicano in the context of a university political organization, *Tejano* to distinguish himself from relatives who live in Mexico or in Illinois, and Mexican-American when filling out a census form or job application. (Of course this situation is not unique to Latinos. Consider, for example, someone from Rochester, NY, who speaks of herself as a New Yorker while talking to cousins from California, as an American while on a trip to Canada, and as someone from upstate to distinguish herself from residents of *the City*.) If in doubt, you should ask the people with whom you are working what term they would like you to use in describing them. It may also be instructive to notice if group members use this same name among themselves, that is, if they are treating you, the researcher, as an insider or outsider.

In preparation for field research on Latino folklore it is also essential to find out something about the history of the group under study, both by asking the people about it and by doing some background research in the library. It is easy to get the impression that folklore is timeless and quaint, but in fact many of the forms of cultural expression that people cherish, preserve, and share have been generated in very specific and not necessarily pleasant historical circumstances. For Latinos, as for all ethnic and immigrant groups, the researcher who knows how they came to live in a country where they are a minority will understand the importance of their lore much more fully.

Most people, given the chance, would rather stay in a country where the majority population shares their language and culture. With the signing of the 1848 Treaty of Guadalupe Hidalgo between the U.S. and Mexico, residents of long-established Hispanic settlements in Texas, New Mexico, and California became U.S. citizens with the stroke of a pen. While the treaty guaranteed citizenship and land rights, the rapid influx of *Anglo* settlers brought discrimination and eventual dispossession for many Spanish-speaking residents, who would have preferred to remain Mexican citizens. Tejano folklore preserves the memory of oppression and local resistance to it. Latinos who have moved to the U.S. were usually forced to do so because of the economic or political situation in their home countries. Periods of immigration to the U.S. correspond to periods of economic hardship and political turmoil in specific countries, for example, the arrival of Cubans in the late 1950s and early 1960s and of Central Americans in the 1980s. Expatriate communities often strive to retain a life like that *at home* before the political or economic upheaval that forced their departure. Miami's Little Havana section is said to resemble the Cuban capital in the pre-Castro period.

METHODOLOGICAL CONSIDERATIONS

Subsequent sections of this article will introduce the range of genres within Latino folklore and the kinds of theoretical issues that research projects in Latino folklore should address. While pondering which genres and issues to explore, you as researcher should also consider your own abilities and situation. Your ability to speak Spanish will have a practical effect on what kinds of folklore you can reasonably collect and from whom and will also influence your acceptance by the community, even though speaking the language will probably not be strictly necessary for communication. With the exception of very recent immigrants or elderly, very traditional people, your informants will speak English. However, the researcher with no command of Spanish will have to rely on interviews and cannot expect to gain as much through observation. If this is your situation, direct your attention to topics like *foodways* or *festivals* or instrumental music (but even then look for contacts who can provide explanations of ongoing activity). A non-Spanish-speaker might also focus on the activities of young people who retain a Latino style while speaking mostly English. Having studied Spanish in school will be an asset, but be prepared for the fact that people may not speak like your textbook models. Coming to appreciate the local variant of Spanish could be a tremendous learning experience, but it will take time. If possible, enlist the help of a bilingual insider to help you make idiomatic translations of any verbal lore you intend to analyze and to clarify cultural background you may have missed. Remember that jokes and other forms of speech play that depend heavily on situation, rapid apprehension, and the use of multiple languages or styles will be the hardest forms of folklore to follow. Stories, legends, songs, proverbs, or other verbal forms with fixed phraseology may be better to start with.

Keep in mind also that your approach to the material and the people must take into account your status as insider or outsider to the community and culture. If you are having your grandmother tell you stories you remember from your childhood, you'll need to start by getting some distance. Do some research to track down comparative variants. Bring a friend along so that you can watch your grandmother telling the stories without yourself being the entire audience. Get your friend to ask explicitly for the kinds of cultural explanations that you may know at such a deep level that you wouldn't think to articulate them.

If you are an outsider, you will need to be especially careful lest you unintentionally interpret the data you collect in terms of the many unflattering stereotypes of Latinos prevalent in American culture. Américo Paredes's article, "On Ethnographic Work Among Minority Groups: A Folklorist's Perspective" is required reading for any Anglo embarking on field research in a Latino community. Paredes cites numerous humbling and instructive examples of situations in which even well-intentioned scholars have radically misinterpreted their data because they couldn't recognize a joke, took as literal a patient's metaphorical characterization of the *animalito* (little animal) that made him sick (compare the English colloquial, "the flu bug bit me"), or accepted at face value comments people made sarcastically about their own supposed stupidity.

CONTEXTUALIZING THE STUDY

A research project of the type modeled in this book will require the student in most cases to focus on one type of folklore as practiced by one circumscribed group of people. It will, however, help you to ask appropriate questions and enhance your understanding of the social importance of the lore you find if you can view your project in light of the overall picture of Latino folklore. In general terms, the type of lore in a particular group will be influenced by seven major factors.

1) What is the group's original homeland?

2) How long they have been in the U.S.? The general category of Latinos includes both recent immigrants and people whose ancestors have lived in the same part of the U.S. for decades or even hundreds of years. A population that has been settled for a longer time is more likely to have developed distinctive cultural forms adapted to the American environment, whereas recent arrivals will be in the process of figuring out what aspects of their old culture they can retain. You may also find interesting differences and even conflicts within a community where there have been multiple waves of migration (for example, Cuban immigrants from 25-30 years ago mixing with more recent Mariel boatlift arrivals). Earlier immigrants may have preserved cultural forms that have passed out of style in the home country in intervening years, spawning disagreement about what is truly authentic folklore for that group.

3) Does the group under study live in an urban or a rural area? This will have an obvious influence on the types of occupations in which the people engage and the occupational lore generated. Look for other influences as well. Rural Latinos may have more opportunities to grow food varieties not favored by the general population. In urban areas the survival of traditional foodways may depend on local markets that cater to group tastes.

4) What is the socio-economic class of the people with whom you are working and how does that relate to their degree of **acculturation** to mainstream American culture? In some instances wealthy immigrants may create their own enclaves and have the means to retain more of their language and culture than working class people who must accommodate themselves to what they can afford. In other instances (particularly among Mexican-Americans in the southwest) the poor retain more of the traditional *folkways* as part of their pattern of mutual support, while those who have moved up into the middle class tend to adopt Anglo ways.

5) Does this group of people live permanently in a single location or do some or all of the members move during a part of the year, especially to find agricultural work in other parts of the country? When studying migrants you should also take into account: a) whether you are studying them in the place they consider their home area or in the area where they go to spend part of the year working, and b) whether these are people who come from Mexico or some other country or Latinos who think of Texas, Florida, California, or some other part of the U.S. as home, but travel for seasonal labor opportunities

(with recent changes in immigration laws, the latter is now the most common situation). These factors are likely to have a strong influence on the types of folklore practiced, since a long-established urban neighborhood may have regular festivals, gathering places, and shops, while migrants must carry their culture with them in less tangible ways, for example, narratives or food.

6) What is the racial background of the group? Most Latinos count both Spanish colonists and the native peoples of their homelands as ancestors. Some prejudices do still exist among Latinos regarding one's relative proportion of Spanish and Indian ancestry and these may influence association and settlement patterns in the U.S. In areas of the Caribbean where African slaves were imported the populations and cultures have in general mixed more harmoniously than in the U.S. Thus a person may easily be culturally Latino, but racially Black, and a move to the U.S. may entail encountering either more or less prejudice from the surrounding society.

7) Is the political stance of the group an important factor in its cohesion? The self-ascription Chicano indicates not only Mexican ancestry but also a dedication to promoting political equality and economic opportunity for persons of Mexican descent. In the past 30 years political changes in Latin-American countries have been a major reason for people to come to the U.S. Thus Cubans and Nicaraguans who left in the wake of those countries' Communist revolutions are likely to be politically conservative, while the Hondurans and Salvadorans arriving in the 1980s and 90s are likely to espouse more liberal policies than those currently practiced by the right-wing governments in those countries. The relative conservatism or populism of these groups may in turn be a significant factor in their retention or discontinuance of traditional practices.

GENRES

Latinos in the U.S. practice a wide variety of folklore. Other chapters in this book will provide guidance on how to approach particular genres; combine what you find there with these suggestions. This section includes descriptions of some types of folklore that are important in Latino cultures. Consult this list for ideas about the kinds of folklore that you might go looking for or ask people about.

Folk Speech. If you have some training in linguistics you may want to investigate local dialects and special speech styles, termed *folk speech* by folklorists. Everyday speech styles are an important aspect of folklore because they are the medium through which

all other verbal forms—narrative, jokes, songs, etc.—are communicated. The type of Spanish spoken by a Latino community is probably not identical to textbook Spanish. You might try studying the distinctive features of a particular dialect. Most Latinos are bilingual in English and Spanish, but some older people may insulate themselves from situations where English would be required, while some younger people may understand Spanish but rarely speak it. You might investigate the correlation between age or *gender* and language use, or you might look at *code-switching*, asking when and why people use one language in preference to the other or what rules they follow in mixing the two in a single conversation. Younger people especially may also speak regularly in a Spanish-English mix known, depending upon the region, as Caló, Caliche, soul English, Pochismos or Spanglish.

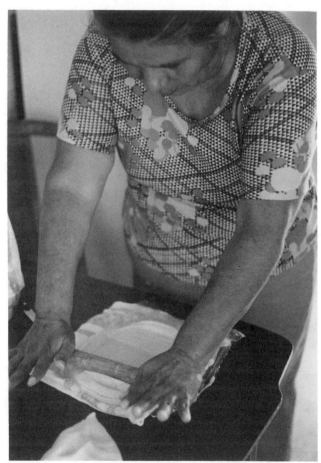

Figure 1. Maria Pozos of Homestead, Florida, demonstrates traditional Mexican foodways, making tortillas. (Photo by Nancy J. Nusz, courtesy Bureau of Florida Folklife Programs.)

The Emergence of Folklore in Everyday Life

Foodways. Foodways, that is, specific foods and eating customs, are often an important marker of identity for Latino groups. Eating the things that you are used to can have an enormous impact on a person's comfort in a new situation. *Foodways* also serve as means for differentiating oneself from the majority Anglo culture. The foods favored by a particular community will reflect home-country resources and preferences and probably bear little resemblance to the homogenized *Mexican* food served in fast-food franchises: Texas *fajitas* (grilled strips of beef marinated in lime juice and served in a flour tortilla with onions, guacamole, and salsa) and Cuban "Moors and Christians" (black beans and rice) served with fried plantain (a starchy banana) are two examples (see Fig. 1). In situations of contact with Anglos, Latinos sometimes use food as a means of subtly drawing cultural boundaries, testing the resolve of an Anglo to appreciate Latino culture, or gain temporary power by grossing out the unwitting visitor. *Menudo* (tripe/cow's stomach) and tacos made with meat from the head of a goat are especially suited for these uses. Keep in mind also that local specialty restaurants and grocery stores may serve as focal points for community sociability and sites where other forms of folklore are enacted.

Religious Celebrations. A majority of Latinos are Catholic, and religious celebrations and displays of devotion are important in the culture. Countries, communities, and individuals adopt particular saints as patrons (see Figure 2). The community as a whole may hold public celebrations and parades for the feast day of their patron saint; immigrant groups may retain and modify the patron of their home country. Individuals or families may keep small niches or altar areas in their homes or display shrines in their yards. In some areas folk religious practices have developed that are tied to Catholic tradition but not directly under church supervision. In New Mexico the Brothers of Our Father Jesus the Nazarene (known to outsiders as **Penitentes**) struggled for many years to gain official approval for their penitential and community support activities.

Figure 2. The altar of the Capilla del Señor Milagroso (Chapel of the Miraculous Lord), San Antonio, Texas. (Photograph by Patricia Sawin)

In the Caribbean area sects have developed that mix African religions with Catholic symbolism. The most prominent Afrocuban sect, **Santería**, has many adherents among white as well as Black Cubans in the U.S. Practitioners address petitions for healing, help, or blessing to the **orishas**, deities introduced by Yoruba slaves from West Africa which have become partially associated with particular Catholic saints. **Santería** rituals may involve practitioners in spirit possession and ecstatic dancing and usually require a sacrifice of money, food and drink, or animals. Because Anglo-Americans have often mistakenly identified **Santería** with *devil worship* adherents may be reluctant to speak to outsiders. Always be especially careful to show proper respect when observing and documenting religious activities. Even those that appear unfamiliar to you are of great importance to the participants.

Secular Celebrations. Secular celebrations also reveal much about the values of the Latino culture. National holidays from other countries, like Mexican Independence day and **Cinco de Mayo**, may be focal points for community identity. Family-based activities held for certain life-cycle rituals, including baptisms, weddings, anniversaries, and birthdays provide interesting comparisons with Anglo-American family celebrations. One special celebration common to most Latino cultures is the **quinceñera**, an elaborate party held to celebrate a girl's 15th birthday. Such celebrations are an interesting arena in which to study culture retention and change and the influence of economics on folklore. Formerly only wealthy families could afford such a party—like a debutante ball—while in the U.S. more families have the means to do it so that in some cases this custom is becoming more popular. Modern young people may reject the **quinceñera** as old-fashioned, but one Indiana student recently wrote a paper reporting that his sister usually rejected the family's Mexican traditions but had asked to have a **quinceñera** because it was a good opportunity to get a lot of presents!

Narrative Forms. Latino cultures are rich in narrative forms including wholly fictional folk tales that may have themes running back to medieval Europe and legends about purported actual occurrences in the home country or the U.S. It is interesting to see which of these survive the immigrant experience and changing cultural situations. In immigrant groups there may also be stories circulating about personal experiences during immigration, although little scholarly work has yet been done on that topic.

Jokes. Jokes in any culture tend to highlight and probe areas of tension and discomfort. U.S. Latinos frequently joke about their relation to the larger Anglo culture. Jokes may lampoon the incompetence of a cultural newcomer or turn on sophisticated bilingual punning. The meaning of a joke can change radically depending on who tells it, to whom it is told, and under what circumstances. Understanding what makes a joke funny requires a lot of compressed cultural knowledge. If you observe a joke as it is being told and can describe and explain it clearly that in itself may form the core of an illuminating research project.

Music. Latin American cultures support a tremendous variety of popular and folk music. Some types——like Mexican mariachi bands with their distinctive combination of guitar and trumpet——are already familiar to many Americans (see Fig. 3). Many kinds of Caribbean dance music——cha-cha, merengue, rhumba, mambo, and salsa——have had an impact on U.S. popular music, although musicians from different areas retain distinctive local variations that would be interesting to explore. Other kinds of folk and popular music are known only locally, for example the narrative **Corridos** that describe conflict along the Texas-Mexico border, the distinctive, accordion-based **Conjunto** music that became the central cultural symbol for border Tejanos starting in the 1930s, and the **Entregas** sung for weddings in New Mexico. Many young Latinos are forming bands that play mixtures of American rock and various Latin styles. You might also want to investigate reflections in the U.S. of the South American **Nueva Canción** (New Song) movement (started in Chile in the Allende period) in which local musics were reinterpreted for purposes of political protest, or the use of traditional ethnic musical forms in Catholic religious services in this country. The Afro-Cuban musical forms that accompany ritual dancing in **Santería** comprise yet another topic for study.

Drama. Some communities in Texas and New Mexico still stage various forms of ritual drama including the Matachines dance and the Christmas play "Los Pastores" (The Shepherds). Since the late 1960s many local, informal *teatros* (theater groups) have developed in communities of Chicano and Puerto Rican workers. The best known is the "Teatro Campesino," which was originally brought together to dramatize workers' demands during the grape boycott and strike and later developed into a professional avant-garde theater, dedicated to creating a distinctively Chicano form of theater. More informal teatros may assemble occasionally to address political and

Material culture. I can only suggest the wide range of material objects whose form and use reveal Latino aesthetics. Piñatas, candy-filled paper figures for children's parties, are popular in many Latino cultures, but Mexicans make animal figures that must be broken open with a stick while Cubans favor boxy shapes that fall open with yanks on replaceable paper streamers (see Fig. 4). New Mexican wood carvers specialize in making figures of the saints in a local style, while Mexicans and Cubans use mass-produced saints' images, but design their own yard shrines to display them. The decoration of graves reflects an adaptation of traditional practices, but still departs from an Anglo aesthetic.

Vernacular architecture. In Texas, New Mexico, and California the architectural styles and techniques favored by the original Mexican inhabitants have been taken up in part by the wider Anglo culture and give a distinctive look to those areas. Local architectural

Figure 3. Guitarron player from the Mexican-American "Mariachi Jalisco" band, Miami. (Photograph by Nancy J. Nusz, courtesy Bureau of Florida Folklife Programs)

labor issues of concern to the community. Their use of elements of traditional Latino culture to express contemporary problems would make an interesting study.

Occupational folklore. Latinos engage in all kinds of occupations, but if you are interested in occupational lore you should try to find out which jobs are particularly common among a certain population or especially important to the ethnic identity of the group. Cuban cigar makers (see Fig. 5), Tejano saddle makers, and Mexican bakers (panaderos) all practice traditional crafts that hold symbolic as well as practical significance for their communities. Agricultural laborers also hand on their skills in a traditional manner, orally and by example. In cities there is often a hierarchy of jobs available to recent immigrants: the service positions held by Asian refugees last year are passed on to Salvadorans this year as the previous generation of new arrivals moves up the ladder.

Figure 4. Cuban piñatas at a specialty shop in Miami. (Photograph courtesy Bureau of Florida Folklife Programs.)

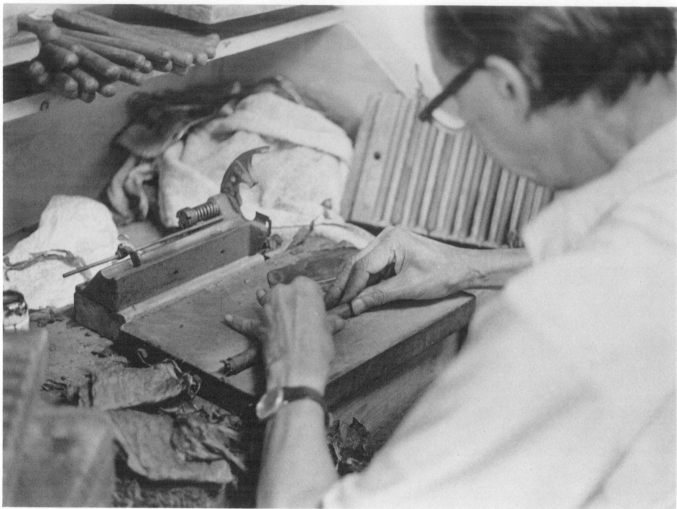

Figure 5. Erebento Kavel rolling cigars at the Ramar Cigar Co., Miami. Photograph by Tina Bucuvalas, courtesy Bureau of Florida Folklife Programs.

styles are often the most difficult part of a culture for immigrants to bring along to a new country, but the Havana-esque style of parts of Miami and the retreats called *casitas* that Puerto Rican New Yorkers build in the midst of vacant lot gardens attest to the ingenuity and determination of Latinos who want to recreate a piece of home.

Folk Medicine. Folk medicine in Latino cultures (as in most) involves a combination of religious faith, magic, and knowledge of healing techniques and pharmacologically effective substances. The techniques of Mexican-American folk healers, called **curanderos** or **curanderas**, have been fairly well-documented, although updates are always useful. Little work has been done as yet on the folk medicine of recent immigrant groups; this might provide an interesting study in retention and change.

THEORETICAL ISSUES

For each of the genres listed above other articles in this book may suggest avenues for exploration, but there are certain issues especially relevant to the experience of Latinos (and other minority or immigrant groups) in the U.S. that apply across genres. Consider addressing one or more of these in your research project.

1) Change and persistence in folklore forms over time is an especially important issue for minority groups that have to maintain their culture while constantly exposed to the aesthetic and cultural forms of the surrounding majority culture. In researching almost any of the suggested genres you may find it instructive to ask the people you are interviewing or to try to figure out: how does this compare to the way they did it back in the home country or the way it was done by community members a few generations

earlier? why does this group keep or reject certain practices? what do retained customs do for the group in their current, changed circumstances? Look especially for evidence that a practice is changing function (e.g., from religious celebration to secular festivity), is dying out for lack of opportunity or appropriate places to perform them, or is acquiring even greater significance to a group as a symbol of ethnic identity.

2) A large proportion of migrant agricultural laborers are Latino, and their folklore has been little explored. If you work with migrants you may want to explore questions such as: what aspects of your culture can you bring along? what do you do differently when you are back home in Texas or Florida? does the verbal lore reflect the particular pressures of a migrant existence or of the relatively low pay and difficult working and living situations these people experience?

3) Many aspects of Latino folklore from foodways to architecture to folk religion are the result of an earlier *syncretism* between the culture of Spanish colonists and that of the native population and/or of African slaves. Do elements from one source or the other persist more strongly when these forms are transported to the U.S.? Why?

4) Contemporary Latino authors have often drawn upon the folklore of their community for literary depictions. Consider comparing the situation you have observed with the representation in literature of people from the same culture and region.

5) A major goal of **La Raza Unida**, the Chicano political organization, has been to attain political and economic equality for Chicanos while promoting and gaining respect for Mexican-American culture. The use of specific folklore forms in some specific facet of this struggle would make a conceptually complex, but rewarding research project.

6) In considering the folklore of any ethnic or minority group, especially those who have suffered discrimination from the majority culture, one must recognize that folklore can be practiced unselfconsciously or it may be used quite deliberately as a marker of ethnicity or a means of displaying identity or negotiating the boundary between *us* and *them*. Much Latino folklore may serve a dual purpose, being directed outward to the majority culture as well as inward and communicating different messages to the two groups. This double-meaning might be an interesting issue for your paper, providing that you are sure you are able to grasp both meanings accurately. I have mentioned the use of traditional favorite foods to emphasize in-group solidarity while

testing Anglos. Look for similar negotiations both in large scale public arenas like *festivals* and in smaller, more intimate contacts between Anglos and Latinos.

7) You should be alert to issues of **gender**. Don't be too quick to jump to conclusions about machismo and the domination of women, but do consider gender roles. Latino women often have very specific duties and spheres of action. For your research project you might consider the folklore about women or folklore in which women participate, relating that both to what you have observed about women's roles and aspirations and to stereotypes about Latino women current in American culture.

STARTING THE FIELD RESEARCH

You have identified the predominant Latino groups in your area; done some background reading on their history; identified a genre that interests you and that you should be able to collect given the time constraints of the project and your linguistic ability and cultural familiarity; and made up your mind to do your research project on Latino folklore. If you plan to learn more about the culture of people with whom you have already established contact through work, common interests, or mutual acquaintances or to study a group of which you are yourself a part, you're all set. If you need to make contacts specifically for this project, I can offer a few suggestions. Specialty stores in a Latino neighborhood are a good place to begin—groceries, restaurants frequented by the locals, bakeries, even the **botánicas** that sell supplies for **Santería** rituals, if that is practiced in your area. People who work in stores are used to dealing with the public and may be willing to answer your questions about their work and its significance in the community or refer you to others who specialize in the kinds of folklore in which you are interested. *Festivals*, either in Latino neighborhoods or city-wide gatherings where many ethnic groups are represented, are also good places for making contacts because people have come prepared to present their culture to outsiders. You might speak to the priest at the Catholic church in the areas where the population you wish to study lives; he may be able to connect you with community leaders who work with him on feast days or book his parish hall for their group activities. Soccer clubs are a major focus of social activity for many of the recent immigrants from Central and South America. These social clubs sponsor all sorts of cultural activities for men, women, and children, but you might be able to get to know them on the soccer fields or to contact the group leaders through the local recreation coordinators.

You can never be sure that people will be willing to talk to you. Don't be discouraged if the first people you ask turn you down. Try to stay open; let the topic for your paper emerge from what is important to the people you are studying. By reaching out to another sector of your community you may find whole new dimensions of what it means to be American.

Acknowledgements

The following people graciously contributed to this article by supplying information to fill gaps in the author's knowledge and/or reading and correcting drafts. I am glad to acknowledge their expertise and kind assistance: Tina Bucuvalas, Olivia Cadaval, Martha Davis, Suzanne Gott, Michael Mason, John McDowell, Kenneth Pimple, Kay Turner.

Selected Annotated Bibliography

Much of the scholarship on recent Latino immigrant groups is just starting to be published and may exist only in festival and museum brochures and other publications that your library probably won't have. Ask your teacher for guidance in looking at recent issues of the folklore journals. For sources relating to the immigrant and ethnic experience, you should also consult the bibliography to the Ethnic Folklore chapter.

Amastae, Jon and Lucía Elías-Olivares. 1982. *Spanish in the United States: Sociolinguistic Aspects*. Cambridge: Cambridge University Press.
The articles in this collection presuppose some understanding of linguistics, but provide detailed data on the many ways Spanish is used in the U.S.

Bauman, Richard and Roger D. Abrahams. 1981. *"And Other Neighborly Names": Social Process and Cultural Image in Texas Folklore*. Austin: University of Texas Press.
Created in honor of Américo Paredes, this volume touches on many of the important issues concerning the folklore of the Texas-Mexican border region. Relevant articles include:
Abrahams, Roger D. Shouting Match at the Border: The Folklore of Display Events.
González, Alicia Maria. "Guess How Doughnuts Are Made": Verbal and Nonverbal Aspects of the *Panadero* and His Stereotype.
Graham, Joe. The *Caso*: An Emic Genre of Folk Narrative.
Jordan, Rosan. Tension and Speech Play in Mexican-American Folklore.
Limón, José E. The Folk Performance of "Chicano" and the Cultural Limits of Political Ideology.
McDowell, John H. The *Corrido* of Greater Mexico.

Brandon, George. 1983. *The Dead Sell Memories*. Ann Arbor, Michigan: UMI Press.
Brandon provides a thorough and complex account of Santería, although he focuses more on history and development than on the current practice of the religion.

Briggs, Charles. 1980. *The Woodcarvers of Córdova, New Mexico*. Knoxville: University of Tennessee Press.
Córdova, NM is known for the distinctive wooden figurines that local residents carve, mostly for the tourist trade. Briggs traces the development of this local practice, starting with the first man who revived and adapted the 19th-century New Mexican tradition of carving religious figures. He analyzes the influence of Anglo patrons on the revival of *authentic* Hispanic folk arts and explores the tensions involved in adapting a religious art to secular purposes.

Cadaval, Olivia. 1985. "The Taking of the Renwick": The Celebration of the Day of the Dead and the Latino Community of Washington, D.C. *Journal of Folklore Research* 22:179-94.
Cadaval describes what happened when members of the Washington, D.C. Latino community were invited to stage a traditional religious celebration in a major art gallery. She explores how traditional activities must be adapted to changing circumstances (and to the exigencies of a performance situation), yet also reveals how participants may be carried away by the power of a ceremony, even in incongruous surroundings.

Curtis, James R. 1981. *Santería*: Persistence and Change in an Afrocuban Cult Religion. IN *Objects of Special Devotion: Fetishism in Popular Culture*, ed. Ray B. Browne. Bowling Green, Ohio: Bowling Green University Popular Press.
Curtis provides a brief and very basic account of Santería. See Brandon and follow his bibliography for more extensive treatments.

Dorson, Richard M. 1964. *Buying the Wind: Regional Folklore in the United States*. Chicago and London: University of Chicago Press.
Section VI, "Southwest Mexicans," will introduce the reader to a basic sample of folktales, legends, corridos, and other forms of verbal lore (in translation).

_____., ed. 1983. *Handbook of American Folklore*. Bloomington: Indiana University Press.
See the articles by Marta Weigle and José Limón for brief but insightful introductions to the theoretical issues involved in the contemporary study of the folklore of New Mexico and the Texas-Mexico border, respectively.

Espinosa, Aurelio M. 1985. *The Folklore of Spain in the American Southwest: Traditional Spanish Folk Literature in Northern New Mexico and Southern Colorado*, J. Manuel Espinosa, ed. Norman: University of Oklahoma Press.
This is the culmination of life-long labors by the pioneer scholar of New Mexican folklore. As the title suggests, it is designed to emphasize the Spanish retentions, rather than Mexican or native influences in New Mexican folklore.

Jordan, Rosan. 1985. The Vaginal Serpent and other Themes from Mexican-American Women's Lore. In *Women's Folklore, Women's Culture*, ed., Rosan A. Jordan and Susan Kalcik. Philadelphia: University of Pennsylvania Press, pp. 26-44.
Jordan focuses on the kinds of folklore shared by women in a Mexican-American family, interpreting it as a reflection of the specific anxieties attendant upon living as a woman in this culture.

Kanellos, Nicolás. 1978. Folklore in Chicano Theater and Chicano Theater as Folklore. *Journal of the Folklore Institute*. 15(1):57-82.
Kanellos provides an insider's view of the Chicano and Puerto Rican *teatro* (theater) movement. Beginning with a single group brought together to dramatize workers' concerns during the Grape Boycott and Strike in the late 1960s, community theater groups have sprung up all over the country. Kanellos argues that *teatro* is folk theater not only because the performers draw upon recognized folk songs, jokes, stories, etc., but also because these groups "unselfconsciously reflect the life, mores, and customs of the grass-roots communities from which they have sprung, performing mainly for those communities."

Paredes, Américo. 1977. On ethnographic work among minority groups: A folklorist's perspective. *New Scholar* 6:1-32.

_____. 1976. *A Texas-Mexican Cancionero*. Urbana: University of Illinois Press.

_____. 1958. *"With his pistol in his hand": A border ballad and its hero*. Austin: University of Texas Press.
Paredes, now professor emeritus at the University of Texas, grew up in the Texas-Mexico border culture and has become an eloquent spokesman and interpreter for his natal culture as well as the teacher of many of the scholars currently doing research on Mexican-American folklore. *"With his pistol in his hand"* is the classic study of the border corrido. The *Cancionero* depicts the range of songs sung on the border in full cultural context. "On ethnographic work" reveals common mistakes made by outside ethnographers working in Mexican-American communities.

Peña, Manuel. 1985. *The Texas-Mexican Conjunto: History of a Working Class Music*. Austin: University of Texas Press.
This is an exemplary extended study of a single musical style. Peña describes the history of this popular, commercial music, traces its probable origins in the earlier folk and popular musics of Northern Mexico and the border, and demonstrates its importance and adoption as a symbol of Mexicano identity in the U.S. in the 1940s and 50s.

Turner, Kay. 1982. Mexican American Home Altars: Toward Their Interpretation. *Aztlan* 13:309-26.
Based on work with four Mexican-American women in Austin, Texas, Turner's article describes the altars many Mexican-American women maintain in their homes and offers a feminist analysis of the sometimes uneasy relationship between this women's folk religious practice and the official Catholic church.

Weigle, Marta. 1976. *Brothers of Light, Brothers of Blood: The Penitentes of the Southwest*. Albuquerque: University of New Mexico Press.
Weigle's book is an exhaustive study of the New Mexican religious association for men, its probable origins, development during the 19th and 20th centuries, religious and community support functions, and rituals.

_____., ed., with Claudia Larcombe and Samuel Larcombe. 1983. *Hispanic Arts and Ethnohistory in the Southwest*. Santa Fe: Ancient City Press.
This compendium emphasizes material culture, folk art, and architecture, focusing especially on Hispanic New Mexico. The articles are exhaustive and authoritative and provide both descriptions of Hispanic arts and crafts and records of their historical development, including critical understandings of the roles played by Anglo art patrons and the development of the tourist trade in the Southwest in the 20th century.

Williams, Brett. 1984. Why Migrant Women Feed Their Husband Tamales: Foodways as a Basis for a Revisionist View of Tejano Family Life. IN *Ethnic and Regional Foodways in the United States: The Performance of Group Identity*, ed., Linda Keller Brown and Kay Mussell. Knoxville: University of Tennessee Press, pp. 113-26.
Williams breaks through the stereotypes Anglos often hold regarding Latino women's subservience to men, arguing that making tamales "because my husband expects it" actually enables Mexican-American migrant women to create opportunities for female interaction and reinforce kin networks essential to the economic survival of their families.

CHAPTER 17
Collecting Children's Folklore

Sean Galvin

WHAT IS CHILDREN'S FOLKLORE?

The designation *children's folklore* can be problematic to the neophyte folklore collector. What are the boundaries of "childhood"? What constitutes children's narrative, customary, or material lore? Are items of children's folklore inherently recognizable? For example, can you remember singing this little "ditty"?

It's raining, it's pouring,
the old man is snoring.
He jumped into bed
And bumped his head
And couldn't get up in the morning.

Or, perhaps, this counting-out rhyme?

Eenie meenie meinie mo,
Catch a tiger by the toe.
If he hollers,
make him pay,
fifty dollars every day.
My mother told me
to pick this very one-
O-U-T spells out!

And finally, this riddle?

Q: What's black and white and read all over?
A: A newspaper.

The above examples immediately spring to my mind but could have been culled from many different oral sources from across America and beyond. They are also the *tip of the iceberg* of what has come to be known as *childlore*. Children's folklore and folklife may encompass such diverse subjects as autograph album inscriptions, catch riddles, cheers, counting-out rhymes, folksongs, folk toys, games (competitive and non-competitive), hand claps, hobbies, insults, jokes, jump-rope rhymes, limericks, lullabies, nicknaming, nonsense jokes, nursery rhymes, play party games, popular songs, proverbs, puppets, scout (brownie) songs, secret languages, swapping, taunts, true riddles, and tongue twisters, to name some of the more prominent areas of study.

COLLECTING CHILDREN'S FOLKLORE

For the simple reason that we were all children at one time, we might assume that collecting or recording children's lore would be as simple as pie. Upon closer examination, however, we find that the world that children inhabit is not as open to adults as we would like to believe. Because adult figures are almost entirely *the authority*, and could hardly be accepted as *friend* (equal), children will not easily let down their guard; in fact, they will go out of their way to tell an adult what they think the adult wants them to say. Therefore, some simple precautionary measures may be in order to be able to establish contact and to successfully document children's folklore.

STRATEGIES FOR COLLECTING

Let us begin with the notion of folklore as artistic communication created or passed on by individuals or folk groups, either informally or by example. Within these parameters, we can make several generalized statements: first, children's folklore emphasizes the concerns children have negotiating daily life in the home or school environment. Most of children's lore pertains to play, the mastery of the skills intrinsic to play, and the relationships with age mates, siblings, and adults while engaged in play. Play can encompass anything from alternative realities to role-reversals to mirroring the activities of actual people and events. If you are interested in collecting children's lore but are uncertain where to begin, begin by observing children in their most natural habitat—at play.

Beginning a collection project with siblings or children already known to the collector is an obvious first-step for gathering data. Going to a place where children play, whether it be a schoolyard, a local playground, or someone's backyard might be a second source for data, but do not expect immediate acceptance by a group if you are not known to them. Children deserve the same respect we would give to any potential informants and require the same investment in time and energy.

If you are unknown, the best procedure is to observe quietly and then approach the group with your collection proposal; or if that is not possible, to approach the group straightaway and await their decision. Again, do not be put off if children are suspicious about you because it is very likely that they might think you odd for not asking anything more of them than to watch. Bribes (such as candy, gum, etc.) have generally been found to be counter-productive to collecting because the nature of the collection is put on a rewards system.

Finally, in most instances, it is not advisable to collect on a one-to-one basis. A child may be able to recreate a song or a joke for the collector but it would not be in the context or *spirit* of play, hence it might feel forced or self-consciously offered. Once the rapport is built with a group, you can perhaps take children aside individually and ask them more specific questions about the context or nature of the games, lore, or objects you are collecting.

Throughout the play activity, one finds that children always maintain a fierce sense of *fairness* about the rules and regulations, and only rarely are rules altered once play has begun. Hopscotch and jump-rope games for girls, or marbles and stick-ball for boys are just a few examples of competitive play that involve pre-negotiation of rules before the commencement of the game. The competing teams of players are chosen democratically (captains will pick sides), or the one who is *it* is determined, usually by a counting-out method or by some other commonly accepted procedure. Actions within the game are monitored closely, and if someone *cheats* or ignores a rule, reprimand is unanimous and punishment is meted out immediately (although sometimes *warnings* are given with first infractions). The greater part of children's play is competitive, and this may provide you with a starting point for a collection project on some aspect of games: on game strategy; on inclusionary/exclusionary practices in games; or perhaps, on gender determined games.

Secondly, children's folklore comprises part of the child's educational and maturational process. Where children derive tremendous benefit from the formal school, church, or adult-child informational channels, they begin to apply what they have learned in the informal child-child conduit. As peers who generally enjoy daily contact, they create their own behavioral norms and fashion an exclusive community in which they reinterpret rules to their advantage, replay scenes with their own dialogue, and often cast themselves in the position of the authority figure. One method children frequently employ to empower themselves is the parody of a known song:

Mine eyes have seen the glory of the burning of the school,
We have tortured every teacher, we have broken every rule
The truth is marching on.
Glory, glory hallelujah, teacher hit me with a ruler
Met her at the door with a loaded .44
The truth is marching on.

This is a parody of *The Battle Hymn of the Republic*, a song commonly learned in school. This variant reverses the reverential sentiment of the song and portrays a scene that most school children would love to see: the school building in ashes and the teachers forcefully humiliated by the students. Parody allows the children not only to poke fun at the form and content of something which is considered sacrosanct by an authority figure, but also allows them to play with a "what if . . . ?" type of scenario, knowing that the possibility of it actually happening is slight. This version would not be welcomed if performed within hearing range of the teacher, however. A particularly bold child might happily risk the chance of being caught in a public performance of the song if he thought he could enhance his status by doing so.

Another creative use of parody involves the modern media: children might lip sync the performance of an entertainer from MTV, parody the featured singer, and then parody their own (or a friend's) parody. By symbolically substituting themselves for the performer and then satirizing themselves as the performer, the children exhibit their mastery of a complex media form while they simultaneously negate the *power* of that singer's performance in their parody.

The above examples demonstrate how children take material from formal settings and rework it into their own informal contexts of games and enjoyment. Role playing, then, is another general topic of interest that can provide grist for the collector's mill. Although props such as dolls, toy soldiers, or ghostbuster guns may be used, children do not need much to kindle their imaginative powers. I was recently sitting at an outdoor pool when two dripping, chattering, towel-draped five- or six-year olds sat themselves next to me by the side of the pool. The first, who was clearly *in charge* said: "You are wearing red, so you should be Little Red Riding Hood, and I'm Granny . . . no . . . I'm the Wolf and I have to get through the forest before you, and . . . ." They proceeded to act out their resourcefully adapted interpretation of that well known tale for about four minutes before they shifted to another imaginary realm. Children bring everyday, public images into their world and personalize them. They freely adapt commercials from television, songs from scouts, or characters from comic-strips and cartoons to their own needs, making the familiar intimate by imaginative role playing.

One technique which has been tried with relative success has been for the collector to join in with children as they play, although, again, it is doubtful whether you, as the adult figure, could be accepted as an equal. But if you are interested in variations of jump-rope rhymes, or hand-clapping games, or ball-bouncing games (such as *Jacks*), then a move from participant observation to actual participation is in order. With the ready availability of portable tape recorders, it should not be too dificult to secure recording permission from the children. This technique may be the closest to a *natural* context that a collector will ever get, save starting a recorder and leaving the room to let it run unhindered.

INTERPRETING THE COLLECTION

Children's folklore, then, has a great deal to do with power and authority. For most of children's lives they are virtually powerless, except for those times when they are with peers or children younger than themselves. It is at this time that children also find that cooperation is as or more important than competition within the framework of play; after all, the idea is to achieve competence and to have a good time. Therefore, play should never be seen solely as the antithesis to work. Mastering skills associated with play, organizing games, and leading group activities are all properties of the power negotiation which is a prelude to the nascent responsibilities the child will have to assume, first as an adolescent, and later as an adult.

When children exhibit mastery of verbal lore within their peer group, for example, by telling a joke successfully, they are emulating their adult models. That is to say, in bringing attention to themselves, they gain competence in the performance of a narrative routine, and acquire personal power as well as a developing a sense of self. Imitating an authority figure is a very common method of assuming the cloak of power, at least temporarily. Satirizing that power figure by imitation, by ridicule, or by role playing reduces the authority to equal status with children and gives them momentary authority over that figure.

We must not be misled, however, into thinking that children's play and children's lore is simply a mawkish or parodic copy of the adult world. Children's folklore takes place largely out of the sphere of adult influence or intervention. Often children role play using dialogic exchanges with each other to practice the skills of being adult-like (playing *House*, *Doctor and Nurse*, *dressing-up*, *School*, etc.), but they set their own parameters for the interaction. Once having learned the rules of behavior or etiquette with their equals, children then creatively re-apply those rules in their child-adult interactions. Neither should we confuse *children's language* with *children's literature*. The play that children engage in is the doing; children's literature is the stylized record of what was done, stories mostly written by adults for an audience of children. Children's language is special because it is not based on the principle of literacy, but rather it is a formative stage of literacy influenced by the language they hear or read in the media, in school or church, or from adults. Children are aware of their language deficiencies and seek to master language as they would a game or a task. Nonsense jokes, sick jokes, nicknaming, tongue twisters, and parodies would all be examples of creative use of language, and these are usually embedded in larger forms of play activity.

The majority of children's folklore has at least some verbal component. Even when children play alone they often accompany their actions with rhyme, song, dialogue, or nonsense chatter. In group situations, which are by far the most commonly collected examples of lore, the motivation behind the riddle or taunt or role playing may be a verbal or linguistic learning process. For example, McDowell (1979) shows how children must go through a *pre-riddling*, a literal riddling stage, before they can handle true riddles, a task which requires the ability to understand and use metaphor. A pre-riddle (because it is merely referential) might be "What's green and says *ribbit*?"; whereas a true riddle (one which employs a ludic transformation) might be "What's black and white and read all over?"

A taunt, on the other hand, provides children with a chance to learn the boundaries of permissibility with regard to action and to speech, whether with peers, siblings, or adults. The subject matter of the taunt can either invite a reply ("If you had brains, you'd be dangerous") or provoke a fight ("Your mother wears combat boots!"). Tongue twisters, which demand more verbal acuity than wit, are especially popular if they can cause someone to say a *dirty* word (also stretching the bounds of permissibility):

> I slit a sheet,
> A sheet I slit.
> Upon this slitted
> sheet I sit.

Many of the rhymes associated with play feature subject matter which is important to the ongoing socialization process of children. For example:

> Suzie and Billy sittin' in a tree,
> K-I-S-S-I-N-G
> First comes love,
> Then comes marriage,
> then comes Suzie with a baby carriage.

Although innocuous in its simplicity, this rhyme does reflect a child's awareness of *where babies come from* and what societal expectations precede that end, regardless of whether it is used to tease or to affirm behavior. In other words, the contents may remain the same but the function of the rhyme may vary with the contextual setting. A parody of the implied action in the above example might be:

> Jack and Jill went up the hill,
> each with a buck-and-a-quarter.
> Jill came down with two-fifty
> Did they really go up for water?

Although it may be a variant of the well known nursery rhyme *Jack and Jill*, this parody concerns sexual matters of a more sophisticated nature than marriage, and reflects the wide range of sexual topics children can and do explore.

DOCUMENTING THE COLLECTION

Finally, we must remember that many of the topics of children's lore are not usually found in isolation. As is the case with many aspects of folklore, specific items (texts, performances) are clustered within this general framework of play. Depending on the specific nature of your collection project, different aspects of what you have collected will stand out. Suppose you are analyzing variants of *it* games played by a core group of children in the yards of a specific local neighborhood (the title of your collection is "An Analysis of 'It' Games in South Park, Indiana").

You might find a group of children playing a game (*Swing the Statue*) governed by rules which are very strictly negotiated before the game begins (the one who is *it* swings; the others must remain frozen in the position in which they land, hence *statue*). Players can employ a great deal of imaginative play within the game itself (e.g., who can make the most interesting statue). This game usually incorporates a counting-out rhyme to see who's *it* (for example, "One potato, two potato, three potato, four . . ."), and during the course of the game there may be a taunt by a player ("I see London, I see France, I see Susie's underpants. . ."). If a player is accused of breaking a pre-agreed rule (moving before judging the best statue), he may cry out: "Liar, liar, pants are on fire, your nose is longer than a telephone wire!" to the accuser (taunt and reply), or protest (swearing an oath) that he did not move: "cross my heart and hope to die, stick a needle in my eye."

This performance may have been indicative of the general spirit of play generally undertaken by this group you have been following for several weeks. Or, it may have seemed somewhat lackluster in terms of previous performances of this (or another) game. Your job as collector is to use as much of the contextual data which supports your thesis as possible—that counting-out strategies (to determine who is *it*) are controlled by certain members of the group—to demonstrate the artistic and communicative patterns of speech and play activity among a specific group of children.

All data are essential to the collection. In your final draft, you should at least include (but not limit yourself to):

> a. the make-up of the neighborhood (with a map or drawing) and the composition of the group;
> b. informant data for each of the children;
> c. copies of tapes made when observing or interviewing (including copies of field-notes);
> d. illustrations of play-sites, or photographs made for the purpose of contextualizing the individual games, and;
> e. comparisons from your own experiences or from published literature to compare and contrast with your findings.

To paraphrase the *Trix* rabbit, "Childlore is for kids," and the domain of collecting children's lore should rightfully be left to children themselves to preserve and protect in its most natural state. Failing that, it is our responsibility as adults to *let the child in us* rule when we attempt to document a very complex and meaningful form of artistic communication.

Selected Annotated Bibliography

Abrahams, Roger D., ed. 1969. *Jump-Rope Rhymes: A Dictionary*. Austin: University of Texas Press.
A pioneering collection of 619 (English language) rhymes from print, collections, and archives. It is alphabetized according to first word, cross-indexing, and an excellent bibliography. With minimal contextual data to support it, it sets the stage for further analysis and comparison.

_____, and Lois Rankin, eds. 1980. *Counting-Out Rhymes: A Dictionary*. Austin: University of Texas Press.
An excellent companion piece to the example above. Entries are alphabetized according to first word with a valuable chronological listing of sources. Some history and theory; excellent source for parent, teacher, or student.

Avedon, Elliott M, and Brian Sutton-Smith. 1971. *The Study of Games*. New York: John Wiley Sons.
An anthology of articles arranged by types of games. The chapter on *Folklore Sources* focuses primarily on childlore. Bibliography on children's games, first for English, and then for non-English language sources.

Bronner, Simon J., ed. 1988. *American Children's Folklore*. Little Rock: August House.
A compilation of contemporary childlore culled from several different folklore archives, offering minimal interpretation and a good bibliography.

Brunvand, Jan Harold. 1978. Folk Games. IN *The Study of American Folklore*, 2nd, ed. New York: W.W. Norton, pp. 226-242.
In his genre-based text, Brunvand breaks games down into such types as games of physical action, mental activity, manipulation of objects, practical jokes, and kissing or drinking games, each illustrated with examples and a short but useful bibliography.

Emrich, Duncan. 1970. *The Nonsense Book of Riddles, Rhymes, Tongue Twisters, Puzzles and Jokes from American Folklore*. New York: Four Winds Press.
Designed and illustrated for popular consumption but remains an important source for librarians or teachers—excellent bibliography. Riddles are most prominently featured; includes jump-rope and counting out-rhymes and autograph verse.

Georges, Robert A. 1972. Recreations and Games. IN *Folklore and Folklife: An Introduction*, ed. Richard M. Dorson. Chicago: University of Chicago Press.
Georges offers an important historical survey before he introduces his model of four principal types: nongames, games of strategy, competitive games, and games of chance. Annotated bibliography and ample examples.

Glassner, Barry, and Gary Alan Fine. 1979. Participant Observation with Children. *Urban Life* 8:153-74.
Two participant observation studies done by the authors: the first (Fine) on two communities of Little League Baseball players in Massachussets and Rhode Island; and the second (Glassner), in a St. Louis elementary school environment (playground, cafeteria, etc.) with equal numbers of black and white, and boys and girls in the sample.

Gomme, Alice B. 1964 [1894-98]. *The Traditional Games of England, Scotland, and Ireland*. 2 vols. New York: Dover Publications.
A photo-offset edition of the original. This landmark study was remarkable in its comprhensivenesss as well as its inclusion of musical notation. Beware of the Victorian sensibility, however, and the resultant censorship.

Goodwin, Marjorie H. 1985. The Serious Side of Jump Rope: Conversational Practices and Social Organization in the Frame of Play. *Journal of American Folklore* 98:315-330.
Concentrates on the social interaction which occurs within the game rather than focusing on the rhymes themselves. Analyzes the inherent conflict and resolution speech patterns that stresses the cooperation factor within the game.

Grider, Sylvia. 1980. A Select Bibliography of Childlore. *Western Folklore* 39:248-265.
A working bibliography specific to the folkloric theory and study of children's folklore, designed to study the major areas that have interested scholars. Alphabetical by author.

Halpert, Herbert. 1982. Childlore Bibliography: A Supplement. *Western Folklore* 41:205-28.
Designed to supplement Grider, this useful collection of sources deals with books outside of the US and Canada, particularly England and Scotland, with some entries from Ireland and Wales; then Europe and South America.

Knapp, Mary, and Herbert Knapp. 1976. *One Potato, Two Potato . . . The Secret Education of American Children*. New York: W.W. Norton and Co. Inc.
A collection of lore from 43 states from observation, interviews, and questionnaires, made by two English teachers, designed for teachers or parents rather than academics.

McDowell, John H. 1979. *Children's Riddling*. Bloomington: Indiana University Press.
An interesting and provocative collection of riddles from children of working-class Chicano and middle-class Anglo Autin dwellers. Provides a theoretical grounding along with a structural and functional analysis from pre- to true-riddles.

Melching, Jay. 1986. Children's Folklore. IN *Folk Groups and Folklore Genres*, ed. Elliott Oring. Logan: Utah State University Press, pp. 91-128.

Newell, William Wells. 1963 [1883]. *Games and Songs of American Children*. New York: Dover.
A reprint of the 2nd (1903) edition of Newall's classic collection. 190 examples of songs, rhymes, and games with somewhat outdated analyses and interpretations.

Opie, Iona, A. and Peter. 1951. *The Oxford Dictionary of Nursery Rhymes*. Oxford: The Clarendon Press.
A compilation of over 500 rhymes, nursery lore, and songs from tradition, many of which are reprinted from original sources. Very few American examples.

_____. 1960. *The Lore and Language of Schoolchildren*. Oxford: The Clarendon Press.
Oral traditional lore of 5000 children from ages 6-14 collected over a ten-year period by headmasters and teachers from 70 public schools in England, Scotland, and Wales.

_____. 1985. *The Singing Game.* Oxford and New York: Oxford University Press.
A collection of 133 games, of which 82 are sung and the rest are chanted, acted out, or involve clapping. Little theory or interpretation offered.

Roemer, Danielle. 1983. Children's Verbal Folklore. *The Volta Review* 85:55-71.
An analysis of the riddling and narrative competence of children in the context of the ethnography of speaking.

Schlereth, Thomas J. 1985. The Material Culture of Childhood: Problems and Potential in Historical Explanation. *Material History Bulletin* 21:1-14.
A profoundly interesting article which discusses some of the reasons for collecting artifacts and the importance of their exhibiion and interpretation in the last century.

Sutton-Smith, Brian. 1972. *The Folkgames of Children.* Published for the American Folklore Society. Austin, Texas: University of Texas Press.
A collection of previously published articles by the author using four principal approaches to games: historical, anthropological, psychological and unified.

_____. 1976. *A Children's Games Anthology: Studies in Folklore and Anthropology.* New York: Anno Press.
A collection of previously published articles on children's games from Oceania, Europe, and America. No annotation or interpretations offered to tie them together.

_____. 1981. *The Folkstories of Children*, in collaboration with David M. Abrams. Philadelphia: Univeristy of Pennsylvania Press.
Stories of over 350 children between two- and ten-years of age collected in and around New York City over three years with accompanying interpretations of language development and related skills.

_____. 1986. *Toys as Culture.* New York: Gardner Press.
An anthropology of toys written for the lay reader using mostly commercially produced toys as examples. Situates toys in the context of play and social interaction.

CHAPTER 18
Family Folklore

Charles R. Frederick

My earliest Christmas memory is of a group of small, brightly painted, wooden sleighs. On Christmas morning my sisters and I would run down the stairs to find the sleighs, sitting on the kitchen table full of small gifts. It did not matter what was under the tree we always ran to the sleighs first. Inside mine there might be a pocket knife, a flashlight, or a small puzzle, and usually there was a Christmas orange and maybe some candy.

Figure 1. The author's Christmas sleigh. (Photograph by Charles R. Frederick, Sr.)

At that age I did not know that many American families put small gifts into Christmas stockings. But I did know that the sleighs were special. My parents made them, cutting out the pieces and gluing them together. Each was painted differently, mine red and white, and each had our name on the front. We still use the sleighs each Christmas. And they help now to provide an entry into a brief discussion of family folklore.

Barre Toelken (1979) has referred to the family as "the first and basic dynamic traditional system encountered by most people the world over." Toelken views the family as the basis for "social education" and allows that "folk learning" (often family based) produces "harmony" or social understanding and cooperation. Each family serves as a vast repository of knowledge, some of it widely held and some of it intensely private. Amidst this knowledge, most of which is unrecorded and passed on informally, are various items that serve to provide the family with a singular sense of identity. Ironically those same items help to bond all people together. Let me illustrate. As you now know part of my family's Christmas celebration involves the use of small, wooden sleighs. I have never met another family with this particular custom. In this, the sleighs help to reinforce my family's singular nature. However because this practice can be seen as a variation of the Christmas stocking tradition it clearly links my family to all others who celebrate the holiday in a similar manner.

I believe that the dual nature of folklore, simultaneously illustrating singularity and evoking commonality can be observed to good effect through the study of family materials. In order to further clarify the scope of folklore we can divide the field into three areas as mentioned earlier in this handbook. They are: 1) things people make, 2) things people do, and 3) things people say. My family's Christmas sleighs are examples of categories one and two but we also speak about them. Please remember that these categories are not exact nor are they mutually exclusive. Human behavior is exceedingly difficult to quantify and attempts at analysis are speculative at best. For the beginning student of folklore a project involving the collection of family materials may open a rich resource as well as provide a comfortable atmosphere in which to do fieldwork.

Margaret R. Yocom (1982) has detailed various strategies that a fieldworker might use when introducing a collection project to one's own family. You should provide a clear description of the project to your family, discussing the focus of the research as well as the methods involved. Be prepared to calm fears about the use of confidential materials or to justify their inclusion in the project. You should discuss the use of family possessions, (i.e. my Christmas sleigh), and also describe the potential uses for the completed project. Yocom also points out the need to emphasize the historical importance of your own family history. Along these lines you may stress the singular nature of the family's knowledge and emphasize the value of their collective experience. By appealing to your relative's favorite topics of interest you may encourage a more free exchange of information.

I began this discussion by referring to my family's Christmas sleighs. Families make many items that are worthy of your consideration as a folklore student. Quilts, toys, clothing, costumes and furniture are all items that come to mind (see Chapter 12 **Folklife and Material Culture**). In my own fieldwork I have concentrated on another aspect of family life. Many families create and maintain distinctive foodways. Whether as a result of ethnicity, region, or a particular personal or group preference foodways often reveal much about a family.

In the case of my family, gardening, preparation, and preservation of food are reflective of historically rural roots, large family size, and religious beliefs. The values that perpetuate these practices are still in place.

My mother grew up on a large Iowa farm in the 1930s. Her family raised and grew the majority of their own food. My father grew up in western Pennsylvania and his family also gardened extensively. These habits, preferences, and skills were present as I grew up and they were passed on to my siblings and me.

A recent field project of mine involved studying the making of a homemade horseradish condiment. My mother's family has a long history of horseradish making and now my brother and sisters are involved in the practice. As we worked, I took notes and asked more questions than usual. Then I used the data I had collected to compare our finished horseradish with commercially prepared products. The results shed some light on the value system of my family as well as documenting the process of horseradish making and the differences between a family effort and a commercial enterprise.

FAMILY CELEBRATIONS

Often families do things in conjunction with specific events. Birthdays, weddings, funerals, holidays and vacations commonly provide the impetus for distinctive family celebrations or observances. You may choose to focus your fieldwork around one of these seemingly ready-made occasions. Does your family celebrate Thanksgiving? If so, in what manner? How is the celebration similar to or different from others you know?

Amy J. Kotkin and Steven J. Zeitlin (1983) have noted that family celebrations, from the mundane to the most ornate are often re-creative in nature. Families attempt to "symbolically re-create" past celebrations. We also try to duplicate successful celebrations. These attempts often become "patterned, recurring activities." Each of these celebrations, from a holiday to the weekly game of dominoes, provides an opportunity for you to put the experience into a larger human context.

In *A Celebration of American Family Folklore* the authors cite numerous examples of family customs, from Sunday afternoon drives to family reunions, all of which may provide excellent opportunities for you as a folklore fieldworker. A colleague has cited her family's annual vacation as a rich source of family lore. The long drive from New Jersey to Orlando, Florida to visit Disney World provided many episodes that contribute to her family's folklore.

Virtually everything that can be collected has a verbal component (see chapter on Oral Narrative). My Christmas sleigh is an interesting artifact, but the more I can learn about it, the more important it becomes. Whether you choose to study things people make or things people do, you will inevitably move into our third area of concern, that is, things people say. In this area I wish to focus on two specific forms of expression.

The first of these is the personal experience narrative. As defined by Sandra K. Dolby-Stahl, the *personal experience narrative* is a first person narrative based on a real incident in the life of the teller. Its worthiness is recognized by the teller who then combines the experience, its perception and context to form a self contained narrative. These stories are steeped in the teller's ethical code. The personal values of the teller influence his/her perception of the incident and the retelling of the incident as well. Recognition and identification of the values that inform the personal experience story are keys to the eventual interpretation of the material. Once you have collected a personal experience story from a family member you may apply questions similar to these to reveal the value structure that lies within the story.

1) Why is this story important to the teller?
2) How does it reflect the values of the teller?
3) Do those values conform to or conflict with those held by the society at large?
4) Why would the teller choose this particular story in the given circumstance?

There are many more questions to ask. As you consider matters of interpretation try to think of the different layers of meaning contained in each item that you collect.

My father tells a story about his first trip (by himself) to the movies. He was quite young and he stayed through several Gene Autrey features. When he decided to leave night had fallen and he got lost coming over *Hogback*, a mountain over which his shortcut ran. He was frightened by the night, the sounds of animals, and maybe by the anticipation of what would happen to him once he got home. He eventually made his way back but not without an ordeal. As my father tells it, this story is filled with various meanings. Notions of independence, assertiveness and persistence are only three of the values in evidence in the story.

Another form that fits into the general category of things people say is the life history. I have used an abbreviated version of this form in my own investigation of cooperative labor practices on my mother's family's farm in the 1930s and 1940s. I conducted an interview with my mother that centered on her memories of farm work. I wanted to get some feeling for the range of farm work, how labor was divided among family members and to what extent there was cooperation between neighbors. My mother's responses covered these topics and they also included valuable information about technological changes during those years.

A complete life history is a massive undertaking for even the most accomplished scholar. However, you may focus your energies on a specific topic or time frame as I did and gain tremendous satisfaction from your efforts. I have assigned life history projects that focused on the lives of grandparents to my undergraduate students. The results at the end of the semester were particularly gratifying because of the warmth that manifested itself from this family interaction. Several students collected Depression Era stories, others collected stories of military service or recollections of natural disasters. Each story provided the student with material for academic use but more

importantly these exchanges between generations fostered an appreciation for and an understanding of one's own family.

These are all examples of common experiences. Many people share histories of military service, natural disasters, etc. but no two experiences are ever exactly alike. They are singular in nature, and yet, they are held in common by many. In my view, that is the ultimate value of family folklore studies. During your project I hope you will come to a more complete understanding of what it means to be a family member, sharing common experiences; and also gain a finer appreciation for your own family, realizing that they are truly unique.

Selected Bibliography

Baker, Holly Cutting, Amy J. Kotkin and Steven J. Zeitlin. 1982. *A Celebration of American Family Folklore*. New York: Pantheon.

Baldwin, Karen. 1985. "Woof!": A Word on Women's Roles in Family Storytelling. IN *Women's Folklore, Women's Culture*, eds. Rosan A. Jordan and Susan J. Kalcik, pp. 149-162. Philadelphia: University of Pennsylvania Press.

Boatright, Mody. 1958. The Family Saga. IN *The Family Saga and Other Phases of American Folklore*, eds. Mody C. Boatright, Robert B. Downs and John R. Flanagan. Urbana: University of Illinois Press.

Brandes, Stanley. 1975. Family Misfortune Stories in American Folklore. *Journal of the Folklore Institute* 12:5-17.

Dolby-Stahl, Sandra K. 1983. Personal Experience Stories. IN *Handbook of American Folklore*, ed. Richard M. Dorson, pp. 268-276. Bloomington: Indiana University Press.

_____. 1989. Family Settlement Stories and Personal Values. IN *The Old Traditional Way of Life: Essays in Honor of Warren E. Roberts*, eds. Robert E. Walls and George H. Schoemaker, pp. 362-366. Bloomington: Trickster Press.

Kotkin, Amy J. and Steven J. Zeitlin. 1983. In the Family Tradition. IN *Handbook of American Folklore*, ed. Richard M. Dorson, pp. 90-99. Bloomington: Indiana University Press.

Ridlen, Susanne S. 1989. Copy Books: A Reflection of Family Tradition. *Midwestern Folklore* 13(2):45-105.

Roberts, Leonard. 1983. A Family's Repertoire. IN *Handbook of American Folklore*, ed. Richard M. Dorson, pp. 100-105. Bloomington: Indiana University Press.

Šmidchens, Guntis. 1989. Latvian Folk History and Family Stories in America. *Lituanus* 33(3):62-72.

Stone, Elizabeth. 1988. *Black Sheep and Kissing Cousins: How Our Family Stories Shape Us*. New York: Times Books.

Yocom, Margaret R. 1982. Family Folklore and Oral History Interviews: Strategies for Introducing a Project to Ones Own Relatives. *Western Folklore* 41(4):251-274.

CHAPTER 19
Contemporary Native American Folklore

Melanie LaBorwit

The theories and approaches American folklorists have used to describe traditional expressive culture in general, have influenced the study of the lore and life of American Indians in North America. In the early 1900s anthropologist Franz Boas encouraged the rigorous collection of tales and myths because he saw Native American folktales as an important reflection of the culture from which they sprang. Huge numbers of recordings were made so that folklorists could listen to the oral performances of these tales, compare data, and map perceived patterns in the spread of folklore. Later on, the literary folklorist, Stith Thompson, looked at the same data from a different perspective. Rather than studying Native American folktales as indexes to the culture of a specific group, he was interested in isolating and indexing characteristic motifs and tale types found in the tales of many cultures, in order to gain a better understanding of the texts themselves. Both kinds of folklorists, the anthropologically oriented and the text oriented, however, dedicated themselves with vigor to documenting the folklore of Native Americans because they believed the *primitive* indigenous cultures of America were fast-disappearing. This dedication and sense of urgency resulted in the regular publication of Native American oral narratives in the *Journal of American Folklore*. Many of these articles were direct field reports from the Bureau of American Ethnology at the Smithsonian Institution, which pioneered field research to enrich the collection of the early museum.

So much folklore was amassed from the turn of the century until the advent of World War II that some collections have not yet even been analyzed. Up until the 1940s, most Native American populations were not very visible to the rest of American society, either *demographically* or culturally. During the World War I, however, many Native Americans served in the armed forces, and afterwards, urban communities of Native Americans multiplied. For the first time the larger American society was more fully exposed to a way of life many had thought had ceased to exist. Native American cultural survival no longer seemed as tenuous as before, and the sense of urgency accompanying the collection of Native American folklore waned. Though a few folklorists continued to study Native American lore, Native American scholarship was dominated for a time by anthropologists and linguists. Scholars in these fields contributed a great deal to modern approaches to Native American folklore. Yet, the many social changes Native American communities experienced and the inevitable meeting and blending of cultures led some to regard the folklore of these modern communities as *muddied* and not as *valuable* for research as that of earlier, isolated communities.

Recent shifts in the study of folklore generally to include a wide range of genres and many different ways of looking at forms of cultural expression has prompted a renewal of interest in Native American folklore today. Native American folklore is especially exciting to observe and study, because it provides a key to the vast changes and growth in modern Indian life and culture. Documenting contemporary Native American folklore also presents a challenge, as the number of modern folklore studies, though growing, is still small. As tribes adapt to new conditions and effect changes in their society, many are expressing renewed interest in their own historical and traditional roots. This chapter addresses some of the different areas for research and collection in Native American folklore, and some of the different approaches towards interpreting that material.

THE ROLE OF HISTORY

The influence of history is especially apparent in Native American studies. The not-so-distant history of the conquest, colonialization, captivity and conversion of Native America had an impact that is still felt today. We often learn about different historical eras as if they were neat chronological units of time with corresponding lists of important events. In Native American communities, however, history is viewed as one long continuum firmly connected to the present day. Historical events may take on a personal meaning. For example, in 1990, one hundred years after the massacre of many Sioux men, women and children camped at Wounded Knee, South Dakota, descendants of survivors have gathered together to share remembrances at this site, nestled in the heart of the Pine Ridge reservation. Indian political activists in the twentieth century evoke strong emotional responses from Native American communities by drawing upon metaphors from the past. The *Longest Walk*, a trans-national demonstration for Native American rights in 1978, reminded many participants of the *Trail of Tears*, the forced walk which removed tribes from the southeastern United States to Indian Territory in Oklahoma in 1838, or the *Long Walk* of the Navajos from their traditional homes to internment at Fort Sumner in Bosque Redondo, New Mexico.

Therefore, if you are not a member of the group among whom you are doing fieldwork, you may miss many historical referents in the folklore and conversation you hear. If you can, try to familiarize yourself with tribal and regional history before beginning your fieldwork. How do historical events and figures influence the way people live today? In what ways has the culture changed? What factors have contributed to change over time? What has contributed to cultural continuity? Which events have affected the integrity of tribal traditions? Your knowledge of the past will put you in a better position to understand the present, and make more informed observations of contemporary Native American culture.

CULTURAL DIVERSITY

As noted by Guntis Šmidchens in Chapter 14 on **Immigrant and Ethnic Folklore**, one must be aware of the many subgroups within an ethnic group. Native Americans have often been treated in popular culture as a monolithic group. While there *is* a broad pan-Indian, or intertribal culture in the United States, we must remind ourselves of the enormous variety of distinct tribal groups existing today. A quick look at the 1980 census of Native American groups will give you an idea of the cultural diversity contained within the general label. Moreover, the expressive culture, and certainly the language spoken by one tribe may be as different from that of another tribe as the

cultures and languages of different countries in Europe. The bibliography at the end of this chapter gives some examples of the kinds of in-depth studies on individual tribes written by scholars who *specialize* on a particular tribe or region.

This is an important distinction to remember if you are going to do a project on Native American folklore. Some people will identify themselves as Native Americans or as Indians, some will prefer to name a specific tribal affiliation, and some may be even more specific in identifying themselves by their geographic region, clan, kinship group, or by family. You might ask yourself what it is that defines *self* and *other*? How do people assert Native American identity in different situations? What do these definitions say about ethnic identity and its importance? If people identify themselves in their own community differently from when they are interacting in the dominant culture, what does that say about intercultural communication or about how Native Americans fit in *Anglo* culture? How do people from different tribes interact with one another? You should also keep in mind how your role as a fieldworker fits in these systems of relationships.

Figure 1. Tepees at Cheyenne River Pow Wow, Eagle Butte, South Dakota.

PAN-INDIAN MOVEMENT

Pan-Indian culture today is in many respects the most visible expression of Native American cultures in general. Pan-Indian refers to the modern merging of tribal symbols, motifs, rituals, and enactments of many groups through which contemporary Native Americans assert their *Indianness*. To a certain extent, the federal government's push during the 1930s through the 1950s for total Indian immersion and assimilation into Anglo American culture fed into the development and growth of a Pan-Indian culture. Native American children were sent to attend schools far away from their homes with members of other tribal groups, and English became the common language for intertribal communication. Increased geographic mobility has also helped foster Pan-Indian attitudes. Moreover, Pan-Indianism may be seen as a response to the dominant culture's singular notion of *Indianness*, a notion that has rarely acknowledged unique tribal identities. On the other hand, it constitutes a means of preventing further loss of Indian culture and avoiding total assimilation.

Emphasizing cultural cohesion and retention, the *pow wow* may be said to be the principal cultural expression of the pan-Indian movement. The *pow wow* is irrefutably *Indian*, unique, and vastly different from anything in non-Indian culture. Hundreds of participants and visitors throughout the United States travel to weekend pow wows hosted by Indian communities throughout the summer months. Pow wowing is not limited to the reservation culture, but thrives in urban areas with large Native American populations as well. Together these events and their corresponding social networks are known as the *pow wow circuit*. The pow wow will be addressed later in this chapter.

In the Field

There is an old proverbial phrase: *When in Rome, do as the Romans do.* This bit of folk wisdom is valuable on the reservation as well as in an urban Indian community. Without being imitative, it is important, and polite, to observe rules of cultural propriety when working in a traditional community. In fieldwork, you will also want to be sensitive to the many sources from which you will gather data and, above all, to your informants. As a cultural outsider, you'll want to try and tap the cultural frame of reference which forms the context for folklore performances.

Sources for this kind of information may include such things as phrases of speech (or kernel narratives) used in passing which may refer to long traditional stories. What kinds of images are used repeatedly in drawings, or even posters used to publicize tribal events? Which colors are culturally preferred? Are there any recurring patterns in verbal, customary, or material folklore? Is there a tribal radio station nearby? What kind of programming do they have? Ask yourself how these things might reflect the culture of the contemporary Native American community. Regarding the nature of the material collected, remember to consider the interests of the culture when recording this information. Did you hear any sacred stories? Should you describe them in detail if they have not been recorded before? Are you allowed to take photographs or make recordings of the materials that interest you? While most folklorists use a camera and a tape recorder as standard equipment, you may want to find out if the people you work with find these study tools offensive or intrusive.

Clearly, it is important to plan ahead for a good project. It is a good idea to enlist the advice or assistance of some local leader or educator who is a well-known and respected member of the ethnic community you are visiting. Perhaps you already have a friend in mind who has introduced you to some other people you were thinking of working with. News of your visit will likely precede your arrival, and your consultation with friends, tribal leaders or educators will help establish rapport with the people you wish to interview for your research. Make several visits to your research site. It will be time well spent. As people get to know you better and feel comfortable with you, you will find that the community will open up to you and share information about the group you might otherwise not have the chance to learn about.

While some cultural events are well-publicized, such as pow wows or art shows, many more are not. Some times dances and ceremonies are so local and community or family oriented, that everyone just assumes that all those interested in attending already know about them. Perhaps there is a special honoring ceremony to mark an elder's birthday, or the naming of a child. Often special events occur in a spur-of-the-moment fashion. Native American people occasionally use the phrase *Indian time* to explain how their conception of the passage of time is different from that of Anglo Americans. One might say that *Indian time* progresses through patterns in daily life, guided by known events in the past, but with little concern for anticipating events which will take place in the future. This attitude towards time is aptly expressed in the sign, writer Harry Paige, noted in a store window in South Dakota:

> Championship softball game tonight!
> Starts somewhere around sundown.

Just *being around* can make a difference in your observing and experiencing a more complete, more rounded picture of Native American life.

FROM BEADWORK TO BINGO: SYNCRETIC TRADITIONS

To begin a good project on Native American folklore, it is probably a good idea to take stock of what we already know, or assume we know about Indian culture, and then to shed ourselves of our invalid exoteric notions. Romantic images of *noble savages* or *strong, silent Indians*, or stereotypical notions of braids and feathers, pottery and throbbing drums left over from fragments of out-dated and inaccurate ethnographies are the only exposure some people have to the complex life and culture of American Indians. While some of the things you know about Native American culture, and their history, now that you have studied it too, are certainly valid, it is important to enter the field with an open mind and heart. A broad spectrum of topics for research exists. Each demands attention not only from a historical perspective but also to document cultural transformations and re-emergences in the twentieth century. Traditional pastimes of Native Americans may vary from tanning hides to playing bingo. The examples described in this section should give you some ideas, but the possibilities are endless.

Syncretism refers to a social dynamic in which two dissimilar cultures come into contact and merge to produce new cultural forms that draw from both histories. Much of contemporary Native American culture is marked by a kind of weaving together of European and Native American traditions, long overlooked by formal scholarship which concentrated on *pure* and *authentic* Native American traditions. These adaptations do not, however, make Indian lore or artifact any less Indian, or traditional, or authentic. Unbounded by historical preconceptions, one can document today how contemporary Native Americans pick the best from both worlds and work to make them meaningful by joining them together.

MATERIAL CULTURE

Whether traditional knowledge of jewelry-making, sheepherding or special food preparations, the material culture of Native American is especially revealing of and symbolically important for ethnic identity. One need not look only for examples of traditional meaning embedded in material cultural forms. For example, many of the older Sioux women today practice cross-stitch embroidery learned from German and Swiss nuns in missions schools, but they now employ Sioux motifs in this introduced medium. Different blends of tradition allow people to make sense of their own heritage in a new way. Star quilts are another example of Plains tribes craftswomen adopting and adapting a European skill for their own

Figure 2. Porcupine quillwork medallion by Alice New Holy Blue Legs. Photograph courtesy of Elaine Thatcher.

uses and purposes. Originally an adornment painted on buffalo robes symbolizing war-bonnets, the star-like motif is now a common quilting pattern. Star quilts play an important part in ceremonial give-aways, and ownership of these quilts is an emblem of pride. Many innovations are made today by some of the master quilters. There are often multi-dimensional patterns embedded in the star design, including multiple-pieced stars, tepees, peace pipes, buffaloes and eagles.

Beadwork, a well-recognized material cultural form throughout Native American communities, has changed too. Where new material and techniques are introduced, they may be added to existing creative forms. A variety of beaded stitches and design styles have emerged as well as a current trend reflecting a preference for the smallest cut glass beads. Uses extend beyond jewelry or dress adornment to beading on canes, salt shakers, lighters, bingo markers, cigarette cases, pen sets and key chains. As you examine the material culture of your chosen communities, look for other materials used today in the manufacture of Native American crafts. Are they man-made? What traditional raw materials have been replaced by materials introduced from the larger culture? Which have not? How far is innovation allowed in tradition? What kinds of choices or decisions does the artist you are observing make? Are the objects made for traditional use in the community or for sale to tourists? If you are working with a folk artist, remember to consider not only the object and its form, but the process involved and the traditional skills required in its production. Find out how these skills were learned. Native American crafts serve in many ways today as traditional icons for cultural

Figure 3. Blessing of drum with tobacco before song. Pow wow at Pine Ridge reservation (Sioux) Oglala, South Dakota.

Figure 4. Junior grass dancers at pow wow, Oglala, South Dakota.

identity. Skilled artists are often especially knowledgeable about their cultural history and are able to share it with you. The chapter on **Folklore and Material Culture** should be helpful for recording and interpreting Native American objects, their manufacture, origin and cultural significance.

MUSIC, SONG AND DANCE

For each region of the United States, the research questions regarding material culture will vary according to available materials and different tribal aesthetics. The same holds true for studying different forms of celebration, ceremony and performance. Special occasions, such as rites of passage, may be marked by religious ceremony accompanied by a particular corpus of songs or dances. Certain seasons will feature particular kinds of dances or music performed only at that time of year, much like the Anglo-American tradition of singing Christmas carols in December.

Some musical forms have spread and have become part of the new traditional culture of Native America. The *pow wow* is a vibrant music and dance phenomenon nationwide, replacing in many ways now lost traditional social gatherings once frequent among each tribe. *Pow wows* are open to the public, and whether your attention is piqued by colorful dress, music or traditional foodways, a *pow wow* is a good place to learn more about the community you are looking at.

What are today Pan-Indian pow wow dance forms are diffused from predominantly Plains Indian cultures' dance traditions. Various *drums* or invited groups of organized singers from different tribes travel to pow wows, and their families and the families of

the dancers add to their number. Many others come to the pow wow encampment or modern arena to sell traditional crafts, jewelry and pow wow paraphernalia for costumes, such as dance rattles, beadwork and feathers. Throughout the weekend event, traditional meals are often served, such as stew, fried bread, and pudding, and the ever-present *Indian tacos*.

Songs are sung at pow wows in many different tribal languages. New pow wow songs are composed annually, and pow wow regulars carry their tape recorders along with dance shawls and suitcases full of jingle dresses and colored feather bustles. This music travels rapidly today. More often than not, favored groups will sell their own cassettes of top hits through commercial distributors.

While pow wow and other older musical traditions are thriving, new Indian music is being written for older songs, staying in tune with modern musical tastes and rhythms. From Lakota pow wow drum songs to Chippewa fiddle playing, to polka-inspired Papago *chicken-scratch* bands to Navajo western swing—a rich diversity of cultural performances is emerging in modern Native American communities.

NATIVE AMERICAN LITERATURE

Stimulating a great deal of interest from many viewpoints, contemporary Native American written literature is flourishing today. Folklorists have not historically studied culture through the written word but this approach is more acceptable today. Though writing may seem new to Native American, traditionally oral societies, storytelling is not. As with adaptations in material culture, the written poetry and novels of new Native American authors constitutes an extension of old forms to a new medium. Among writers and their readers, there is a strong sense of continuity between ancient oral literature and modern written expression. These two kinds of artistic expression exhibit similarities in style, content and form as well. Yet modern Indian writers are acutely aware that their literacy and the very *act* of writing sets them apart from the oral tradition. They see their current writing as an attempt to adapt to twentieth-century culture, while at the same time maintaining their own Indian cultural identity. Through their works, writers from many different tribes negotiate their Indian identity, their sense of place in society, and provide a reflexive window into Native American thought through which we can often learn much about ourselves.

POW WOW

Hair the color of
tobacco ash, the fair lady
anthro asked, Excuse
me please, . . . sir
(guess it beats Chief),

does that red patch
on your blanket symbolize something?

    Yes mam,
it surely does, it
symbolizes that once
upon a time ther
was a hole
in the blanket

        Carroll Arnett/Gogisgi
        (Cherokee)

Customary lore, games, children's lore, narrative, and jokes are also living traditions you may consider for your project. Before getting started, review some of the other chapters in this book on different genres and approaches to recording folklore in traditional communities. You will find it helpful to review many of the ideas and suggestions in this book. Finally, keep in mind that there is more to American Indian folklore than *memory culture*, and there are many ways we may look at *new* material cultural expressions, events and expressive forms learn from the Native American people who are here *today*. Voices from the field increasingly now are Native voices, and collaborative efforts increase the depth of our knowledge.

Acknowledgements

I am grateful for the patient coaching of editor George Schoemaker and Louis J. LaBorwit. I would like to thank Sue M. Johnson, Ron Smith, Gail H. Bickel, Butch Thunderhawk and Robert Walls for their helpful comments and contributions in the writing of this chapter.

References Cited

Paige, Harry W. 1987. *Land of the Spotted Eagle. A Portrait of the Reservation Sioux.* Chicago: Loyola University Press, p. 35.

Arnett, Carroll/Gogisgi. 1979. POW WOW. IN *The Remembered Earth*, ed. Geary Hobson. Albuquerque: Red Earth Press (1980- University of New Mexico) p. 127.

Selected Annotated Bibliography

This bibliography is not meant to be exhaustive, but is representative of the scope and variety of sources available for researchers in many disciplines. Many of the folkloristics and anthropological sources have excellent bibliographies of their own for further study of a particular group or genres of folklore.

Journals:
Journal of Ethnic Studies
American Indian Quarterly
American Indian Culture and Research Journal
Indian Historian
Cultural Survival Quarterly
Journal of American Indian Education
American Indian Art Magazine

See also regional journals, such as the *Turtle Quarterly Review*, or *Dine Ba-iina Journal of Navajo Life*, as well as tribal newspapers, such as the *Navajo Times*, the *Lakota Times*, *Akwesasne Notes*. Some tribal colleges now have extensive archives and research centers well worth visiting. Also look for other media resources such as the nationally syndicated public radio program, "First Person Radio".

1)   **Reference**
Clements, William M. and Frances M. Malpezzi., eds. 1984. *Native American Folklore, 1879-1979. An Annotated Bibliography.* Chicago: Swallow Press.

Fogelson, Raymond. 1978. *The Cherokees: A Critical Bibliography.* Bloomington, IN: Indiana University Press.

Frazier, Gregory. 1985. *The American Indian Index*, ed. Randolph Punliy. Denver: Arrowstar Publishing.
This volume has a wealth of information and is full of names and addresses of sources, resources and more. A good place to begin for the novice doing fieldwork.

Green, Michael D. 1978. *The Creeks: A Critical Bibliography.* Bloomington, IN: Indiana University Press.

Green, Rayna, ed. 1983. *Native American Women: A Contextual Bibliography.* Bloomington: Indiana University Press.

Grumet, Robert Steven. 1979. *Native Americans of the Northwest Coast: A Critical Bibliography.* Bloomington, IN: Indiana University Press.

North American Indians: A Dissertation Index. 1977. Ann Arbor, MI: University Microfilms International.

Sturtevant, William., gen. ed. 1978-1988. *Handbook of North American Indians.* Washington, D.C.: Smithsonian Institution.

2) History and Culture

Cappe, Walter Holden, ed. 1976. *Seeing with a Native Eye: Essays on Native American Religion.* New York: Harper and Row.

Cox, Bruce Alden. 1987. *Native People, Native Lands: Canadian Indians, Inuit and Metis.* Ottawa: Carleton University Press. Should also be of interest to residents of those states on the Canadian border with similar tribal groups.

Cunningham, Keith. 1988. Native Americans as Folk: Collecting and Compiling Indian Traditions. IN *100 Years of American Folklore Studies.* ed. William M. Clements. Pp. 33-35. Washington, D.C.: American Folklore Society.

Debo, Angie. 1977. *A History of the Indians of the United States.* Norman: University of Oklahoma Press.

Farris, Glenn J. 1989. Recognizing Indian Folk History as Real History: A Fort Ross Example. *American Indian Quarterly* 13(4):471-480.

Fenton, William N. 1989. Return of Eleven Wampum Belts to the Six Nations Iroquois Confederacy. *Ethnohistory* 36(4):392-410. Addresses the very current issue of repatriation of Indian artifacts from museum collections to their tribes.

Fowler, Loretta. 1986. *Shared Symbols, Contested Meanings: Gros Ventre Culture and History, 1778-1984.* Ithaca: Cornell University Press.

John, V.P. 1972. Styles of Learning—Styles of Teaching: Reflection on the Education of Navajo Children. IN *Functions of Language in the Classroom,* eds. C. Cazden, D. Hymes, and V.P. John, pp. 331-343. New York: Teachers College Press.

Kirk, Ruth. 1986. *Tradition and Change on the Northwest Coast: The Makah, Nuu-Chah-Nulth, Southern Kwakiutl and Nuxalk.* Seattle: University of Washington Press. Includes a wealth of valuable photographs. Useful for understanding a contemporary Native American group on the Pacific coast.

Lowie, Robert H. 1956[1935]. *The Crow Indians.* New York: Rinehart and Company, Inc.

Olson, James B. and Raymond Wilson. 1984. *Native Americans in the Twentieth Century.* Chicago: University of Illinois Press. Offers a clear explanation of United States history in relation to Native Americans, from first contact to the present time. Extremely valuable for background research in any area.

Tedlock, Dennis and Barbara Tedlock, eds. 1975. *Teachings from the American Earth: Indian Religion and Philosophy.* New York: Liveright.

3) Renewals and Revisions

Bahr, Howard M. Bruce A. Chadwick, and Robert C. Day., eds. 1972. *Native Americans Today: Sociological Perspectives.* New York: Harper and Row.

Berkhofer, Robert. 1978. *The White Man's Indian: Images of the American Indian from Columbus to the Present.* New York: Vintage Books.

Coe, Ralph T. 1986. *Lost and Found Traditions: Native American Art, 1965-1985.* New York: American Federation of Arts.

Josephy, Alvin H. 1982. *Now That the Buffalo's Gone: A Study of Today's American Indians.* New York: Alfred A. Knopf.

Lincoln, Kenneth, with Al Logan Slagle. 1987. *The Good Red Road. Passages into Native America.* San Francisco: Harper and Row.

McNickle, D'Arcy. 1973. *Native American Tribalism: Indian Survivals and Renewals.* New York: Oxford University Press.

Waddell, Jack O., ed. 1971. *The American Indian in Urban Society.* Boston: Little, Brown & Co.

4) Native American Folklore and Related Fields

Abrams, George. 1985. American Indian Tribal Museums: Conserving Tradition with New Cultural Institutions. IN *1985 Festival of American Folklife* program. Washington, D.C.: Smithsonian Institution.

American Indian Art: Form and Tradition. 1972. Walker Art Center/Minneapolis Institute of Arts/Indian Art Association. New York: E.P. Dutton & Co., Inc. In addition to lavish photographs, drawings and descriptions of art on display in this collaborative exhibit, this catalogue includes numerous scholarly essays on various different historical eras and interdisciplinary commentary on tribal arts nationwide up to the present time.

Amoss, Pamela. 1978. *Coast Salish Spirit Dancing: The Survival of an Ancestral Religion.* Seattle: University of Washington Press.

Basso, Keith. 1979. *Portraits of "the Whiteman": Linguistic Play and Cultural Symbols Among the Western Apache.* New York: Cambridge University Press. Discusses the uses and function of ethnic joking.

Blackburn, Thomas. 1975. *December's Child: A Book of Chumash Oral Narratives.* Berkeley: University of California Press. Native American literature from California.

Boas, Franz. 1940. *Race, Language, and Culture.* New York: MacMillan Co. An extraordinary collection of Boasian writings from his career, still valuable as a model for intensive and thorough fieldwork and thoughtful observations of many different cultural groups throughout the United States.

Brady, Margaret K. 1984. *"Some Kind of Power": Navajo Children's Skinwalker Narratives.* Salt Lake City, UT: University of Utah Press. Raises important questions of culture change, and the roles children play in shaping cultural understanding.

Brinton, Daniel G. 1905. *The Myths of the New World*. Philadelphia: D. McKay.
Written as "a treatise on the symbolism and mythology of the red race of America," this is but one of Brinton's important early contributions to Native American scholarship. Though the language may be dated, you may find the early folklore studies interesting and helpful.

Bunzel, Ruth. 1972[1929]. *The Pueblo Potter*. New York: Dover Books.

Clark, LaVerne Harrell. 1966. *They Sang for Horses: The Impact of the Horse on Navajo and Apache Folklore*. Tucson, AZ: University of Arizona Press.

Coe, Ralph T. 1976. *Sacred Circles—Two Thousand Years of North American Indian Art*. London: Arts Council of Great Britain.

Conn, Richard. 1974. *Robes of White Shell and Sunrise: Personal Decorative Arts of the Native American*. Denver: Denver Art Museum.
Though not a well-known exhibit, photographs and essays on this museum show focus on traditional dress and elaborate costuming of tribes from all over the United States, and fill a gap in this area of material culture for Native American folklore.

Cullin, Stewart. 1975[1907]. *Games of the North American Indians*. New York: Dover Books.
An ambitious collection by an early folklorist and ethnographer, filled with many drawings, diagrams and rich in description of games and recreational activities of Native Americans throughout the United States at the turn of the century.

Curtis, Natalie., ed. 1907. *The Indians' Book*. New York: Harper and Row.
Subtitled "an offering by the American Indians of Indian lore, musical and narrative, to form a record of the songs and legends of their race, recorded and edited by Natalie Curtis." An ambitious early publication, may give you many ideas for research today.

DaMallie, Raymond J. and Douglas R. Parks., eds. 1987. *Souix Indian Religion: Tradition and Innovation*. Norman: University of Oklahoma Press.

Dockstader, Frederick J. 1987. *The Song of the Loom: New Traditions in Navajo Weaving*. New York: Hudson Hills Press.

Dundes, Alan. 1964. *The Morphology of North American Indian Folktales*. Folklore Fellows Communications, no. 195, vol. 81. Helsinki: Suomalainen Tiedeskatemia.
A technical analysis of the structural components of Native American Oral Literature.

Evans-Pritchard, Deirdre. 1987. The Portal Cases: Authenticity, Tourism, Tradtions and the Law. *Journal of American Folklore* 100:287-296.

Farrer, Claire., ed. 1979. *Forms of Play of Native North Americans*. St. Paul, MN:West Publishing Co.

Fenton, William N. 1987. *The False Faces of the Iroquois*. Lincoln: University of Nebraska Press.

Frisbie, Charlotte., ed. 1980. *Southwestern Indian Ritual Drama*. Albuquerque: University of New Mexico Press.

Grinnell, George Bird. 1968[1892]. *Blackfoot Lodgetales*. New York: Scribner's and Sons.

Hofmann, Charles. 1968. *Frances Denamore and American Indian Music*. Contributions from the Museum of the American Indian, Haye Foundation, #23. New York: Museum of the American Indian.
A short but informative work on the important contributions of this pioneer ethnomusicologist.

Hymes, Dell. 1981. *"In vain I tried to tell you": Essays in Native American Ethnopoetics*. Philadelphia: University of Pennsylvania Press.

_____. 1988. Preservation of Indian Lore in Oregon. IN *The Conservation of Culture: Folklorists and the Public Sector*, ed. Burt Feintuch, pp. 264-268. Lexington: University of Kentucky Press.

Jacobs, Melville. 1959. *The Content and Style of an Oral Literature: Oklahomas Chinook Myths and Tales*. Chicago: University of Chicago Press.

Kroeber, Alfred L. 1976. *Yurok Myths*. Berkeley: University of California Press.
An excellent collection of myths from Northern California. Includes insightful annotation and folkloristic commentary.

Kroeber, Karl., ed. 1981. *Traditional American Indian Literatures, Texts and Interpretations*. Lincoln: University of Nebraska Press.
A valuable collection of articles addressing intepretation of oral and written literatures.

Lankford, George. 1983. *The Unfulfilled Promise of North American Indiana Folklore*. In Handbook of American Folklore, ed. Richard Dorson. Bloomington: Indiana University Press. For those interested in texts, discusses many ideas for potential projects.

Marshall, Alan G. 1985. Prairie Chickens Dancing . . . Ecology's Myth. IN *Idaho Folklore, Homesteads to Headstones*, ed. Louis W. Attebery, pp. 101-109. Salt Lake City: University of Utah. Exemplary of writings dedicated to studying a culture's relationship with the environment, an important theme in Native American tradition.

Martin, Christopher., ed. 1988. *Native Needlework: Contemporary Indian Textiles from North Dakota*. Fargo: North Dakota Council on the Arts.

Merriam, Alan P. 1967. *Ethnomusicology of the Flathead Indians*. Chicago: Aldine Publishing.

Milton, John., ed. 1969. *The American Indian Speaks*. Vermillion: University of South Dakota Press.

Niethammer, Carolyn. 1974. *American Indian Food and Lore*. New York: Collier Books.
This dense and informative book is still a good source for traditional recipes, food preservation techniques and agricultural practices of many different Native American groups. Entertaining.

Ortiz, Alfonso., ed. 1972. *New Perspectives on the Pueblos*. Albuquerque: University of New Mexico.

_____. and Richard Erdoes., eds. 1984. *American Indian Myths and Legends*. New York: Pantheon Books.

Reichard, Gladys A. 1970[1950]. *Navajo Religion: A Study of Symbolism*. Bollingen series #18. Princeton, NJ: Princeton University Press.

Sebeok, Thomas., ed. 1976. *Native Languages of the Americas*. New York: Plenum Press.

Swann, Brian., ed. 1983. *Smoothing the Ground: Essays on Native American Oral Literature*. Berkeley: University of California Press.

_____. and Arnold Krupet., eds. 1987. *Recovering the Word. Essays on Native American Literature*. Los Angeles: University of California.

Tafoya, Terry. 1989. Coyote's Eyes: Native Cognitive Styles. *Journal of American Indian Education* (August):29-42.
An excellent article written from an insider's view of how people learn and understand the world, using models from traditional stories. Good companion to Barre Toelken's "Seeing With A Native Eye."

Tedlock, Dennis. 1972. *Finding the Center: Narrative Poetry of the Zuni Indians*. New York: Dial Press.

Toelken, Barre. 1977. Folklore, Worldview and Communication. IN *Folklore: Performance and Communication*, eds. Dan Ben-Amos and Kenneth S. Goldstein, pp. 265-286. The Hague: Mouton.
Toelken challenges the reader to think about how worldview may affect learning patterns and aptitudes through his observations of Native American students at school in Oregon.

_____. 1976. Seeing with a Native Eye: How Many Sheep Will It Hold. IN *Seeing with a Native Eye*, ed. Walter Capps, pp. 9-24. New York: Harper and Row.
An insightful presentation of alternative worldviews and understanding of the Navajo universe from the inside.

Trimble, Stephen. 1987. *Talking with Clay: The Art of Pueblo Pottery*. Santa Fe: School of American Research.

Vogel, Virgil J. 1970. *American Indian Medicine*. Norman: University of Oklahoma Press.

Walker, James. 1980. *Lakota Belief and Ritual*, ed. Raymond DeMallie and Elaine Jahner. Lincoln: University of Nebraska Press.

Witherspoon, Gary. 1977. *Language and Art in the Navajo Universe*. Ann Arbor: University of Michigan Press.
Describes correlation of native use of language and arts, valuable for study of any group.

Worth, Sol and John Adair. 1972. *Through Navajo Eyes: An Exploration in Film Communication and Anthropology*. Bloomington: Indiana University Press.
Explores worldview and different ways of structuring reality through film (as filmed by Navajos themselves).

Young, M. Jane. 1988. *Signs from the Ancestors: Zuni Cultural Symbolism and Perceptions of Rock Art*. Albuquerque: University of New Mexico Press.
An important discussion of the contemporary significance of rock art to a Native American culture of the Southwest.

5) Syncretism—Weaving New Traditions with the Old

Campisi, Jack. 1975. Powwow: A Study of Ethnic Boundery Maintenance. *Man in the Northeast* 9:33-46.

Corrigan, Samuel. 1970. The Plains Indian Powwow: Cultural Integration in Prairie Canada. *Anthropologica* 12:253-277.

Dyck, Noel. 1983. Political Powwow: The Rise and Fall of an Urban Native Festival. IN *The Celebration of Society: Perspectives on Contemporary Cultural Performance*, ed. Frank Manning, pp. 165-184. Bowling Green, OH: Bowling Green University Popular Press.

Gill, Sam. 1987. *Native American Religious Action: A Performance Approach to Religion*. Columbia: University of South Carolina.
A new contribution to Gill's many works exploring meaning in Native American religion. Especially relies on Southwest models.

Graburn, Nelson., ed. 1976. *Ethnic and Tourist Arts: Cultural Expression from the Forth World*. Berkeley: University of California Press.

Green, Rayna. 1989. Beaded Adidas. IN *Time and Temperature*, ed. Charles Camp, pp. 66-67. Washington, D.C.: American Folklore Society.

LaBorwit, Melanie. 1989. Contemporary Native American Folklore. *North Dakota History* (In press).

Lincoln, Kenneth. 1983. *Native American Renaissance*. Berkeley: University of California Press.
Addresses the renaissance of Native American literature and culture during the past few decades.

Lurie, Nancy Oestreich. 1971. The Contemporary American Indian Scene. IN *North American Indians in Historical Perspective*, eds. N.O. Lurie and E.B. Leacock, pp. 421-469. New York: Random House.

Powers, William K. 1970. Contemporary Oglala Music and Dance: Pan-Indianism versus Pan-Tetonism. IN *The Modern Sioux Social Systems and Reservation Culture*, ed. Ethel Narge, pp. 268-288. Lincoln: University of Nebraska Press.

_____. 1975. *Oglala Religion*. Lincoln: University of Nebraska Press.

Wade, Edwin L. 1986. *The Arts of the North American Indian: Native Traditions in Evolution*. New York: Hudson Hills Press.

6) Native Voices

Allen, Paul Gunn. 1985. *The Sacred Hoop: Rediscovering the Feminine in American Indian Tradition*. Boston: Beacon Press.
A strong section on Indian literature; discusses the traditional roles of Indian women, woman's perspectives on tradition, and future visions of the direction of Indian scholarship.

_____. 1982. *Between Sacred Mountains: Navajo Stories and Lessons from the Land.* Chinle, Ariz.: Rock Point Community School.

Blowsnake, Sam. 1963[1920]. *The Autobiography of a Winnebago,* ed. Paul Radin. New York: Dover Books.
An early collaborative effort between informant and anthropologist.

Bruchac, Joseph. 1987. *Survival This Way: Interviews with American Indian Poets.* Tucson: The University of Arizona Press.
Discusses, in essays and letters, personal approaches to asserting Native American identity, especially through writing.

Cook-Lynn, Elizabeth. 1977. *Then Badger Said This.* New York: Vantage.
A compilation of poetry, narratives, tribal stories and history.

DeLoria, Vine Jr. 1969. *Custer Died for Your Sins: An Indian Manifesto.* New York: Macmillan.

Green, Rayna. 1984. *That's What She Said: Contemporary Poetry and Fiction by Native American Women.* Bloomington: Indiana University Press.
A good anthology with contributions from throughout the United States.

Herbert, Belle. 1982. *Shandaa: In My Lifetime.* Anchorage, Alaska: Alaska Native Language Center, University of Alaska.

Hobson, Geary., ed. 1979. *The Remembered Earth: An Anthology of Contemporary Native American Literature.* Albuquerque: University of New Mexico.
One of the earliest and best anthologies published; includes outstanding essays on Native American culture and language by N. Scott Momaday, Leslie Harmon Silko and Paula Gunn Allen, among others.

Krupat, Arnold. 1985. *For Those Who Came After.* Los Angeles: University of California Press.
Excellent treatment of Native American autobiography in cultural context.

_____. 1989. *The Voice in the Margin: Native American Literature and the Canon.* Berkeley: University of California Press.

Momaday, N. Scott. 1969. *The Way to Rainy Mountain.* Albuquerque: University of New Mexico.
Written in three voices representing mythic, historic and present time; a beautifully written approach to a traditional Kiowa story with much autobiography and narrative history woven in. Challenges one's perspective of chronological time and the writing of history.

Neihardt, John G., ed. 1961. *Black Elk Speaks.* Lincoln: University of Nebraska Press.
Discusses history and philosophy; this autobiography of Black Elk, a prominent Sioux leader, describes his vision quest and observes the changing of the Indian universe at the turn of the century.

Ortiz, Simon., ed. 1984. *Earth Power Coming: Short Fiction in Native American Literature.* Tsaile, Ariz.: Navajo Community College Press.

Silko, Leslie Marmon. 1981. *Storyteller.* New York: Seaver Books.
Fiction and autobiographical essays blended together as the author negotiates her Indian identity and role as storyteller.

Vizenor, Gerald. 1984. *The People Named the Chippewa: Narrative Histories.* Minneapolis: University of Minnesota Press.
The author, Chippewa, is a wonderful resource on tribal narrative, and his work is a good model for the kinds of stories one might collect.

Welch, James. 1974. *Winter in the Blood.* New York: Harper and Row.
A moving novel about one Native American man's perspective of contemporary Indian life and culture.

CHAPTER 20
Documenting the Fieldwork Project

Katherine Borland

Alright. You've read something about folklore and have a general idea of what it is. You've been asked to go out and do some folklore fieldwork. You've identified the individual or group who will act as your collaborators, and you've done an initial tape-recorded interview. You've realized (probably) that far from being a difficult, unpleasant task, interviewing has been fun and interesting. Now, with your own body of folklore examples, you feel more confident in talking about the concepts, issues and problems in folklore research that are being discussed in class. The next step is to assemble your project and prepare a description and analysis of the lore you've collected.

There are many different approaches you may have taken in the initial stage of conceptualizing and planning your project. You may have identified a particular *kind* of folklore (a local legend, for instance) and collected numerous versions of one *type* from many individuals. You may have assembled a particular folk *group* and recorded a story- song- or joke-swapping session. You may have identified a folk practice (quilt-making or a holiday celebration) and visited practitioners to observe how they perform their folklore. Or you may have interviewed just one person and collected a variety of folklore genres from his/her repertoire. Each of these approaches provides an initial *focus* for your project (the item/type, the social interaction, the process, the individual). None, however, provides you with the specific questions you will want to ask about the meaning of your material.

It is at this point that many beginning folklorists throw up their hands in dismay. Faced with a wealth of interesting material, how does one locate an organizing principal that would draw it all together in a meaningful way? While each project will be unique, there are some general practices that will help you construct a good solid folklore document. In what follows I will identify the general steps you should

take and the questions you'll need to ask yourself as you write up your research.

ON THE MULTIPLE PURPOSES OF DOING A FOLKLORE PROJECT

The first thing you need to do is to reflect on the purposes of doing a collecting project. Most instructors identify a variety of purposes for the assignment. The first set of purposes concerns your own personal and intellectual growth. The second set concerns your audience, or the community of scholars who may find your work useful in the future. Try to keep these purposes in mind as you review and organize your data.

Personal satisfaction

One of the basic values of doing a collecting project resides in the personal satisfaction you and your collaborators derive from the experience. Whether you work with people you know well or with people you have never talked with before, the interviewing process provides you with an opportunity to learn more about your collaborators' special talents, knowledge or experiences than you knew before. Likewise, *you* provide an appreciative audience for the people you work with. In some cases you may be the first audience for some of the material you collect, since the beliefs and practices of "ordinary" people are often trivialized even by the people who possess them. Moreover, the sharing involved in collecting folklore often creates or strengthens bonds of respect and intimacy among interview participants.

The value that you personally derive from the fieldwork experience should be reflected in your final write-up of the project. One useful way to document *this* aspect of the collecting experience is to keep a journal of your thoughts and feelings as you move through the various stages of your fieldwork. Then, when you are ready to assemble your project you'll already have a written record of your personal reflections to draw on.

Sharpening observational skills

Folklore fieldwork also provides you with an opportunity to sharpen your observational skills. Remember, folklore is immersed in the ordinary practices of daily life, and is often taken for granted in the course of our everyday activity. The fieldwork project forces you to pay close attention to those aspects of everyday life that are specially marked and to ponder their significance.

For instance, if you are collecting verbal folklore (stories, legends, jokes, special turns of phrase), for which the natural context is conversation, you will have attempted to construct your interview so that it comes as close to the ordinary flow of talk as your situation allows. When you review what you have on tape, your job is to pull out chunks of artful talk that correspond to the forms (genres) of folklore you have learned about in class. Since the interview constitutes a special kind of conversation (usually more structured and artificial than ordinary talk), you will need to pay close attention to the ways in which people communicate. You must distinguish a true performance of folklore (the dramatic telling of a legend, for example) from a mere description or report of a folklore item.

If you are working with a group, you should also note the conversational rules that are operating. For example, in what ways do various people take turns at talk? What allows one person to interrupt another? How do people encourage each other to perform? Who gets to perform? How does one performance activate (lead to) another?

This kind of heightened observation demands careful watching as well as listening. Watching will be even more important if you are collecting customary folklore, folklore that has to do with actions rather than words. For instance, say you are documenting a game of hopscotch. You'll need to record in as much detail as possible the physical, social, and verbal aspects of the game. Where is it located? How many participants are there? Who are they? What determines admission into or exclusion from the game? What is the design of the hopscotch? How is it made? What are the steps taken in playing the game? What gestures, words, or other activities surround the game? How long does it last? What determines the beginning and end of the activity? Are there variations in the performance of the game?

For a good, thorough description of an activity like hopscotch, you will need to supplement your own written or taped observations with drawings, photos, and interviews with the participants. The fieldwork activity often involves looking closely at something with which you are quite familiar. But for the purposes of creating a folklore document, you will need to suspend your knowledge and look at/listen to the performance with new eyes and ears. (For more on ethnographic observation, see Spradley, 1979 and 1980.)

Exercising Analytical Skills

If good observations are important to creating your folklore record, good analysis is essential to determining the meaning of the folklore you collect. What is the difference between observation/description and analysis/interpretation? Most simply, description is the activity of telling about something, limiting oneself to the verifiable, observable facts. Analysis takes this activity a step farther. When you analyze something you look at the relations between its parts or its relation as a part to a larger whole in order to find patterns of significance that are not immediately obvious through straightforward description.

Let's take a simple example——the gesture of waving. If we were to describe that gesture we might say:

> Person X lifts his/her right hand and forearm, slightly in front of the body, palm out, to a height of about a hand's-breadth above the head. Then, keeping the lower arm stable, the hand begins a back and forth motion, right to left, left to right, inscribing a semi-circle pivoted at the wrist and/or elbow. This motion is repeated several times.

Here we have a physical description of a particular wave. But what does it mean? The first, most common meaning would be that it acts as an American form of greeting. However, a wave may have other meanings depending on the context and on the intent of the waver. If the waver were at a football game waiting for a friend to join him/her, the wave might signify, "Here I am, up here!" If the waver were seated in a classroom, the wave might mean, "Pay attention to me, I have something to say." You can probably think of other possible meanings in other contexts. The point is that an *interpretation* of a wave involves viewing the action as one component in a larger constellation of communicative activity.

When one looks at other, more elaborated communicative forms, like folklore, the ways in which something can mean become much more numerous and complex. One way to think about the meaning of an item of folklore is to ask yourself what the doing of it accomplishes for the persons involved in the interaction. How does it transform the interactive situation? How does it reflect or challenge commonly understood rules for social behavior or commonly held beliefs or values? (For more on interpretation, see Geertz, 1973).

Providing a folklore record

Moving away from the purposes related to you, another fundamental purpose for doing a collecting project is to build up a folklore record. Folklore's definitive characteristic is that it varies across time and space. That is, a folk practice that thrives over a period of time will exist in numerous versions. Additionally, as the folklore that is tied to older ways of life fades away, new kinds emerge. Since folklore is ever changing, it is difficult to grasp in its entirety. Only by writing down, or otherwise fixing, specific instances of folklore can we amass the body of materials necessary to understand general folklore patterns and processes.

While most immediately, your collection provides you with the materials upon which to construct an analysis, it should also provide future folklorists with the material they need for broader comparative or historical studies. For this reason it is important that you construct a record that is as detailed, accurate and complete as possible.

Since you are the person who collected the folklore in the field, you are the expert on the particularities of your fieldwork project. But to make your material useful to others, you must keep in mind what your readers will need to know to understand that material. Having gotten to know each other during the fieldwork project, you and your collaborators will share a common frame of reference—a body of understandings that will not be spelled out, because they are considered obvious. Your readers will not have access to this dimension of the communicative exchange, and therefore, you will need to make those share but unstated understandings explicit in your final project.

Assembling Data for the Archives

A related purpose for the collecting project is to assemble data for the folklore archive at your school or institution. While each archive will be organized in a particular way, most require the same basic information for each of your collected items so that they can be filed and cross-referenced effectively. For each item you will need to provide:

1. a genre label

2. a title
3. the folk group to which the item belongs
4. the time, date, and place the item was collected
5. the names of collaborator(s), interviewer, and audience members present
6. the typical context in which the item is performed
7. a verbatim transcription or representation of the item itself
8. collaborator comments about the item.

Each piece of information about the item should be clearly marked, so that the archivist can file the item in the appropriate categories.

Try to be as specific as possible in labeling your materials. Perhaps the most important labels for archiving purposes are genre and folk group. For instance, hopscotch can be characterized as a folk game, generally played by children. Yet, the folk game is not usually played by boys or by very young or high school-aged children. Therefore, a more specific definition of the folk group would be grade-school, female children. If you have trouble identifying the genre to which your item belongs, you may want to consult some of the folklore textbooks that are organized by genre. Jan Brunvand's *The Study of American Folklore: An Introduction* (1986), and Richard Dorson's *Folklore and Folklife: An Introduction* (1972), both provide definitions and examples of the more common folklore genres.

You should consult your instructor about the particular format he/she wishes you to use in presenting your material. But you may also find it helpful to review the following format, taken from the paper of a beginning folklore student at Indiana University. (See Figures 1 and 2)

ASSEMBLING ADEQUATE DATA

Having reviewed the five purposes for doing a collecting project, you are now ready to review and organize your data. Let's begin with the primary source for most projects, the tape-recorded interview. One simple fact that you should bear in mind is that the first-rate collection project depends upon good, thorough, interesting data. Everyone possesses folklore. Theoretically, this means that you should be able to collect an abundance of folklore from anyone. Why, then, do interviews sometimes prove disappointing? There are several reasons.

Some people are just not as verbally communicative as others. Some, who seem very willing to share folklore in ordinary social situations, "clam up"

Title: Safe Sex
Genre: Proverbial Phrase
Primary Folk Group: Young Men

Contextual Information: This proverbial phrase was collected by Jeff A. Eckert from Walter Lampert, age 82, on October 14, 1989, at the informant's home in St. Anthony, Indiana. Typically this proverbial phrase is told by the informant whenever other people are teasing an unmarried male or reciting jokes.

Item: Do you want to hear one?

(Yeah!)

(Laughter) I read in a book one time . . . you know old Ben Franklin he's supposed to have been a smart man; so one young feller got in trouble with a girl so he said, "I told you from now on, take'em from 70 years (old)." He said, "they won't tell and they won't swell".

(laugh)

"They won't tell and they won't swell."

Oral Literary Criticism: Walter learned this proverbial phrase as a younger man but recites it usually as a riddle or a joke. Walter does not tell or even listen to "ornery" jokes, "but I did take an interest in this one." He sets this one as the limit and says this is "kind of dirty" but justifies it by saying "Franklin said it!"

Classification: According to Borland and Livesay, "Folk Speech", in The Emergence of Folklore in Everyday Life: A Fieldguide and Sourcebook, ed. George H. Schoemaker, pp. 43, a proverbial phrase is "a shortcut that helps to make a point quickly and effectively. They are often repeated because they are easy to remember."

Figure 1. Illustration of how folklore item might be documented.

Mrs. D.D. Anderson
Longview, Washington
1981

Legend
"Indian Story"

The informant of this story is my mother. She was born and raised in Salt Lake City, Utah. She is 51 years of age and has raised eight children. My mother is a housewife. She enjoys reading in her spare time, sewing, handicrafts, and target shooting. She is an active Catholic.

****

This story was told to my mother by her grandmother when she was a small child. My mother used to help my grandmother bake pies every Saturday morning and my grandmother would tell her all these stories about when she was a little girl. I think the telling of these stories helped to bond them together because they were very, very, close. This event actually occurred to my great grandmother in the 1890s near Rock Springs, Wyoming.

****

When my great grandmother was living in Rock Springs, Wyoming, around 1895, she had a frightening experience. In those days, Indians would often come to settlers' homes and ask for food or even trade small items. My great grandmother had a one-month old child at the time. One day some indians showed up at her home and instead of asking for food, they wanted to take her baby. Eventually, they went away and she lay the baby down for a nap. She then went to visit one of her neighbors. Upon returning home, she found the baby missing. Later on that evening, however, one of the squaws from the Indian village returned the baby safe and sound. As it turned out, that baby was my grandmother, and she still has the Indian blanket that she was wrapped in.

Robin Anderson
640 E. 900 N.
Logan, Utah
Utah State University
History 124
Spring 1982

Figure 2. Another example of how to document an item of folklore.

in the presence of a tape recorder. Some people have a hard time grasping what you want when you askthem to share their folklore (especially when you are not very clear yourself), and therefore claim not to know any folklore. If your collaborators fall into any of these categories, you may find that you just don't have enough material on tape to work with.

Another common problem with interviews is that while you may have gotten a wealth of background material, you don't seem to have much in the way of folklore. Or, you may have collected many folklore items but what you have on tape provides only the barest description of these items. In all these cases the solution is the same: do another interview.

There are several rules of thumb that will help you collect good, solid data. **First,** try to be as clear as possible with your collaborators about what you are after in the interview. You've probably already noticed or know about folklore practices that they engage in. You might want to start by requesting a particular story, joke or other piece of folklore you've heard from your collaborator before. If this is the case, you may want to bring along a companion to act as a fresh audience, since people sometimes dislike repeating things they know you've heard already.

Second, try to make the interview situation as relaxed and informal as possible. While interviews are by their nature more structured than ordinary talk, your aim is to get people to interact in a natural way. Sometimes a dry-run interview is helpful to accustom your collaborators (and yourself) to the presence of the tape recorder.

Third, when you think about what questions you want to ask a collaborator, remember that not every individual will actively practice all the folklore he or she is familiar with. While everyone amasses folklore throughout his or her lifetime, at each stage of life some folklore practices will be more central and meaningful to the individual than others. Similarly, not everyone in a community shares the same repertoire, though they will be familiar with the repertoires of their friends and acquaintances. Therefore, when you interview people to find out what kinds of folklore they possess, you'll need to distinguish between their active and passive repertoires, for your interview will be more successful if you concentrate on recording items your collaborators actively perform.

We know, for instance, that the folk group that actively transmits most folk games is children. Of course, older people will have participated in this folklore and may sometimes remember quite well the games they used to play. Since they no longer participate in these games, however, they are understood to be passive bearers and are not likely to be your best sources for this genre of folklore. Therefore, if you are fascinated by children's games, find some children to observe and talk to.

Teenagers, on the other hand, are a good source for urban legends and supernatural stories. While other groups may know of and even perform these legends, the most common situation in which this kind of folklore is transmitted is the teenage slumber party, camp out or weekend gathering. Likewise, older relatives are better sources for life stories and family history than younger brothers and sisters, since they have experienced more and have had time to reflect upon those experiences. Often, an older relative will have a rich store of tales that he or she has told repeatedly, and through repetition, has refined to a high degree of artistry. Therefore, when you chose a folklore topic to investigate, try to locate the *active* bearers of the tradition. If you begin with a person you want to interview, try to identify the kinds of folklore he or she actively performs.

Another rule of thumb is to aim for a full description of a few items rather than a superficial description of many items. Often, beginning folklorists feel the need to collect as many examples of the genres they have learned about as they can, and their taped interviews proceed like a rapid-fire game of twenty questions. The result is often a minimal description of each item, sometimes so minimal that it does not constitute folklore. Consider the following example of a student who asked her grandmother if she remembered any of the songs she used to sing as a child. Her grandma responded:

> Ohh . . . up a lazy river by the old mill sun. (See I don't remember all of it, but that's how it started out. I love that song. That was one of my favorites; it's by the Mills Brothers.)

The grandmother's response provides several clues for the alert fieldworker. Obviously, this song is important to her——"I love that song." She even remembers the group that performed it. However, the interviewer has not succeeded in collecting the song, nor has she delved into the possible meaning the remembered fragment may have for her grandmother. So actually, we have no record of the item itself. This is an example of inadequate description. If the fieldworker had conducted a second interview, she might have focused upon this fragment and asked her grandmother to expand upon the description of the song (perhaps she might even have been able to prod her grandmother's memory, and get a full performance of the song). Alternately, she might have refocused her question, asking her grandmother what songs she sings (actively performs) now.

Another common difficulty in interviews is that the beginning collector regards talking as the *only* medium through which folklore is transmitted and the tape-recorder as the only tool for documentation. Yet, there are many kinds of nonverbal folklore that require other collecting methods. For example, if you are documenting Italian-american foodways, you need to ask your collaborator not only *what* is served but how it is prepared. Better yet, you should ask your collaborator to *demonstrate* the process of preparing the meal, if possible, and take careful notes of your observations. Photographs of the important steps in cooking the meal will greatly enhance your description (For examples of photographic documentation of folklore practices, see Toelken, 1979:178ff). And, of course, a tape-recording of your collaborator's instructions and comments as she goes about preparing the meal will give you additional data for your analysis.

In short, a line recited from an old, half-remembered song is not a folksong; a list of dishes at an Italian-american dinner is not a foodway. These fragments are signs of the existence of folklore, and you should pursue those signs in an attempt to uncover the folklore performance or process you are after.

MAKING A WRITTEN RECORD

Now that you have gathered as much material as possible, you need to begin to make a written record of your folklore collection. Most likely, you will not be able to include everything you have collected, so you'll need to make some careful choices. You may have to narrow or even change your original focus. To do this, you'll find it helpful to review your tapes, notes, and visual documents, separating your materials into categories of stuff. These categories may be based on form (genre), theme, time period, steps (in a process), or other relevant distinctions. Now see if you can break down the materials in these categories into smaller subcategories.

As you sort out your materials, look for emerging patterns that might tie them together in some meaningful way. For example, I once did a collecting project with my grandmother in which I asked her to talk about growing up in a small town in Maine. Over a period of five days she told me about aspects of everyday life, customs and practices, and she performed a number of personal experience narratives and tales about the other characters who lived in her hometown. While my original intention had been to

identify regional characteristics in my grandmother's lore, I became fascinated by her tales. One, in particular, dealt with an amusing incident that had happened to her when she went to see the horse races with her father. Focusing on this one story, I noticed a very sophisticated pattern in the way she constructed her account. I also discovered that the incidents of that day provided a picture in miniature of some of the issues that she had discussed in her more general description of women's lives in the town. At this stage, I decided to abandon my original purpose and write an analysis of the racetrack narrative.

Once you have identified your new focus, you can then select from your data the items you will use to represent that focus in your final project. You will also be able to organize the materials that will function as background information for your discussion. Thus, in my study of a single narrative from my grandmother's repertoire, I incorporated much of the other material I had collected to demonstrate the meaning and value of that story. You may also wish to include any oral literary criticism your collaborator has made about the items you select. Oral literary criticism constitutes any comment or explanation your collaborators offer that conveys their view of an item's meaning. While you and your collaborators may not always agree on the meaning of an item, oral literary criticism can enrich your analysis by providing a perspective on the data from the *native's* or *author's* point of view. (For more on oral literary criticism, see Dundes' "Metafolklore and Oral Literary Criticism," 1980[1966].)

On Accuracy

The next step is to transcribe the taped materials you will use in your project. Since your aim in documenting folklore is to preserve it in as natural a state as possible, you must transcribe your materials accurately. Listen carefully to your tapes as you transcribe, and check your transcription repeatedly against the original oral version. You will find that you need to work slowly, since most people cannot write as fast as the speed of a normal conversation. Remember, a transcription should represent the tape-recorded performance with word-for-word exactness.

As you transcribe, you will notice that oral communication differs significantly from ordinary written forms. Oral conversation contains no punctuation. People rarely speak in complete sentences. They often make false starts or change their grammatical constructions mid-utterance. Indeed, while written works most often represent the finished product of numerous revisions, oral communication represents an ongoing compositional process. Your transcription should reflect that process, so don't revise or polish your collaborators' words.

Since there are many aspects of oral communication, like pause, loudness and voice quality, that cannot be conveyed by using the traditional written code, you will need to employ a system of symbols to use in transcription to indicate these features of the oral message. To indicate a pause, use three dots: . . . For longer pauses you may want to use words in parentheses: (long pause). Special voice qualities, gestures or other extraverbal factors should be recorded in parentheses as well: (in a high, squeaky voice), (points to the door), (laughs). If you or someone else comments during the performance, indicate a change of speakers. If you or the audience responds during the flow of talk, include these in brackets: [laughter], [groans]. If the speaker breaks off in the middle of a thought to start a new thought, indicate the break with a dash: It was, it was in-- Now this was before we moved to Boston, remember... All other punctuation should follow the ordinary rules for written discourse. (For a more thorough discussion of transcription making see Edward Ives 1974.)

Providing Context

Once you have a record of your item, you will need to consider the relevant contexts for that item. There are several kinds of context that will be important both for archival purposes and for your analysis. I have already discussed the interview and generic contexts in the section on archives. But there are other contexts that you might want to consider in analyzing your data——the situational, biographical, and sociocultural contexts.

Situational context. The situational context (also called the typical context on archiving forms) represents the immediate context in which the folklore is normally performed or practiced. Notice that the situational context does not usually correspond to the context of the interview. For instance, a beginning student collected a folk legend from her younger (teenage) sister, entitled "The Porcelain Doll." On her item form she writes:

"This item was collected by Terri Smith from Amanda Smith, age 16, in their parents' home on September 29, 1989. Typically, this legend would be told as a *ghost Story* among girls at a slumber party. Tales like this would usually be proceeded [sic] by a seance."

Here we have a brief sketch of the kind of situation in which this story would naturally be told, including the emic genre (*ghost story*) and the surrounding activities (slumber party, seance).

Why is the situational context important? It shows folklore as purposeful activity, linked up to a larger complex of communicative activity. One exemplary study of folklore in its situational context is Barbara Kirshenblatt-Gimblett's exploration of a Jewish-canadian woman's use of a parable to settle a family dispute (1975). The parable professor Kirshenblatt-Gimblett collected did not, in itself, display its usefulness. However, by carefully questioning her collaborator about the specific situation in which she had told the parable, professor Kirshenblatt-Gimblett found that the story provided a means of indirectly criticizing the behavior of a family member. It also allowed the family member to recognize his error by showing him that his actions were parallel to those related in the parable.

Sometimes the meaning of a folklore item will be ambiguous if the situational context is not recorded. The proverb, *a rolling stone gathers no moss*, for instance, can function as either an admonition against or a defense of the wanderer's life, depending, of course, on the speaker's understanding of the metaphorical meaning of moss. Only by examining the conversational context in which the proverb arose can we determine which meaning the speaker intends. Analyzing folklore in its situational context shows how folklore does social work. If you decide to look at the situational context for your folklore, you will need to find out how the folklore came up in a specific situation. For instance, you might ask you collaborator: When was the last time you told this joke/story/proverb? What was going on at the time? What was your intention in performing the folklore? How was the folklore received by your audience? Why did you select this particular item of lore rather than another?

Biographical context. Another important kind of context is biographical context. If you are focusing on the folklore of one person, you will want to collect a life history so that you have a sense of who he/she is and what folk groups he/she belongs to. You may find, as I did with my grandmother, that particular items of folklore become meaningful as expressions of the tensions, problems or successes of a particular period in that person's life. More generally, a person's folklore may reveal a particular set of values or beliefs that have guided them to become who they are today.

Socio-cultural context. If we expand our vision of context outward, we come to the social and cultural contexts for interpreting folklore. The social context includes the structures and institutions set up by a particular group that govern the actions of its members. The cultural context involves the symbolic dimension of the social world: beliefs, attitudes and symbols shared by the members of the group. Often the cultural and social contexts are difficult to separate from one another, since the institutional life of a group is based upon, and at the same time provides the basis for, shared beliefs and values. Thus, scholars often talk of the socio-cultural context of folklore.

The social structure provides a way of organizing people so that the work of everyday life can proceed (relatively) smoothly. It also assigns individuals social *roles*, to which they are expected to conform. The expectations a society has for people in different social roles will be conveyed through a number of symbolic forms. For instance, Erving Goffman looked at the presentation of men and women in advertisements and found that the placement of women with respect to men (below or behind) and their stances (averted gaze versus straightforward gaze; tilted posture versus erect posture) reinforced the cultural idea that women are subservient to and less serious than men (1979). Folklore is made up of symbolic forms. Existing within the social structure it may reflect, reinforce or challenge that structure.

Let's return to the example of the legend told at a slumber party to see how the socio-cultural context might provide an analytical frame for understanding the folklore. First, we can say that slumber parties constitute a socially accepted practice among white, middle-class, teenage girls. But, they also represent a break from ordinary social practice. Consider, parents, the household authorities, are usually banished from the house (or at least restricted to their bedroom) during the slumber party. Moreover, the girls involved are released from normal restrictions governing appropriate sleep and eating practices. If you were to analyze the folklore that arises in the context of a slumber party, you might want to look at how the slumber party itself is related to socio-cultural expectations for teenage girls. One of my former students compared an American slumber party to the more formalized puberty rituals of African societies and found many similarities in the activities. This led her to interpret the slumber party as not simply a form of entertainment but as a rite of passage in which girls' anxieties and expectations about becoming adult women were aired.

While you will not be able to describe the socio-cultural context in its entirety, you may be able to identify aspects of it that will help you interpret your collected material by connecting it to elements of the larger symbolic system, of which it is a part. Numerous ethnic cultures, occupational cultures, class cultures, even age cultures in America exhibit their own unique set of symbols and organizational structures. You may wish to explore how your folklore relates to one of these socio-cultural systems. If you choose to study a particular folk group at your university or college, you may wish to consult Jay Mechling's article on academic folklore (1989). In this article Mechling stresses the importance of doing research on your own campus, since the university provides a meeting ground for public and private worlds and a site for the enactment of American pluralism.

Alternately, you may wish to view your folklore within the larger context of American society and culture. In his essays in *Interpreting Folklore* (1980), Alan Dundes sees American culture as future-oriented, racist, sexist and homophobic. Does your collection of folklore support or challenge Dundes' assertions?

To sum up, when you explore what a particular item means, you may find clues at a variety of different levels: the immediate situation, the background of an individual's life, the socio-cultural organization of a community, or the socio-cultural organization of the entire nation. These contexts can and do overlap in real life, but they provide you with alternative analytical frames for interpreting your folklore.

CONSTRUCTING AN ARGUMENT

Now that you have assembled and transcribed your data and developed some ideas about how you might interpret that data, you are ready to write your analysis. Remember, your analysis represents your own interpretation of the folklore you have collected. Although you may use ideas and concepts from your readings, don't feel bound by someone else's interpretation. Be creative. Use your own knowledge and experience to weave together a unique perspective on the topic. There are no right or wrong interpretations; there are only better or worse ones.

What makes a good interpretation? First, it should be thoughtful and well-organized. If you stick to the surfaces of things, if you point out only the obvious, you will probably bore your readers. If you flit from one idea to the next without showing your readers how they are connected, you will lose them altogether. You will need to strike a balance between good, thought-provoking generalizations and supporting details. Remember, each time you make a claim about the significance or meaning of your data, you will need to present support for that claim in a well developed paragraph. Throughout your analysis you will need to move back and forth between general ideas (claims) and the specific examples from your data (evidence).

On Proper Citations

When you write an analysis of folklore fieldwork, you place your material within the context of folklore scholarship. You may decide to explore the ways in which the folklore you have collected compares with other collected versions. (If so, you should consult Elliott Oring's article "Documenting Folklore: The Annotation" (1989) for resources and methods for comparative folklore.) You may employ ideas or interpretive strategies you have discovered from reading other authors. Even if you develop your own interpretive strategy, you will still need to discuss how that strategy relates to other accepted scholarly interpretations.

For instance, after reviewing your folklore materials, you may find that some of them reveal the future-oriented American world view that you read about in Alan Dundes' article "Thinking Ahead" (*Interpreting Folklore* 1980:69-85). Alternately, you may discover that your material does not support Dundes's thesis about the American world view because it reveals a profound concern for and valuing of the past. Either way, in order to locate your discussion within the larger scholarly debate over American world view, you'll need to cite relevant material from the work of Dundes and others.

A proper citation includes an accurate quotation or paraphrase from your source, the author, title, publication information, and page number(s). There are many different styles of citation, however, and you should choose one and stick with it throughout your essay. For guidelines on citations for folklore papers, see the Style Guide in *Journal of American Folklore* 101:219-226. You may also find it useful to refer to the latest edition of the *MLA Handbook for Writers of Research Papers, Theses, and Dissertations*.

One final note. As you have probably gathered from reading this chapter, documenting folklore requires you to exercise a number of different skills: observational, analytic, organizational, and creative. All of these require thoughtfulness and, above all, time. Try to start your project early so that you have enough time to arrange and conduct your interviews,

review your data, make accurate transcriptions, develop an analysis, and provide proper citations. In the long run you'll find that the time spent is well worth it, for a good, solid collecting project is a tribute not only to your scholarly abilities but also to those friends, new or old, who have taken the time to share their folklore with you.

Acnowledgements

I would like to thank my teachers, Richard Bauman and Beverly Stoeltje for many of the ideas and approaches contained in this chapter. Also, thank you to George and Phillip, Vicki, Chip and Colleen, Jennifer and Michelle for your support and friendship in teaching folklore together.

References Cited

Brunvand, Jan Harold. 1986[1968]. *The Study of American Folklore: An Introduction*. 3rd edition. New York: W. W. Norton.

Dorson, Richard M., ed. 1972. *Folklore and Folklife: An Introduction*. Chicago: Univ. of Chicago Press.

Dundes, Alan. 1966. Metafolklore and Oral Literary Criticism. *The Monist* 50:505-516.

_____. 1980. *Interpreting Folklore*. Bloomington: Indiana University Press.

Geertz, Clifford. 1973. *The Interpretation of Culture*. New York: Basic Books.

Goffman, Erving. 1979. *Gender Advertisement*. Cambridge, MA: Harvard Univ. Press.

Ives, Edward D. 1974. *The Tape-recorded Interview: A Manual for Field Workers in Folklore and Oral History*. Knoxville: University of Tennessee Press.

Kirshenblatt-Gimblett, Barbara. 1975. A Parable in Context: A Social Interactional Analysis of Storytelling Performance. IN *Folklore, Performance and Communication*, eds. Dan Ben-Amos and Kenneth Goldstein, pp. 105-130. The Hague: Mouton Press.

Mechling, Jay. 1989. Mediating Structures and the Significance of University Folk. IN *Folk Groups Folklore Genres: A Reader*, ed. by Elliott Oring. Logan, Utah: Utah State University Press.

Oring, Elliott. 1989. Documenting Folklore: The Annotation. IN *Folk Groups and Folklore Genres: A Reader*, ed. by Elliott Oring. Logan, Utah: Utah State University Press.

Spradley, James P. 1979. *The Ethnographic Interview*. New York: Holt, Rinehart, and Winston.

_____. 1980. *Participant Observation*. New York: Holt, Rinehart, and Winston.

Toelken, Barre. 1979. *The Dynamics of Folklore*. Boston: Houghton Mifflin Company.

Selected Annotated Bibliography

1) Fieldwork

Bauman, Richard. 1983. The Field Study of Folklore in Context. IN *Handbook of American Folklore*, ed. by Richard Dorson, pp. 362-368. Bloomington: Indiana University Press.
Outlines the various kinds of context important to consider in doing field research. Fairly theoretical.

Briggs, Charles L. 1986. *Learning How to Ask: A Sociolinguistic Appraisal of the Role of the Interview in Social Science Research.* Cambridge: Cambridge University Press.
Examines the false assumption that ethnographic interviews represent unmediated reality. Argues for an examination of the sociolinguistic rules of interaction in a community before doing fieldwork.

Dorson, Richard M. 1964. Collecting Oral Folklore in the United States. IN *Buying the Wind: Regional Folklore in the United States*, pp. 1-20. Chicago: University of Chicago Press.
Provides an anecdotal account of the author's fieldwork methods and experiences. Stresses the importance of identifying the active bearers of folklore in a community.

Georges, Robert A. and Michael Owen Jones. 1980. *People Studying People: The Human Element in Fieldwork.* Berkeley: University of California Press.
Argues against the notion that the successful fieldworker is detached, objective and emotionally distant from the people he/she studies. Focuses on the human element of fieldwork in deciding on a project, establishing rapport, and negotiating relationships with collaborators.

Goldstein, Kenneth. 1964. *A Guide for Fieldworkers in Folklore.* Hatboro, PA: Folklore Associates, Inc.
An early fieldwork guide that calls for placing folklore fieldwork on a scientific basis. Advice on technical equipment now outdated.

Jackson, Bruce. 1987. *Fieldwork.* Urbana: University of Illinois Press.
A good, up-to-date discussion of technical matters in fieldwork research. Also includes a discussion of ethics and interesting accounts of personal experiences to illustrate the do's and dont's of fieldwork.

Paredes, Amèrico. 1977. On Ethnographic Work Among Minorities: A Folklorist's Perspective. *The New Scholar* 6:1-32.
Important discussion of miscommunication between culturally insensitive fieldworkers and their collaborators. Offers a warning to those studying groups who belong to a culture different from their own about the powerful distorting influence of stereotypes.

Wilson, William A. 1986. Documenting Folklore. *Folk Groups and Folklore Genres: An Introduction*, ed. by Elliott Oring, pp. 225-254. Logan, Utah: Utah State University Press.
A good introductory article on how to set up a field work project, what to look for, what to look out for. Contains examples from student papers.

2) Interpretation

Bauman, Richard. 1977. *Verbal Art as Performance.* Prospect Heights, IL: Waveland Press.
A theoretical presentation of the most influential recent approach to interpreting verbal folklore.

Dorson, Richard M., ed. 1983. *Handbook of American Folklore.* Bloomington: Indiana University Press.
A collection of short articles by experts in the field about various kinds of American folklore. Articles provide useful introductions to the basic concepts and existing scholarship in particular fields of folklore.

Dundes, Alan. 1980[1966]. Texture, Text and Context. IN *Interpreting Folklore*, pp. 20-32. Bloomington: Indiana University Press.
An important work describing how to analyze and interpret a folklore item.

Oring, Elliott, ed. 1989. *Folk Groups and Folklore Genres: A Reader.* Logan, Utah: Utah State Univ. Press.
A collection of interpretive essays by experts in the field on various kinds of folklore. Useful for getting ideas about possible interpretive approaches.

EXAMPLES OF STUDENT FIELDWORK PAPERS

APPENDIX A
WORKING TOGETHER:
THE SUCCESS OF A FEMALE FIRE FIGHTER
Jennifer Hickman
Indiana University

This paper illustrates how a folklore paper focusing
on gender issues might be carried out.

APPENDIX B
DISCUSSING RURAL FOLKLORE
IN CONTEXT AND IN CHARACTER
Gwendolyn M. Filosa
Indiana University

This paper illustrates how a *Fieldwork Project* might be done. The paper consists
of biographical information, an analytical essay, and ten items of folklore.

APPENDIX C
THE COMPLEX SURROUNDINGS OF A MUSICAL EVENT
Ericka J. Schumacker
Indiana University

This paper illustrates how a *Musical Observation Paper* might be carried out.

WORKING TOGETHER: THE SUCCESS OF A FEMALE FIRE FIGHTER

Jennifer Hickman
Indiana University

In an earlier paper about occupational folklore in the fire department, I began a discussion of common stereotypes the public has of fire fighters. I noted that these stereotypes are of two extremes. There are those people who idolize the fire fighters as brave heroes risking their lives to save others, while some consider them to be lazy, overweight bums who get paid for sitting around the station all day and doing nothing. Though wildly different in their representations of the profession, these stereotypes do have one thing in common--both are images of males. Since women have only been active in the fire service since 1974 and there are still relatively few of them (1908 in 483 U.S. fire departments), the public has not really had the opportunity to develop stereotypes of female fire fighters (Firework: Women in Fire Suppression, January 1989).

Within the profession itself, however, it is quite a different story. As recent issues of Fireworks (a monthly newsletter for women in fire suppression) indicate, sexual stereotypes and discrimination are very much a problem in this traditionally male dominated occupation. Robert McCarl offers an explanation for the difficulties that women face:

> A basic tenet of the fire fighting tradition is the strength of the male group; it is difficult for the men to conceive of women as equals in the work place. As one female fire fighter put it: 'Our being here takes away from their pride in their job--their egos are deflated having a woman on the job!' The women who go into the fire service see it as unchartered territory, offering financial and personal rewards not available elsewhere, while the men see them as affirmative action beneficiaries who have gotten the job due to special treatment (The District of Columbia Fire Fighters' Project: A Case Study in Occupational Folklife. Washington, D.C.: Smithsonian Press, 1985, p. 110).

When I went to interview Alice Thompson (a pseudonym), the only female amongst the eighty professional fire fighters in the city of Fairfield (fictitious name), I expected to collect data that would illustrate this tension. For the sake of my paper, I hoped to find dramatic examples of how she uses folkloric performances to negotiate her status in this male dominated arena of work activity. Instead, the data I collected seemed to indicate that Alice fit in very nicely with her male colleagues. As a woman myself, I found this to be very encouraging news about what lay ahead for me when I would enter the work force. But as a student who was counting on collecting data of a very <u>different</u>

type (some sort of conflict around which I could build my paper), I was very disappointed.

However, after a great deal of thought about this lack of tension and conflict, I now realize that the very fact that Alice fits into this group so well is in itself worthy of discussion. It occurred to me that both she and the men on her shift must share some sort of common sense of what is and is not appropriate behavior. These cultural "rules" are very significant in that they operate as a form of social control. Any violation of these norms of individual behavior (e.g. joking relationships or physical contact or job performance) would affect the entire group and disrupt its harmony (McCarl 174-5).

When Alice joined the department three years ago, she was an outsider in two ways. First of all, she was a rookie on a shift with very experienced fire fighters and secondly, she was a woman in a previously all male domain. Being the new kid on the block, so to speak, made it necessary for her to learn to adjust to the already established patterns of behavior in this group. Though my data is scant, I do have evidence that she did this quite well. But I also have data that suggests that her gender as a woman influenced some of these patterns of behavior to change.

Throughout his book, McCarl argues that a solid knowledge of the "canon of work techniques" is the crucial factor in determining if a person is inside or outside the group. In fact, much of the expressive behavior in any occupational sub-culture is really a mechanism for recognizing and evaluating the performance of these work techniques (160). This expressive behavior often takes the form of oral narratives about specific incidents. Discussing past experiences is a way of learning about work techniques and also evaluating job performance. This latter function is especially important when the narrative centers around a rookie's actions.

> This is how reputations go. We had a crazy woman up here at college set her place on fire. For some reason we went to the wrong address or something, so we were the second truck in. Well, they were trying to get in the front and we pulled around the back and I jumped off the booster and went on in the back door and was knocking down the fire. I didn't either hear them or something, but they couldn't get in the front door. and they didn't know it and they were standing there [imitates a male's voice] 'Where the hell is 331?'--that's our truck, you know. And all of a sudden about that time they bust that door down and that door came down on top of me. Her I am and they say, [imitating male voice again] 'Well, there they are!' And I had the fire out, you know, and I was the only one in there. So you see, that story gets around a lot. You know, there she was in there all by herself and had that fire out. And hence, you're a good fire fighter and I will be forever more-- that's the only story [first on told about her] that will qualify me, I'm sure.

Although Alice told this story herself, she indicates that it is often told by others. This incident played an important role in changing her status from a rookie fire fighter to one that is considered equal. Just like any other rookie, Alice's first few job performances were very crucial in establishing her competence as a fire fighter. The fact that the rookie involved in this incident is female (automatically considered by many to be less capable of doing the job) is not even mentioned in the telling of this narrative. However, it would be interesting to hear a male fire fighter tell this same story. Would it be just another evaluation of a rookie's performance, or would it be an evaluation of a woman's job performance? Regardless, the fact that stories are told about Alice indicates that she is a part of the group. And the fact that she is aware of them and good naturedly allows them to be repeated indicates that she has adjusted to one of this group's cultural norms.

Another cultural norm that she has adjusted to is the abundance of joking behavior that goes on in the fire house. McCarl says that insults, putdowns and "verbal dueling" are ways in which the solidarity of the group is reinforced. "If the individual cannot exchange this kind of abuse with equanimity, then his opportunities for acceptance as an equal in the culture are severely limited" (177). Several things that I recorded indicate that Alice is teased a lot and is often the butt of practical jokes.

> I could leave $20 here [points to the window sill] and it would be here when I get back [three days later on her next shift], but they get the biggest kick out of breaking into your food locker and stealing your peanut butter. I mean, they're just as honest as the day is long, but that's just such a challenge to do something like that.

> [referring to the Firework newsletter] The [battalion] chief calls this my "monthly." I'll say, "Look at this!" and he'll say, "Oh, God--you got your monthly again!"

> [referring to the exercise bike she just finished using] I made them buy that one. They [male fire fighters] said, "You ask them [administration]. You get everything you want." Well, hell. I was the only one that came in here and showed any interest.

The brief narrative about stealing food is common of many practical jokes fire fighters play on each other. However, the last two references to teasing behavior seem to be tailored specifically because Alice is a woman. Obviously, the chief's calling Alice's newsletter her "monthly" is an allusion to her menstrual cycle. The tease "You get everything you want" is perhaps tinged with a little bit of jealousy because, being the first and only female fire fighter, Alice gets a lot of attention and is "taken care of" by the administration. But again, the fact that Alice herself told me these things shows that she is more than willing to take her turn at being the victim of jokes.

Although none of them gave specific examples, all of the men on her shift agreed that Alice is able to "dish it out" as well as take it. She has established herself in this group because of her equal participation in its joking relationships.

The examples I gave above illustrate that Alice has successfully patterned her behavior to fit the norms of this culture. Like an other rookie, she had to learn the rules of the group and then play by them or face exclusion. These rules of behavior that I have discussed are part of the group's folklore and always have been. This is how they communicated before Alice arrived, and they will continue to behave long after she leaves. It is simply a part of the fire fighting culture. Although a few examples of these folkloric expressions seem to center on the fact that Alice is a woman, gender per se is not really the issue. Based on my reading of McCarl's book, my contact with men on my brother's fire department, and my interview with the rest of Alice's shift, the examples I have cited appear to be like any other folklore of this type. It is tailored to fit individual characteristics rather than group stereotypes. For example, just as Alice is teased about her alleged special treatment by the administration, Dicky is teased about his habit of going to bed much earlier than everyone else, Chuck is hassled about the extraordinary amount of time and equipment he uses to groom himself, and my brother is called "Jewels" because of the fancy wedding ring and watch he wears.

However, I do have some evidence that Alice's specific qualities of being a woman have shaped and influenced the norms of behavior on this shift. Modifications of the bathroom and the lack of changes in the sleeping quarters are very interesting examples of how a woman's presence has (or has not) influenced the use of community space, but I will limit my discussion by considering only other examples of oral folklore. Primarily I am concerned with how the fact that Alice is a woman has influenced the language used in this group. My personal experience with fire fighters is that they are notoriously crude and vulgar. Alice said that she used to work for a utility company, so there is nothing that shocks her any more. But sometimes the language the others use does bother her. My interview tapes show that she uses mild expletives herself (hell, damn), so presumably it is some off the more foul language that really bothers her. when she first arrived on this shift, one of its members tried to use this to his advantage.

> We had one guy that was really pretty bad. When I first come on he would--I don't know if I told you this--he would use a lot of profanity which he didn't use before. Well, it was really obvious tot he guys what he was doin'. I've worked at utility departments so there ain't nothin' that phases me, you know--I've heard it all. And he just didn't know what to do then because I wasn't reacting to it, so he had to just keep up that act. He was just making a fool of himself. He was the one I had areal hard time with. He was just a little perverted for me.

This fire fighter was an exception. He reacted to a woman's presence by increasing the foulness of his language. Apparently he wanted to make her feel so uncomfortable and out of place that she would leave. However, his unusual behavior made <u>him</u> out of place. Many of the men had just the opposite reaction when Alice arrived. It amuses her that fire fighters from different shifts (who are not as comfortable in her presence) will often apologize if they swear in front of her. But it is not this conversational swearing that is offensive. Thought we did not get into details, I suspect that what she really objected to and caused a change in was the language that had sexual connotations. Not the following conversation that took place during my interview with the entire shift.

> F.F.1: That's the biggest change. Poor Alice--it was "girls, girls, girls" up here. Now there's none of that.
>
> Alice: Now it's just "girls"--and more "girls!"
>
> F.F.1: Naw, we've cleaned that up.
>
> Me: [to Alice] Did you ask them to change?
>
> Alice: They probably know I'm some sensitive.
>
> F.F.2: She got Chuck. She helped Chuck out quite a bit. [Group laughter]
>
> Me: [to Chuck] Did she put you in your place?
>
> Chuck: There you go.[smiles]
>
> Me: What did she do?
>
> Alice: [imitating what she said to him] DAMN, Chuck! <u>Enough</u> already!

A potential conflict in this group was prevented because each let the other know what his or her limits were. The above example is unusual in that a request for change in behavior was more or less directly made. Usually there is some sort of "silent negotiation" that goes on which causes people to unconsciously adapt their behavior.

> I don't think any of us changed. We didn't change our language, I know that. Some women might have pressed that issue. But probably [we didn't swear] any more than we do now. . . . Some of us are crude. We don't do it specifically to hurt her. Oh, no. We don't do it to upset her or shock her. It's just a way of life. But a bunch of women by theirselves would be just as bad.

This fire fighter claims that the language of the men did not change when Alice joined the department. However, his remarks clearly indicate that he is aware that foul language could upset women. Once aware of this issue, how could he possibly not change? It may not have been conscious on his part and Alice may not have demanded a change, but the rough fire house language appears to have mellowed somewhat. As one very wise fire fighter remarked, "It would be like throwing a guy in with a bunch of girls--they're bound to change." Although I do not have any examples of folkloric performances that directly indicate this change, I do believe that it has happened. The only way to know for sure would be to have collected data from this shift before Alice arrived and then compare it to data collected when she was part of the shift. Since this longitudinal study was not possible, I have had to speculate and draw inferences from what people told me about how their behavior did or did not change. One thing that Alice told me in our private interview sounded remarkably like a success story.

> There's constantly remarks about women. They sit and look out this window here . . . But they get another perspective, I think, when a woman is sitting up here with them, you know? Bill, the other night they had that Playboy swimsuit kind of thing on or somethin' and--now he had never heard of the word 'exploit' 'till I came up here, you know? And he got up there and said, 'I sure hate to see them women exploited like that,' he said. 'But seein' as they already are, I think I'll watch it.' I said, 'Okay. I can live with that.'

This seems to have been the key factor in the department's comfortable acceptance of Alice as a member of the group-- compromise. As an outsider, Alice had to learn the rules of this group and then play by them like any other rookie would have had to. At the same time, she being a woman caused certain changes in these norms of behavior. Alice says that the shift she got assigned to had a lot to do with her success.

> I think the underlying thing you find in terms of success is your captain, your supervisor. It makes all the difference in the world. . . . I think you lose friends as you go up the ladder, naturally, but it just happened that Bill and Dicky [higher ranking officers] they're not--they're not assholes at all. Their promotions didn't affect them.

At the same time, the shift she got assigned to says that Alice herself had a lot to do with her being accepted.

> F.F.1: She could make things really difficult around here, but she never. If she didn't like it, she didn't say anything. She didn't push or expect to be treated differently or somethin' like that exactly. That would have made it hard on all of us--her and us . . . She can do the job, but her personality--it made it work easier than what a lot of it could have been.

F.F.2: See, after a couple of years, she realizes this is the best place [shift] she could be.

Me: [to Alice] So you really lucked out, huh?

F.F.1: We all lucked out.

Alice: Yeah, it was a wise choice (putting me on the shift).

At this point the interview ended. Though I did not realize it then, I do now. This shift functions together so well, despite the "intrusion" of a woman into their previously all male world, because of the respect they have for each other and the rules of their culture group. Each fire fighter knows that he or she must operate within the boundaries of the group's social norms, yet be willing to adjust those norms, when change becomes necessary. The entry of women into this profession has been controversial ever since the idea was first suggested. Some departments have been very slow to change and not all attempts at integration have been successful, but the Fairfield Fire Department is proof that qualified men and women can work together. In a profession where cooperation often means the difference between life and death, respect for and compromise with others are essential traits to have. Although there are no guarantees in any relationship—personal or professional—this combination of mutual respect and compromise is the formula that yielded success in Fairfield.

DISCUSSING RURAL FOLKLORE IN CONTEXT AND CHARACTER

Gwendolyn M. Filosa
Indiana University

Introduction

This project contains a selection of folklore items from the repertoire of my informant, Mr. Ray E. Vaughn, who lives in North Vernon, Indiana and is a chemistry teacher at Jennings County High School.

My primary objective is to examine the inhabitants of small rural communities like North Vernon, where rich culture and much character lie deep in the town's roots--and like to keep to themselves. In his book, Amish Society, Mr. John A. Hostetler claims that "small communities, with their distinctive character--where life is stable and intensely human--are disappearing."[1] Mr. Hostetler is correct in his statement. Small towns like North Vernon, Indiana are growing, population-wise as well as industrial-wise, with new businesses moving in and real estate booming, thus creating a mini-city. But even as the small town continues to grow, the sense of stability among the residents still remains. These communities have always been the back-streets of the American dream and within their tiny frames, they hold and protect the promise of the future and at the same time, provide a glimpse of what can and will eventually become.

Through reviewing the life of Mr. Ray E. Vaughn, one can sense the essence of the small rural community. Mr. Vaughn is sharp, honest, wise, very proud of his family, and a refreshingly outspoken individual. But more important is the fact that Mr. Vaughn enjoys life. This may sound like a simple thing: however, it is sadly becoming a rare quality among Americans as we enter the twenty-first century.

I would like to extend many thanks to Mr. Vaughn, who so graciously offered his cooperation and time which was needed to complete this project. I hope I can give justice to this truly exceptional individual whom I have grown to admire and respect at first as one of his students and now as a friend.

PART I: THE INFORMANT

The bell to begin the seventh and the last period of the school day at Jennings County High School has just rung and Mr. Ray Vaughn's Chemistry I students are up and about, scattered around the room chatting about the five fights that broke out during the long school day.

Mr. Vaughn appears from out of his prep room. he is clad in blue work pants, a faded blue and red striped short sleeved dress shirt with a paisley necktie streaming down his front. In his left breast pocket rests a nerdy pocket protector with about two hundred pens sticking out. His light reddish brown hair is cropped closely to his skull and with a slight adjustment of his gold colored wire rim glasses he prepares to bring the class to order.

"Jus LOOK at this outfit!" a blond teenybopper boldly smarts off to him.

Vaughn's lips purse slowly. The student continues, "I can't believe you're wearing that tie with that shirt!"

The reply comes back slowly but surely.

"You think I care?" Vaughn bellows, laughing loudly in her face. His stocky pint-sized frame rocks back and forth.

What this forty-nine year old teacher lacks in height, he makes up for in smarts and voice. Firmly believing that the teacher is the boss in the classroom, Ray Everett Vaughn never lets a "lowly scrud" (Vaughnese for a smartass student) get away with a cheap shot at his expense.

"Your seat's calling you, Miss Julie," he informs the student, and she, knowing fully that she has been put in her proper place, disappears into the back of the room.

He starts to address the class but can't be heard fully over the din of young voices.

"People, I'm gonna say this in the nicest way possible. Shut up. Thank you."

Silence. Class has now begun and the boss starts in on today's agenda. First order of business: checking the homework, and cheaters had better beware.

This is how Mr. Vaughn gets through to his students: crudely, simply and effectively. And in a school system where violence, intolerance, racism and disrespect are an everyday occurrence, he reigns over his colleagues.

Vaughn is stalking down the aisles, checking and recording homework credit in his grade book, most widely known as "The Book of Life."

"What's this? Looks like a drunk chicken walked across this paper," he jokes with a student. "How about a 96 percent. No, I don't give 100s. Everyone knows 100s are scarcer than hens' teeth."

Talk turns back to the fighting that occurred today. His students want to know what he thinks.

"I will make one statement. We don't need those kind of people in school. You people are here to get an education and an education is so important. You don't realize how important it is. So these people that insist on fighting--get rid of them. Now I said this but I never said this. If I could have my way if you get caught fighting, you're done for the semester."

A student pipes up, "But what if you didn't start the fight? That's not fair."

Vaughn explains, "Well, if someone comes up and whacks you on the head then no, it's not your fault and you shouldn't be punished. But that person ought to be out for the rest of the semester. You see what I'm saying? Now. Homework, homework, homework. Burgmeier, let me see your homework, Burgmeier."

"Lit me seee yer homewerk, Burrgmiier . . ."

His southeastern Indiana dialect soars at full capacity in a squeaky roar that commands respect in this classroom.

His students either love him to death or they can't stand
him. There is no middle ground when you talk about Ray Vaughn in
this high school. But whatever they think of their teacher is no
matter to Vaughn himself. He doesn't want to be liked, he wants
to be respected and obeyed.

* * * * * * * * * *

The firstborn of Edna Taylor Vaughn and Harold Henry Vaughn,
delivered on the fifth day of August, 1940 in Seymour Community
Hospital, Ray Everett Vaughn spent his boyhood days fishing,
camping and chumming around with grade school friends on a
stretch of land in the Muscatatuk Refuge area. Jennings County
is located in the southeastern corner of Indiana, about sixty
miles southeast of Bloomington. The county seat is historic
Vernon, where Morgan's Raid took place during the Civil War.
    The Vaughn's were a closely knit family, influenced greatly
by father Harold's German and Lutheran background. Harold
operated heavy equipment for a living and farmed on the side.
Edna was a standard housewife, taking care of the children: Ray
and his two younger brothers, Stevan and Logan, and little sister
Christina Jean, as well as taking care of the cooking, putting up
canned goods, gardening, and cleaning, among other various
household chores.
    The most important folk group in Ray's background is
probably the German ethnic group. For his father instilled a
deep rooted sense of the importance of hard honest work as well
as the importance of strong family ties. Believing in oneself is
another prominent trait passed down from generation to generation
in the history of the Vaughn family. Mr. Ray Vaughn firmly
believes in standing up for yourself and for what you believe in,
even if some perceive it as just being stubborn.
    Ray attended Hayden School, grades one through twelve and
was disillusioned by school until he reached high school. Then,
his interest in veterinary science grew with a passion and he
went from a self-described "poor student" to valedictorian of his
senior class. As well as excelling in academics, Ray ran track
and was a 4-H member for several years. But Ray changed his mind
about careers when he entered Franklin College in the fall of
1958, choosing a double major in math and chemistry.
    "I've been kicking myself about that ever since," Vaughn
confided about his change of heart about becoming a vet.
    Graduating with a bachelor of arts degree in math and
chemistry in 1962, Vaughn did his student teaching at Columbus
North High School. This turned out to be quite a disaster for
young Vaughn. His students were from the upper crust of the
small city, and "spoiled and snotty" did not set well with this
student teacher. He ended up failing the whole apathetic class.
School administrators and parents were in an uproar over the
incident and Vaughn was told by his adviser that he would
"definitely not be recommended for a teaching license."
    Vaughn would not buckle under to his adviser's, the school's
or the parents' pressure. Brushing off the experience as a
career choice mistake, he chose to be a semi-truck driver for a

contractor in Seymour, Indiana. At this time, life was simple, good and carefree. Marriage was not even thought of until he met Karen Ruth Stout. Ray, 22, and Karen, 21, were married in the summer of 1962, and have been for the past 27 years.

This new commitment left Vaughn no choice but to change jobs. With the help of a Freetown High School principal, Ray was able to get his teaching permit, and later on his license and for "pure economic reasons," he gave teaching a second change. He taught mat at Freetown for two years and then transferred to the newly consolidated Jennings County High School in North Vernon, Indiana. Mr. Vaughn taught some math as well as Chemistry I and II. Presently he is only teaching the chemistry program.

Ray and Karen Vaughn have two sons, Brian Keith, age 26, and Jonathan Lemarr, 19.

* * * * * * * * * *

I first met Mr. Vaughn as junior at Jennings County High School in the fall of 1986. I only knew him as a teacher that school year and I was surprised to find chemistry as being my favorite class. Mr. Vaughn's unorthodox teaching techniques were refreshingly honest compared to my other classes, which were nothing but exercises in memorizing rhetoric. In chemistry class, we learned more than just equations and math. Mr. Vaughn would often allow us some time during each period to discuss important issues whether they were school-related or national events. Jennings County High School is full of problems: disrespect, students fighting almost every day, racism, theft, drug abuse, etc. Mr. Vaughn allowed us to open up a forum to talk about these things and to figure out solutions. He would usually give us his opinion. "I will make one statement on this..." he would start, and then he would allow us students to make comments and bring up ideas.

Yes, sometimes this would conflict with the day's schedule of standard academic study; however, sometimes getting the problem out in the open, discussing alternatives and finding solutions takes precedence over following a curriculum guidebook. Mr. Vaughn was never afraid to speak his mind and let others do the same in the classroom. He felt it was important to talk about things instead of wringing one's hands about it, like many other teacher at Jennings County did and still do.

During my senior year, I was in Mr. Vaughn's Chemistry II class and helped out during fourth period as a teacher's assistant. This was the year I really got to know him. I could always count on him for an honest opinion or a piece of advice. He was the teacher you could always depend upon to stick up for you if you were in a bind. Through working with him on this project, I have found a new respect for him. Perhaps it is because I see him in a different perspective, now that I have graduated from Jennings County High School, that I can greater understand the valuable source of knowledge he possesses.

PART II: ANALYTICAL ESSAY

The items of folklore selected from the repertoire of the informant, Mr. Ray E. Vaughn, for use in this project were all "verbal" genres, by choice of the collector as a means to probe deeper into the personality of Mr. Vaughn. The language that Mr. Vaughn uses to express himself is as important as the ideas he holds, and his self-designed proverbs, personal experience narratives and memorates illuminate this one individual, who was brought into this world and raised by customs and beliefs that can be classified under "Rural Folklore."[2]

Rural Folklore, used in this context, will refer to the Midwest, especially southern Indiana. The term can be used to label a people, a people bound together by more than just physical means like endless fields of corn, brick streets, gravel roads or barns painted with the Mail Pouch chewing tobacco logo, but a people sharing a "human" environment, where you support the Union, get married young, and learn to earn your living by the sweat of your brow.

The residents of North Vernon, Indiana, however, are now seeing changes in this philosophy, save for the huge amount of teenage pregnancies and young marriages. Today the Union's on strike, jobs are hard to come by, and the cost of living seems to be getting harder and harder to afford.

There are thirty-two years between Mr. Vaughn and myself, but I lived in North Vernon for thirteen years. And there was where I was educated, had my First Communion, was confirmed, got my driver's license, and my first job. I, along with Mr. Vaughn, have been a witness to the great changes that North Vernon has gone through. We both can remember when there was no department store or even a McDonald's, when they leveled grassy fields to build grocery stores, when a small forest of trees was destroyed to put up a Wal-Mart. We both can remember the Danner's 5 and 10 store, the old junior high school (est. 1925) which was closed down last may, the King Restaurant (now a Dairy queen), the Burger Chef, the pool hall, and the train depot.

But the thirty-two years do make a difference in accepting these changes. I saw them only as fantastic improvements, economic growth, and industrialization. Mr. Vaughn saw the changes as a seal on the past and as an end of his youth, and it was all a little hard to deal with.

Ray Vaughn's youth took place in possible the most turbulent time America has ever seen: the late 1950s and the widely publicized 1960s, when people chose sides between white and black, between rich and poor, and between Vietnam and the United States of America. Perhaps in San Francisco or Alabama, these events reshaped lives, but in places like North Vernon, Indiana it all seemed distant and separate. There were hardly any blacks in North Vernon or in Franklin College, where Mr. Vaughn graduated from in 1962, middle class was the norm and war was something your father and his father went through and if you don't love your country, you can just leave.

Beliefs in this low-context group were givens: attitudes your parents instilled in you practically at birth, and which you

210   *The Emergence of Folklore in Everyday Life*

taught your own children, and so on and so on. these attitudes were made up of a set of values, like hard work, earning your own way and being proud of it all. As for religion, church was, and still is, an important social gathering consisting of pitch-in dinners, holiday parties, baptisms, weddings and funerals. Mr. Vaughn grew up in the age where "everybody knew everybody," you didn't even think of locking your doors, and you could trust your neighbors.

Through the study of folklore, we can connect all of the aforementioned observations, the context of customs and beliefs, with the functions of the rural folk group. "A group's image of itself and its images of other groups are reflected in its folklore repertoire," writes William Hugh Jansen in his article "The Esoteric-Exoteric Factor in Folklore,"[3] knowing that the esoteric factor is what the group thinks of itself and that the exoteric factor is what outsiders think of the particular group, we can begin to discuss further Rural Folklore.

As the wheel chart on page 9b of this project shows, the informant is a 49-year-old white male middle-class resident of North Vernon, Indiana (population averaging around 5500). His occupation is of a teacher, his immediate family is rather closely knit and he chooses the Lutheran religion. These are all esoteric factors and determine what Mr. Vaughn, as well as his family and friends, thinks of Mr. Vaughn. For example, Mr. Vaughn is a member of the white race, and it is the closest ethnic label that can be put on him. An exoteric view would be that being white, coupled with being a male, makes him superior over blacks and other minorities. And even though, Mr. Vaughn has repeatedly claimed not to be a racist, he often uses phrases such as "that's mighty white of you" or call a foreign-made sander as a "squint-eyed" sander. In Mr. Vaughn's worldview on racism, saying these phrases does not make him a racist; however, an exoteric view would automatically stamp the racist label on him and his folk group. When approached on the "squint-eyed" remark, Mr. Vaughn refers to his father, who "spent the best two years of his life 'over there' fighting 'those people.'" In his eyes, as well as in the eyes of the majority of his folk group, this justifies the remark. And when Mr. Vaughn says "you gotta be careful" when saying the "mighty white of you " statement, he is confirming the attitude that it is okay to say it as long as there are no black people present. This collector assumes that the function of this attitude stems from a subconscious fear of black people, which then stems from an ignorance of not ever being closely related or involved with blacks.

In the social network category, Mr. Vaughn would be considered absolutely middle class by the standards of the rural folk group, by having a steady, respectable job and able to support his family. An exoteric view, let's say someone living in an urban environment, like Chicago or New York, would assume that he is of a lower class of the social network by comparing his lifestyle to that of an urban resident. The function of this unfair assumption on the exoteric's part is the way people from small towns, or "the country" are portrayed in motion pictures or books. Just compare the reaction of an urban professional tot he book or film "Deliverance" with that of a farmer or a factory worker living in a small town. The reactions would be totally different and possible extreme. The same observation could be made with the two parties viewing "Wall Street."

Thus, the functions being established for the context and the character of this member of the rural folk group all depends on verbal exchange. What is said is linked to what is believed and the language with which the informant chooses to express himself tells all. The informant is a high school teacher and this would lead to an assumption that he is a highly educated individual. This is true. Mr. Vaughn shows brilliance with his knowledge of chemistry and math. He seems to have not lost, but rather increased his retainment of this type of information throughout his many, many years of teaching. But one would never know this if one was to have just a simple conversation with the informant, excluding science. Mr. Vaughn's language is relatively simple and coupled with mismatched and poor grammar, an exoteric view would classify the informant as uneducated, lower-class, or a "country bumpkin." Yes, this is an unfair assumption, but it is made every day. The words we choose to use for expression of an idea tend to become more important than the idea itself.[4] This superficial function is the heart of the exoteric world view.

The continuities of the items of folklore collected for this field project exemplify the above function. On paper, the personal experience narratives "That's Mighty White of You" and "A Summer Place" are more difficult to follow and appreciate than if hear aloud firsthand from the informant. This informant's word choice and language pattern remaining intact. The only exception is item number seven, Personal Experience Narrative: "Work for Your Own Dime," which was presented in a paraphrased form, to allow the reader to make the distinction between a verbatim account and an edited version of the personal narrative.

On the other side of the perspective, the discontinuities are more difficult to pinpoint; however, there is a shift from a sort of "standard" folklore, ie. the folk remedies, to more "modern" types of folklore, such as the personal narratives and the memorate "Well-Witchers." This is referring to misconceptions of what is and is not considered "folklore." For example, one who has never studies folklore would not consider a story like "Well-Witchers" to be a piece of folklore, but they would readily accept a folk remedy like "The Peroxide Method" as "true folklore."

Again, all of the items in this collection are mainly "verbal" as opposed to photographs of crafts or personal articles. This project exemplifies how important the verbal skills of an informant are when studying a folk group. The rural folk has its own personalized jargon, and while it unites the members as a singular group, it can lead to a feeling of being ostracized from "outsiders," especially in a society that generally associates content with appearances. It might appear that these rural folk are stupid, ignorant, uninformed, apathetic, etc., by their style of dress, or accent or word choice, but it is simply not the case. Eloquence may be lacking

The Emergence of Folklore in Everyday Life

in certain members of the group, but that does, in no way, alienate the whole group as inferior to society.

Mr. Ray Vaughn is an honest, hardworking man, a passionate patriot, and a brilliant scholar of physical science. Mr. Ray Vaughn is a singular personality, although he identifies and relates to the rural folk group, of which he is a truly qualified representative.

1.   Folk medicine: "A Cure for Rheumatism"

Folk group: American Rural; Ethnic: White

This remedy was collected by Gwendolyn M. Filosa from Ray E. Vaughn, age 49, on September 29, 1989 at the informant's high school classroom in North Vernon, Indiana. The remedy was used by the informant's grandfather, who was convinced of it power.[5]

*****

Mr. Vaughn's grandfather would gather a couple of ounces of pokeberries, squeeze out the purple juice and mix a concoction of one part pokeberry juice and one part whisky. The grandfather would commonly refer to this as his "rheumatism medicine."

Mr. Vaughn offered this item of folklore with much laughter; however, he later emphasized how seriously his grandfather was in his method of "curing" the rheumatism.

2.   Folk Medicine: "The Peroxide Method"

   Folk group: American Rural; Ethnic: White

   This remedy was collected by Gwendolyn Filosa from Ray
Vaughn, age 49, on September 29, 1989 at the informant's high
school classroom in North Vernon, Indiana.   The remedy was used
by the informant's parents and by his brothers and sisters as
well as himself when one of them had a sore throat.

*****

   The remedy for a sore throat is to simply gargle with
peroxide for one or two minutes while being very careful not to
swallow too much of it.

   The above item is the way Mr. Vaughn himself treats a sore
throat and he often recommends the method to his students.   He
considers it the best remedy.

3.   Folk Medicine: "A Remedy for Cuts and Scrapes"

Folk group: American Rural; Ethnic: White

This remedy was collected by Gwendolyn Filosa from Ray Vaughn, age 49, on September 29, 1989 at the informant's high school classroom in North Vernon, Indiana. The remedy was used mostly by the informant's mother for use on cuts and scrapes.

*****

Mr. Vaughn's mother would put a handful or so of fat raw meat on cuts or scrapes to draw out the infection. "It always worked," Mr. Vaughn said.

While Mr. Vaughn reported his family had other remedies to alleviate the pain of a cut or scrape, this was the first one he recalled.

4.   Proverb: "Reprimand for Discipline Problems"

Folk group: American Rural; Occupation: Teacher

This proverb was collected by Gwendolyn Filosa from Ray Vaughn, age 49, on October 10, 1989 through the mail. Mr. Vaughn, as a high school teacher, has his own jargon and his own classroom rules.[6] The following two related "proverbs" are commonly snarled (usually in general humor) to misbehaving students and underachievers in and out of the classroom.

*****

"if you were any lower, you'd be out there scratching for worms with the chickens."

And:

"THINK! It might be a new experience."

Both of these proverbial sayings are used by Mr. Vaughn to get a point across in a quick and clear manner. He does not feel that either will greatly offend anyone. The sayings are used to get attention and are said often. The repetition delights his students and provide an air of familiarity inside Mr. Vaughn's classroom.

5.   Proverb: "Classroom Talk"

    Folk group: American Rural; Occupation: Teacher

    This collection of related proverbs were collected by Gwendolyn Filosa from Ray Vaughn, age 49, on October 6, 1989 in the teachers' lounge at Jennings County High School in North Vernon, Indiana. These are just a sample of the informant's countless "sayings" which are said with good humor to the delight of students.

*****

"Is this spoon feeding time?!?"
(This is said when students ask for help on a test.)

"Use your teeth and restaple it!"
(When students ask repeatedly for use of the stapler.)

"ROT in study hall!!"
(This is said to an undeserving student who asks for a library pass.)

"Take it on the chin!!"
(This is said to whining students.)

"Passes are scarcer than hens' teeth!"
(Another response to library pass seekers.)

"If all else fails, READ THE BOOK!"
(This is advice for all students.)

"My heart bleeds for you..."
(A sardonically unsympathetic response to whining students.)

"Enroll in the Theory of Study Hall."
(A response to a student who threatens to drop chemistry.)

"If 'Hillstreet Blues' is a rerun, we'll have a written test."
(A saying used during the heyday of the series which was Mr. Vaughn's favorite show of the time period.)

The above proverbial sayings have become a mainstay in Mr. Vaughn's classroom for as long as he had been a teacher at Jennings County High School (almost 25 years). They are usually said in jest and have made Mr. Vaughn a very popular teacher and even his students have been known to say them to each other.

6.   Proverb: "A Teaching Tool"

Folk group: American Rural; Occupation: Teacher

This proverb was collected by Gwendolyn Filosa from Ray Vaughn, age 49, on October 6, 1989 at the informant's high school classroom in North Vernon, Indiana. This proverbial saying is said not only for amusement purposes, but to also remind students what sulfuric acid is and how dangerous it can be when not handled properly.[7]

*****

"Here's to little Willy, for Willy is no more. For what he thought was H 2 O was really H 2 SO 4!"

Mr. Vaughn considers the above saying as a teaching tool in which students can easily remember what H 2 SO 4 is. Also, sayings like this make a class period easier and more enjoyable.

7.   Personal Experience Narrative: "Work for Your Own Dime"

Folk group: American Rural; Ethnic: White

This personal experience narrative was collected by Gwendolyn M. Filosa from Ray E. Vaughn, age 49, on Friday, November 3, 1989 in the teachers' lounge at Jennings County High School in North Vernon, Indiana. The factual story took place in the early 1970s on the campus of Indiana University at Bloomington, Indiana. Mr. Vaughn has told this to several of his classes for years. His point being that there is not substitute for hard work and that everyone who is able to work should do so.[8]

*****

Mr. Ray E. Vaughn was registering for a couple of chemistry classes at Indiana University's Bloomington campus one day in circa 1971. As he was leaving the building he was approached on the sidewalk by a young fellow who looked like "a hippie," in Mr. Vaughn's words.
Now, Mr. Vaughn has never believed in asking for, receiving or giving handouts. Especially to someone who looked physically able to work and earn a living on his own.
The young man asked, "Can I have a dime to get a cup of coffee?"
Mr. Vaughn turned to the man and said calmly but firmly: "Why don't you go work for your dime just like I do."

Mr. Vaughn cites this story as an example of how important the value of hard work is.
"I was always taught that you worked hard and not to go looking for handout," Mr. Vaughn explained.

8.   Personal Experience Narrative: "That's Mighty White of You"

   Folk group: American Rural; Ethnic: White

   This personal experience narrative was collected by
Gwendolyn M. Filosa from Mr. Ray E. Vaughn on Friday, November 3,
1989 at around 1:30 pm in the teachers' lounge at Jennings County
High School. Also present was Mr. David Cheatham, a government
teacher at JCHS and a state representative.
   This story emerged as the informant and the collector were
discussing racism. Mr. Vaughn often will use the expression,
"That's mighty white of you" but in a light, jokingly manner and
he does not believe that by use of the saying he is racist.[9]

                              *****

   "Well, I don't get uptight about racist remarks because I'm
not really a prejudice person but yeah you gotta be careful
because one time down in the Ashland terminal down in Louisville
about three years ago they had this colored lady working in the
terminal, you know, and we're in there every night carrying on in
this pretty loose, you know, and and I know everybody, and so I
didn't know she was still working. This guy did something, I
said, 'Oh, that's mighty white of you' and she stuck her head
around the corner. [Laughs, remembering.] got mad, you know,
started chewin' on me for racial remarks and I said, now look I'm
not a prejudice person, and if you can't take that that's just
tough. And I just got in my truck and left.
   "I've heard it a long time, you know. I suppose it's
racially oriented. 'Mighty white of you', inferring that white
would be better than black whatever. But some people really et
uptight about it being a racial remark."

9.   Memorate: "Well-witchers"

Folk group: American Rural; Ethnic: White

This memorate was collected by Gwendolyn M. Filosa from Mr. Ray E. Vaughn on Friday, November 3, 1989 at around 1:45 pm in the teachers' lounge at Jennings County High School. This memorate describes certain people who can predict where water is inside the ground by running a forked stick over the ground.

*****

"Growing up in the wildlife area we had this old guy, he wasn't old at the time but he grew old and passed away, but there wasn't anything that he wasn't an authority on. I mean just one of these kinds of guys, and I heard this story for years and years and did you ever hear about the old time 'well-witchers'? You know, they would take a peach limb, a forked stick and they...there's a term used for these people who can predict where water's at. So this guy claimed he was a well-witcher, well, so some people were somewhat skeptical but there wasn't nothin' he wasn't an authority on. So they got this other fella, whose name that I can remember when he was still living, this guy's name was Leo Maschino, of course this was years and years ago. So they got him to witch this well. So he gets out there and he walks around and he walks around and he says, 'All right, right here there's two water veins that cross. So they said, fine, so this guy that owned the property, name was Jim Howard, put a little stick in the ground, covered it and just put some grass on it. So this other fella's name was Carl Mras, happened to drive a school bus, so he's coming up the road one morning, he's been going his route. So he flags him down and says, 'Come over here and witch this well. We're gonna dig a well here, I want you to witch it.' So he cuts him a limb off an old wild cherry tree, and gets out there walking around, walking around and so on and so on. He says, 'Right here, there's two veins that cross.' He was within six inches of this other guy. So they dug the well and I'll take you and show you where the well was at it's now been covered up it's down in the refuge area. But they dug down twenty some feet and hit two veins that crossed, laid the well up and so on and you couldn't pump it dry, no you just could not pump the well dry. And this is a story that was told and retold and told again. This time period, it happened probably in the early 1940s when the well was dug in that area but so from then on if you wanted a well witched and you couldn't get this Leo Maschino you got the Carl Mars guy so, you know, it was quite a phenomenon."

When asked if he knew any ghost stories, Mr. Vaughn laughed and replied, "No, I don't believe in that ghost story stuff." But he did recall the above story that he first heard as a young boy and continued to hear again and again throughout his formative and young adult years. It was quite apparent that Mr. Vaughn believed this story and believed in the "Well-Witchers."

10. Personal Experience Narrative: "A Summer Place"

Folk Group: American Rural; Ethnic: White

    This personal experience narrative was collected by
Gwendolyn M. Filosa from Ray E. Vaughn on Friday, November 3,
1989 in the teachers' lounge at Jennings County High School.
This narrative emerged as the informant and the collector were
discussing the many changes that North Vernon has gone through
since the informant's youth to the present. The talk led to the
old Parke Theatre, which was located in downtown North Vernon in
the mid-1950s.

                            *****

    "It (North Vernon) was probably a lot better back then
because you had a theatre and stuff to go to. You know what I'm
saying? We got no theatre, even though the last time I went to
the Park Theater I got hit in the back of the head with a pop
can. [Laughs.] You can't remember this, but right where the
First National Bank is right along there, there was a theater
there. Do you remember that? Yeah. Parke Theater. Yeah, I
used to go there all the time when I was in highs school and so
on. Last movie I went to see there was "Summer Place." You ever
seen that movie? It was the beginnings of all this stuff. The
jist of the story was they had this rich family and another rich
family and the two, the boy and girl got together on the beach
one night and, of course, got the host for one another and it was
little bambino time. [Laughs.] But, you know, the movies of
course, just like changing in our American society. When I was
growing up the drive-in theater was big. But nowadays with the
advent of the VCR and all that kind of stuff, drive-in movies are
out of it and I really feel like that movie theaters are about
out of it because of the home video stuff. It's all changing."

    This narrative was one example Mr. Vaughn used when talking
about all the many changes he has lived to see happen. He spoke
of how things "were better back then" in Jennings County, rather
wistfully, as the collector observed. Mr. Vaughn predicted that
"your people" (referring tot he present youth, myself included)
would have hard times to face but at the same time managed to
convey some hope for today's generation.

Endnotes

[1] John A. Hostetler, <u>Amish Society</u>. 3d. ed. (Baltimore: Johns Hopkins University Press, 1980), p. 3.

[2] Alan Dundes, <u>Interpreting Folklore</u>. (Bloomington: Indiana University Press, 1980), pp. 4-5.

[3] William Hughes Jansen, "The Esoteric-Exoteric Factor in Folklore," in <u>The Study of Folklore</u>, ed. Alan Dundes, pp. 43-51. (Englewood Cliffs, NJ: Prentice-Hall, Inc., 1965)

[4] William R. Bascom, "Four Funtions of Folklore," in <u>The Study of Folklore</u>, ed. Alan Dundes, pp. 279-298. (Englewood Cliffs, NJ: Prentice-Hall, Inc., 1965)

[5] Jan Harold Brunvand, <u>Folklore: A Study and Research Guide</u>. (New York: St. Martin's Press, 1976), p. 108.

[6] Dundes, pp. 23-25.

[7] Ibid.

[8] Ibid.

[9] Brunvand, p. 110.

References Cited

Bascom, William R. 1965. "Four Funtions of Folklore." In <u>The Study of Folklore</u>, ed. Alan Dundes, pp. 279-298. Englewood Cliffs, NJ: Prentice-Hall, Inc.

Brunvand, Jan Harold. 1976. <u>Folklore: A Study and Research Guide</u>. New York: St. Martin's Press.

Dundes, Alan. 1980. <u>Interpreting Folklore</u>. Bloomington, IN: Indiana University Press.

Hostetler, John A. 1980. <u>Amish Society</u>. 3d. ed. Baltimore: Johns Hopkins University Press.

Jansen, William Hughes. 1965[1959]. "The Esoteric-Exoteric Factor in Folklore." In <u>The Study of Folklore</u>, ed. Alan Dundes, pp. 43-51. Englewood Cliffs, NJ: Prentice-Hall, Inc.

Stahl, Sandra Dolby. 1989. "Interpreting Personal Narrative Texts." In <u>Literary Folkloristics and the Personal Narrative</u>, pp. 27-49. Bloomington, IN: Indiana University Press.

THE COMPLEX SURROUNDINGS OF A MUSICAL EVENT

Ericka J. Schumacker
Indiana University

The Blue Mountain Coffee Company, in Fort Wayne, Indiana, is a restaurant known for its gourmet coffee, its large selection of imported beers, and its homemade cheesecake. But the culinary delights are not what sets this restaurant apart from others. Rather, it's the musical performances that draw the crowds. The Blue Mountain is a place of cultural rebellion for many Fort Wayne youth. The music played is rarely Top 40 or heavy metal, and the art work is changed monthly to promote local, abstract artists. Though the music is a main part of the atmosphere at the Blue Mountain, the audience, the fixtures, and the proxemics distract from the performance to give a feeling of contained disorganization.

An example of contained disorganization is that of a musical performance on a street corner. An integral part of the experience is the hustle and bustle going on despite the performance, the background noises, and the attitudes and reactions of the "audience." Though the music is simple, the atmosphere is complex.

The Blue Mountain is located on "The Landing," a historic Fort Wayne street, and it occupies the bottom floor of an old limestone building which stood at the time when Fort Wayne was composed of many waterways. The front of the Blue Mountain is glass allowing the patrons to view the pedestrians, and vice versa. Upon entering the restaurant, the performers are immediately visible, behind a 3-foot high glass showcase. The counter where the hostess stands is piled high with coffee jars, tea, and coffee paraphernalia available for purchase, as well as a basket for donations to the band and a cash register.

The restaurant is divided into two sections, each side identical to the other. The decorations consist of burlap coffee bags hung over pipes hanging down from the ceiling, ceiling fans, hanging lights, and whitewashed cinder block walls. The first impression is that of a warehouse, very mechanical looking and barren. The tables and chairs are nondescript wood and are not fixed, this includes the tables in the booths, which are simply tables placed between two partitions. The thing that sets the booths apart from the tables in the open area, besides the partitions, is that the booths are built on a one-foot high platform. On the wall in each booth and around the restaurant, art work done by local artists are hung, and changed monthly. On each table is a Perrier bottle with a daisy in it.

Other prominent features are the partitions in the middle of each section, which further separates the audience from the performers. In the center of each partition is a hollowed out area in which thrives a Boston fern. The glass showcase in front of the performers houses an empty bottle of each type of beer

227

served in the Blue Mountain. And, the tables nearest to the front windows have "Cinzano" patio umbrellas on them, giving a sidewalk cafe effect.

The "stage" is nothing more than a space without tables. There is no platform or permanent fixture to signify the stage, rather the performers transform the space into a stage. On September 30, the performers were "Bob and Zena," a couple from Auburn, Indiana. The instruments used in the performance were a tambourine, a harmonica, a wood block, and a guitar. Bob played the guitar, and Zena played all the other instruments. They lead off with "Lemon Tree," made popular by Peter, Paul, and Mary. The following songs included: "Homeward Bound," "Proud Mary," "Tracks of My Tears," "Blowin' in the Wind," and "The 59th Street Bridge Song." Zena had a fairly low alto voice, but could reach into a second soprano range. bob had a tenor voice. They sang mostly together, harmonizing, and Zena sang the solos, when there were any. The musical structure was predominantly homophonic. When ending a song, Zena would nod her head at Bob to cue him to play one more refrain. In between songs, they would talk amongst themselves to decide what song to play next. The only equipment, other than the instruments, on stage were two bar stools, two microphones, and an open guitar case for donations.

Because the Blue Mountain is separated into two parts by the walls in the middle, and then further separated by the partitions on each side, it is difficult to see the performers from most tables. During this performance, I was seated behind the partition on the right side, making it impossible to see Bob and Zena without a great effort. Since the proxemics are such that the performers are singing to the glass showcase, the audience tends to continue talking, and even raise their voice levels during the performance. The performers, in turn, directed their performance towards a group of their friends or loyal fans who were seated to the right of the stage. This group applauded loudly after each song, whereas the rest of the patrons rarely contributed more than a smattering of applause. The performers did not react to any other applause except that of their friends, nor did they seem to expect applause from the audience, or become annoyed by the lack of it. The lack of applause was not because the performers were not liked, but because in the Blue Mountain, the music blends into the background, and the show becomes the people in the audience. The waiters and waitresses walk across the "stage" instead of around it, detracting from any formality involved with the performance.

The patrons of the Blue Mountain become the show because they are such an odd mixture of Fort Wayne's youth. They include the few punk rockers in Fort Wayne, the preppy high school crowd, and a few die-hard fans in their twenties. Surprisingly, there is little open conflict between the groups. Each group observes the other in a mocking, curious sense, but they will never combine into one group.

When I was there, the art work was tie-dyed material stretched into frames, and abstract scenes of Fort Wayne. Nothing in the Blue Mountain is easily classified.

The reason the Blue Mountain's performances are not much more formal is most likely because of the proxemics and the attitudes of the people. The proxemics make it impossible for the performers to dominate the patrons' attentions. The walls and partitions seem to separate the participants, and give the performers a second priority. Also, when you first enter the Blue Mountain, loud talking is heard first, and then the performers. Another detraction from the performance is the casual attitude of the employees and the audience. When being seated, it is often necessary to walk across the stage to get to the table. And, as previously mentioned, the employees always walk across the stage when serving. The customers are usually there to see their friends and talk, but they like the idea of live performers, which is why the Blue Mountain is so popular. Also, the diverse crowd tends to distract attention from the performers.

The idea of contained disorganization comes from the fact that there are many different unrelated acts going on in one setting, and this is emphasized by the contrasting decorations. There are people deep in conversation, there are employees intent on doing their jobs, and there are people observing other people in the restaurant. The musical event is also separated from everything else, not only by the proxemics, but because the performers seem to be performing and reacting only to their friends. These concurrent events are emphasized by the attempt to make the front of the restaurant appear as a sidewalk cafe with the patio umbrellas, the continuously changing art work, and the Perrier bottles on the tables. All seem unrelated, but yet all are combined in one place. All this is revolving around the musical event, with an underlying complexity.

GLOSSARY

Acculturation: The process a person goes through in adapting herself to a culture other than the one she was raised in; distinguishable from *enculturation*, the process a child goes through in absorbing the culture into which she was born. The term many also be applied to entire cultures or social groups. In this sense, *acculturation* refers to the massive borrowing of cultural components by one group from another group with which it has had prolonged contact. In effect, the smaller or less powerful group adapts to the ways of the dominant society.

Aetiological Legend: A narrative that explains the origin of things in the world. An aetiological legend is more properly classified as myth, but scholars long ago fell into the habit of calling origin stories aetiological legends, and the name has stuck. Examples include the story of how the rattlesnake got his fangs, why the thumb is separate from the rest of the hand, why the sun goes down in the east, why the cat looks like the lion, or why the sky is separated from the earth. In one Turkish version of the last example, the sky was separated from the earth after a leper wiped his hand on the sky. The deity was so offended that he raised the sky up.

Alliteration: Poetic language involving the repetition of sentence-initial consonant sounds. Example: *b*usy *b*ee, *b*usy *b*ody.

Anglo: A term used by Latinos especially in the Southwestern U.S. to refer to the non-Latino, non-Native American population. It is a shortened form of Anglo-American, but in practice it is not restricted to those of English descent. *Anglo* is regularly used to describe all whites regardless of their actual ethnic background and is sometimes applied to Blacks as well.

Animal Tale: A simple folktale in which animals play major roles, such as The Three Little Pigs. These often involve tales of cleverness in which the under-dog wins. *Trickster Tales* feature animals that play tricks or behave mischievously.

Artistic Communication: A mode of communication which is specially marked and calls attention to itself. *Artistic communication* is specially marked because it informs the person(s) or recipients of the fact that there is something out of the ordinary which is transpiring and that one should take notice.

Assonance: Poetic language involving the repetition of vowel sounds within words. Example: long gone.

Belief: A conviction or acceptance that something is true. See also *folk beliefs, superstition, world view*.

Belief legends, belief tales: See *Supernatural legend*.

Blues: A form of song which began in rural south, noted for sharp social commentary.

Body attitude: The way the body is held and can be erect or slouched, rigid or loose. *Articulation* refers to where the body is bent.

Catch Joke or Riddle: Related to a catch tale (see formula tales), plays a trick on the listener. For example, here's one which was once posed to high school girls:

> "Do you know what virgins eat for breakfast?"
> "No."
> "Gee, I never would have guessed it. You sure had us fooled."

Chicano: Many Mexican-Americans refer to themselves as Chicanos. This self-ascription emphasizes their pride in the Indian as well as the Spanish background of Mexican culture and signals their involvement in movements to promote civil rights for Latinos.

231

Code switching: People who are fluent in two languages often develop regular patterns of usage, employing one language in preference to the other in certain settings, while speaking with certain people, or when discussing certain topics. They may even switch from one language to the other in the course of a conversation or mix the languages in a single sentence. The study of code-switching seeks to understand the regularities and social correlates behind this dual language use.

Community: The bonds of social relationships which emerge through accepted modes of expressive interaction. Community interaction generates the experience of identity within a group. A *community* is a group of people who identify with each other and participate in large and small scale celebrations.

Complex tale: *Complex tales* are those which have more than one episode: these include *Märchen*, *religious tales*, and *novella*.

Consonance: Poetic language involving the repetition of consonant sounds within words. Example: ha*c*king cough.

Conjunto: A form of music developed by Tejanos starting in the 1930s which became a central cultural symbol for working-class Mexican-Americans in the ensuing decades. An accordion, played in a distinctive style, and accompanied by a bajo sexto (double coursed, 12-string bass guitar) are the basic components. Conjunto groups also included guitar, stand-up bass, and vocalists.

Contagious Magic: Also called the *magic of touch*, the principle operating with this kind of magic is that things never lose contact or their natural tie. For example, if you are able to obtain a lock of hair from your lover, you will be able to have control over that individual. This kind of magic will work with hair, nail parings, personal items, or old clothing.

Conte Fabulaire: See *Märchen*.

Context: Context has many dimensions. In a general sense, it has to do with the performance situation of an item of folklore, everything that is going on at the time an item of folklore is presented. But this is misleading because there are many things which happen at the time of a performance of folklore. There can be two categories of context, *cultural* and *social*. In sum, the cultural and social contexts deal with six broad categories: a) *context of meaning* (what does it mean?); b) *institutional context* (where does it fit within the culture?); c) *context of communicative system* (how does it relate to other kinds of folklore?); d) *social base* (what kind of people does it belong to?); e) *individual context* (how does it fit into a person's life?); f) *context of situation* (how is it useful in social situations?). (See Chapter 1 **Introduction: Basic Concepts of Folkloristics**)

Conversational Genres: Small, relatively fixed and traditional forms of expression used in everyday conversation such as proverbs, proverbial phrases, traditional greetings, curses, insults, etc. The legend, which develops in conversation, can also be considered a conversational genre.

Corrido: A Mexican ballad (narrative song) genre, developed in the mid-19th century. Corridos are composed in 4 or 6 line stanzas, with eight syllables to a line; even numbered lines rhyme or display assonance. This was the dominant song form along the Texas-Mexico border from the 1830s to 1930s; most of the border ballads celebrate Mexicanos who defended their rights against Anglo domination. Corridos continue to be composed not only in Mexico but also in the U.S. to commemorate events of importance to the Mexican-American community, for example the assassination of John F. Kennedy.

Counter-culture: A culture group that takes a position counter to or against the established mainstream culture. Behavior which develops in defiance of traditional or majority norms and values. The term has been used to describe youth movements like the hippie movement of the 1960s, British working-class punkers of the late 1970s and early 80s.

Cult: A type of religious group which deviates from a dominant religious tradition and centers attention on a particular religious leader. Religious groups which have a belief system centered upon a person or entity other than a deity. Specialists of cults perform rituals and practice certain beliefs just as would be done in a religion, except that there is no deity at the center of their belief system.

Culture: A whole way of life, those aspects of society that are learned and acquired by its members. *Culture* has also been used to mean a particular civilization or group who share certain traits which are distinct from other groups. Culture is learned through familial, religious, political, educational, and even economic conventions, as well as through the informal daily interactions involving face-to-face communication.

Culture trait: Isolable culture elements which may be either material or non-material.

Cultural Performance: Events in which culture is enacted and put on display both for those within a *community* and for others. Cultural performances include public display events, festivals, rituals, and other performances such as theater.

Custom: *Traditional* or habitual forms of behavior within a particular culture group. It is behavior that is required and often expected in certain cases.

Demographic: The mapping of the geographical space occupied by a particular group of people.

Diachronic: Happening at different times. A *diachronic* study emphasizes how a culture develops and changes over time as a result of its own internal dynamics and external influences. (See also *synchronic*)

Dialect. A social or regional variation from standard pronunciation, grammar and vocabulary. Dialects often have their own grammatical rules that are as logical as those operating in official written grammar.

Divination: A ritualized set of actions designed to contact the dead, demons, the divine, one's own innate psychic abilities, or one's unconscious, usually in the hope of gaining advice, hidden information, or predictions about the future.

Dozens: Short for "playin' the dozens." A genre of verbal insult prevalent in African American youth culture, usually directed at one's opponent's mother. For example, "At least my mother ain't no doorknob; everybody gets a turn."

Enculturation: The process of learning and acquiring a culture, other than the one you were born into.

Emic/Etic categories: *Emic* categories are native or indigenous to a specific culture group. They are derived by members of a particular group and are not usually found outside of that particular culture group. In contrast, *etic* categories developed by scientists studying culture, describe that culture interms relevant to traditional Western scientific thought, but possibly not in ways that make sense to members of the society in question.

Entrega: A kind of improvised ritual song found only in the Hispanic areas of New Mexico and southern Colorado. There are entregas for baptisms, funerals, and other occasions, but the most popular are for weddings. A singer, usually accompanying himself on guitar and perhaps joined by a fiddler, addresses formulaic improvised verses to the bride, groom, and assembled company in which he describes the wedding service, thanks those who have helped with the celebration, and offers good advice for the success of the marriage.

Episode: A unit of action in a story that is part of the larger whole of a story. A tale about a prince's quest to marry a princess might contain several episodes; in one episode, for example, the prince might seek and slay a dragon; in another episode, he might search for a magic potion; and in another episode, he might defeat an entire army single-handedly, before marrying the princess.

Esoteric/Exoteric Factor. Attitudes, beliefs, and concerns a group has about *itself*, and those the group supposes *others* to have about itself constitute what is called the *esoteric factor*. Attitudes, beliefs, and concerns that a group has about another group, and those it supposes the other group to have about itself make up the *exoteric factor*.

Ethnicity: A sense of shared cultural heritage and traditions which identifies individuals with a distinct group. (see Chapter 14 **Ethnic and Immigrant Folklore**)

Ethnocentrism: The practice of interpreting other cultures from the perspective of one's own culture. It is also the condition where a culture believes that it is superior than others.

Ethnography: The act of describing and writing about culture.

Ethnomusicology: The study of music in its cultural and social contexts. The cultural context is where we look to determine the meanings that people assign to music. Different cultures have different ways of categorizing what we in English-speaking America call *music*.

Etic: See *emic/etic* categories.

Evolutionary/Devolutionary theory of culture: The evolutionary theory of culture regards *folklore* as the survivals of *primitive* cultures, of earlier stages of cultural development. Implicit in this notion is the idea that culture is evolving into a more civilized form. The devolutionary premise views *folklore* as survivals of an ancient golden age when culture was in its pristine and most pure form.

Exemplum: (the plural of this word is *exempla*). An instructive tale told by a religious specialist to illustrate a religious moral.

Exoteric: See *esoteric/exoteric* factor.

Fable: A simple folktale that illustrates an ethical point and often features animals. The main difference between fables and animal tales is that a fable has a *stated* moral as its conclusion, e.g., "Thus, people should not tell lies."

Fairy tale: *Fairy tale* is used to refer to a Märchen that has been printed in a book.

Festival: A regularly recurring *cultural performance*. Like other public display events, they are public and large scale, but their link with an annual cycle sets them apart. Traditional festivals are based on agricultural or religious calendars, more recent festivals continue this annual schedule. All festivals feature community participation, and multiple purposes and expressive forms.

Folk: (See also *Social Base*) The term *folk* has had many meanings. It can denote:
   1) *A nation*, as in the German *das Volk*, and *Volkskunde* (folk knowledge) characteristic of the German Romantic-Nationalism of Johann Gottfried von Herder, and Jacob and Wilhelm Grimm.
   2) *A social group* connected by a common tradition and a unique sense of communion, characteristic of the work of Ferdinand Tönnies, and Émile Durkheim.

   3) *That portion of society that has not evolved to the point of being *civilized*, as characterized by the writings of *cultural evolutionists* like Edward B. Tylor. Tylor's idea was that culture evolved through three stages of social development:
   savagery——> *barbarism*——> *civilization*
Folklore in these terms is the remnants or survivals of an earlier stage of social development.
   4) A group that is "*small, isolated, nonliterate, and homogeneous, with a strong sense of group solidarity. . . .*" writes Robert Redfield about the folk. This notion contrasts the folk with modern, and urban populations.
   5) *The lower stratum*, the old-fashioned, rustic, rural segment of society.
   6) *Anyone*. As formulated by Alan Dundes, "The term *folk* can refer to any group of people whatsoever who share at least one common factor."

Folk architecture: Consists of artifacts, usually buildings, that are based on traditional non-academic design, with construction techniques learned through oral communication or by imitation. Such architecture is built by *untrained* individuals or craftsmen utilizing materials which can be obtained locally.

Folk art: The manipulation of the material environment for the purpose of making an expressive or artistic statement, usually within the boundaries of the aesthetic conventions of a specific group of people.

Folk beliefs: As argued in the chapter on Folk Beliefs, these should be considered as *perspectives* rather than definitions. Numbers 3, 4, and 5 are most useful.
   1) Folk beliefs are beliefs that are false.
   2) Folk beliefs are beliefs that have not been demonstrated to be true.
   3) Folk beliefs are beliefs that are held uncritically, are taken for granted, or are never examined very closely by their believers.
   4) Folk beliefs are beliefs that members of a (folk) group hold because they are members of that group.
   5) Folk beliefs are *traditional* beliefs; that is, they are beliefs that are circulated by word of mouth or by observation and imitation and, as a result of this circulation, undergo change.

Folk craft: The manipulation of the material environment for the purpose of creating an item that has significant practical use in the activities of everyday life.

Folk Narrative: A *folk narrative* can be any oral prose narrative that has been repeated at least twice and therefore exists in at least two versions.

Folk Speech: The local dialect or speech style, considered a kind of folklore because it serves as the medium through which all forms of verbal lore are communicated.

Folklife: The totality of traditional life in a given region, rural or urban. Folklife encompasses all aspects of material folk culture, as well as associated oral and customary traditions.

Folklore: Artistic communication in small groups. These groups may have shared social identities or on occasion, *difference* may be the only social base on the basis of which folklore is performed. It is that part of culture which is disseminated through time and space by many processes including visual or oral transmission, and imitation and repetition.

Folkloristics: The study of folklore as an academic discipline.

Folktale: Folktales are stories that are completely fictional. The characters are not believed to be real people, and the purpose of folktales is usually to entertain, although they may also be instructive.

Folkways: While the term *folklore* directs the researcher's attention to discrete, artistic aspects of the culture of a group, *folkways* may refer to the same body of knowledge, practice, and verbal and material culture, but emphasizes the everyday, customary use of the lore and the underlying belief system and way of conducting social relations.

Foodways: The study of foodways begins with attention to actual recipes and ingredients, but also inquires into the social uses of food and food preparation, the customs surrounding special foods, and the symbolic importance of particular kinds of food.

Formula Tales: A kind of simple folktale that depends less on the content than on the formulaic structure of the story. "The House that Jack Built" is an example of a *cumulative* tale, also known as a *chain tale*: "This is the house that Jack built. This is the malt that lay in the house that Jack built. This is the rat that ate the malt that lay in the house that Jack built," etc. An *endless* tale, as its name implies, never ends until the listener becomes impatient and brings the telling to a halt. Some endless tales, known as *rounds*, *circular tales* or *clock tales*, continually return to their beginning:

> Once upon a time as we sat around the campfire telling funny tales, a stranger rode into our mist on an old grey mule, and we said, "Stranger, tell us a funny tale," and he began something like this: 'Once upon a time as we sat around the campfire telling funny tales, a stranger rode into our mist on an old grey mule, and we said, "Stranger, tell us a funny tale," and he began something like this . . . .

A *catch tale* plays a trick on the listener. An old-timer in Texas told his nephews and nieces how he had been surrounded by Indians with tomahawks, spears, and bows and arrows, and he described in detail how the Indians started closing in on him. Suddenly the uncle quit telling the tale, and the children said,

"Uncle Will! What happened?"
"Well, they killed me!"

Frame Tale: A tale that holds several tales together. One such frame is that of Princess Scheherazade, in the *Thousand and One Nights* who marries a king who each day kills his bride to marry another woman. Princess Scheherazade saved herself from this fate by telling the king a story on her wedding night and stopping at the most interesting point. The king decided to postpone her execution until hearing the end of the tale. Each night she told a new tale and was able to stall her death for many nights until the king decided to change his ways. The overall tale of Princess Scheherazade is the frame. The tales she tells are the tales within the frame.

Function: What the performance of a folklore genre does for the people who use it. A functional analysis considers the inter-relationships between folklore and other dimensions of human experience (i.e. culture, society, psychology, religion, ecology, etc.)

Gender: The totality of cultural attitudes and definitions of maleness and femaleness, the ways that the members of a culture understand what it is to be a woman or a man and what the rules of interaction between the two are.

Genre: A particular category of lore. Myths, folktales, legends, jokes, and personal narratives are examples of the many genres of oral prose narratives. Everything that falls under a certain genre shares characteristics with other examples in that genre. For example, most jokes share the characteristic of having a punchline which immediately ends the joke. Most folktales begin with a standard formula like "Once upon a time." It is important to listen to what genres the people themselves actually distinguish, because in doing so you may actually discover a new genre. Some folklore may overlap genres or fall in the fuzzy boundaries between known genres.

Gesunkenes Kulturgut: From the german meaning sunken culture. This notion refers to the sinking of culture from the elite to the peasant strata. *Gesunkenes Kulturgut* views folk culture as that part of a former high culture that has trickled down to and been preserved among the *backward* sectors of society.

Hero tale: See *Märchen*.

Hispanic, Hispano: Some residents of Northern New Mexico refer to themselves as *Spanish-american*, *Hispanic*, or *Hispano* to emphasize links with European Spanish culture, since many of their ancestors moved to the region as early as the 1600s, before Mexico was politically independent or had developed a distinctive culture. The U.S. Census Bureau uses *Hispanic* (rather than Latino) as the general term, but one should be careful in employing that term when interviewing, because to many people it has a negative connotation of political conservatism.

Historical Legend: A legend based on actual people and/or events, although the stories about them greatly expand and multiply through the years, usually with the help of mass media such as movies, television, magazines, and books. Wild Bill Hickock's reputation was greatly enhanced by dime novels. Davy Crockett's legendary fame spread through newspapers and almanacs. Billy the Kid was a real person who has been the subject of many movies; people still argue about who is buried in his grave. A recent legend asserts the Elvis Presley faked his own death in order to get some peace and quiet from his fans. Numerous sightings of him in grocery stores have been reported; other people claim his corpse was a wax dummy or the corpse of a look-a-like. Whether these stories are believed to be true or not, they do have some link to reality.

Homeopathic Magic: Also called *sympathetic magic*, operates on the principle that things that are alike will produce or experience the same effect. An example of homeopathic magic is the voodoo doll. It has the likeness of another person and when certain actions are done towards the doll, the actions are supposed to produce the same kinds of experiences in the person.

Humorous Anecdote: A short tale that usually involves a historical character. An example would be the "I cannot tell a lie" story about George Washington and his purported chopping down of a cherry tree.

Identity: How one perceives oneself as an individual and as a member of a group. Identity can also be extended to how a group perceives itself in relationship to other groups. The sense of identity is built on the ability to operate effectively within a cultural framework.

Ideology: The belief system or pattern of ideas peculiar to a specific culture group. The term has been used synonymously with worldview.

Immigrants: People who once chose to leave another country and live in America. Some wish to escape economic hardship in their homeland, and arrive in the "land of plenty," hoping to start a new life. Other immigrants arrive to escape political oppression in the old country. In a world plagued by wars and totalitarian governments, millions of people today have fled from their homelands to save their own lives. Thousands of these refugees are allowed to enter America each year.

Jargon: A specialized language or vocabulary usually related to a particular occupation.

Joke: A tightly structured narrative with a recognizable beginning, such as "Did you hear the one about——" and with a climactic punchline that usually pivots on double meanings of words or a reversal of expectations. (See Chapter 8 **Jokes and Practical Jokes**.)

Kinesics: Body movement which includes but is not limited to dance. Other types of body movement include facial expressions and gestures, like shaking hands, rolling the eyes, shrugging the shoulders, arm waving and winking.

Latino: A person who traces his or her cultural and family background to the Spanish-speaking areas of the Western hemisphere, including Mexico, most countries in Central and South America, parts of the Caribbean, and parts of the United States that were occupied by Spanish and Mexican settlers before the U.S. takeover in 1848.

Legend: Legends are stories people tell about events in the recent past that purportedly really happened. The protagonists in legends are predominantly human but can involve supernatural beings like ghosts, revenants, deities, saints, and so forth.

Linguistic: Having to do with language. In speech, that part of the message that is conveyed through words.

Malapropism: The incorrect use of a word in discourse, often leading to humorous utterances or unintended double-entendre. Example: *Don't smooch from my cupboard.*

Magic tale: See *Märchen*.

Märchen: *Märchen* means *little short story* in German, and the German term is used because the first great collection of this type was made in Germany by the Grimm brothers in 1812. Other terms that have been used in the past for this type of tale include *magic tale, ordinary tale, hero tale,* and *conte fabulaire*. A märchen has a distinctly recognizable beginning, such as "Once upon a time, . . ." as well as a standard ending, such as ". . . And they all lived happily ever after," or "A rat went in a hole, and now my story's whole." Set in a world of fantasy, the stories are highly complex, with multiple episodes, high adventure, and magical acts.

Memorate: A *memorate* is a narrative told in first person that usually expresses a personal encounter with the supernatural. These stories may involve an individual's encounter with a dead relative or friend (a revenant) or may contain more traditional supernatural characters.

Mexican, Mexicano: Some Mexican-Americans refer to themselves (especially when speaking to other members of the same group) simply as Mexicans or, in Spanish, Mexicanos.

Mexican-American: The most general term (often employed by scholars and government agencies) to refer to persons of Mexican ancestry now residing in the U.S. (See also *Mexican, Mexicano*).

Motif: A *motif* is the smallest meaningful component of a story; for example, a pumpkin which turns into a carriage would be a motif in the folktale of Cinderella. Motifs can be considered the building blocks or bricks of a story.

Music event: The observable sound and behavior in a specific place and time. With such a broad definition, we can use nearly any event that has music in it as the subject for a musical observation.

Musiqa: Linguistically similar to "music," refers only to instrumental music.

Myth: A *myth* is a sacred narrative set in the primordial past. The word *myth* is sometimes used by nonfolklorists to mean something that is fallacious or silly, but folklorists do not use the word in this sense. Myths are the tales people tell about the beginnings of things. They are powerful social forces, often connected with a person's religion, and as such, are associated with ritual and ceremony. The characters in myths are believed to be real, even though they may exist in a time and space remote from ordinary life. Myths explain the creation of the earth and all things in it; they explain why things are the way they are.

Narrative jokes: These are short narratives that end in a punchline.

Novella: A complex folktale similar to a märchen, except that its setting is in the real world. An example of a novella would be the story about "a pound of flesh" which was dramatized in Shakespeare's *The Merchant of Venice.*

Numskull Story: A form of simple folktale that focuses on the behavior of alleged morons, such as Texas Aggies or Kentuckians.

Observation: The careful collection or documentation of events and materials as they occur in performance. Rather than attend an event and simply absorb the music, researchers listen to music with a heightened awareness of their surroundings, noticing and taking notes on not only the sounds, but also the sights, surroundings and even the smells and tastes of the performance.

Oral prose narrative: See *folk narrative*.

Oratory: The language used in formal public speaking.

Ordinary tale: See *Märchen*.

Paralinguistic features: Aural qualities of a speech performance. Includes speed of delivery, voice quality, loudness and breath pauses.

Participant observation: A common research strategy used in folklore and ethnomusicology fieldwork. Participant observation can allow you to experience the event as more than just a passive observer and can sometimes give you insights into the performance that would not otherwise occur to you. Participant observation is when the fieldworker takes an active part in the performance of folklore or other forms of cultural expression.

Performance: At its most basic, the concept of performance refers to the practice or use of a communicative form. Performance is also used to describe a special kind of event separate or distinguishable from routine life which involves audience and performers, expressive forms, and action of a heightened or artistically framed nature.

Personal narrative: A first person narrative based on a real incident in the life of the teller. Its worthiness is recognized by the teller who then combines the experience, its perception and context to form a self contained narrative. These stories are steeped in the teller's ethical code. The personal values of the teller influence his/her perception of the incident and the retelling of the incident as well. Recognition and identification of the values that inform the personal experience story are keys to the eventual interpretation of the material.

Place-name Legend: An explanation of how a place got its name. The name of Gnawbone, Indiana, is said to have resulted from the sight of a poverty-stricken inhabitant gnawing on a bone to stave off his hunger; others say the original name was Norbonne, original home of some of the town's French settlers.

Popular culture: Literally, *people's culture*.

Proverb: A short, pithy, traditional saying that sums up an argument or a point of view; well-known examples include *A stitch in time saves nine*, *People who live in glass houses shouldn't throw stones*, and *You can lead a horse to water but you can't make it drink*.

Proverbial Phrase: A traditional turn of phrase that does not constitute a complete sentence. For example: He was *three sheets to the wind* last night.

Proxemics: The use of space by participants.

Public Display Event: A large scale cultural performance involving public participation. In public display events identities are created and negotiated, communities are reaffirmed and experience is intensified through game, performance, celebration, ritual and other modes of collective human action.

Pun: A play on words.

Rap: A form of song which began in large urban cities, noted for stylized language and sharp social commentary.

Region: The literal geographical location where people live. A region's spatial boundaries can be determined by economic, political, cultural, ethnic, religious, topographical, ecological and historical criteria. Identification with a region shapes folklore, cultural practice and informs personal and group identity.

Register: The form of speech adopted for a particular social setting (occupation, hobby, etc.).

Religion: *Religion* can be defined in terms of sacred experience. It is the organization of life around this kind of experience, however varied in form or in content. It is a system of belief along with the accompanying rituals involving a deity of some kind which constitutes religion.

Religious legend: A story of a miraculous event involving gods, saints or humans that groups of people attest to but that are not officially recognized or sanctioned by a religious institution. For example, many Mexican-Americans in New Mexico and Texas tell stories of miraculous cures performed by Pedro Jaramillo, also known as the Healer of Los Olmos.

Religious tale: A type of complex folktale that is not considered sacred but is based on religious themes.

Repertoire: The items of folklore a person or group knows.

Rhyme: Metrical or poetic language that involves the exact repetition of end sounds. Example: Sl*im* and Tr*im*.

Riddle joke: This form uses a question and answer format. Unlike real questions, in riddles the person asking the question already knows the answer, and assumes that the person being asked does not know it. In true riddling, people may make serious efforts to guess the answer, but in riddle jokes they are more likely to simply ask for it. The question exists so the teller will be invited to reveal the answer, and thus the joke.

Rite of Passage: A special occasion during which a person moves from one social stage into another. This includes three separate ritual stages, that of separation, that of transition or liminality, and that of reincorporation. This model was developed by the Belgian folklorist, Arnold Van Gennep. An example of a rite of passage would include marriage, the first day on the job, and the initiation ceremonies of fraternities and sororities.

Ritual: A category of symbolic behavior occasionally associated with but not necessarily dependent on religious myth. The meaning of rituals is complex and ambiguous because of the use of symbols.

Ritual Language: Language used in a patterned or symbolic way in religious or ritual contexts.

Schwank: A simple but lengthy narrative that depends on humorous description of a situation and/or character rather than on a punchline. The characters themselves are funny, the humor is low-class, and the characters are small-town.

Sermons: Form of preaching in many Judeo-Christian religions. This form of artistic communication is multi-generic (uses many genres). It is also a form of Black preaching style used in Black churches, characterized by rich metaphor and simile.

Sex: A biological classification as male or female based largely on chromosomal differences.

Shaggy Dog Story: A long, drawn-out type of joke that builds up to an anti-climactic punning punchline, such as "People who live in glass houses shouldn't stow thrones." As in this example, a familiar expression is slightly twisted by switching words or beginning letters, and the drawn-out story that leads up to it is a mere ruse leading to the play on words.

Simple tales: *Simple tales* have only one episode or a simple formula: these include *animal tales, fables, exempla, jokes, humorous anecdotes, Numskull tales, schwank, tall tales, shaggy dog stories*, and *formula tales*.

Slang: Unofficial words or expressions that are no longer a part of a register, but have entered into common use in colloquial speech. Example: *groovy, man* or *bust a move*!

Social Base: Answers questions having to do with the WHO of a social situation where artistic communication, or folklore may be created and disseminated. Shared social identity (see *folk*) is one factor contributing to the proliferation of artistic communication in situations of social interaction. Differential identity is another way. Social interactions between people with differing (and occasionally opposing) social identities and role relationships can actually provide situations where folklore is produced and disseminated. For example, race conflicts, border disputes, gender differences, religious conflicts, or socio-economic differences, can provide the spark for the creation and performance of artistic communication. In the above cases, folklore may be the only reason that people interact with each other.

Socialization: The process by which human beings become social beings, capable of interacting one with another, and capable of interacting within a particular society.

Sociolinguistics: The study of language in its social and cultural contexts.

Spanish-American: see Hispanic.

Spoonerism: Humorous word play produced by switching the initial sounds of words, as in the following joking question: What's the difference between a lawyer and a rooster? Answer: a rooster wakes up in the morning *cl*ucking *d*efiance.

Stereotype: A *stereotype* is a preconceived idea, image, or attitude that an individual or group has about another person or group. *Stereotypes* are not based on experience but are learned as part of our socialization process.

Supernatural legend: *Supernatural legends* (also known as *belief legends* or *belief tales)* include stories of ghosts, spirits, witches, the dead, haunted places, voodoo, and other supernatural creatures and events. Supernatural legends flourish at night, in the shadows, when people are most susceptible to their fears, and when they are mentally prepared to be scared.

Superstition: A belief, usually about luck or concerned with the successful completion of a specific task, often accompanied by ritual behaviors, that the believer recognizes is probably not valid, but that the believer continues to hold.

Symbol: Something that stands for something else, which encapsulates and expresses cultural and personal meanings. Any one symbol can possess multiple meanings for the people who use or interpret it. An obvious example of a symbol is the American flag. Symbols charge folkloric communication with a complexity and richness that transcends literal interpretation.

Synchronic: Happening at the same time. A *synchronic* study describes a culture at a particular point in time, without references to past history or possibility of historical change. This is a valid and important approach, but can be misleading if used to imply that a given culture is timeless or changeless. (See also *diachronic*)

Syncretism: The blending or reconciliation of differing belief systems, particularly characteristic of folk religious practice in areas where Catholicism or another world religion has been introduced to (or imposed upon) a native population. The tendency evident in many parts of the world to attribute to the Virgin Mary the qualities of an earlier earth or moon goddess is a classic example.

Taboo: An action or object that is considered off-limits, as in speaking four-letter words, which are *taboo* in many social situations.

Tale Type: A recurring pattern of narrative plot elements or the broad framework of a story. A particular tale type might be found in various versions in several different cultures. While no two manifestations of a particular tale type are ever exactly alike, the broad genetic outline can be discerned. Barre Toelken points out that no single cat can be called *the* cat; rather, the concept of cat is a theoretical prototype, and this is the way we can look at a tale type.

Tall Tale: A deliberate, exaggerated lie told with a straight face to humorous effect. A tall tale is also called a *windy*.

Tejano: Mexican-American residents of Texas use this term to distinguish themselves from Mexican residents and Mexican-Americans living elsewhere in the U.S.

Text: The item of folklore itself, a version or telling of a folklore item.

Texture: How any item of folklore is presented. It takes into account the *linguistic, paralinguistic,* and *kinesic* aspects of communication. In verbal or aural forms (narrative forms, music, folk speech) this would include:
1) Tempo of speech (how fast or slow)
2) Dynamics (loud or soft)
3) Pitch (high or low)
4) Repetition of sounds (alliteration, rhyme, assonance, consonance, repetition of words and phrases)
5) Types of comparisons (simile and metaphor)
6) Figures of speech
   In visual, performance, or mixed-media forms (dance, festival, material culture, etc.) texture would also include:
1) Tempo
2) Color
   a) intensity

b) value

c) hue

3) Repetition of motifs and patterns (the interplay between repetition and innovation)

4) Use of textures in material objects

5) Use of space and line

6) Movement

Toasts: Long, metrical narrative poems, usually involving *blue* language, that are primarily performed by men in urban Black communities.

Tradition: A belief or a story (or whatever) is traditional if it exhibits continuity over time and space. Traditional items are communicated by word of mouth or by observation and imitation. The term has also come to mean interpretations of practices of the present in terms of its connection (sometimes real, sometimes symbolic) with the past.

Trickster tale: See *animal tale*.

Twin Laws of Folklore Process: The seemingly paradoxical process characteristic of folklore—one dynamic, the other conservative—these are what folklorist Barre Toelken calls the *twin laws of folklore process*. Says Toelken, "Conservatism refers to all those processes and forces that result in the retaining of certain information. . . and the attempted passing of those materials, intact, through time and space in all the channels of traditional expression." On the other hand, "Dynamism comprises all those elements that function to change features, contents, meanings, styles, performance, and usage as a particular traditional event takes place repeatedly through space and time." In any kind of artistic communication, there will be a constant interplay between conservatism and dynamism, between tradition and innovation. As a result of the twin laws of folklore process, items of folklore exist in numerous *versions* and *variants* as they are performed in different situations, at different times.

Urban legend: *Urban legends* are also stories of horror or eeriness, that involve weird happenings, close calls, horrible deaths, and other real-world phenomena. These stories have developed out of the contemporary urban and industrial setting and may involve people's fears about technology. Stories about microwaved cats and babies cooked in the oven are examples of urban legends.

Variant: A *variant* is a radical deviation from a standard text of a folklore item.

Version: A *version* is created when an item of folklore is performed in a certain way so that certain motifs, stylistic devices, and structural features differ from other renditions.

Wellerism: A traditional quotation ascribed to a particular person, as *"It won't be long now," said the monkey as he backed into the fan*. The name *Wellerism* derives from a character in a Charles Dickens novel who had a fondness for these sayings.

Windy: See *tall tale*.

World view: The system of values, attitudes, and beliefs that provides a person's fundamental understanding of the way the world works; world view is closely related to what we call common sense.

INDEX